The Toughest Beat

THE TOUGHEST BEAT

Politics, Punishment, and the Prison Officers Union in California

Joshua Page

OXFORD
UNIVERSITY PRESS

OXFORD
UNIVERSITY PRESS

Oxford University Press is a department of the University of Oxford.
It furthers the University's objective of excellence in research, scholarship,
and education by publishing worldwide.

Oxford   New York
Auckland   Cape Town   Dar es Salaam   Hong Kong   Karachi
Kuala Lumpur   Madrid   Melbourne   Mexico City   Nairobi
New Delhi   Shanghai   Taipei   Toronto

With offices in
Argentina   Austria   Brazil   Chile   Czech Republic   France   Greece
Guatemala   Hungary   Italy   Japan   Poland   Portugal   Singapore
South Korea   Switzerland   Thailand   Turkey   Ukraine   Vietnam

Oxford is a registered trade mark of Oxford University Press
in the UK and certain other countries.

Published in the United States of America by
Oxford University Press
198 Madison Avenue, New York, NY 10016

© Oxford University Press 2011

First issued as an Oxford University Press paperback, 2013.

Library of Congress Cataloging-in-Publication Data
Page, Joshua.
The toughest beat : politics, punishment, and the Prison Officers' Union in California / Joshua Page.
   p.   cm. — (Studies in crime and public policy)
Includes bibliographical references and index.
ISBN 978-0-19-538405-5 (cloth : alk. paper); 978-0-19-998507-4 (paperback)
1. Criminal justice, Administration of—California.
2. California Crime Prevention Officers Association. 3. Prisons—California.
4. Corrections—United States. 5. Prison administration—California. I. Title.
HV9475.C2P34   2011
331.88'113659794—dc22   2010028266

Printed in the United States of America
on acid-free paper

This book is dedicated to my grandfather Charles Page, a source of endless inspiration, love, and encouragement.

CONTENTS

PREFACE

On August 4, 2009, a panel of federal judges ordered California to release 40,000 prisoners (roughly one-quarter of the inmate population) within two years. Operating at nearly twice their capacity, the state's prisons had become unconstitutionally overcrowded and unmanageable. Because the facilities were "bursting at the seams," the judges argued, prisoners did not receive adequate medical and mental health care. "As of mid-2005, a California inmate was dying needlessly *every six or seven days*," they wrote.[1] The judges concluded forcefully: unless the government stepped in to relieve the incredible overcrowding (the fundamental reason for the inadequate medical and mental health care), prisoners would continue to suffer and die. After decades of sending floods of people to prison without providing enough space to house them or resources to care for them, California's chickens had finally come home to roost.

The judges were correct: California's "correctional crisis" was not new. The state's prisons had been dangerously overcrowded, unmanageable, and extraordinarily costly for years. The government, while acknowledging the problem, had simply failed to deal with it. In this regard, the judges wrote, "Tough-on-crime politics have increased the population of California's prisons dramatically while making necessary reforms impossible."[2] *The Toughest Beat* is about the "politics" behind the state's penal catastrophe. More precisely, it focuses on key organizations that have entrenched (and continue to reinforce) the penal status quo in California. It shows that the state's prison boom in the 1980s and 1990s created the ideal conditions for the ascent of the California Correctional Peace Officers Association, the labor union that represents prison officers and other penal employees in the state, which, along with allied crime victims' groups and other law enforcement associations, has made it so difficult to alter California's penal policies and priorities. *The Toughest Beat* unpacks the phrase "tough-on-crime politics," explains how the Golden State's politics currently make "necessary reforms impossible," and suggests ways for making what is now impossible—major and long-term prison and sentencing reform—possible.

* * *

The Toughest Beat is the culmination of roughly a decade of research, analysis, writing, and rewriting. Without the contributions of numerous people and organizations, this book would not have been possible. I am deeply grateful to past and present members of the California Correctional Peace Officers Association for sharing their views and feelings, allowing me to tag along at union functions, and answering my endless questions. Thank you to the lobbyists, politicians, staffers, journalists, crime victim advocates, attorneys, activists, prison administrators, and others involved in the criminal justice arena who generously allowed me to interview them and, in many cases, follow up with pestering phone calls. They provided me with an invaluable education.

I would also like to thank my mentors at the University of California, Berkeley and University of California, Santa Barbara: Dick Flacks, Avery Gordon, Chris McCauley, Cedric Robinson, Kim Voss, and Franklin Zimring. Thank you also to Jonathan Simon and the late John Irwin for challenging me with insightful questions and pointed critiques of chapters. I am particularly grateful to Loïc Wacquant for guiding me during my often-bumbling sojourn through graduate school, infecting me with his passion for the sociological enterprise, and continuing to provide advice and friendship after I left the East Bay for the Midwest.

The following colleagues at the University of Minnesota graciously gave feedback on drafts and helped me navigate the book publishing process: Ron Aminzade, Michael Goldman, Teresa Gowan, Doug Hartmann, Candace Kruttschnitt, Ross Macmillan, Joachim Savelsberg, Rachel Schurman, Teresa Swartz, Michael Tonry, and Christopher Uggen. Mary Drew, Ann Miller, Hilda Mork, and Kerrie Deef provided administrative support and have truly made the sociology department such a great place to work. A number of wonderful graduate students at the University of Minnesota helped with this project. Jeannette Hussemann and Sarah Whetstone commented on chapters, Kia Heise and Essam Sater collected data, and Sarah Shannon gave feedback on the manuscript and made the great map of prison officer unions in the United States (see chapter 1). I appreciate their work immensely.

Special thanks goes to Dan Ibarra, amazing artist and dear friend, for designing the cover and formatting images. I cannot thank Gretchen Purser enough for providing incisive feedback on several versions of the entire manuscript and being so supportive throughout the publishing process. And Jody Lewen commented on multiple drafts of multiple chapters, talked through innumerable thorny issues with me, and supplied limitless encouragement. Thank you!

James Cook, my editor at Oxford, inspired me with his patience, support, advice, and, most importantly, commitment to this project. James was instrumental in transforming my dissertation into a book, a tough task for editor and author alike. Several anonymous reviewers also helped with this task. I thank each of them for their careful readings and shrewd advice for enhancing the book's readability, clarifying its arguments, and broadening its appeal. The book benefited greatly from their suggestions.

I am also deeply appreciative of my family's love and encouragement. Thank you to my parents John, Sharyl, Mona, and Ed; grandparents Dorothy, Charles, and Roxie; siblings Andrea, Bryan, Jason, Jennifer, and Jenny; nephew Shane; and nieces Mady and Seger. The following friends continually picked me up, pushed me forward, and helped me maintain perspective: Jason Alexander, Marit Appeldoorn, Melanie Boyd, Megan Comfort, Mark Cutmore, Chad Jamrozy, Heather McCarty, Amy Lerman, Jesse Nissim, Tony Rasic, Trevor Shoemaker, and Chris Thompson.

Finally, my wife Letta Wren Page deserves major credit for this book. She edited each draft of the manuscript and helped me clarify countless conceptual, organizational, and editorial issues. Her boundless love and friendship kept me going when I was burned out, frustrated, and just plain sick of the book. I am lucky and grateful to have such an amazing partner.

The Graduate Division at the University of California, Berkeley, and the University of California Institute for Labor and Education provided financial support for this research.

ABBREVIATIONS

ACLU: American Civil Liberties Union
AFL-CIO: American Federation of Labor and Congress of Industrial Organizations
AFSCME: American Federation of State, County, and Municipal Employees
API: Alternative Programs Inc.
BU 6: Bargaining Unit 6 (CCPOA's Bargaining Unit)
CAHP: California Association of Highway Patrolmen
CCA: Corrections Corporation of America
CCF: Community Correctional Facility
CCOA: California Correctional Officers Association
CCPOA: California Correctional Peace Officers Association
CDAA: California District Attorneys Association
CDC: California Department of Corrections
CDCR: California Department of Corrections and Rehabilitation
CHP: California Highway Patrol
CIRP: Corrections Independent Review Panel
CSEA: California State Employees Association
CTA: California Teachers Association
CUPS: Californians United for Public Safety
CUSA: Corrections USA
CVB: Doris Tate Crime Victims Bureau
CVUC: Crime Victims United of California
CYA: California Youth Authority
DPA: Department of Personnel Administration
IE: Independent Expenditure
LAO: Legislative Analyst's Office
MTA: Medical Technical Assistants
MTC: Management Training Corporation
NAPO: Native Americans and Peace Officers
NYSCOPBA: New York State Correctional Officers and Police Benevolent Association

OIG: Office of the Inspector General
PAC: Political Action Committee
PCAP: Prison Creative Arts Project
PERB: Public Employment Relations Board
PIC: Prison Industrial Complex
POBR: Peace Officers Bill of Rights
PUP: Prison University Project
SEIU: Service Employees International Union
YACA: Youth and Adult Correctional Agency

KEY DATES

1944: Prison Reorganization Act establishes California Department of Corrections

Beginning of the "Era of Treatment"

1957: California Correctional Officers Association is formed

1961: Youth and Adult Prison Agency is established

1975: Governor Jerry Brown takes office

1976: Legislature eliminates indeterminate sentencing, the cornerstone of rehabilitation

Official purpose of imprisonment changed from rehabilitation to punishment

1978: Ralph C. Dills Act establishes collective bargaining rights for California state employees

First issue of CCOA Folsom chapter's newsletter, *The Granite*

1982: Passage of Proposition 8, Crime Victims' Bill of Rights

1982: California Correctional Peace Officers Association is formed with Don Novey as president (replaces California Correctional Officers Association)

1983: Governor George Deukmejian takes office

First issue of CCPOA's *Peacekeeper* magazine

1990: Crime Victims United of California and Doris Tate Crime Victims Bureau are formed

1991: Governor Pete Wilson takes office

1994: Passage of "Three Strikes and You're Out"

1999: Governor Gray Davis takes office

2002: Mike Jimenez replaces Don Novey as CCPOA president

2003: Gray Davis is recalled from office

Governor Arnold Schwarzenegger takes office

2004: Defeat of Proposition 66, initiative to reform Three Strikes

2005: Governor's Reorganization Act creates California Department of Corrections and Rehabilitation (replaces YACA as umbrella corrections agency)

2009: CCPOA fires political consultant Don Novey

Federal judges order California to release 40,000 prisoners

The Toughest Beat

CHAPTER 1

Welcome to the "Toughest Beat"

Just 50 years ago, it was unthinkable that California would one day have a gigantic, overflowing, and notoriously tough prison system. In fact, at the end of World War II the Golden State embarked on a large-scale, idealistic mission to rehabilitate—rather than simply warehouse—convicted felons. State officials and penologists reasoned that if the Allies could defeat Fascism abroad, surely California could transform socially and psychologically afflicted offenders into well-adjusted, law-abiding citizens. Toward that end, the state built "correctional institutions" and hired "treatment professionals" such as psychiatrists, sociologists, and social workers to diagnose, classify, and cure the prisoners. Nearly all offenders served open-ended sentences. In theory, these prisoners earned their freedom by completing individualized treatment programs that typically included education, vocational training, therapy, and group counseling.[1]

California's governor, and future U.S. Supreme Court justice, Earl Warren, established a governmental agency, the Department of Corrections, to coordinate and monitor the state's dozen prisons and its parole system, which had hitherto functioned without coordination or an overarching vision. Led by renowned correctional expert Richard McGee, the department was to ensure that the rehabilitation express stayed on track. A state official who worked for McGee describes the spirit that marked California corrections in the immediate postwar years:

It is hard to recapture the excitement of those days . . . It is an exhilarating experience to engage in an enterprise in which all participants are convinced that they are leading the world to great improvements in the established order of things. We knew that that was the case; we could see the improvements and their effects, and we heard the acclaim from travelers who came from all over the world to see for themselves.[2]

Those travelers were prison administrators and penologists, many of whom returned home committed to emulating this grand correctional experiment. During this period, California earned a reputation as a national, if not international, leader in progressive imprisonment.[3]

It was not long, however, before the Golden State flipped from being a leader in *correctional* incarceration to a forerunner in *retributive* confinement. In 1976 the California legislature eliminated discretionary sentencing (the cornerstone of rehabilitation) for all prisoners except those with life terms, and, in the ensuing decades, politicians and voters (via the ballot initiative) approved numerous laws, including the nation's most severe "three strikes and you're out" law, which mandated long prison sentences for an ever-growing list of crimes. Between 1980 and 2000, California's prison population skyrocketed from about 25,000 to approximately 160,000. In 2008 the state had roughly 172,000 people behind prison bars; about 30,000 more were in county jails and another 123,665 were on parole.[4] Blacks and Latinos comprised approximately 68% of the total prison population but only 40% of the general population.[5] "The scale of criminal justice in the state of California is by far the largest in the free world, much larger than the U.S. federal system," according to prominent legal scholar Franklin Zimring and his colleagues. "California's prisons incarcerate a larger volume of offenders than the penal systems of France and Germany combined."[6]

To house the constant flow of new inmates, California has expanded its prison system on a scale no one would have imagined possible even as recently as the late 1970s. Whereas the state built only 12 penitentiaries from 1852 to 1965 (and none from 1965 to 1984), it has erected 21 new prisons since 1984, for a current total of 33, in addition to 40 camps, 12 community correctional facilities, 5 prisoner-mother facilities, and 6 youth correctional facilities. State spending on imprisonment has also grown exponentially since the 1980s. In 1981 incarceration accounted for approximately 2% of the state's general fund, but by 2007 that figure had jumped to 7% and totaled $9.7 billion.[7] The Department of Corrections and Rehabilitation is now the state's largest governmental agency, with approximately 62,000 workers.[8]

As the penal system ballooned, state policy and funding decisions made prisons increasingly stark, depressing, and punitive. Thousands of prisoners now serve long periods—sometimes decades—in austere, technologically sophisticated, super-maximum-security housing units, which purposefully deprive inmates of sensory stimulation. Many literally go crazy.[9] California's prisoners have few genuine opportunities to change their lives, as quality educational, vocational, chemical dependency treatment, and counseling programs are sparse (and those that do exist are always full, with very long wait lists).[10] Because, for the most part, the penal facilities simply punish and incapacitate offenders, some critics now refer to the state's prisons as human warehouses.[11] Unlike their idealistic predecessors, prison officials in California today have little hope for "correcting" their charges (much less "leading the world to great improvements in the established order of things"); instead they obsessively focus on managing their enormous, gang-ridden, ethnically polarized, often violent, and over-packed institutions.

While California's penal transformation unfolded, a parallel narrative developed. At the end of the 1980s and beginning of the 1990s, observers of incarceration in the Golden State began commenting on the rise of a new player in state politics: the California Correctional Peace Officers Association (CCPOA). In its first decade (1982–1992), this labor union representing prison officers[12] and other correctional workers nearly tripled in membership, from 5,000 to approximately 15,000. Between 1992 and 2002, the CCPOA grew from about 15,000 to roughly 30,000 dues-paying members. As it expanded, the union became one of California's largest financial contributors to local and statewide electoral candidates, lavishing money on both Democrats and Republicans and establishing a formidable stable of lobbyists to advance its agenda in the state capitol. It spent millions on media campaigns to change the image of prison officers from "knuckle-dragging thugs" to professional public servants who, according to the union's motto, "work the toughest beat in the state."

Having become a significant political player, the CCPOA won contracts that greatly improved pay and benefits for its workers. Prison officers in California today earn at least twice as much as their counterparts in other states.[13] Journalists and activists charge that, in addition to improving officers' compensation, the union promotes prison expansion by pressuring politicians, sponsoring and lobbying for laws that increase prison terms (e.g., "Three Strikes and You're Out"), and fighting reforms designed to shrink the state's prison and parole populations. The CCPOA's motivation for promoting prison expansion is simple, according to the union's detractors: prison growth increases the number of prison officers (i.e., dues-paying union members), they provide the CCPOA with money for lobbying and campaign contributions, and these tools are used to promote prison growth. And the cycle continues.[14] According to this formula, critics maintain the CCPOA helps fuel and greatly benefits from California's imprisonment spree. Because of the union's alleged conflict of interest, detractors argue that it is immoral for the CCPOA to support "tough on crime" laws. Anthony Kennedy, a U.S. Supreme Court justice, stated publicly in February 2010 that "the three-strikes law sponsor is the correctional officers' union and that is sick!"[15]

The developing story of the CCPOA is about more than just lucrative contracts, severe sentencing laws, and prison expansion. It is also about public versus private incarceration. The CCPOA fights efforts to privatize prisons in the state, going so far as to "take out" legislators (i.e., bankroll efforts to unseat them) who buck the union's zero-tolerance policy on for-profit prisons. Again, critics charge self-interest: private penal facilities employ nonunion labor. Stories of the prison officers' union also describe the CCPOA's alleged authority over prison management and operations. Reportedly, managers are unable to implement programs or discipline rank-and-file workers without the union's approval. About the union's influence on prison functions, Jackie Speier, a former state senator and current U.S. congresswoman, asserted in 2004 that the state had "turned the keys over to the guards, in virtually every way."[16] The CCPOA's detractors also argue that the union uses its ties with high-level politicians to block the confirmation of prison wardens who oppose its interests. More salaciously, district attorneys in prison towns are said to fear the reprisal of the CCPOA if they prosecute "rogue" officers—effectively, then, officers like those accused of staging "gladiator fights" between rival gang members at Corcoran prison can allegedly continue with impunity.

This prevailing story of the CCPOA portrays an almost omnipotent organization that, in many respects, shapes the state's penal policies and priorities. It is not surprising that the *Los Angeles Times*, in a 2004 series of editorials on California prisons titled "State Prisons' Revolving Door," asserted that the CCPOA "threatens political retribution on politicians who suggest reform" and "keeps lawmakers intimidated." Not mincing words, the *Times* continued, "The union, among the largest political contributors in the state, has defeated all major reform efforts for well over a decade," and, "Today they run the system." Against the CCPOA's claim that it serves the common good, the *Times* concluded, "No other California union's success for its members has been so disastrous to public safety."[17]

Journalists, activists, and scholars have suggested that the stories of California's flip from a national leader in progressive imprisonment to a leader in hyperincarceration and the ascent of the CCPOA are causally related.[18] But this causal imputation is largely rhetorical. No one has thoroughly examined the connection between the Golden State's punitive turn and the rise of the union. This book does just that. Drawing on archival research, several years of fieldwork, and nearly 100 interviews, this book examines two interrelated questions. First, how and why did the CCPOA become a powerful and successful labor union—at a time when other unions in the public and private sectors lost members and clout at the bargaining table—and one of the most important actors in California politics?[19] Second, how has the CCPOA affected policies and priorities regarding crime and punishment?

By analyzing these questions, this book enhances our understanding of the scope and character of criminal punishment in California. It helps us comprehend how the penal system became so large and dysfunctional and why the state is now so resistant to change—two questions that have received surprisingly little intensive scholarly attention.[20] California's stubborn refusal to change its penal course in the face of pressure from the federal courts, extreme budgetary crises, and mounting evidence that the penal system feeds on itself is remarkable. While many other states—even notoriously "tough on crime" states like Louisiana and Mississippi—have implemented new policies and rescinded old ones to decrease their prison and parole populations, California has barely budged.[21] And even though from 2003–2010 California had a Republican governor who supported criminal justice reform and Democrats controlled the legislature, the Golden State's very punitive penal culture and policies remain firmly entrenched. *The Toughest Beat* addresses why California obstinately refuses to implement sensible reforms, alter the penal status quo, and seriously address what seems like a perpetual "correctional crisis."

My thesis is that the prison boom and related developments in the second half of the twentieth century produced the CCPOA—or, rather, created a fertile environment that facilitated the union's remarkable ascent. As it grew and became a formidable political force, the union influenced the nature, purpose, and scope of imprisonment and associated functions in California. In addition to shaping policies, the CCPOA promoted particularly moralistic conceptions of lawbreaking and tough penal policies, helped redefine penal expertise, and empowered actors that supported its interests and views on criminal punishment (most notably, like-minded crime victim organizations) while marginalizing those with competing perspectives. The CCPOA, in short, worked to shape the penal landscape in its own image *as part of its unionization strategy*. A major unintended consequence of the rapid, astronomical increase of the penal population, then, was the growth and empowerment of interest groups that now frustrate efforts to seriously roll back hyperincarceration, the phenomena that facilitated their growth into major political players in the first place.

In this book I focus specifically on the CCPOA and punishment in the Golden State, but the implications stretch beyond California's borders. It is well documented that California is a bellwether state that sets national trends in a variety of policy areas, such as taxation, affirmative action, immigration, and environmentalism.[22] This is particularly true with criminal justice. In both the pre– and post–World War II eras, California has been a harbinger of influential penal experiments, including indeterminate sentencing, victims' rights laws, sex offender treatment and surveillance, and "Three Strikes and You're Out."[23] Rather than waiting to see how these experiments play out in California, other states frequently rush to implement similar measures—often with disastrous consequences. *The Toughest Beat* provides useful lessons about prison officer unionization; politically active crime victims' organizations; and the widespread politicization of penal policy that scholars, policymakers, and citizens outside of California are currently wrestling with or may confront in the future. The map in Figure 1.1 shows that prison officer unionization has taken root in more than half of the United States and that more than one-third of all American prison officer unions are independent (i.e., unaffiliated with both the American Federation of Labor and Congress of Industrial Organizations

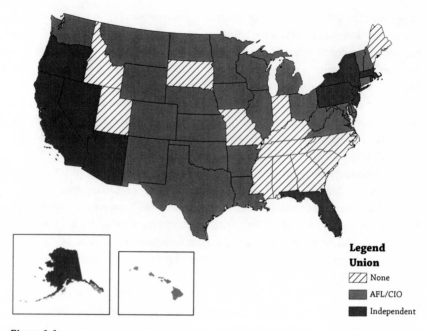

Figure 1.1.
Prison officer unions in the United States.
Essam Sater and I collected the data on prison officer unions in the United States, and Sarah Shannon created the map.

[AFL-CIO] and the Change to Win coalition), like the CCPOA. Prison officer unions also operate in countries such as England and Australia.

More generally, public sector labor unions are a recent and growing phenomenon. Some studies chronicle the history and organizing strategies of these unions, while only touching on their relationship to the state.[24] The CCPOA's ascent suggests how state workers' unions can become important governmental actors by influencing the design and implementation of salient state policies. Successful state workers' unions can change the character and expanse of state government. After all, these labor organizations strive to affect public policy, state spending, and institutional operations in schools, prisons, and the like.[25] Here, the CCPOA shows that through its achievements, the union affects the nature and scope of imprisonment and related state functions in California.

THE CONTEXT OF CONTEMPORARY CRIMINAL PUNISHMENT

The remarkable transformation of criminal punishment in California during the second half of the twentieth century was part of a larger national trend. It is now well known that the U.S. prison population exploded in the 1980s and

1990s. The number of people in state and federal prisons per 100,000 residents increased from 139 in 1980 to 508 in 2008.[26] When including jail inmates, the 2008 number jumps to 754—higher than any other nation. Approximately 2.3 million people—1 in 100 American adults—are now behind bars in the United States.[27] Even more remarkable, *one in nine* black men are incarcerated.[28] As a result of this penal explosion, imprisonment and associated practices (especially probation and parole) consume large portions of county, state, and federal budgets, threaten other social services such as education, and deepen social inequality.[29]

A related transformation has occurred in the rationale of criminal punishment. For most of the first half of the twentieth century, the central purpose of imprisonment and related forms of punishment was rehabilitation. But from the mid-1970s onward, the central aim and logic of incarceration switched to retribution and incapacitation.[30] In other words, reformation of individual offenders gave way to the control and containment of populations defined in terms of dangerousness.[31] With rehabilitation no longer a major aim of imprisonment, funding for educational, vocational, and treatment programs dried up, making it ironic that states still refer to their prisons as "correctional facilities" and their penal agencies as "departments of correction."[32]

The United States' punitive turn and its disproportionate effects on African Americans have been major subjects of scholarly research for at least two decades. Studies demonstrate that these phenomena were not automatic responses to rising crime and public fear of victimization. In fact, while crime increased substantially in the 1960s and 1970s, it went up and down in the 1980s and dropped steadily from the early 1990s onward.[33] In a landmark study, Katherine Beckett shows that conservative politicians raised the call for "law and order" well before opinion polls registered notable increases in public fear of crime. Starting in the mid-1960s, conservatives such as Barry Goldwater and Richard Nixon promised to crack down on "street crime" as part of a larger effort to restore conventional moral and social order shaken by the civil rights and other social movements. It was also a strategic tactic to break up the New Deal coalition and bring white voters into the Republican fold.[34] Since the 1960s, politicians of both major political parties have used "tough on crime" to appeal to voters—particularly middle-class whites made uncertain by the major economic, cultural (including technological), social, and demographic changes associated with "late modernity."[35] The "war on crime" and "war on drugs" are means of containing and controlling African Americans in the ghettos who, having very limited chances of obtaining work that pays a living wage, participate in the violent drug trade ruled by the "code of the street."[36]

Although the United States has become increasingly punitive since the 1970s, punitiveness in general and imprisonment in particular differ considerably from state to state.[37] Recent research demonstrates that large-scale national and international trends play out in particular ways at the state level because of local legal and political institutions, cultural traditions, economic transformations, and ethnic and racial relations.[38] Several studies also highlight the pivotal role interest groups play in shaping state penal policy.[39] As one of the leading scholars on contemporary criminal punishment, Zimring argues that "single issue lobbies committed to crime and punishment issues" are central to the "new politics of criminal justice." He contends that crime victim groups, pro-gun organizations like the National Rifle Association (NRA), prison officer unions, and law enforcement associations mobilize "citizen fear and hostility, shaping these emotions into a hard-line consensus for additional punitive legislation." And, they "push the public consensus into legislative directions where big operational changes [in criminal law] are produced." Punitive-oriented interest groups, Zimring maintains, are powerful engines that mold the penal agenda in California and other states.[40] Other scholars show that private prison companies, prosecutors' associations, and coalitions of law enforcement workers are pivotal penal actors that anchor "law and order" in states such as Arizona, Florida, Pennsylvania, and Texas.[41]

INTEREST GROUPS AND THE SHAPE OF STRUGGLE

Interest groups are essential to contemporary criminal justice policymaking. These groups' actions help explain why politicians and state officials (and in some cases, the voters) *choose* "tough on crime" responses to crime and related social problems such as drug addiction, mental illness, ethnic and racial inequality, and poverty. They also help account for why it is extremely difficult for policymakers and pundits to even envision alternative ways of dealing with criminal victimization. In addition to validating the proposition that *interest groups matter* in contemporary criminal justice policymaking, this book enhances our theoretical understanding of *how* they matter. By doing so, it further fleshes out the dynamics that shape state-level penal polices and priorities.

My analytical framework draws heavily on sociologist Pierre Bourdieu's methodological and theoretical innovations.[42] The core concept of this framework is the *penal field*. The penal field is the social space in which agents struggle to accumulate and employ penal capital—that is, the legitimate authority to determine penal policies and priorities. It is a semiautonomous, relatively bounded sphere of action (one might picture a sporting field; but a sporting field in which the boundaries, rules, and goals of the game are continually challenged).[43] The penal field intersects the bureaucratic,[44] political, and legal fields, and neighbors the economic, academic, and journalistic fields. It includes agents (people, groups, and organizations) that participate in and affect these struggles and the rhetoric, signs, and symbols that are both weapons in and products of the struggles that take place in this social microcosm.[45] The actors occupy specific positions, which are organized hierarchically. Whether agents occupy dominant or subordinate positions depends on their relative amount of penal capital. Players in weak positions tend to struggle to alter their distribution of capital in the field, so as to improve their position and potential for affecting penal outcomes. Those in strong positions typically work to retain the existing distribution of capital, thereby maintaining their ability to shape justice policies and priorities.[46]

Agents' positions in the field greatly affect their possible paths of action.[47] The actions they do take occur in relation to other actors in the field. In other words, the players in the field (often unwittingly) orient their behavior to other players in the field (and typically disregard those outside of the field). They take particular actions to thwart opposition from more powerful actors or quash potential resistance from less powerful players. Alternatively, they may simply not act at all for explicit or implicit fear of potential reactions from others in the field. For example, organizations that want sentencing reform may not "waste their time" lobbying lawmakers to reform mandatory-minimum prison sentences because they "already know" that dominant actors in the penal field (such as crime victims' groups), with strong ties to the governor or major political party leaders, oppose and will easily defeat such reforms. Thus, actors' positions in the field help determine which possible moves are worthy of pursuit.

Like all fields, the penal field has an orientation consisting of its guiding principles and values. The orientation defines the purposes of action in the field and indicates proper means for achieving those ends. Along with its structure, the penal field's orientation determines what is and what is not thinkable as concerns criminal punishment. For instance, when the "rehabilitative ideal" was the dominant orientation of California's penal field in the years following World War II, it was "thinkable" that prisoners should have access to higher education and the state should help support convicts who decided to get college degrees while behind bars. Today, however, when "punitive segregation"—an orientation that promotes long sentences in austere prisons and extensive and intensive postrelease supervision—is the prevailing orientation in the penal field, college education for prisoners (particularly that which is paid for by taxpayers) seems unthinkable if not "taboo" or "crazy."[48]

Agents within the penal field intuitively grasp the mores, expectations, and acceptable actions of that field; they have a distinct "feel for the game." Therefore they have at least a sense of what is and is not presently conceivable in the field, as well as who are the dominant and subordinate players. Seasoned players can confidently predict the outcomes of penal struggles because the outcomes are determined, on the one hand, by the composition of the field (which they unthinkingly grasp) and, on the other hand, by the orientation of the field, which defines appropriate and inappropriate penal possibilities.

Although I focus centrally on the relationship between the CCPOA and the penal field, I also examine the relationship between the union and the *imprisonment field*. Nestled within the larger penal field (and therefore technically a subfield), the imprisonment field is the institutional arena of state bureaucracies and bureaucrats responsible for youth and adult incarceration, which began to develop with the establishment of the Department of Corrections in the mid-1940s. Within this field, actors, including the prison officers union, vie to shape policies and priorities concerning imprisonment.

The CCPOA and its allies have been very successful in altering the composition and orientation of the penal field and the imprisonment subfield. Changing the structure or shape of a field has major implications. Fields are like prisms; they refract external pressures like economic downturns, moral panics, and war. How they do so depends on the architecture of the field.[49] There are, for instance, innumerable ways in which California might deal with the combined crises of massive budget shortfalls and disastrously overcrowded prisons. Responses might include releasing categories of prisoners, shipping prisoners to other states, or building tent cities on prison grounds. How the state actually responds to external pressure depends on the composition of the field and which actors have the authority to shape the response.

Affecting the orientation of the penal field also has important implications. The orientation—the guiding principles and values that orient action within the field—not only helps define what is thinkable or possible in terms of criminal punishment, it influences the allocation of resources, operation of institutions, and the relative positions and status of actors. By affecting the field's orientation, interest groups and other actors indirectly influence penal outcomes.

The analytical perspective used in this book encourages a thick, nuanced view of interest groups that goes beyond framing issues, pressuring politicians, whipping up public fervor, and taking sides on legislation. It leads us to analyze the *relationship* between these actors and the fields in which they operate, seeking to comprehend how they shape each other. The perspective also directs us to investigate which actors occupy dominant and subordinate positions. It guides us to focus on the battles between dominant and subordinate players in the field, along with efforts from actors outside of the field to enter and change the field.

The CCPOA and its allies are dominant actors in California's penal field, and they greatly affect the state's penal policies, priorities, and practices. Which groups dominate the penal field in other states is an empirical question. It is a question, however, that needs to be answered to understand the nature and scope of criminal punishment in those states. The analytical approach used in this book can be employed to understand penal outcomes in other contexts—including contexts in which prison officers' unions are relatively powerless.

HOW THE PENAL FIELD AND THE CCPOA SHAPE EACH OTHER

Each of the book's chapters serves to describe how the penal field and the CCPOA have affected each other. Chapter 2 sketches the historical evolution of the imprisonment subfield in California and locates prison officers within that social microcosm in the decades following World War II. It then details the transformation of the California Correctional Officers Association (CCOA), from a marginal professional group founded in 1957 into the CCPOA in 1982. It demonstrates that the CCPOA's fiercely independent, ultramasculine, militaristic model of unionization and stances on criminal punishment were shaped by the union leaders' dispositions (which grew primarily out of their experiences working in prisons) and by the then-subordinate position of prison officers within the imprisonment field.

Chapter 3 continues to explain the CCPOA's rapid ascent, showing how converging social, political, and penal developments in California during the 1980s and 1990s created necessary but insufficient conditions for the union's success. The expanding CCPOA developed a novel unionization strategy that, ironically, mirrored the lessons Saul Alinsky laid out for progressive community organizers in his book *Rules for Radicals*. This *politically realistic* strategy centered on three tenets: public sector unions are political organizations; the political field is an arena of fierce competition; and political actors must frame their interests and actions in moral terms. Employing this strategy, the CCPOA achieved remarkable successes and facilitated the politicization of imprisonment and related functions, encouraging like-minded politicians to affect penal policies and priorities while directly and indirectly keeping other lawmakers out of the penal game.

As outlined in chapter 4, the CCPOA's success flowed in part from the union's ability to develop mutually beneficial alliances with other organizations. It contends that the union's most important allies are uniquely political and punitive crime victims' groups, which the union effectively created. Since their inception in the early 1990s, the victims' organizations have helped the CCPOA achieve *power by proxy*. As these groups became *the* voice of crime victims in California, they fundamentally altered the architecture of the state's penal field.

Chapter 5 argues that the CCPOA and its allies have promoted policies and popularized images and rhetoric that harden penal "common sense" in the Golden State. It details the groups' efforts in 1993 and 1994 to pass California's "Three Strikes You're Out" law—the granddaddy of "tough on crime" sentencing provisions across the country—and analyzes the organization's work to protect Three Strikes from reform efforts once its costly and deleterious effects had become evident. The CCPOA and its allies constitute an organizational bloc within the penal field, promoting the strategy of punitive segregation.

Chapter 6 demonstrates that the CCPOA affects criminal punishment in California by fighting against actors who potentially threaten the union's dominant position in the penal field. Specifically, it shows that the CCPOA, in concert with diverse groups (including traditional foes), has protected the penal field from intrusion by actors in the economic field: private prison companies.

Chapter 7 analyzes struggles between the CCPOA and the state over "managerial rights"—the ability to make and implement policies concerning prison administration. It traces how the CCPOA has reduced managerial authority and discretion over key workplace functions, decreased managers' capacity for monitoring and disciplining workers, and enhanced the ability of the CCPOA and its members to contest and influence workplace policies and procedures. The union's success in the battle over managerial rights is due, in large part, to the comparative weakness of the state's penal agencies—that is, California's perennial lack of administrative capacity. The CCPOA's victories in the battle over managerial rights further weaken the state bureaucracies, thereby reinforcing the union's superior position in the field, in a cyclical fashion.

The concluding chapter brings the story to the present, showing how the CCPOA has negotiated major developments in the penal, political, and bureaucratic fields. In doing so, it examines recent claims from the media and the CCPOA that the union has changed from a staunch "tough on crime" organization to an agent of progressive reform. The chapter then draws lessons from the study about the prospects of long-term, consequential penal transformation, arguing that such change requires altering the current shape and culture of the penal field. The final section indicates how *The Toughest Beat*'s core concepts and analytical perspective can be used to understand penal trends beyond the Golden State.

CHAPTER 2

The Birth of the "Correctional Officer" and His Union

In 1957, disgruntled sergeants and lieutenants at San Quentin State Prison formed the California Correctional Officers Association (CCOA). According to the history of the CCOA, Al Mello, a supervisor, proposed the group after a coworker committed suicide and a newspaper article about the death noted tangentially that guppy keepers at San Francisco's Steinhart Aquarium earned more money than prison officers at San Quentin.

In its early years, the CCOA resembled a social club or fraternal organization; it was not a labor union and could not bargain with the state on behalf of officers. Steve Fournier, a retired prison officer and former member of the CCOA, recalls:

> I actually signed up with CCOA as I went for my final interview [for an officer position at Folsom State Prison]. I was actually a member of the organization before I was an employee. And about six months later I had cause to go to the [CCOA] over the way I felt I was being treated . . . So I went, and the [CCOA] president at that time said, "Grievance? What do you mean, grievance? We do pizza and beer." . . . It was like the Elks Club kind of thing. Pizza and beer.[1]

Larry Corby, another former member of the CCOA who started working at Folsom State Prison in 1969, says similarly:

> It was just an employee association . . . we managed the snack bar, we managed a dry cleaning plant there on the site. Inmate labor. And then everybody could take their laundry in there to get it done. And we had a snack bar—it was actually pretty good back in those early days.[2]

Tommy Marich, an ex-CCOA member and California Correctional Peace Officers Association (CCPOA) activist who worked in the California Youth Authority (CYA), describes CCOA as "a 'good old boy' organization. Put it like that . . . It was going nowhere. It wasn't doing anything. But it had . . . kind of like having a boy's club, you know what I mean? That's what it was."[3]

In retrospect, it is difficult for these officers to even imagine that this little "pizza and beer" outfit would eventually develop into the CCPOA. This chapter analyzes that transformation, showing that events inside and outside of the penitentiaries and the low position of prison officers in the imprisonment field and larger penal field during the 1960s and 1970s shaped the CCOA, and later the CCPOA. The battles officers fought in those earlier decades are part of the CCPOA's DNA, continuing to influence its unionization model, worldview, relationships, and positions on issues such as prisoner rights, labor relations, rehabilitation, judicial involvement in prison matters, and the nature of penal expertise.

THE IMPRISONMENT FIELD IN THE POST–WORLD WAR II YEARS

The imprisonment field in California did not develop until after World War II. Before the mid-1940s, the state's four prisons and youth reformatories existed as relatively autonomous fiefdoms. From 1880 until 1944, a board of directors appointed prison wardens and oversaw prison conditions and management. In practice, the board did little more than appoint the autocrats who controlled the penal facilities.[4] The sole purpose of California's "Big House" prisons of the nineteenth and early twentieth centuries (San Quentin and Folsom) was to securely confine prisoners.[5] State bureaucrats, politicians, and journalists typically stayed out of prison affairs. With only a few prisons and roughly 7,000 prisoners, incarceration was not a major state function in the first decades of the twentieth century.[6]

By the early 1940s, though, politicians and penologists took actions that spawned the gradual formation of the imprisonment field. In 1942 Earl Warren became California's thirtieth governor. He had previously worked as a prosecutor and state attorney general, and was committed to the rehabilitative ideals propagated by the "new penologists."[7] Warren entered office in a time of national idealism and general faith in government's ability to solve social problems. A year earlier, state legislators had responded to a series of prison scandals by passing a constitutional amendment that permitted the state to establish a government agency to take control of "all institutions for all persons convicted of felonies."[8] In November 1943, after another highly publicized scandal, Warren established a committee to investigate the state's penal facilities, which reported that "con bosses" effectively controlled sections of Folsom and San Quentin prisons with implicit, if not explicit, approval from prison staff.[9] The committee concluded that the state's prisons were corrupt and mismanaged, and its report provided Warren with cause to establish a centralized prison system, around which the imprisonment field would grow.[10]

In 1944 Warren signed the Prison Reorganization Act, which created the California Department of Corrections (CDC), and appointed Richard McGee, a renowned penologist committed to the rehabilitative ideal, to be its first director.[11] The Prison Reorganization Act also established the Adult Authority, which determined prisoners' release dates on a case-by-case basis. The law's passage marked the beginning of the "Era of Treatment" in California.[12]

During his 23 years as leader of the prison system, McGee oversaw the development of a centralized penal bureaucracy.[13] Historian Shelly Bookspan argues that the changes wrought by the Prison Reorganization Act "certainly put into place, for the first time, a structure through which to interpret and effect penological thinking."[14] This structure (what I call the imprisonment field) had two primary aims: securely confining *and* rehabilitating prisoners. During this Era of Treatment, legitimate authority in this field was based primarily on penological expertise developed through training in colleges and professional schools (e.g., social work) or administrative experience in prisons and other penal institutions.

By now the state's penal agencies wielded the most authority in the imprisonment field. McGee and his colleagues in the CDC had near sole authority to shape and monitor the daily operations of prisons. McGee was a charismatic leader, and unwavering support from Governor Warren helped him effectively insulate his agency from political pressures.[15] He also had high esteem for "correctional experts" (as defined by credentials and other indicators of penological expertise) and gave them ample opportunities to influence decisions about imprisonment and related practices, such as parole—particularly with respect to rehabilitation techniques and programs. Professional penologists were joined by criminologists, sociologists, psychiatrists, and psychologists who participated in policy discussions and helped implement rehabilitative routines inside the prisons and on the streets (in the case of parole).[16] Consequently, correctional experts occupied a relatively dominant position in the imprisonment field. These experts helped shield penal policy from actors inside and outside of the field who criticized the practice and philosophy of rehabilitation and attempted to shape penal policy according to nonpenological criteria (e.g., politics). Their scientific evidence bolstered the prevailing ideas of crime and punishment and helped McGee and his contemporaries fend off threats from those who did not possess penological expertise.

The three main components of McGee's postwar rehabilitative enterprise were evaluation, classification, and individualized treatment. Upon entering the prison system, prisoners received a thorough evaluation, including a battery of physical and psychological tests, to determine their treatment needs and security risks. Based on the evaluation, prisoners were classified and housed in the appropriate prison, where they began an individualized treatment program that typically included a mix of educational and vocational training and counseling. The government hired large numbers of "treatment staff"—including social workers, psychiatrists, psychologists, educators, and sociologists—to work alongside prison officers in the state's penal facilities.[17] Because of their ostensible penological expertise (or willingness to develop that expertise through work experience) and their responsibility for implementing rehabilitative practices, treatment staff occupied a position in the imprisonment field slightly higher than custody staff, who typically lacked penological credentials.

With the advent of the Era of Treatment, the state reclassified "prison guards" as "correctional officers." At this same time, prisons became "correctional institutions," the prison system became the "Department of Corrections," midlevel prison managers became "correctional supervisors," and prisoners (or convicts) became "inmates." The name changes signified the state's commitment to *correcting* people through incarceration. Changing the occupational titles of "prison guards" and other prison staff was also supposed to show that the state (and Director McGee in particular) wanted these employees to become "professionals."

In addition to maintaining order behind the walls, prison officers were to be part of the inmates' rehabilitation. In its 1959–1960 biennial report, the CDC described the transformation of the "prison guard" into the "correctional officer":

> From the fist to the helping hand.
> This is the story of the transition from the gun carrying guard of old prison years to today's correctional officer.
> More than the name has changed.
> Time was when a man equipped with a muscle and a good rifle eye was considered the best candidate for a post as guard.
> These qualifications are not adequate today. The old time guard has been replaced by men qualified in many special fields. And rehabilitation now starts at the prison gate.
> First and in most cases constant contact with the inmates there are the Correctional Officers, men whose training far surpasses any ever asked of the historic prison guard. These men are asked to help—not merely herd—the inmate.[18]

There is scant evidence to support the CDC's claim that "correctional officers" were central actors in the rehabilitative project. Scholars who have studied California prisons in the post–World War II era argue that prison officers did not partake in the majority of "corrective" activities. Rather, they engaged in traditional custody tasks such as counting and escorting prisoners; moni-toring recreation yards, mess halls, and treatment programs; report writing; searching for contraband; and breaking up fights between prisoners.[19]

The historical record also does not support the CDC's claim that the state provided prison officers with adequate training. In fact, it suggests the oppo-site: officers received little training for traditional custody duties and even less for rehabilitative tasks. In 1972, nearly three decades after the passage of the Prison Reorganization Act, a government report explained that recruits rarely got more than five days of training before they were "expected to perform the multifarious tasks of a correctional officer."[20] The report went on to say that even the employees charged with training prison officers were unqualified. And without a CDC academy to train new officers, officers received "on-the-job" or "in-service" training.[21] Finally, equipped with this informal and inade-quate training, prison officers earned relatively low wages—even though they now were supposed to accomplish lofty custody *and* treatment tasks.[22]

Prison personnel were increasingly divided along that very line: treatment and custody. These two factions began to struggle against each other for power and recognition. Custody staff—officers—saw treatment workers as naive foreigners who bought into softheaded sociological theories about crime that excused criminal behavior. Moreover, treatment workers, who sought to tailor prison routines and disciplinary measures to prisoners' particular circum-stances and needs, were accused of undermining institutional order. It infuri-ated custody staff when treatment personnel received preferential jobs, status, and appreciation. For the officers, the rehabilitation workers received these goods *at their expense*.[23]

Officers grew ever more certain that prison officials, academics, and treatment personnel alike disrespected and denigrated their beliefs and values regarding crime and punishment. These slights came atop their inadequate training, poor to moderate wages and benefits, and limited means for profes-sional advancement. In short, prison officers' perceptions of their situations matched the subordinate position they occupied in the post–World War II imprisonment field. They knew were they stood.

THE WAR ON REHABILITATION AND THE "GUARDS"

During most of Richard McGee's tenure as the leader of rehabilitative incar-ceration in California, the imprisonment field stayed relatively stable and insulated from political and other external pressures, and correctional experts and prison officials remained dominant actors in the field. However, during the mid-1960s, actors inside and outside of the imprisonment field challenged the field's orientation (the rehabilitative ideal) and the dominant positions of the state officials, penal professionals, and correctional experts who comprised the rehabilitative regime. Developments within and beyond the imprisonment field in the 1960s and 1970s produced forceful reactions from prison officers and their organization, the CCOA.

A major challenge to the status quo came from the supposed benefactors of rehabilitation: the prisoners. After initially welcoming the advent of the Era of Treatment, prisoners increasingly felt that rehabilitation was more symbol than substance. When they left prison, ex-convicts faced many of the same difficulties finding decent jobs and fitting into the conventional world as they did before the rehabilitation era. Prisoners grew disillusioned as their counterparts left prison only to end up in the joint again. By the end of McGee's time as head of the prison system, numerous convicts simply went through the motions to quicken their release from prison.[24]

Prisoners increasingly claimed that prison staff and members of the parole board used rehabilitative rhetoric and routines to manipulate and mistreat them. Prison officers and managers could jeopardize prisoners' chances for parole by placing negative reports in prisoners' files, which parole board members considered when determining parole verdicts. In addition, the parole board had vast discretion to determine whether prisoners had become "rehabilitated." Convicts believed that parole board members considered extrapenological factors when making parole decisions (such as race and ethnicity, socioeconomic status, political beliefs and activities, and peer groups).

The composition of parole boards intensified prisoners' distrust of the parole process. Richard McGee and the other architects of the Prison Reorganization Act had envisioned that parole board members would be correctional experts. In practice, however, parole boards primarily consisted of former law enforcement workers who, in the eyes of prisoners, did not have penological expertise or the prisoners' best interest in mind.[25] In short, the parole process was highly unpredictable and nontransparent. Joan Petersilia, an expert on parole in California, writes, "there were few standards governing the decision to grant or deny parole, and decision-making rules were not made public . . . Prisoners argued that not knowing their release dates held them in 'suspended animation' and contributed one more pain to their imprisonment."[26]

Prisoners' increasingly vocal opposition to rehabilitation (and manipulation by prison staff and officials generally) was part of a larger trend behind the walls: the politicization of convicts. During the late 1950s and 1960s, prisoners developed political identities and engaged in political activities, as calls for "rights," "power," and "free speech" rang throughout American society.[27] Convicts increasingly viewed themselves as victims, on the one hand, of social-structural inequality and, on the other hand, of a repressive prison system. They insisted that, although incarcerated, they had certain inalienable rights, including the right to humane treatment. (Since 1871, the California penal code stated that prisoners were "civilly dead slaves of the state."[28])

The Black Muslims was the first organized group to demand that the state recognize prisoners' rights. It started organizing in California prisons during the mid-1950s; because of its Black Nationalist and separatist ideology and their collective discipline, custody staff feared the group. Prison administrators attempted to clamp down on the organization—going so far as to forbid inmates in some prisons to participate in it. The Black Muslims took its case to the Supreme Court, arguing that convicted felons retained the constitutional right to practice their religion.[29] In 1965 the high court sided with the Black Muslims; this was a crucial development in American imprisonment. For the first time, a federal court deemed that prisoners had constitutional rights. The court's ruling opened the floodgates for lawsuits concerning "prisoner rights."[30]

Also in 1965, a federal court ruled that a prison in Arkansas had to "change its practices and conditions" because they violated the Eighth Amendment of the U.S. Constitution, which forbids "cruel and unusual" punishment.[31] Before this ruling, the courts had taken a "hands off" approach with prisons, allowing states to run their penal facilities as they saw fit. Legal scholars Malcolm Feeley and Edward Rubin explain: "No American court had ever ordered a prison to change its practices and conditions . . . Within a decade of that decision, prisons in twenty-five of the fifty states [including California] and the entire correctional systems of five states had been placed under comprehensive court orders."[32] The 1965 federal court decisions regarding prisoners' rights and prison conditions and practices firmly placed the federal courts within the imprisonment field.

Prisoners, in concert with attorneys, brought the civil rights movement into the prison system. After the legal rulings of the mid-1960s, prisoner rights lawyers and the federal courts would be permanent features of California's penal system. Whereas convicts and their supporters celebrated court intervention into prison affairs, custody staff opposed it. Prison officers, in particular, alleged that lawyers and judges were meddlers who knew nothing about running a prison and consistently facilitated policy changes that benefited prisoners while compromising staff safety. They were convinced that the attorneys and judges sided with convicts at the workers' expense.

In the late 1960s, a growing number of prisoners (especially African Americans) not only demanded rights, they called for revolution. Sociologist John Irwin argues that politically radical prisoners increasingly identified with and joined revolutionary groups like the Black Panthers, which advocated overthrowing the government "by any means necessary."[33] Black radicals inside and outside of prisons were extremely critical of law enforcement workers, claiming that officers on the streets and in the prisons were, like Hitler's jackboots, ground-level enforcers of an oppressive, fascistic state. Radicals, such as the notorious black revolutionary George Jackson, regularly used terms like "sadistic pigs" when referring to prison officers.[34]

In addition to demeaning custody staff, Jackson and his comrades threatened officers' physical safety. On January 13, 1970, a white prison officer named Opie G. Miller fired four shots to break up a fistfight between convicts in an exercise yard at Soledad prison. Miller's bullets killed three black prisoners, including one of Jackson's close friends. The killings intensified the battle between black prisoners and white officers. Historian Eric Cummins explains:

> Following the yard deaths known as the Soledad Incident, black prisoners throughout the California prisons readied themselves to take the most extreme reprisals. George Jackson and others had already begun to preach a doctrine they termed "selective retaliatory violence" in an attempt to devise a strategy by which black inmates could band together to survive the quickly escalating number of prison gang murders. Basically, the rule was "If you kill one of ours, we'll kill one of yours." This was nothing new in the gang dynamics of the prison yard. But after the Soledad Incident, Jackson added a unique twist. *The threat was now extended to corrections officers as well as other convicts, a move that redefined the guard staff as just one more gang in the political struggle for control of the yard.*[35]

A white officer at Soledad was murdered three days after the Soledad Incident. The state charged George Jackson, Fleeta Drumgo, and John Clutchette with the crime. Because he was already serving time for a capital crime, George Jackson, if convicted of the officer's murder, would receive the death penalty.

Activists in the Bay Area argued that prison administrators falsely accused Jackson and his fellows, who they dubbed the "Soledad Brothers."[36] Fay Stender, a renowned San Francisco "prison movement attorney" and founder of the Prison Law Office, defended George Jackson and established a legal defense fund for all three Soledad Brothers.[37] The Black Panther Party recruited Jackson to serve as a field marshal inside San Quentin Prison (Jackson and his codefendants were transferred from Soledad to San Quentin when their trial was moved to San Francisco). Jackson's star status grew when a book of his letters from prison, *Soledad Brother*, was released in the fall of 1970. The book was an instant bestseller.[38]

In August 1970, the saga surrounding George Jackson took another deadly turn, which included his 17-year-old brother Jonathan. In February 1970, prison officers in San Quentin forcibly removed a recalcitrant black prisoner named Fred Billingsea from his cell. The following morning, news spread throughout the prison that Billingsea was dead. Black prisoners accused the prison staff of murder. Prisoner James McClain allegedly tried to implement the "one-for-one" doctrine when he stabbed, but failed to kill, a San Quentin officer. On August 7, 1970, the state transported McClain and two other prisoners who were to testify on McClain's behalf, Ruchell Magee and William

Christmas, to a courthouse in Marin—a wealthy, liberal county in northern California. During the court proceedings, Jonathan Jackson (George's younger brother) rose out of his seat, pulled out a sawed-off shotgun, and threw two other guns to McClain and Magee. Jackson and the prisoners took several hostages: the judge, the district attorney, and three jurors. As they left the building, one of the prisoners allegedly demanded that the state free the Soledad Brothers. Shortly after the captors and their hostages drove off in a van, law enforcement officers fired numerous rounds of bullets into the moving vehicle, killing the judge, Jackson, McClain, and Christmas. Prisoners in San Quentin vowed to murder prison officers to avenge McClain and Christmas.

While George Jackson and the other Soledad Brothers awaited trial in San Quentin's Adjustment Center (the "prison within the prison"), prison movement activists continued to describe Jackson as a beloved, elite revolutionary. Custody staff inside the prisons viewed Jackson as a "superhuman threat, a superconvict now held personally accountable for each and every San Quentin guard death and suspected as well of being the elusive leader of the emerging Prisoners' Union." (I discuss the "Prisoners' Union" later.) Cut off from most people inside and outside the walls, Jackson plotted an act that would confirm both his supporters' and detractors' Herculean images of him.

On August 21, 1971, several days before the scheduled start of his murder trial, the 29-year-old Jackson allegedly brandished a gun as an officer escorted him back to his cell. Cummins describes what followed:

> First, [Jackson] released his fellow AC (Adjustment Center) revolutionary convicts, shouting, "The Dragon has come!" Certain AC prisoners then helped Jackson take six officers and two white convict tier tenders as hostages. Five of these men, three guards and the tier tenders, were later found dead in Jackson's cell, stabbed with their throats slit. Three other wounded guards would recover.
>
> As a call for aid went out to Marin County law enforcement agencies and scores of heavily armed California highway patrolmen and Marin County sheriff's deputies began converging on the prison, blocking off all access roads, George Jackson made his final stand. "It's me they want," he said simply. Gun in hand . . . the Dragon bolted out through the AC lobby and into the prison "plaza." There he was killed instantly by a marksman on the yard gunrail with one shot to the middle of his back, which according to official reports, then ricocheted off his spine or pelvis and exited the top of his skull.[39]

Jackson's supporters argued that San Quentin officers set up and then assassinated Jackson. Activists inspired hatred among custody staff when they protested outside San Quentin on the day of the funeral for the murdered officers. The protesters called officers murderers and chanted "Three dead pigs ain't enough!"[40]

The violence against staff only intensified after Jackson's death. Black prisoners, particularly those affiliated with the Black Guerilla Family (BGF), a revolutionary group-*cum*-prison gang that had splintered off from the Black Panther Party and Black Muslims, continued to carry out Jackson's "one-for-one" doctrine.[41] Between 1970 and 1971, prisoners killed 9 prison officers (24 prisoners were killed in that same period).[42] In comparison, prisoners had killed four officers in the previous 16 years (1953–1969).[43]

As prisoners physically assaulted staff inside the prisons, Irwin maintains, radical activists (and even mainstream liberals) denigrated officers outside of the facilities:

> The activists' vituperative condemnations of guards and the prison staff enraged the custody force. The radical movement spokespersons eloquently articulated a world view in which the *prisoners were elevated not to equality, but to superiority, and the prison staff, particularly guards, were relegated to the lowest level of humanity* . . . The condemnations were not restricted to the radical activists. Radical and even liberal criminologists, civil rights-minded citizens, and sections of the media accepted and circulated a highly derogatory conception of guards and prison administrators. At least, this is the way in which many guards and prison administrators perceived it.[44]

Making matters worse, custody staff felt that prison officials and legislators typically sided with the kept rather than the keepers. In the eyes of officers, when violence erupted behind bars, prison officials and politicians appeased rather than cracked down on prisoners. For example, after convicts conducted a "unity strike" in 1968 (prisoners of various ethnic and racial groups collectively refused to work), legislators met with a group of inmates to hear their grievances. In the wake of these meetings, the legislature passed the "Convict Bill of Rights," which removed nineteenth-century penal code language that declared prisoners "civilly dead" and extended prisoners' reading, writing, and correspondence rights.[45] During this period, politicians held hearings, formed committees, and authorized investigations to try to understand prisoners' grievances and propose ideas for improving prison conditions specifically *for convicts* (not officers). Prison officials also considered granting (but ultimately denied) prisoners the right to form a "prisoners' union," which would have had the authority to negotiate with managers about prison conditions and routines.

In the wake of these events, custody staff at San Quentin "increasingly felt beleaguered by a threatening pattern of left-wing legal and legislative victories against the prison."[46] Their counterparts at California's other prisons felt similarly besieged and forlorn. It was in this context that the CCOA went on the offensive.

THE RADICALIZATION OF THE CALIFORNIA CORRECTIONAL OFFICERS ASSOCIATION

The CCOA transformed in relation to what Cummins terms the "radical prison movement."[47] As radicals inside and outside of the prisons threatened prison officers' lives and worldviews, the CCOA became increasingly militant. The association (and its successor, the CCPOA) became pugilistic and radical, in part because it developed within this pugilistic and radical era in California prisons. In that bloody and tense time, from the perspective of prison officers, the public, politicians, courts, and prison administrators favored prisoners over prison officers.

In the 1960s through the mid-1970s, the CCOA did not have strong connections with politicians or state bureaucrats and lacked the means to significantly influence prison-related policies and priorities. Although the legislature granted state workers' associations the right to "meet and confer" with agency administrators in 1971, the meet and confer process only provided a forum in which CCOA representatives voiced their concerns—it did not allow the association to negotiate binding policies.[48] Because the CCOA had limited economic resources and political connections, the association relied primarily on protests and other informal means to express prison officers' indignation.

The CCOA's representatives logged protests of prison policies with the media, politicians, and state agencies, such as the Public Employees Relations Board. In addition, the association urged investigations into prison conditions and policies, and threatened to take drastic actions if the status quo did not change. For example, the CCOA called for the "investigation and prosecution" of organizations such as the National Lawyers Guild and Citizens for Prison and Parole Reform that reportedly helped prisoners organize radical (even violent) political actions.[49]

The CCOA's representatives also demanded that prison administrators institute changes to protect staff. On August 19, 1971, the CCOA announced that it intended to file a complaint with the State Department of Industrial Relations, Division of Industrial Safety, claiming that San Quentin officials' policies compromised workers' safety. A newspaper report stated, "If the State Department of Industrial Relations rules in favor of the Officers, the San Quentin prison administrators could face a year in jail or a fine of up to $5,000." As part of the complaint, the CCOA proposed safety-related recommendations, including a "buddy system" for all staff on prison grounds; additional gunners and other custody staff throughout the institution; an emergency alarm system; the division of cell blocks into smaller, more manageable units; and closed-circuit televisions in industrial and vocational areas.[50]

Two days after the CCOA announced that it would file a complaint against San Quentin officials, George Jackson unleashed "the Dragon" in San Quentin's Adjustment Center. After the bloody incident, prison administrators locked down the institution. Five days later prison authorities infuriated custody staff by allowing attorneys to meet with prisoners inside the walls. Arnold Thompson, CCOA chapter president at San Quentin, demanded that the prison remain shut until "strict procedures are written to insure the safety of all employees." He warned, "If they open this thing up, resignations may well come in mass." Thompson also insisted that prison administrators immediately implement the "buddy system," so that no officer would ever be out of sight of another officer, and 24-hour "gun coverage" in certain areas of the prison.[51]

As prison authorities reopened San Quentin, 13 officers resigned.[52] In their resignation letters, the officers echoed Thompson and the CCOA's message regarding lack of safety behind the walls. The *San Francisco Chronicle* printed one of the resignation letters:

> It is my intention to tender my resignation effective 12:25 p.m. on 27 August 1971. I am not in accord with the trend toward return of so-called "normal" conditions at this institution.
>
> In order to maintain complete control of the inmate population in a manner which will assure the safety of all correctional employees here, there would have to be a sweeping change of administration policies, which, due to many Supreme Court decisions and softened policies by the California Department of Corrections relating to inmate rights, would be an impossibility . . .
>
> I have struggled through WWII, Korea, and Vietnam, I see no future in laying my life on the line for a convict, nor do I see any future for other correctional officers to lay their lives on the line either.[53]

As this letter expresses, prison officers felt alienated, unsafe, and relatively powerless because, from their perspective, the courts and prison officials cared more about "inmate rights" than officers' safety.

Along with lobbying for enhanced safety measures, the CCOA pushed for a clampdown on militant convicts. For example, in September 1971, the CCPOA made several recommendations for curbing prison violence, including finding a way "to accommodate revolutionary prisoners who request renouncement of citizenship and transfer to other countries." CCOA's director, Ken Brown, explained:

Our prison serves a dual purpose . . . To provide for the safety of society and to provide rehabilitative programs aimed at producing useful and productive citizens . . . The revolutionary segment of [the] population in our prisons prevents our accomplishing either purpose and we think it might be well to pursue the idea that such violent-prone [sic] revolutionaries be provided the means to leave our great country when they express a desire to do so, and when they are accepted by other countries.

The CCOA also wanted the CDC to study prison hiring practices "to prevent revolutionary elements and their sympathizers and other subversive elements from infiltrating our ranks."[54]

In 1971 a congressional subcommittee held hearings as part of an investigation into the violence at San Quentin. During the proceedings, Moe Camacho, speaking on behalf of CCOA, recommended the creation of a "supermaximum" prison to isolate and control revolutionary prisoners, and demanded tighter control of the rest of the maximum-security population.[55] Further, in 1972 the CCOA reserved $50,000 for the campaign to reinstitute the death penalty in California.[56] The association claimed that the death penalty was necessary to deter prisoners with long sentences (especially life sentences) from assaulting officers and other prisoners. In the absence of the death penalty, they argued prisoners with little chance of release (essentially those with little to lose) could attack their fellows and staff with impunity.

The CCOA made headlines when it threatened to organize a labor strike in 1976. An organization of prisoners, ex-convicts, and relatively moderate (compared to their revolutionary counterparts) prisoners' rights activists calling themselves the Prisoners' Union had reached a tentative agreement with CDC administrators. The deal would allow prisoners to form a Soledad prison "union" to represent inmates in grievance proceedings and regularly confer with administrators to hash out nonbinding solutions concerning prison operations and routines. The union would not have the right to organize work stoppages or other contentious collective actions.[57] The day before representatives for the Prisoners' Union and CDC administrators were scheduled to announce the agreement, the press learned of the deal and informed the CCOA, which "flew into a rage and denounced the proposal in the strongest terms, threatening to strike and demanding that [CDC Director Jiro] Enomoto be fired."[58]

The CCOA distributed a press release that inaccurately claimed that the Prisoners' Union would enjoy the same rights as a traditional labor union. The press echoed the CCOA's misleading characterization of the Prisoners' Union.[59] Stung by the negative media coverage, the CDC vacated the pending deal. A lawyer for the group blamed the officers' association for killing the agreement:

It was the CCOA that eventually shot us down, with allies in the warden's office. We were just faced with the enormous institutional inertia of these thousands of employees who were the people with the keys. They were just seething and resentful . . . And they just chose us as their cause célèbre that they were gonna die over. And they effectively blocked it.[60]

The Prisoners' Union sued CDC Director Jiro Enomoto, claiming that the state had violated their First and Fourteenth Amendment rights. In ruling against the Prisoners' Union, the California Supreme Court concluded, "a prisoner's [sic] union is incompatible with current and lawful policies of penological confinement."[61]

The CCOA was not alone in its call for a return to "law and order" inside and outside prison walls in this period.[62] During the 1968 presidential race, Richard Nixon (following in the footsteps of Barry Goldwater) argued that the country's approach to crime reduction exacerbated rather than alleviated the "crime problem." Nixon and his supporters claimed that the country needed tough laws that would deter and incapacitate (rather than rehabilitate) convicts—who were increasingly portrayed as dangerous, dastardly, and dark street predators who threatened "law-abiding" white citizens.

While Nixon touted "law and order" at the national level, political conservatives advanced the cause in California. State senator Bill Richardson (R-Arcadia), a former employee and member of the John Birch Society (an infamously archconservative, anticommunist, and nativist organization), exemplified the right-wing backlash to the movement for prisoners' rights and ardently promoted "tough" approaches to crime in the streets and behind prison walls. He reasoned, "there are already too many advocates for the rights of the criminals, and I do everything I can to speak up for the rights of the law-abiding. Our side is outnumbered in the legislature, and I am trying to provide some balance."[63] In June 1976, Senator Richardson founded the Law-and-Order Campaign Committee, which aimed to defeat politicians and judges charged with "coddling criminals" and being "soft on crime." Through direct mailings, the committee raised more than $1 million from roughly 220,000 donors in just two months. The committee produced and provided reports on lawmakers' voting records and judges' rulings to voters.[64]

Like the CCOA, Senator Richardson angrily opposed the CDC's negotiations with the Prisoners' Union in 1976, saying, "We're talking about Bolsheviks, inside and outside the prisons who want to foment as much internal strife in this country as they can."[65] Richardson harshly criticized Governor Jerry Brown: "There is some reason to believe that the Brown administration is fronting for the Prisoners' Union and prisoners' rights groups who want to shut down our prison system entirely." Senator Richardson bristled when one of his colleagues in the state legislature, Julian Dixon (D-Los Angeles), tried to secure voting rights for prisoners and parolees. He observed bitterly, "the same liberals who fought the death penalty are now voting to give murderers the right to vote."[66]

During this time, prison administrators and lawmakers implemented increasingly restrictive prison policies. For example, under CDC Director Raymond Procunier, prison officials often segregated groups of prisoners, such as gang members; regularly locked down prisons for long stretches; instituted X-ray examinations and involuntary rectal and body searches of prisoners to look for weapons and contraband; and isolated troublesome convicts in Adjustment Centers. Prison authorities eliminated convict self-help groups and rehabilitative programs, hired more officers, terminated treatment staff, and divided cellblocks into smaller, more-manageable units.[67]

By this point, the correctional enterprise was widely condemned. Mainstream academics had turned on rehabilitation as it was then practiced.[68] And, in general, prisoners viewed it as a sham. The reduction in treatment programs and the corresponding growth of custody measures had dimmed convicts' perceptions of rehabilitation. Since at least the beginning of the 1970s, prisoner rights activists had demanded eradication of indeterminate sentencing and the Adult Authority, which they viewed as inherently biased and punitive. The American Friends Service Committee's book, *Struggle for Justice*, articulated the political Left's critique of rehabilitative programs and indeterminate sentencing. It also strongly advocated for a determinate sentencing model predicated on the legal philosophy of "just deserts."[69]

Using different reasoning, conservative advocates of "law and order" like Bill Richardson also opposed indeterminate sentencing. They felt that judges and parole board members manipulated the system to shorten prison sentences (particularly during state budget crises). The various critiques culminated in the passage of SB 42, the "Determinate Sentencing Act," which in September 1976 broke the cornerstone of rehabilitation in California: the indeterminate sentence.

Even though the political and cultural tides turned in the CCOA's favor, prison officers remained underpaid, underappreciated, and unsafe. A report issued by the Joint Legislative Audit Committee in 1977 found that the 3,843 rank-and-file officers worked "under substantial amounts of anxiety," used "excessive amounts of sick leave," sustained "significant assault and battery rates," and received "salary and retirement benefits below other state law enforcement officers."[70] Prison officers earned between $1,097 and $1,260 per month, roughly $204 less than California Highway Patrol officers' monthly earnings. Prison officers lacked an organization with the power to improve their situation. They were increasingly convinced that a strong labor union was the answer to their problems.

In 1978 the California legislature passed the State Employer-Employee Relations Act (also called the "Dills Act" after its author state senator Ralph C. Dills), which legalized collective bargaining for state workers.[71] Over the next year, the California Public Employee Relations Board (PERB) organized state workers into twenty bargaining units. The state agency put prison officers in Bargaining Unit 6 ("Corrections"), which also included correctional program supervisors, group supervisors, youth counselors (CYA), medical technical assistants (hybrid prison officer/nurses), parole agents, and correctional counselors. To the chagrin of prison officers and other state workers, a state appellate court ruled that the Dills Act was illegal in early 1980. However, in March 1981, California's Supreme Court overruled the lower court and declared the Dills Act constitutional. On March 25, 1981, PERB declared that elections for union representation would occur on May 11, 1981.

In this formative time between 1978 and 1981, three organizations—the CCOA California State Employees Association (CSEA), and the Teamsters— battled to win the support of workers in Bargaining Unit 6. A small group of CCOA activists at Folsom prison developed a strategy for defeating their larger and wealthier foes. Before describing what was actually more vision than strategy, it is necessary to sketch the history and culture of Folsom prison, for they influenced the trajectory and character of the Folsom chapter of the CCOA, and ultimately the CCPOA.

When Folsom opened in 1880, it was the state's second prison. The maximum-security facility housed California's most incorrigible convicts; it was a prison for repeat offenders. Located 20 miles east of Sacramento, in the town of Represa, Folsom was the quintessential "Big House" prison. Covering roughly 400 acres, it was a large fortress, complete with thick walls of concrete and granite, looming gun towers, and gates with thick, creaking bars. As Folsom's architecture suggested, the prison's sole penological purpose was to incapacitate convicts.[72]

Folsom quickly earned a reputation as a tough, roughshod prison. Edward Bunker, an ex-convict and novelist who served time at Folsom in the late 1960s, writes:

> Folsom's history is blood-spattered and brutal. Straightjackets, bread and water, and tricing up by the thumbs were standard punishments well into the twentieth century. Hangings were common. Ninety-one men were topped on Folsom's gallows before California went to the gas chamber and first used it in San Quentin.[73]

Custody staff at Folsom did not maintain order by force alone. In fact, they gave considerable leeway to prisoners who behaved and "did their time." As was typical in most Big House prisons, the vast majority of convicts adhered to the "convict code" and governed themselves. Prisoners who did time in other, more chaotic prisons appreciated the comparative peace at Folsom. Ray Johnson, an ex-convict who served time at Folsom in the 1950s, recalls in his autobiography, "The convicts really ran the joint and there was a smooth routine. The guards didn't mess with an inmate unless he messed with them. It was a live-and-let-live place."[74] Another convict, who requested a transfer from Soledad to Folsom, told CDC officials: "You've got a tighter operation there [Folsom]. Here [Soledad] you have people running all over the place. At Folsom, if somebody is running, you hit the ground. You don't run or they'll start shooting."[75]

Prison officers and administrators at Folsom referred to their method of running the prison (and the general institutional culture) as the "Folsom Way."[76] The culture among prison staff at Folsom was relatively stable because the officers not only worked in close quarters, they also lived in the small, prison-dominated town of Represa. In addition, the officers had similar backgrounds. Until the mid-1970s, nearly all of the prison officers at Folsom were white males, the vast majority of whom had fathers or other relatives who worked at the prison.[77] Former Folsom officer Steve Fournier remembers the insular, nepotistic world of prison officers that he entered in 1975: "Folsom in those days was—If you weren't already related to somebody working there, there was a very slim chance of your being hired . . . It was pretty much a family business. But myself and [two other men] were the first people that weren't related to somebody already working there hired at Folsom in about 45 years."[78] The average prison officer had a high school degree and one year of college credit. The officers were politically conservative men who identified with rugged, ultramasculine, cowboy types like John Wayne. As many of the officers were military veterans, they embraced the prison's paramilitary leadership structure and affectations.[79]

The officers and old-time prison administrators at Folsom intensely resented outsiders—that is, politicians, state bureaucrats, penologists, journalists, prisoner rights activists, and judges—who told them how to run their prison. They also resented that, from their perspective, imprisonment was becoming increasingly "feminine," in two principle ways. First, females began to enter the previously all-male prison officer ranks in the mid-1970s.[80] Prison officers then (as now) prided themselves on working a tough, macho job. The possibility that females could be successful prison officers threatened a main source of job-related pride for male officers—that only "real men" were cut out for this line of work. Consequently, many if not all male officers felt that women should not work as officers in male prisons, particularly in high-security prisons like Folsom and San Quentin. A female officer who worked at Folsom stated in a legislative hearing in 1985: "In the pecking order, women [officers] are placed at the bottom—below the inmates."[81] In a study of prison officers at San Quentin in the early 1980s, sociologist Barbara Owen reported:

"With few exceptions, the male sample declared that 'women do not belong here.'"[82] A female officer in Owen's study insightfully described the threat that she and fellow female officers posed to their male counterparts' masculine self-conceptions: "The presence of [female officers] forces [male officers] to recognize that they can't go home and talk about how bad and mean they are and what a tough day they have had because some little chickie can do the same thing they're doing."[83] The prevalence of sexual harassment at Folsom and other prisons in the late 1970s and early 1980s is further evidence of the psychological threat that female officers posed to male officers.[84] As scholars have shown, male workers (particularly those in traditionally male-dominated occupations) primarily harass female coworkers to assert their power in the workplace.[85] By harassing women who entered their ranks, the male guards communicated that they (and not their female coworkers) were genuine prison officers who controlled the prison beat. Sexual harassment, in short, was a means of reminding women of their subordinate position inside the prison.

From the viewpoint of prison officers, the prison system also became increasingly feminine in its overall mission and operations. As discussed earlier, during the rehabilitative era, the state sent convicts to prison to receive help and even nurturing. Prison personnel (including "correctional officers") were supposed to gently guide their charges along the path of personal transformation. Prison officers felt that the theoretical blending of social work with imprisonment made prisons soft and effeminate. For them, the rehabilitative ideal was perhaps appropriate for schools, hospitals, and therapy offices, but not for rough, masculine prisons like Folsom.

During the Era of Treatment, prison officers and officials at Folsom romantically harkened back to the days when the warden and his staff maintained order the old-fashioned way, the "Folsom Way." The CCOA activists at Folsom (who would later become the leaders of the CCPOA) envisioned their organization as a vehicle for fighting changes at Folsom and throughout the prison system. In other words, the association would defend and promote the "Folsom Way" of running a prison. They also saw the CCOA as a means for making imprisonment in California tough and manly once again.[86]

Leaders of the Folsom chapter of the CCOA disseminated their vision of a labor union *of* and *for* prison officers via a monthly newsletter called *The Granite*. The first issue, edited by Larry Corby and Don Novey, went out to officers in December 1978. *The Granite* was bombastic and sometimes ribald, and its writers ruthless and confrontational. Steve Fournier, who wrote for *The Granite*, described the newsletter to me as the "*Berkeley Barb* of corrections." The *Berkeley Barb* was a militant newsletter put out by radical prison movement activists in northern California. Fournier mentioned (as did several issues of *The Granite*) that state bureaucrats threatened on

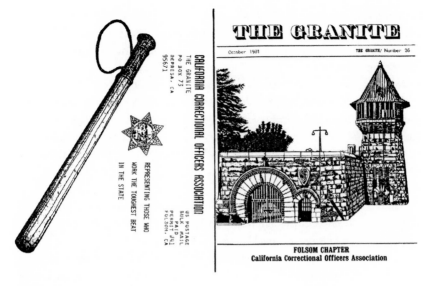

Figure 2.1.
Cover of *The Granite* 1, no. 26 (October 1981).

several occasions to sue the editors of *The Granite* because of its inflamma-
tory content.[87]

The Granite's writers directed shots at various targets. Governor Jerry
Brown received numerous rhetorical whippings, for *The Granite's* staff viewed
him as an unprincipled ultraliberal. Brown's judicial appointments and penal
policies infuriated the Folsom officers. *The Granite's* editor summed up the
CCOA's feelings about Brown's approach to crime and punishment:

> Our ever illustrious Governor is now proposing a "tough, new" $121 million
> assault on crime. In actuality, however, all he's doing is paying "lip service" to a
> very deadly problem caused in part by his previous, and continuous, lackadai-
> sical actions in this field. Remember? He's the one that has appointed the liberal
> judges with their "punish the victim" philosophy. He's the one that has repeat-
> edly vetoed anti-crime bills passed by the legislature. He's the one that fights
> every step of the way against an effective death penalty for heinous crimes. He's
> the one that has achieved, by all his appointments, a Supreme Court balanced in
> favor of the criminal in virtually everything that crosses their bench. "Get tough
> policy," I rather doubt it.[88]

The Granite also targeted leaders of the Department of Corrections. Even
though they disapproved of many of the CDC's policies, they particularly
detested the department's efforts to hire, promote, and train female and non-
white officers. In 1976 the CCOA filed a class-action suit against the CDC,

claiming that the department practiced unconstitutional "reverse discrimination" against white males.[89] In 1977 a San Francisco superior court judge sided with the CCOA; however, the state court of appeals overturned the lower court and deemed the CDC's affirmative action policies legal. The CCOA unsuccessfully appealed to the California Supreme Court.

Even though the courts ruled against them, CCOA activists continued to harshly criticize CDC administrators who supported affirmative action. In April 1979, *The Granite* printed a terse article titled "Loyalty," which addressed CDC Director Jiro Enomoto and Deputy Director Dorothy Stevens-Roby (two of *The Granite*'s favorite targets):

> In the recent CDC's propaganda sheet called "Newscam," we were all treated to a fine example of this administration's threatening way of doing things; "If you aren't nice to me, and kiss my ---, I'll fire you."
> Let me remind you, Mr. Director and/or Ms. Dorothy, loyalty, like respect, is earned, not demanded. To write an article (?) like that, you have once again confirmed to the entire department that you don't give a damn about anyone or anything except your policies of Affirmative Action and Employee be Damned. [Unsigned][90]

The Granite's editors accused the CDC administration of using affirmative action practices to divide and conquer staff, as an article titled "Skin" attests:

> According to those members that have been affected, discrimination of the worst order is being practiced daily here at Folsom Prison. Recently, many job assignments have been made or changed solely on the basis of the officers [sic] skin color, sex, or national origin. No, this was not written in 1900, 1920, 1940, or 1960, but in 1979. We now have, apparently, black posts, white posts, brown posts, male posts, female posts, everything but a fence post. Apparently, the shade or shape of an officers [sic] skin is the criteria that is judged on whether or not that officer can do the job in a professional manner . . .
> It should be quite apparent that someone is making an attempt to get staff grouped against one another . . . They have done their damndest to get the working masses to erupt at each other and in some cases have accomplished it. Hopefully, the professional people we have here at Folsom will see these cases of discrimination for just what they are, and not let them influence their thinking with respect toward dealings with each other.
> Well, your CCOA is now, and has many times in the past, fighting these flagrant cases of discrimination. Your CCOA will continue to fight the practices and the people that initiate them as long as your support and desire for it is present. Support your CCOA, it *will* support you.[91]

The CCOA activists also chided CDC administrators for supporting gender- and race/ethnicity-specific training programs and employee organizations (e.g., Black Correctional Workers Association).

Prison officers and old-time managers resented affirmative action because the policy, they felt, exemplified a trend of outsiders dictating how prison staff should run the institutions. Additionally, the officers, who were primarily working-class white males, felt that affirmative action helped others *at their expense*—hence they claimed that affirmative action created divisions among groups of workers. The officers did not feel privileged. After all, they earned rather meager pay and benefits, and they lacked advanced educational degrees and valuable social connections. Moreover, they did not receive respect or gratitude for their work, and they had little say over work conditions or prison policies more generally. The officers felt that affirmative action reinforced their low social status by blocking avenues of career advancement in order to help members of groups that the government deemed worthy of assistance (many of whom had questionable qualifications, according to the opponents of affirmative action).[92]

Beyond complaining that state bureaucrats at CDC headquarters in Sacramento meddled in prison affairs, articles in *The Granite* insisted that the new breed of professional managers who ran the prison system were incompetent. Unlike their predecessors who were "prison people" (i.e., they had extensive experience working inside prisons, often starting out as prison officers and gradually rising up through the ranks), the new administrators were hired straight out of university management programs or from other state agencies (e.g., the Health and Welfare Agency).[93] A joke in *The Granite* summed it up:

How many CDC Deputy Directors does it take to change a light bulb?
Ans. All of them, plus an Officer to tell them in which direction to rotate.[94]

The jab is telling because CDC authorities, officers alleged, rarely asked their subordinates for input regarding changing light bulbs or anything else dealing with operations.

The CCOA activists argued that prison authorities continually bumbled their duties, creating problems in the institutions. Moreover, staff felt that administrators did not take responsibility for their miscues; rather, they blamed the workers. An article in *The Granite* that made recommendations for decreasing prison violence provides insight into officers' feelings about management:

The saddest part of it all, however, our illustrious leadership undoubtedly won't do anything [about violence and unrest]. They'll sit and talk about rehabilitation, whine about wanting more institutions, and do nothing about obtaining the [safety] devices we need. Then after the explosion, they'll wander in, blame some of the local staff, initiate disciplinary procedures against them, and rebuild what is destroyed, except the lives, knowing full well they could have spent the same money on security devices and training before the riot and just possibly prevented it altogether.

CDC hierarchy wants to stop violence and assaults? No way. The proof is in history and actions. Both prove them to be just what they are . . . administrators incapable of curbing the problem who can always point to some poor slob they can shift the blame to. Of course I guess that's the answer to being an administrator in this administration, one who can show in writing how great he is and how the fault lies with somebody else.[95]

Officers felt that management routinely initiated disciplinary procedures against officers out of spite and to shift blame for mishaps from the bosses to the workers. As the article suggests, officers felt that managers used their education (in this case, their writing skills) to manipulate situations and punish less educated prison officers.[96]

Whereas officers felt that the authorities were quick to blame and punish staff, they believed CDC had "long been against any policy and/or procedure that humiliates and/or degrades any prisoners in custody." The CCOA concluded that the state should "return control of the institutions throughout California to the people who should have it: the Wardens and Superintendents . . . In so doing, the 'Central Office' could be completely done away with," and the "good old days" of local control would return.[97]

In addition to blasting politicians, the courts, management, and prisoners' rights advocates, *The Granite* criticized the CCOA's competitors: the CSEA and the Teamsters. The Folsom activists contended that the CSEA did not care about prison personnel; it only wanted their dues:

The reason CCOA was started was because of a lack of concern displayed by CSEA towards the professional Correctional Officer . . . The problem is, though, whether CSEA were to win the election or lose it, their concern, representation, and visibility would be the same, little or nothing. The Clerks, [sic] Secretaries Employees Association is just that, for Clerks and Secretaries.[98]

The CCOA activists maintained that because prison workers would comprise roughly 5% of CSEA's 60,000-plus membership, the workers would have little control over the CSEA's policies. They further insinuated that tough, masculine prison officers would not have the same concerns as effeminate secretaries and clerks (the bulk of CSEA's membership), therefore officers would continually have to fight to have their voices heard in their own union. Moreover, the Folsom officers insisted that CSEA was a "dictatorship" that raised dues without members' consent, made political donations to candidates of its (not the members') choice, and supported issues that were important to the so-called labor movement (understood as politically liberal). Perhaps most importantly, CSEA's "bosses" knew little if anything about prisons and even less about the plights of prison officers.

The Granite's writers similarly described the Teamsters as an undemocratic, dictatorial, and greedy organization. Whereas the officers referred to CSEA as "secretaries and clerks" (effeminate, "pink collar" workers), they depicted the Teamsters as "used car salesmen" and "crooks." For example, when comparing CCOA's legal resources with those of the two other organizations, the Folsom officers said about the Teamsters: "most of their legal staff is kept busy fighting criminal charges against their own elected officials."[99] They described the Teamsters as carpetbaggers who would take officers' money and run—and possibly commit acts that could land them in prison. Former CCOA and CCPOA lobbyist Jeff Thompson explains: "with the Teamsters we made the point that there was a potential irony [because] a lot of Teamster officials were in prison themselves. And how would they like to be guarding their own?"[100]

Along with castigating the CSEA and Teamsters, the Folsom officers described the benefits of the CCOA. First, the CCOA was an *independent* association comprised solely of prison personnel (primarily rank-and-file officers). Moreover, its leaders were prison employees (not hired hands) and the organization was a representative democracy:

> Remember, unlike our counterparts (CSEA and Teamsters) you, the CDC/CYA employee, set the order of priorities and give the orders to your elected leadership of what will happen. They don't dictate to you, or tell you what you want or will get. And even more importantly, you are represented only as a peace officer in CDC/CYA, not as a member of all state services (i.e., cooks, bakers, and candlestick makers; or clerks, secretaries, and Cal-Trans workers). CCOA is just what the name implies, The Association of Correctional Workers for the State of California.[101]

The CCOA would not send its members' dues to the American Federation of Labor and Congress of Industrial Organizations (AFL-CIO) or any other international labor organization; it would keep the money "in house." It would not take positions on behalf of "labor" or the "labor movement"; it would only address issues specific to CDC/CYA workers.

The Granite's editors claimed that CCOA could have similar success to the independent California Association of Highway Patrolmen (CAHP), which rebuked CSEA years earlier. As A. K. Scribner, president of CCOA's chapter at Duel Vocational Institute, wrote:

> What does the CHP have, 4,000 members. A pretty small group according to CSEA, but can they explain why the wages for Patrol Officers is [sic] 22% above

that of a Correctional Officer? I can, it is because their organization represents only CHP officers, lobbys [sic] only for CHP Officers and don't [sic] give a hoot about anyone else. They have EXCLUSIVE representation! Does this sound a little like CCOA? It may be noted that when the CHP made their big move, they asked CDC to join them. Unfortunately we, at that time, refused. Look where we could be at this moment. People, now we have a second chance to be recognized as an elite group of Professional Peace Officers.[102]

In contrast to the girly CSEA and crooked Teamsters, *The Granite* assured its readership that the CCOA would be a tough, macho, and upright union. The group's colors and motto exemplified this toughness, as Larry Corby explains:

> During those election fights for two or three years, a lot of the foundation was laid for what the vision of CCPOA would be. And "The Toughest Beat in the State" came out of that. Black jackets and black hats with gold. And the reason we were black and gold was because the [Oakland] Raiders [the notoriously pugnacious professional football team] were silver and black, and we figured, okay, we're better than the Raiders so we're gold and black. So we became gold and black.[103]

The Folsom chapter sold SWAT baseball-style caps that had the CCOA's black-and-gold logo to signify that the association was battle ready.

Don Novey and his associates developed a motto for CCOA (which remains the CCPOA's motto today): "The Toughest Beat in the State." Their credo expressed the toughness of prison officers, prison officer work, and the CCOA. Jeff Thompson describes the origins of the motto:

> We were sitting in a back office and trying to brainstorm themes and arguments . . . Sitting in a back room and coming up with slogans—you know, one-liners . . . And it just kind of . . . we were grinding around in it, and I said what about this, "walking the toughest beat in the state." Because they wanted to redo their letterhead with the name change. And they had . . . I'm trying to think. The old correctional officer look was green and gold. And it had something about . . . It was sort of academic sounding. It sounded kind of salesman stuff, right? And we wanted something a little grittier. We went from green and gold to black and gold as our colors, and the black element was brought in because we considered ourselves the Oakland Raiders of law enforcement, you know?
>
> . . . It was a tough job. And so when I came up with the toughest beat in the state, that's it. We're tougher than . . . you ask any cop—they don't want our job. We're in here, outnumbered with our wits and a whistle. That was another one of our little phrases, "Nothing but our wits and a whistle for survival." As I described it many times to legislators who never argued with me—these guys are only in a reaction mode. Inmates always have first strike capability.

And [officers are] outnumbered the moment they step on the yard or a tier, or whatever.

. . . Of course, in the '70s we came off of some years where we had lost as many . . . I think they had one year where they lost . . . multiple officers were murdered and there was kind of . . . They had about thirteen killed in the last ten years or something like that. So anyway, it was a tough, tough, tough job.[104]

The "Prison Officer's Survival Creed" expressed the CCOA's militaristic view of prison officers and their work environment.

THE WILL TO LIVE, TO SURVIVE THE ATTACK,
MUST BE UPPERMOST IN EVERY OFFICER'S MIND.

FIGHT BACK AGAINST THE ODDS. TURN THE TABLES.
GET UP OFF THE GROUND. SEIZE THE INITIATIVE.

TAKE EVERY ADVANTAGE: KICK, PUNCH, SCRATCH, BITE.
DON'T EVER GIVE UP.

YOU DON'T BLEED, YOU DON'T HURT.
YOU'RE GOING TO MAKE IT.

YOU'RE NOT JUST FIGHTING FOR GOD AND COUNTRY,
YOU'RE FIGHTING FOR YOURSELF, TO SEE THE KIDS AGAIN.

IF YOUR ATTACKER KNOCKS YOUR TEETH OUT,
SWALLOW THEM AND KEEP ON PUNCHING.

DON'T LET THEM WASTE YOU
IN SOME DIRTY, STINKING PRISON.[105]

The Granite crew felt that the public, press, politicians, and other law enforcement groups treated prison officers as undeserving, faux cops. Although *The Granite*'s writers begrudgingly respected the state's highway patrol officers for forming a successful, independent association, they intensely resented the highway patrol officers' positive reputation and solid material compensation. In addition, they felt betrayed by the CAHP because the CAHP lobbied against a CCOA-sponsored retirement bill. The Folsom officers disparaged highway patrol cops as "traffic officers." In the May 1980 issue of *The Granite*, the editor wrote:

At the recent legislative hearing on the 2.7% Retirement for Correctional Workers, the CAHP testified in strong opposition to our receiving it. This is a matter of some consternation among those of us that have felt we deserved it. A typical CHP officer *might* run up against 5 or 10 felons during his entire career, and when he does, he's got a .357 [gun] to help him. We work with several hundred each day, with our trusty whistle. It seems to us that the [CAHP] doesn't wish to work with us. Let it be known, [CAHP], we're very liable to return the favor at your next legislative session.[106]

Don Novey linked CAHP's smug treatment of prison officers to CCOA's (and later CCPOA's) efforts to show that prison officers are vaunted officers who work "the toughest beat in the state." Novey's article also demonstrated that the CCPOA's public relations activities have been tied to instrumental goals for two-and-a-half decades.

> For years the Correctional Officer has been considered subservient to the Highway Patrol Officer. Permeating the crusty exterior of the Highway Patrol, one realizes their present high position in our "Peace Officers" field was a creation of lobbying and inculcated public relations.
>
> The California Association of Highway Patrolmen has been able to protect the lofty position of the "Traffic Officer" by programming the public and legislature. They downplay other state peace officers during legislative action by displaying the outstanding differences that exist between the other peace officer groups and the traffic officer . . . This type of contrived and calculated operation has been going on for many years. Therefore, with the above in mind, we consider it imperative that we produce to the public and our legislative representatives, the plight of the individuals in Corrections. The Correctional Staff Member that deals on a daily basis with wards, residents, inmates, or convicts, face the peril of a continual volatile situation, one of working exclusively with convicted felons.
>
> . . . The CAHP has belittled our field too long. With that in mind, I suggest we break our supposed ties with that organization and get out a campaign for the plight of the individuals working in the Correctional endeavor.[107]

Novey and his colleagues' resentment toward and grudging respect for the CAHP influenced their vision of an independent prison officers' union.

In order to implement that vision, the Folsom activists had to obtain leadership positions within the CCOA. With that goal in mind, Don Novey ran for statewide president in 1980. Steve Fournier recalls that the CCOA activists at Folsom "spent from 1976 to 1980 challenging [CCOA's statewide leadership] election-wise internally, until we got Mr. Novey elected [in 1980]. And then we changed direction."[108] Novey did not like that the CCOA had an "executive director," Ken Brown, who was a former reporter—not a prison worker. During his campaign for statewide president, Novey championed one main issue: eliminating CCOA's current leaders, who, according to Novey, were not *of* or *for* prison officers (they were just hired hands).

Upon winning the election, Novey restructured CCOA. As the organizational chart in Figure 2.2 shows, he reconfigured the association so that, ideally, all decisions would trickle down from CCOA's membership. Note that noncorrectional personnel (e.g., officer manager and insurance director) have the least amount of authority in the reconfigured CCOA. As president, Novey focused the organization on what he termed the "three Ls"—labor, legislative, and legal. He would gradually develop semiautonomous divisions within the CCOA (and later the CCPOA) to concentrate on each of these three areas. As I discuss in the following chapter, Novey and his colleagues understood that while all three of the "Ls" are essential, the middle L—legislative—is the heart of unionization in the public sector.

When Novey became CCOA president, 5,000 prison workers were eligible for membership in CCOA. Of the 5,000, 3,500 were members of the association. Each member paid $11.00 per month in dues (the membership approved a $2.50 dues increase in summer 1980 as the CCOA geared up for the PERB elections), which amounted to roughly $462,000 per year. As of 1980, the CCOA had 16 chapters, 7 committees, and 6 full-time employees.[109]

Along with restructuring CCOA, Novey moved it further into politics. The CCOA's formal political activities were limited before Novey took charge, Larry Corby remembers:

> The lobbying was all started by Don when he became the state president of the association. He became the state president and we had a retirement bill every year we would put up. And we never got to first base on it. And Don and I were walking the halls of the capitol one day, wearing our black hats. Just walking the halls of the capitol, trying to figure out how do we get a bill heard? . . . And finally [Don] stopped a guy by the name of Bill Richardson, a state senator. And Uncle Bill, as he became known, said, "Well, you guys want to understand politics? Is that what I'm hearing?" And Don says, "Yes, sir." He says, "Follow me." And so we went into his private office and he said, "If you want the people in this capitol building to listen to you, you have to have a political action committee. You have to participate in the political process." And Don says, "Which means what?" And he says, "Well, I can't really talk about it here at work, but if you have trouble figuring out what it is, let me know and I'll talk to you from my house." And so we just started going around and understanding then that there was such things as a political action committee that had funds that donated to races. And this was how you got your foot in the door. It didn't buy you votes, but it bought you access. Where I could walk in or you could walk into a senator's or an assemblyman's office and ask for a meeting and you might get one in about three years. But if you're playing the political game—as they call it—then you have access to these people. And when you have access then you can argue your position. And

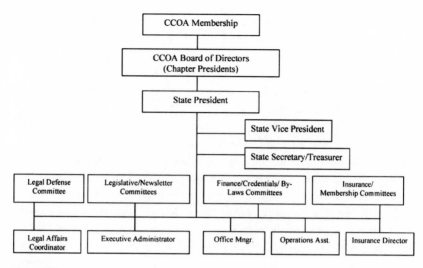

Figure 2.2.
California Correctional Officers Association organizational chart.
The Granite 1, no. 18 (August 1980), 17.

when you can argue your position you can talk them into voting for your bills. And that's what it amounted to.[110]

To help the CCOA gain access to politicians, Don Novey hired Jeff Thompson to lobby full time for the organization.

With Novey at the helm, the association's activists geared up for the PERB election scheduled for May 11, 1981. Jeff Thompson describes the CCOA's strategies:

> We did a direct mail campaign. We did site visits. We handed out literature. We were active in the capitol. We tried to tout as much as we could what we were doing. But our flyers were along the theme that this was our only concern—the toughest beat in the state. And I remember specifically one of the materials that I designed compared the board of directors of the State Employees Association [CSEA], that had everything from maintenance workers to professors of music and all this other stuff, to our board—which was strictly peace officers. Strictly people who walked the toughest beat in the state. And our question was—at the end of the day, when push comes to shove and your scarce dues dollars are being applied for services; which group is going to give you the most bang for the buck?
>
> . . . And we put together an eight-page piece called "Living Targets" and it was a booklet style . . . it was a black enamel cover. Very slick. And it just basically said "Living Targets—the story of the correctional officer," and there was literally a black-and-white target in profile. Or an outline of a body, the

way a target looks. And then there was a series of holes drilled, as if they were bullet holes—in the actual cover. And behind it we had a full blood red page. And then a picture of an officer who unfortunately had been beat to death ... with weights in socks. And it was a grisly photo. But all you saw in the front was this target, and then red behind those holes as if it were blood. And then you open it up and you saw this and it was like—bam.

... [It] was just about their job. We had statistics on people who had been killed on the job; we had statistics on assaults on staff. We had statistics on turnover ... We had how they compared and what it is that they face every day ... And you didn't even know who it was from until you got to the last page and you saw—oh, this is the Correctional Officer's Association.

... And that thing flew out. People couldn't get enough of those things. And when push came to shove on the vote, we were proving the point that that was our only concern—and it was their story, and we were the ones that were carrying it.[111]

Steve Fournier also remembers the campaign against CSEA and the Teamsters:

There was a lot of us involved in it. But what worked the best was what still works best today. When is the last time the central labor council in any district or state stepped forward to assist anybody in law enforcement? And nobody could answer that one. So it was real easy. And ... the president of CSEA ... was the manager of the Department of Motor Vehicles ... CSEA had a bad habit of electing managers to run their association. So the Teamsters was easy. The Teamsters never had a strong foothold in California. And it was real easy to point out that they couldn't even find their president. He was buried somewhere.[112]

The results of the election were closer than CCOA's representatives had expected. The tally was 1,883 for CCOA, 1,707 for CSEA, and 287 for the Teamsters. Although CCOA received the most votes, it did not reach the 50%-plus-one margin needed for outright victory. Therefore the state scheduled a runoff election between CCOA and CSEA for September 1981. In the second election, the CCOA convincingly defeated the CSEA by a vote of 3,370 to 920. With the victory, the California Correctional Peace Officers Association was born. The CCOA changed its name to the CCPOA because now it was not a union solely of "correctional officers." It included other "peace officers"— parole agents, correctional counselors, and medical technical assistants (hybrid officers and nurses). The creation of the CCPOA was also the creation of a new position within the imprisonment field and the larger penal field: that of the independent prison officers union.

CHAPTER 3

A Politically Realistic Union

When prison officers in California established their union in 1982, they found themselves in a very favorable social environment. The ascent of "tough-on-crime" politics and a corresponding "culture of fear" sparked an incredible prison boom in the Golden State, which, in turn, filled the California Correctional Peace Officers Association's (CCPOA's) membership rolls and financial coffers. They also enhanced the CCPOA's (and other law enforcement groups') value in the political arena and offered the prison officers union potential allies. This advantageous environment (what social movement scholars would call a "political opportunity structure") was a necessary but not sufficient condition for the CCPOA's success.[1]

This chapter discusses how the CCPOA's leaders developed an unorthodox strategy of unionization that facilitated their ability to take advantage of the fortuitous environment of the 1980s and 1990s. This strategy, which I term "politically realistic unionism," centered on three tenets:

1. Public sector unions are political organizations.
2. The political field is an arena of Hobbesian competition.
3. Political actors must frame their interests and actions in moral terms.[2]

The CCPOA used the windfall of economic resources wrought by the prison boom to develop a large political infrastructure. It then employed its political resources to reward friends, punish enemies, and construct the "specter of the CCPOA"—an image of an omnipotent, unpredictable, and merciless labor organization. The union also funded expensive public relations campaigns that framed the union's interests in terms of the public good and described prison officers as professionals and victims worthy of respect and substantial material compensation. It was through its politically realistic strategy that the union obtained remarkable success, and as it gained in achievements and power, it fundamentally altered the composition and culture of the penal field.

THE GOLDEN STATE OF OPPORTUNITY

The timing of the California Correctional Officers Association's (CCOA's) victory over the California State Employees Association (CSEA) and the Teamsters could not have been better. With the end of indeterminate sentencing, the rehabilitative ideal lost its standing as the official purpose of incarceration in the Golden State. The state legislature officially declared that punishment (and not rehabilitation) was the primary objective of imprisonment.[3] At the same time, many mainstream liberals and radical activists changed their focus from prison reform to other issues (e.g., the environment and nuclear power), and federal jurists reduced their favorable, interventionist decisions for prisoners' rights.[4]

During the 1960s and through much of the 1970s, strident law-and-order advocates, including CCOA leaders, had been well outside the mainstream regarding penal policies. In addition, they were not well organized and had few influential political allies in Sacramento. However, in the late 1970s and early 1980s, proponents of law and order started to combine their energies and push penal policy away from rehabilitation and toward retribution and incapacitation. These proponents included inchoate victims' rights groups, anticrime entrepreneurs, prosecutors, and several ultraconservative politicians, including "Uncle Bill" Richardson. Legal scholar Candace McCoy describes the loose coalition of law-and-order advocates and their national appeal:

> Ordinarily, suggesting that such close connections existed between conservative politicians, their policy supporters, and planned electoral issue-mongering might strain credibility. But this group of dedicated anticrime entrepreneurs was well recognized in Sacramento and in newspapers and broadcasts as an organized *coterie* of agitators for the conservative agenda. The group also received attention when some of its members later carried its ideas to the national arena. Included were State Senator Ed Davis and Edwin Meese III, who . . . was appointed Attorney General of the United States when Ronald Reagan became president [in 1981]. He provided a conduit whereby the law-and-order agenda developed in California in the 1960s and 1970s was later applied to national policies. These people were united in their demands that California criminal law be transformed, and, to a large extent, they cohered so tightly because of their common experience in attempting to recall the Chief Justice of the California Supreme Court, Rose Bird, in 1978.[5]

The "coterie" tried unsuccessfully to recall Judge Bird (the first female chief justice of California's Supreme Court) because during her tenure (1977–1987) the state's highest court opposed the death penalty, expanded defendants' rights, and undercut mandatory sentencing laws.[6] California voters, in 1986, chose not to reconfirm Judge Bird—the first time that the electorate had ever refused to reconfirm an appellate court judge in the Golden State.

In 1982 the loose-knit alliance of law-and-order advocates organized a campaign to pass Proposition 8, "The Crime Victims' Bill of Rights." The proposition contained a hodgepodge of provisions, some of which did not concern crime victims or their rights. It required prisoners to pay restitution to their victims, curtailed plea-bargaining for major felonies, toughened bail procedures, added an additional five years of prison time for prior felony convictions, and guaranteed victims the right to testify at sentencing hearings.[7] Proposition 8 passed by a vote of 54% to 46%.

Proposition 8 was the first ballot initiative to target penal professionals (in this case, judges and lawyers) in the name of "crime victims." It was also the first major public campaign that juxtaposed "victims' rights" and "prisoners' rights," and depicted a zero-sum game between crime victims and prisoners.[8] The initiative exemplified the intensifying backlash against actors who occupied dominant positions in the post–World War II rehabilitation-centered penal field, especially judges. It also showed that the previously fringe law-and-order activists (or at least their issues) were becoming more mainstream.

At this time, criminologist Joan Petersilia explains, the political establishment in Sacramento increasingly embraced the move toward punitive segregation:

> Once the public lost confidence in rehabilitation, politicians were less willing to defer to criminal justice professionals' judgment on how to reduce crime, and, in response to perceived public demands for a tougher approach, began enacting mandatory minimum prison sentences and increasing sentence lengths for many offenses.[9]

In May 1981 the California Department of Corrections announced:

> "Get tough-on-crime" has emerged as the main theme of the 1981 legislative session. More than 30 bills have been introduced increasing punishment for various crimes. Another half-dozen would forbid the granting of probation. Others create new crimes. Some take away "good time." Elimination of commitment of persons convicted of sex crimes to state hospitals as mentally disordered sex offenders is the object of other bills. Legislators feeling the need to crack down on juvenile [sic] offenders are carrying bills to prohibit criminal court commitments to the Youth Authority [YA], to count criminal court prior YA commitments as

prison terms for purposes of sentence enhancements, and to bar recommitment of minors to the YA if they are convicted of a felony.[10]

When Republican George Deukmejian became governor in 1983, he declared,

> Protecting citizens from crime and fear of crime is, in my view, government's paramount responsibility. For this reason, I have repeatedly expressed my satisfaction over the increasing percentage of convicted criminals who were being sentenced to prison. I would rather have the state have the problem of housing criminals, than for citizens to have criminals entering their houses.[11]

Governor Deukmejian's Democratic counterparts also supported punitive policies (or refrained from policy discussions about crime and punishment) to avoid appearing soft on crime. Democratic state senator John Garamendi said on this topic, "People are afraid of the 'tough-on-crime folk' that want to— afraid of getting beat up in the next election by voting for a bill that might indicate softness on crime."[12] As Senator Garamendi's statement suggests, political candidates more and more appealed to voters by acting tougher on crime than their competitors. To demonstrate this toughness, politicians supported mandatory-minimum sentencing laws with catchy names like "Rob a Home, Go to Jail." Likewise, they opposed relatively innocuous reform bills for fear of getting tagged as "convict comforters." For example, legislators refused to pass legislation that would reduce model prisoners' sentences by 30 to 90 days as a means of making room for new prison commitments.[13] Between 1984 and 1991, the state legislature passed more than a thousand bills that changed felony and misdemeanor statutes, most of which increased prison sentences or changed misdemeanors to felonies.[14]

The blitz of tough-on-crime legislation was one factor among several that fueled an unprecedented increase in California's prison population. Other factors included growth of the state's general population, longer parole sentences, increases in parole violations, and the "war on drugs."[15] In addition, state bureaucrats no longer had the discretion to control prison populations by shortening prisoners' sentences through the parole process, as prisoners now served fixed sentences, and because of mandatory-minimum sentencing laws, judges had limited authority to keep convicts out of prison.[16] In 1981 Governor Jerry Brown described the flood of new prison commitments:

> In the last six years, there has been a 100 percent increase in the number of persons sent to prison. During the early 1970s, judges in California sent an average of about 4,500 felons to prisons each year. Last year, our judges sent 11,000 felons to prison, and this year we expect the number to be even higher. Courts are now convicting 76 percent, or more than three-quarters, of all people arrested for felonies and prosecuted.[17]

California was officially on the path toward hyperincarceration.

The incarcerated population in California had remained relatively constant from the 1950s through the 1970s. Figure 3.1 shows that the prison population had hovered around 25,000, but increased steadily after 1980. As the prison population grew, the state's penal facilities became dangerously overcrowded. Governor Brown and his successor, George Deukmejian, determined that California's 12 prisons could not contain the state's growing number of prisoners. Together, they launched an awe-inspiring prison construction program. The state had opened only 12 penitentiaries from 1852 to 1965, and none from 1965 to 1984. In the last 25 years, though, California has added 21 prisons, for a total of 33 (in addition to 41 firefighting and conservation camps for low-security prisoners).

The Golden State's prison boom forced the state to hire numerous prison officers, swelling the ranks of the CCPOA. From 1982 to 2001, the CCPOA's membership grew by about 600% (from 5,000 to 31,000), as shown in Figure 3.2. Of the CCPOA's nearly 30,000 members in 1999, 19% were women (the largest female representation of any law enforcement union in California), 55% were white, 26% were Hispanic, 15% were black, and 6% were "other."[18] In 2008 the CCPOA represented *one of every seven* state workers.[19] The CCPOA's bank account grew along with its membership. As noted in chapter 2, the CCOA had a budget of approximately $462,000 in 1980. In 2002 union members paid about $60 per month (1.3% of the top salary) in dues, while nonmembers paid an agency fee of $40 per month (about 97% of eligible workers were union members). The union's budget in 2002 was roughly $19 million.[20] In 2009 the approximately 30,000 members of the CCPOA paid nearly $80 per month in dues (1.3% × $6,144, the top-step monthly salary), providing CCPOA with about $29.7 million that year.

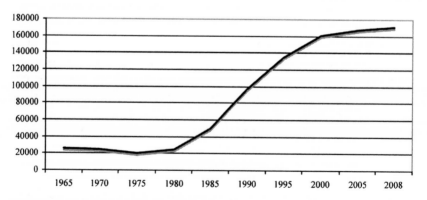

Figure 3.1.
California adult prison population, 1965–2008.
California Department of Corrections, "California Prisoners, 1980" (Sacramento: Youth and Adult Correctional Agency, 1980); California Department of Corrections and Rehabilitation, "Historical Trends, 1985–2005" (Sacramento: CDCR, Data Analysis Unit, 2005); California Department of Corrections and Rehabilitation, "Fourth Quarter 2008 Facts and Figures" (Sacramento: CDCR, n.d.).

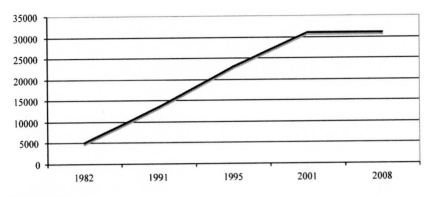

Figure 3.2.
CCPOA membership, 1982–2008*
*Center for Juvenile and Criminal Justice, "California Prisons," II-4; 2008 membership total provided by Joe Bauman, phone correspondence, August 2009.

A Note on Diversity

As the CCPOA's membership grew, it became increasingly diverse, and the union's leadership promoted, even celebrated, the organization's ethnic, racial, and gender diversity. This may seem surprising considering that the CCOA was, in the words of union activist Tommy Marich, a "good old boys" association that virulently opposed affirmative action. Yet, as the CCOA morphed into the CCPOA, it adopted a very different stance toward diversity in its membership. This was made clear during the union's 2004 membership convention when former president, then consultant, Don Novey criticized the California Association of Highway Patrolmen (CAHP) as a "good old boys' club" that is insensitive to its female members, noting in particular its continued use of the phrase "patrol-*men*" rather than patrol officers. In contrast, he proudly referred to the CCPOA as uniquely "open," claiming that the union embraced ethnic, racial, and gender diversity in the 1980s.[21]

As further evidence of the CCPOA's support of diversity, the group established the Minorities in Law Enforcement political action committee (MILE PAC). Novey's biographical sketch claims that MILE PAC was "the first ever political action committee for minorities in law enforcement."[22] Although it is difficult to verify the veracity of the claim, it is perhaps more important that the former union president proudly emphasizes it as a significant aspect of his biography. The union also provided financial assistance to other ethnic- and gender-based criminal justice organizations, including the Association of Black Correctional Workers, the Chicano Correctional Workers Association,

(continued)

and the Women Peace Officers' Association of California.[23] In addition to supporting organizations, the CCPOA has been particularly open about promoting Hispanic and African American officers to leadership positions in the organization. For example, CCPOA's current president, Mike Jimenez, is Hispanic and its legislative director, Stephen Walker, is African American. Although there are no female members on the CCPOA's executive council, women do serve as chapter presidents and committee leaders.

The CCPOA's public celebration of diversity has clear practical utility in increasing both the union's strength and its cohesion. Scholars have documented that strong ethnic, racial, and gender divisions existed among prison officers in California, particularly in the 1970s and 1980s.[24] The CCPOA's leaders clearly did not want such fissures to undermine the union. Given the CCOA's intense opposition to affirmative action and race- and gender-specific organizations before the CCPOA won the right to represent workers in Bargaining Unit 6, this was obviously a legitimate concern. Taken together, embracing diversity was a skillful maneuver that both increased and maintained support from all prison officers (not just white males) as the union rapidly grew. In embracing diversity, the CCPOA smartly made a virtue out of a necessity.

POLITICAL REALISM

As the CCPOA's membership and financial coffers grew during the 1980s and 1990s, the union developed its politically realistic unionization strategy. It was able to fashion its relatively novel approach because it was *independent*— that is, it had no ties to the American Federation of Labor and Congress of Industrial Organizations (AFL-CIO). Thus the CCPOA did not have to report to a parent organization and was free to devise its own strategy. On this topic, former CCPOA lobbyist Jeff Thompson astutely remarks: "And here's another advantage that we had, unlike any other correctional officer union . . . We had a blank slate to write on, so we could set up our politic [sic] any way we wanted."[25] Free from outside interference, the CCPOA's strategists set about learning and eventually mastering politics. (It is important to note that none of the union's tacticians had previous experience working with labor unions. Therefore they were not constrained by dominant paradigms about union organization, and they felt no affinity to the "labor movement." In brief, they were free of the conceptual and social constraints that shaped other large state worker unions, such as the CSEA.)

Don Novey and his colleagues were quick studies on public sector unions and politics. They understood early on that state workers' unions are political entities. Politicians and state bureaucrats—not business owners, CEOs, or boards of directors—create state workers' terms of employment and sign their paychecks. The success of public sector unions depends, in large part, on their ability to become skillful political players, which includes understanding the contours of and players in the political field and learning and manipulating the rules and mores of the political game.[26]

The CCPOA developed a strategy that exemplified what renowned community organizer and political theorist Saul Alinsky characterized as "political realism." Channeling Nicolló Machiavelli, Alinsky defined "political realists" as those who "see the world as it is: an arena of power politics moved primarily by perceived immediate self-interests, where morality is rhetorical rationale for expedient action and self-interest."[27] Alinsky juxtaposed his view of politics with that of people who see the world as it "ought to be." Typical political discourse tends to deny and obfuscate the reality of politics. Like the pluralist perspective that dominated American political science in the first half of the twentieth century, lawmakers and other professional political actors characterize politics as a relatively open and equitable arena of competition in which legislators serve the interests of "the people."[28] For Alinsky (and for the CCPOA), politics is not a pluralist heaven in which any group of individuals can develop an interest group and create political change. Rather, it is Hobbesian world of fierce, self-interested conflict in which only the strong survive.[29]

The CCPOA's leaders intuitively grasped the often ruthless underbelly of politics because it resonated with their experiences in the dog-eat-dog world of prisons and the military, in which a person or group was either with them or against them and brute force was common. Prison officers learn that they must not show weakness, which means responding quickly and, if necessary, forcefully to threats and acts of disrespect. Not responding to acts of disrespect shows weakness and fear. Prison officers who do not respond to challenges, therefore, risk further disrespect from prisoners and chiding and isolation from coworkers. Officers who respond to challenges consistently and appropriately (using force only when it is absolutely necessary) earn reputations as generally fair people who should not be messed with.

Politics felt familiar for the union's officers, who quickly learned to navigate as they did in prison. Lance Corcoran, union vice president, made this point implicitly in 2004, when legislators led by state senator Jackie Speier demanded that the CCPOA give up the raises it received as part of its 2001–2006 contract to help ease the state's financial woes. When asked how the union would respond to threats from the lawmakers Corcoran said, "In the prison system, if you give in to a bully, you're a punk . . . [The CCPOA] has never been a punk. I can't say it any more clearly than that."[30] Just as officers and prisoners intuitively respond to threats and disrespect with force, the CCPOA consistently hits back against its critics, ensuring that it is not a

"punk." In short, the CCPOA's strategists infused their model of unionization with the pugilistic spirit that marked *The Granite*. Don Novey and his
associates did not need to read Machiavelli or Alinsky to develop their
approach to politics (although they may have). Their previous experiences
primed them to play politics *as if* they had studied these political philoso-
phers intently.

The CCPOA's tacticians understood that in order to become a viable political player, they had to develop the requisite political tools—they needed a
political infrastructure. Toward that end, the union, since 1982, has established at least eight PACs that contribute money to (or on behalf of) political
candidates or causes (e.g., ballot initiatives). As detailed in appendix B,
CCPOA's PACs promote the union's interests at the state, local, and federal
levels. Each year the union channels millions of dollars through PACs to influence elections and ballot initiatives, support allied organizations and political
parties, and accomplish other, related goals. Between 2000 and 2010, CCPOA
PACs doled out nearly $30 million.[31]

In addition to having its own PACs, the CCPOA participates in at least
three PACS with other groups, including Native American tribes, crime victim
organizations, and law enforcement unions and associations. The CCPOA also
participates in temporary PACs that consist of several organizations that
share a similar interest (e.g., opposition to a particular candidate or ballot
initiative). For example, in 2006 the CCPOA established an organization of
law enforcement and crime victim groups called "California United for Public
Safety," which allocated money to defeat Proposition 66, a ballot initiative to
reform the Golden State's "Three Strikes and You're Out" law (see chapter 5).
These temporary PACs are useful when the CCPOA (or another group) does
not want to appear as a self-interested architect of a particular ad or campaign. The disguised PACs make it difficult for political observers to "follow
the money." The CCPOA makes this chore ever more complicated by regularly
transferring money between its PACs and contributing money to other organizations' PACs, which then use the money to support or oppose candidates
and issues.

Prison Officers and Native Americans Unite

The CCPOA's joint PAC with Native American tribes is called the Native
American Peace Officers Independent Expenditure Committee (NAPO).
CCPOA ex-president Don Novey argues that NAPO grew out of officers'
and Native Americans' shared history of disrespect: "I see a wonderful
synergy here," he told the *Los Angeles Times*. "We're the second-class
citizens of law enforcement and they've been shafted by the white man
for generations."[32] Reportedly the alliance also grew out of a personal

connection between the CCPOA and a member of the Pechanga tribe, explains former *Los Angeles Times* reporter Dan Morain:

> In 1988, when Pechanga Chairman Mark Macarro was a teenager and the union was not yet a major political force, his father, Leslie, was a California Youth Authority officer. When a delinquent fled from a jail bus at County–USC Medical Center in Los Angeles, Officer Macarro gave chase. A car struck him, and he died. The union used its widows and orphans fund to help the family cover its bills. A decade later, as the tribe's gambling profits ballooned, [Don] Novey and Macarro created the Native American and Peace Officers Political Action Committee.[33]

> Novey and Macarro obviously saw that, together, the CCPOA and the Pechanga tribe, two of the state's largest political contributors, could become an even more potent political force than either was individually.[34] Over the last decade, the CCPOA has contributed $1,140,000 to this joint operation.[35]

In addition to building an extensive and complex PAC operation, the CCPOA established an incredibly effective lobbying presence in Sacramento. Professional lobbyists help advance the interests of groups like CCPOA by building relationships with legislators, legislative staffers, and state officials; "educating" policymakers about the groups' positions; and, unlike regular citizens, maintaining a physical presence in the capitol.[36] In 1990, with the institution of term limits (Proposition 140), lobbyists in California became even more influential and valuable to their employers, for these seasoned political operatives now had far more experience and knowledge about issues (as well as the inner workings of the political and bureaucratic worlds) than the legislators and staffers who cycled in and out of the capitol. Political scientists Bruce Cain and Thad Kousser stated, "Many legislators turned to lobbyists for guidance. A few new members confessed that in their first year, over 90 percent of their bills were drafted or given to them by lobbyists. When members had questions that their staff and other members could not answer, they called lobbyists for explanations."[37] Clearly an unintended consequence of Proposition 140 was enhancement of the political clout of well-funded and professionally represented advocacy groups like the CCPOA.

From 1982 until 2002 Jeff Thompson was the CCPOA's head lobbyist. In 2002 Craig Brown replaced Thompson.[38] Getting Brown was a coup for the CCPOA, since he had served for 13 years (1983–1996) as a top-level administrator in the Youth and Adult Correctional Agency (YACA), including stints as undersecretary (second in command) of YACA and director (first in command) of the California Youth Authority (CYA). He also served as California's director of finance from 1996 until 1999. In that position he was responsible for developing and managing California's budget. Because he was previously a high-ranking state official (he was "management"), Brown essentially switched sides when he went to work for the CCPOA, providing the union with a representative who knew as much, if not more, about politics, state government, and penal bureaucracy than the lawmakers and state officials he now lobbied.[39]

Two other lobbyists, Gavin and Shari McHugh, now lobby with Brown for the CCPOA. Understanding that lobbyists are essential to gaining and maintaining access to politicians and state officials, and ultimately influence in the state capitol, the CCPOA spends millions to retain the services of quality, professional lobbyists. In the last decade the union has spent more than $3.5 million on lobbying.[40]

REWARD YOUR FRIENDS (AND KEEP 'EM HONEST)

For nearly thirty years the CCPOA has spent millions of dollars developing mutually beneficial relationships with public officials. By 1987–1988, the CCPOA spent more than any other state workers union in California on campaign contributions.[41] Whereas other large public sector unions in California, such as the California Teachers Association and California State Employees Association, predictably align with democrats, the CCPOA is—and has been from its inception—nonpartisan.[42] The union's bylaws mandate that the CCPOA's political action "shall be conducted in a non-partisan, objective manner."[43] The organization's commitment to nonpartisan politics flows from its politically realistic philosophy. The CCPOA builds relationships with politicians who advance its cause, regardless of party labels. Because Democrats outnumber Republicans in both houses of the California legislature, the CCPOA supports more members of that party. For example, in 2005, recipients of the union's contributions were 63% Democrat and 37% Republican.[44] As further evidence of the CCPOA's nonpartisanship, the organization spent comparable amounts in contributions to the California Democratic Party ($1,766,310) and California Republican Party ($1,438,225) during the last decade.[45]

The CCPOA's leaders have long understood that Democrats could help them on labor issues and Republicans could assist them on the law-and-order front. Former officer and union activist Steve Fournier explains, "Here's the definition that will always be true in my lifetime. Democrats love unions, hate cops. Republicans love cops, hate unions. Find a way to walk right down the middle of that aisle and they'll all listen to you. And public safety is the key [to walking the middle of the aisle]."[46] Jeff Thompson agrees,

We knew that the Dems were the guys to go to for labor and union issues, and we also knew that no union went to the Republicans for anything. And we thought—you know what, there are so many times when you just need to work with both sides of the aisle. Let's just cut a new swath here. Nobody is doing this; nobody is doing this in the state. Frankly, nobody is doing it in the country. So . . . we got this bipartisan thing going, and we didn't bat an eyelash about endorsing a Republican. As long as they were okay with us on the collective bargaining stuff. We had some issues [with Republicans] on retirement, career incentives. And we had some stuff that we knew that they couldn't go for, but which we frankly thought were fair. The Democrats could always do this for us, and so they always got the extra brownie points.[47]

Because the CCPOA is nonpartisan, both Democrats and Republicans seek (and get in almost equal measure) the CCPOA's endorsement and money.[48] Had prison workers in Bargaining Unit 6 sided with the CSEA or the Teamsters rather than the CCPOA, they would be members of a "Democratic union" and likely would not receive as much support from Republicans as they do today.

In 1982 the CCPOA developed a process for making endorsements that it still uses today. The union conducts face-to-face interviews with electoral candidates, organized around a list of questions called the "Magic 13." The list changes yearly, but always includes "bread and butter" and "silver bullet" questions. The former focus on typical labor issues such as retirement, arbitration, wages and benefits, and sick leave; the latter concentrate on crime and punishment issues.[49] The CCPOA makes endorsement decisions based on interviewees' responses to the "Magic 13" (and related questions) as well as on "subjective criteria." A key subjective criterion is a candidate's chance for victory. The CCPOA funds public opinion polls to determine voters' positions on candidates (and issues) and often makes endorsements late in the election cycle, which helps them choose winners and have the greatest influence on elections. They also examine the political leanings of voting districts. Jeff Thompson explains, "We looked at the entire state. We would examine every district to see who was an incumbent running for reelection, which was an open seat, what the voting patterns were, how reapportionment had affected the voting constituency blocks—Democrat, Republican, Undeclared, Independent, whatever. So you knew the battleground districts."[50]

The "Magic 13" (2006)[51]

1. What are your thoughts on the utilization of private, for-profit companies to perform prison duties?

(continued)

2. Do you support the death penalty?
3. What are your thoughts on the antiquated, dilapidated facilities at San Quentin and on officer safety on Death Row?
4. Do you support binding arbitration for resolution of disputes arising in the following contexts: impasse and grievances?
5. What are your thoughts on maintaining solvency on peace officer retirement benefits?
6. Do you favor or oppose legislation that changes the "three strikes" law?
7. What are your thoughts regarding vacancy rates in the Department of Corrections and Rehabilitation?
8. Over the years, supervisors have had their salaries and benefits deteriorate compared to line officers. Would you support legislation to mandate salary differentials between the two?
9. Are you in support of physically searching packages and physically searching visitors to control drugs and alcohol within prison facilities and to control violence in prisons? What are your thoughts on the utilization of drug-sniffing dogs?
10. Do you believe in more funding for staffing and infrastructure to be used for setting up true rehabilitative services?
11. What are your thoughts on the Peace Officers' Bill of Rights?
12. Do you support the use of lethal force within the Department of Corrections and Rehabilitation?
13. Presently, local police and firefighters incapacitated in the line of duty get one year's pay. Would you support this provision being extended to correctional peace officers?

Reapportionment (also called redistricting) helps determine which districts are "safe"—that is, overwhelmingly Republican or Democratic—and which are competitive. Because of California's redistricting practices, the vast majority of districts are "safe," which makes it relatively easy for the CCPOA and other groups to predict the outcome of elections.[52] For example, in the November 7, 2006, California general election, 71 of the CCPOA's 72 endorsees for state assembly won their elections; 38 of the 71 endorsees received at least 65% of the total vote. Nineteen of the CCPOA's 20 endorsees for state senate won their races, and 12 of them received at least 65% of the total vote.[53] Since the vast majority of districts are safe, the CCPOA can concentrate its resources on the few contested ("battleground") districts.

In addition to studying voters' preferences, the CCPOA studies candidates' records and personal characteristics, Jeff Thompson explains:

Not only would we have our Magic 13 in that loop of consideration of a candidate, we would do as much research on the background as we could. [Inaudible]
things they brought in terms of their pedigree. What had been their experience
in life? You know, how sharp are they—literally? Just how smart a person is
this? Is he going to be someone who can handle the stress and the demands and
the challenges associated with public office? Are they a good candidate? I mean,
Don [Novey] would have all that subjective stuff . . . In the case of an incumbent
we relied a lot on the pattern of their voting over the years. We had to look
at that.[54]

Along with considering candidates' individual qualities and chances for winning, the CCPOA's strategists study the potential effects of election outcomes
on the composition of the state assembly and senate. They examine whether
potential results will shift power in the legislature from one party to another
and the possible effects of power shifts on the union. When control of the
legislature switches, the leaders and members of committees also change, as
do legislative agendas—all of which can affect the CCPOA.

The CCPOA rewards friends and would-be friends with financial contributions. By 1992, only the California Medical Association was a larger campaign contributor than the CCPOA.[55] The union distributes money to
incumbents and challengers in three main ways. First, the CCPOA makes
direct campaign contributions called "hard money." In 2000 California
voters passed Proposition 34, which limited these contributions so that
PACs could only contribute up to $6,000 per legislative candidate; $10,000
per candidate for statewide office (other than the governor), such as lieutenant governor, treasurer, attorney general, and secretary of state; and
$20,000 per gubernatorial candidate.[56] The CCPOA also provides "soft
money" to political parties, which allocate the cash to candidates and
expenses (e.g., conventions and debates). Under California's campaign
finance laws, PACs can contribute $26,600 to political parties for direct sup-
port of candidates, and they can make unlimited contributions to parties for
noncandidate expenses.[57]

The campaign finance restrictions did not reduce the CCPOA's spending
on politics; they only limited its direct contributions to candidates. The union
then shifted its spending to independent expenditures (IEs)—money spent
on behalf of a candidate or issue for advertisements, mailers, and other
expenses—because PACs are allowed to spend unlimited funds on IEs as long
as they do not coordinate IEs with candidates' campaigns. The courts have
ruled that IEs are "speech" and are therefore protected under the First
Amendment of the U.S. Constitution. The CCPOA made its first major independent expenditure during the 1990 gubernatorial election between Republican Pete Wilson and Democrat Dianne Feinstein.[58] Even though the CCPOA
was not the first advocacy group to use IEs, political pundits in Sacramento

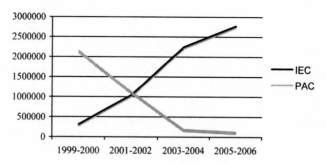

Figure 3.3.
CCPOA IEC and general PAC, total contributions (1999–2006).
California Secretary of State, *Campaign Finance Records*. This chart does not include contributions made by the CCPOA's other political action committees (e.g., "Issues PAC" and "Local PAC") or joint PACs in which it participates (e.g., Crime Victims United PAC and Native American Peace Officers PAC).

consider the union an IE trailblazer, largely because it has spent millions of dollars on IEs since the 1990s.[59] The union has now used IEs extensively for nearly 20 years for such things as the production and airing of commercials in support of or opposition to candidates, direct mailings, radio spots, polling, fundraiser events, and yard signs. As seen in Figure 3.3, the CCPOA's spending on IEs grew exponentially after 1999–2000. During the same period, the money in CCPOA's general PAC decreased precipitously because of limits on direct contributions to candidates.

Gubernatorial Ties

Although the CCPOA contributes to numerous politicians and political aspirants each year, it concentrates resources on leaders in the executive and legislative branches of government. For example, the union has lavished large sums of money on gubernatorial candidates. On this topic, Don Novey states, "If you have an open door with an administration, you can do creative things. A lot of the money that was spent by our group was to get that door open."[60]

The CCPOA made its first foray into gubernatorial politics in 1982. That year the union endorsed Democratic Los Angeles Mayor Tom Bradley over Republican California Attorney General George Deukmejian. In the words of Steve Fournier, it was "a total disaster." The union went with Bradley because he had worked in the Los Angeles County Jail and was better on collective bargaining issues than Deukmejian.[61] When Bradley lost, Don Novey "sent the new governor a congratulatory card and 10 pounds of kielbasa sausage. 'That was only the beginning,' recalls [Rodney] Blonien, then an aide to Deukmejian. 'After that, if the governor had a fund-raiser in Imperial

County, Novey would be there,' atoning for his sin."[62] When Governor Deukmejian attended the CCPOA's convention in 1985, the union gave him a life-size statue of John Wayne, "the other Duke."[63] The CCPOA contributed nearly a half-million dollars to Deukmejian during his tenure as governor.

The CCPOA followed the "disastrous" 1982 election with more than two decades of victorious gubernatorial elections. In the 1990 race for governor, the CCPOA endorsed the Republican mayor of San Diego, Pete Wilson, over the Democratic mayor of San Francisco, Dianne Feinstein. The union's endorsement surprised political analysts because of Wilson's rather poor record on collective bargaining, but Don Novey explained the decision, "Although Feinstein had promised to appoint judges who would enforce California's death penalty law, there's just too much connection between Ms. Feinstein and Ms. Bird . . . We think she's going to be soft on such issues as appointing judges."[64] The CCPOA's endorsement was critical to Wilson because other large unions of state workers—including the California Teachers Association, California State Employees Association, and the California Association of Highway Patrolmen—endorsed Feinstein.[65] The union spent large sums on an IE for Wilson, Jeff Thompson recalls excitedly:

> When Wilson ran for governor in 1990, we did our first significant independent expenditure. And we . . . I say, "we," but Don [Novey] headed this up. And to this day I still remember talking to the press over the IE that we did for Wilson. Because we had some excellent commercials. We did our own polling. We bought our own airtime. We produced our own 30-second spots. We used crime victims [in the commercials] . . .
>
> We also researched the candidates' appeal in certain areas. We knew the battleground was going to be the Central Valley and, to an extent, the Inland Empire. And we thought—well, if Wilson can take these places, he's going to win this race. And so we bought airtime in Fresno, Bakersfield, Riverside. Forget about LA. [because it was a Democratic stronghold]. Forget about San Diego; Wilson will handle San Diego [because he was the city's mayor]. So we had these critical spots all figured out. And we bought airtime during the World Series in October. I mean, we figured it out. Monday night football. We knew. We had done a demographic thing . . . And from that point on we went—[referring to IEs] "That's the big game."[66]

The CCPOA's pro-Wilson commercial featured Harriet Salarno, founder of Crime Victims United of California, a CCPOA-backed organization that I discuss in the next chapter. The spot claimed that Feinstein would support allegedly soft-on-crime judges in the mold of Rose Bird. Wilson's campaign, which had previously castigated IEs as "vicious" and "irresponsible," said that the

CCPOA's commercial was "not bad at all." When asked about Wilson's criticism of IEs, Jeff Thompson said, "He didn't want this kind of stuff to go on. Our board felt so strongly about the issues involved that they wanted to go independently, directly to the voters. Pete's getting our support whether he likes it or not."[67] In other words, CCPOA's tacticians felt that they were better equipped than Wilson's campaign to attack Feinstein in key "battleground" regions of the state. The CCPOA continued to support Wilson after he defeated Feinstein, making a 1994 contribution of $425,000 to Wilson's reelection campaign—the largest single contribution ever made to a political candidate in California.[68] The CCPOA spent more than $1.5 million on Wilson's two successful bids for governor.[69]

An Independent Investment Strategy

During his tenure as governor, Wilson received help from his one ally among state worker unions: the CCPOA. For example, in 1991 Wilson pressured public employee unions to help ease the state's $12.6 billion budget deficit by taking cuts in compensation. All of the state's unions except the CCPOA balked at Wilson's request. Claiming to take the "high road," the prison officers union took a 5% pay cut, which infuriated other unions and CCPOA members. President of the California Teachers Association, Ed Foglia, stated when asked if his organization would take the CCPOA's lead, "We're already taking pay freezes . . . Correctional officers have a total compensation package averaging about $53,000 per year . . . It takes a high school degree and six weeks of training to become a guard. It takes five years to become a teacher and our average pay is about $43,000. So we're not about to play that game."[70] In response to the CCPOA's action, a group of members started an ultimately unsuccessful decertification campaign. A leader of the dissident group, Kurt Bender, told the Sacramento Bee, "CCPOA has been run as a closed little fiefdom for a select few . . . People are ready for new representation."[71] Although the CCPOA's action brought criticism both inside and outside the union, it further ingratiated the organization to Wilson. To show his appreciation to the CCPOA, Wilson approved a 12% pay raise for Bargaining Unit 6 in 1998. At the same time, the governor denied raises to all other state unions except the union representing firefighters.[72]

The CCPOA's acceptance of Wilson's request to take a pay cut and the raise the governor later gave to the union exemplified the CCPOA's independence from other labor unions and the so-called labor movement. The prison officers union explicitly defied fellow state employees groups on behalf of an outright antiunion governor. By taking the pay cut, the

CCPOA made the other unions look greedy in comparison. The action also showed the CCPOA's skill at making long-term investments with politicians, particularly with governors. Whereas union members and other labor groups wanted the CCPOA to refuse the pay reduction, CCPOA's leaders understood that taking the cut and making enormous financial contributions to the governor would likely reap dividends in the future. The 12% raise seven years later proved that the CCPOA's independent support of Wilson was a wise, long-term investment—even if it initially led to harsh criticism from labor leaders and CCPOA members.

In the 1998 gubernatorial race, the CCPOA once again surprised pundits by endorsing Democratic Lieutenant Governor Gray Davis rather than Republican State Attorney General Dan Lungren. The CCPOA had endorsed Lungren for attorney general and contributed more than $100,000 to him. Because of his tough-on-crime credentials, political analysts assumed the CCPOA would side with Lungren. However, Davis appealed to the union because he was prolabor and as tough on crime as most Republicans. As an example of his toughness, Davis vowed that if elected, murderers would not receive parole on his watch (a vow he kept while in office).[73] Whereas the CCPOA's endorsement allowed Wilson to play "the union card," the union's nod for Davis bolstered Davis's claim that he was a bona fide crime fighter.

In addition to endorsing Davis, the CCPOA spent roughly $2.1 million in IEs on behalf of the gubernatorial hopeful. Following a pattern set in Wilson's first race for governor, the CCPOA spent roughly $2 million on television ads, which touted Davis's military record and record on crime. The CCPOA strategically aired the television spots in the hotly contested Central Valley; it also funded a phone bank that placed a million calls to Central Valley voters.[74] When asked to reflect on the CCPOA's support for Davis, Dan Shur, the manager of Lungren's campaign, said, "The day the prison guards endorsed Davis was probably the last day you heard anybody seriously talk about Lungren coming from behind to win."[75]

The union's efforts on behalf of Davis infuriated California's Republican Party, which ran its own television spots in the Central Valley that said, "Don't be fooled by the prison guard union boss' phony ads for Gray Davis. They are spending $2 million because Davis will bow to their demands at taxpayers' expense."[76] Members of the CCPOA also criticized the union's leadership for supporting the Democrat over a conservative, law-and-order Republican. Don Novey said that the CCPOA's support for Davis was "tough for my guys to understand."[77] When Davis became governor and a major benefactor of the CCPOA, Novey's "guys" likely got it.[78] During Davis's

Table 3.1 CCPOA CONTRIBUTIONS TO LEGISLATIVE LEADERS, 1980–2006 ESTIMATED CONTRIBUTIONS (BEFORE AND DURING TENURE)

Position	Tenure	Name	Party	CCPOA
Senate Pro Tem	1980–1994	David Roberti	D	121,000
	1994–1998	William Lockyer	D	62,500
	1998–2004	John Burton	D	895,000*
	2004–2008	Don Perata	D	145,700
Speaker of Assembly	1981–1995	Willie Brown	D	309,000**
	1996	Curt Pringle	R	91,250
	1996–1998	Cruz Bustamante	D	139,700
	1998–2000	Antonio Villaraigosa	D	105,700
	2000–2002	Robert Hertzberg	D	32,500
	2002–2004	Herb Wesson	D	42,700
	2004–2008	Fabian Nunez	D	231,600

*An additional $100,000 from the Native American Peace Officers PAC.
**This figure includes the contributions for only the years 1989–1995. I did not locate contribution amounts for previous years.
Source: California Secretary of State, *Campaign Finance Records.*

tenure as the state's top politician, the prison officers union spent more than $3 million on his behalf.[79]

Legislative Ties

Since the mid-1990s, the prison officers union has become a major player in legislative races. In 1998 the union set a state record by contributing $1.9 million to Democratic and Republican candidates for the state senate and assembly.[80] The following year the CCPOA broke its own record, contributing $2.3 million.[81] Table 3.1 shows that the CCPOA has contributed money to each leader of the senate (senate pro tem) and assembly (speaker) since 1980. Most notably, the CCPOA and its affiliate, the Native American Peace Officers PAC, contributed approximately $300,000 to the long-time, powerful leader of the assembly, Willie Brown, and nearly $1 million to former senator and leader of the senate, John Burton.[82]

The CCPOA supports legislative leaders because they allocate positions on important committees (e.g., budget, public safety, and appropriations), shape their respective parties' positions on important issues, meet regularly with the governor and his staff, and orchestrate the parties' electoral strategies. Legislative leaders, for their part, must build relationships with wealthy advocacy groups like the CCPOA because their capacity to maintain power depends in large part on their ability to allocate campaign dollars to candidates and produce positive electoral results for their parties.[83] These leaders are also attractive allies for the CCPOA because they are generally effective at moving bills through the legislature. For example, between 1998 and 2004, John Burton, leader of the state senate, moved more CCPOA-sponsored bills through the legislative process than any other legislator. Moreover, he did the legislative legwork for three CCPOA contracts, including the 2001–2006 labor compact, which critics labeled a "sweetheart deal" that greatly increased union members' compensation as the state was scrambling to fill growing gaps in the budget.[84]

Even though the CCPOA distributes extensive resources to establish and sweeten relationships with legislative leaders, it also contributes considerable resources to legislators who share the CCPOA's goals and act as "foot soldiers" for the union. These lawmakers side with the CCPOA on issues, represent the union's interests during legislative debates, attend the union's functions, etc. The CCPOA typically honors legislative advocates with awards such as "Legislator of the Year" at its annual convention and events such as the annual crime victims' march on the capitol.

The most obvious legislative "foot soldiers" for the union are lawmakers who are past or present CCPOA members. The union encourages its members to run for local and statewide offices and provides funds to those who take up the challenge.[85] For example, the CCPOA contributed at least $57,000 to former prison and parole officer Joe Baca, Jr.'s campaigns for the state assembly between 1996 and 2006;[86] spent roughly $250,000 on parole officer Albert Martinez's losing bid for the state assembly in 2000;[87] and spent upwards of $200,000 on parole officer Rudy Bermudez's three statewide electoral campaigns (for state assembly in 2002 and 2004 and for state senate in 2006).[88]

During his tenure in the state assembly, Bermudez aggressively championed the CCPOA's causes, to the extent that Don Novey affectionately deemed him "Rudy the Brute."[89] From 2004 to 2006, Bermudez served as chair of the assembly budget subcommittee that oversees state spending for the prison system. He was also a member of the assembly Committee on Public Safety, which has jurisdiction over bills related to crime and punishment. These positions provided Bermudez ample opportunities to assist the union.

Additional Ties

The CCPOA spreads its money and influence beyond the confines of the state capitol. It endorses and makes financial contributions to federal candidates via its "Fed-PAC" and to local political aspirants and incumbents through its "LOPAC." In addition to spending money and issuing endorsements in races for school board, city council, and county supervisor, the union is active in elections for sheriff, judge, and district attorneys.[90] For example, in 1998 the union contributed $25,000 to California Supreme Court Chief Justice Ronald George. The CCPOA's representatives maintain that the union participates in local races because they are the breeding ground for future state legislators. And when asked why the CCPOA involves itself in district attorney races, CCPOA Vice President Lance Corcoran states, "Today's DA is tomorrow's state senator. We get our name out there."[91] In other words, the CCPOA informs local public officials that the union is major player, both locally and statewide, that they should respect. Participating in local politics also provides CCPOA chapters with opportunities to participate in union business and affect their local communities—many of which are "prison towns." The CCPOA uses its local political operation to support like-minded penal practitioners (e.g., judges, sheriffs, and district attorneys) and to oppose penal actors who, in the eyes of the CCPOA, undermine law and order.

In all, endorsing and spending money on behalf of candidates does not guarantee that the candidates will serve the CCPOA's interests once in office. However, it does provide the union with access to public officials. Moreover, the CCPOA expects policymakers it supports to promote the union's interests. In the October 1987 issue of *Peacekeeper*, Jeff Thompson made this point:

> How does CCPOA persuade legislators, who are constantly barraged with inquiries and requests on literally thousands of policy issues before them? The answer is access. CCPOA has built an ability to gain access to legislators and their valuable time. The way we have done this is to examine their voting records on issues of concern to CCPOA. *In return for their support of our issues, we have supported them through legitimate political contributions. As we help insure that they remain in office, they continue to help foster the legitimate goals of correctional peace officers statewide.*[92]

As Thompson indicates, the CCPOA monitors politicians that it supports. If a lawmaker consistently fails to support the union, the CCPOA withholds additional offerings. If the politician betrays the union, he or she risks punishment.

PUNISH YOUR ENEMIES (AND FEED THE SPECTER)

The CCPOA is unique among large public sector unions because it not only rewards its friends; it penalizes its adversaries. Other unions periodically produce negative advertisements (television, radio, or mailing) about a sitting politician, but they have not routinely opposed detractors. Bill Leonard, a former Republican lawmaker who is now on the state Board of Equalization, comments: "If the guards don't like you, they're willing to spend money to get you. Very few special interests go negative quite like they do. That certainly adds to their power—you don't want to be considered hostile to them."[93] Jackie Speier, a former state senator, current U.S. congresswoman, and persistent critic of the CCPOA, says the union is unique because it "take[s] people out. Many of these other groups just raise money and contribute. They don't go around taking people out who don't support them. They don't make demands like CCPOA does."[94]

For followers of Saul Alinsky, the purpose of confrontation is to earn respect, which is distinct from recognition.[95] Politicians and state officials *recognize* numerous unions as players in the political game. However, they do not necessarily *respect* these unions. Unions that dump money into elections force politicians and pundits to acknowledge them. But unions that threaten politicians' careers and back up those threats with action compel politicians to sit up and take notice, to respect and fear their clout. Confrontation helps organizations—in this case, unions—produce exaggerated perceptions of their power. Alinsky's first "rule of power tactics" is *"power is not what you have but what the enemy thinks you have."*[96] Unions develop the perception of power not by confronting every foe all of the time; rather, they periodically confront carefully chosen antagonists.

By attacking their foes (or potential foes), the CCPOA helps create the *perception* of the ruthless, unpredictable, and powerful prison officers union (critics commonly refer to the CCPOA as an "800 pound gorilla"). I call this image "the specter of the CCPOA." The union's officials publicly complain that critics refer to the CCPOA as "the powerful prison guards' union," since they think the name makes it sound like a bully. Jeff Thompson says on this topic, "Well, we were often given that little moniker of 'the powerful prison guard union.' After a while the reference to power begins to be . . . there is a connotation that it is somehow a malevolent power. And they don't say things like . . . I don't know why they don't use words like 'the politically astute' prison guard union."[97] CCPOA Vice President Lance Corcoran says similarly, "We are not politically powerful; we're politically successful . . . Power implies abuse, I prefer 'successful.'"[98] Whereas CCPOA representatives do not like the negative connotation of "the powerful prison guard union" as a phrase, they still want policymakers and other actors in the penal and political fields to view the union as omnipotent and to fear it. Fearful foes are less likely to oppose the CCPOA. The specter of the CCPOA affects actors who do and do not have direct contact with the union. Because of the specter, actors consider possible consequences of their actions before taking positions about penal policy and other issues of importance to the CCPOA. They must think about whether their actions will bring the union's wrath. Therefore the specter of the CCPOA is a *social fact* that has real, practical effects in the fields over which it looms.[99]

The CCPOA breathes life into the specter in two main ways. First, it confronts relatively powerful veteran politicians. For example, in 1990 John

Vasconcellos (D-Santa Clara) opposed a prison-building bond as a member of the state assembly. When Vasconcellos ran for reelection in 1992, the CCPOA contributed $75,000 to his little-known opponent, who put up a tough but ultimately unsuccessful fight against the seasoned lawmaker. Don Novey knew that the CCPOA could not "take out" Assemblyman Vasconcellos—the politician was very popular in his overwhelmingly democratic (and therefore "safe") district. Instead, the CCPOA spent the $75,000 to send the message to *all* politicians (and political aspirants) that the CCPOA would even confront popular and relatively powerful lawmakers who threatened the union's interests. On this topic, former leader of the state senate John Burton says, "Don's not afraid to spend on a losing cause if he thinks he'll get someone's attention."[100]

Vasconcellos is not the only veteran lawmaker that the CCPOA has confronted. In 2002 the union challenged former state lawmaker Richard Polanco. During his tenure in the legislature, Senator Polanco was a constant thorn in the CCPOA's side. He publicly accused the CCPOA of interfering with investigations into staff abuse of prisoners at Corcoran Prison and Pelican Bay State Prison. When talking to reporters about the CCPOA, Senator Polanco infuriated the union by twisting around its motto to emphasize the supposed prevalence of rogue officers: "It's the toughest beating in the state, not the toughest beat."[101] Senator Polanco also enraged the CCPOA by advocating for private prisons.

In 2002 Senator Polanco announced his plans to run for a position on the Los Angeles City Council. The CCPOA sought revenge. It organized a meeting at CCPOA headquarters with East Los Angeles Councilmember Nick Pacheco and Polanco's main challenger in the race, Ed Reyes. "Discussion soon centered on a proposal that the union underwrite an independent anti-Polanco campaign, something in five figures," remembers Reyes.[102] The only plausible reason for the CCPOA's support of Reyes was retribution against Polanco. The City of Los Angeles did not operate any prisons and did not have any plans to build any prisons within city limits. In the end, the CCPOA did not have to contribute the money for Reyes' campaign because Polanco dropped out of the race before it began. The senator's decision came shortly after the media learned of a birth certificate that listed Polanco as the father of an 8-year-old whose mother was a longtime employee of the senator. As the scandal spread in the media, unsubstantiated rumors surfaced that the CCPOA had leaked the story. Don Novey denied the rumors in the *Los Angeles Times*: "I wouldn't do that to another human being."[103] The fact that journalists and legislators believed that the CCPOA was willing and able to leak the story about Polanco's child was an example of the specter at work.

A second way that the CCPOA fuels the specter is by vigorously opposing weak incumbents. For example, the CCPOA spent hundreds of thousands of dollars to defeat state senator Phil Wyman in his bid for reelection to the state assembly. The union ostensibly opposed Wyman because he supported prison privatization. Wyman was an ideal target—he did not have leadership positions in the assembly and was not overwhelmingly popular in his district. Therefore the CCPOA was certain it could tip the electoral scales in favor of Wyman's opponent and receive credit for "taking out" the incumbent. Moreover, if Wyman had won reelection, he would not have had power in the legislature to harm the union. In short, by confronting weak incumbents, the CCPOA sends warnings to actual and potential antagonists without risking retribution from the incumbents.

During his 20-year tenure as CCPOA president (1982–2002), Don Novey contributed to the union's frightening and mysterious aura. Critics routinely compare Novey to Jimmy Hoffa, who embodied the Teamsters' "bare-knuckles" image. Novey regularly touts his experiences as an amateur boxer and military spy, and he rarely appears in public without his trademark fedora (Figure 3.4). While leader of the CCPOA, Novey was reluctant to meet with people outside of his inner circle or who lacked formal political or bureaucratic authority; this reticence contributed to his air of mystery and import. And his elliptical conversation style is known to leave even those people he does meet confused. After conducting a rare, extended interview with Novey, *Los Angeles Times* reporter Jenifer Warren wrote: "In conversation, he veers and rambles, sometimes winking, often leaving cryptic holes in the stories he tells.

Figure 3.4.
Don Novey, CCPOA president, 1982–2002. Image courtesy Zuma Press.

Barrel-chested and never without a hat, he's like the eccentric uncle you whisper about at family reunions."[104] Former CCPOA lobbyist Ryan Sherman says similarly, "It is absolutely mind-boggling to talk to him. You leave a conversation with Don and you are going, 'Maybe it was white or maybe it was black.'"[105]

Novey has a reputation in Sacramento for dressing down politicians, state bureaucrats, lobbyists, and journalists. During my fieldwork, numerous people recounted incidents in which Novey chastised them or other people. A former warden and CDC labor negotiator who asked to remain anonymous revealed:

> I heard Novey say things to people that I could not believe the level of disrespect that money can buy you . . . And the attacks by the union so devastated [prison managers] that it affected their families. It was wrong to do that. When you take people's pride away from them, I just . . . and that was the part of the union stuff that I thought was where they went too far. They really went too far.

Speaking about Novey, former state senator Jackie Speier comments: "He is full of vitriol. At one point we had a press conference, and he walked in with his hat and dark glasses on . . . And I went up to him to say something, and he said something crass, like 'You don't exist.'"[106] Taken together, Novey cultivated the persona of a fearless, unpredictable, and explosive labor leader. The former CCPOA president confronted enough foes to make the rumors about him *seem* true; whether the rumors are true or exaggerated is immaterial. The perception of Novey as a politically sophisticated, Hoffa-esque labor leader enhanced the specter of the CCPOA.

The CCPOA's commitment to rewarding its friends and punishing its enemies has a chilling effect on lawmakers—particularly those who do not agree with the CCPOA's ideas about crime, punishment, or labor unions. Lawmakers are hesitant to support prison and sentencing reform for risk of appearing "soft on crime." Moreover, there is not a sympathetic lobby for prison reform, as there are in other policy domains such as education (e.g., parents of schoolchildren) or health services (e.g., sick and handicapped individuals). I provide examples in following chapters that show that the CCPOA and its allies increase lawmakers' hesitance regarding prison issues, for the lawmakers risk retribution from the union and its allies if they take the "wrong" position.

A MORAL IMPERATIVE

By aggressively rewarding its friends and punishing its enemies, the CCPOA risks looking like a self-interested bully. Students of public sector unions astutely note that these unions must frame their pecuniary or particular interests in terms of the *public good*, since the taxpayers fund public employees' salaries and benefits. State employee unions have to demonstrate that their members provide valuable public services and deserve raises, better training, etc. Unions that do not adequately frame their demands in moral terms risk being labeled "special interests" that harm the public good.[107] Alinsky argues that all political realists—not just unions—must rationalize their actions and goals. Put pithily, "All effective actions require the passport of morality."[108]

As I described in chapter 2, Don Novey recognized that the CAHP's public relations strategy was integral to its success. Novey saw that public relations and politics were two sides of the same coin, and he committed to developing a positive image of prison officers for instrumental, political reasons. Moreover, he and his fellow officers resented that the entertainment industry, academics, and other law enforcement workers (e.g., Highway Patrol officers) depicted prison officers as "knuckle-dragging thugs," "hacks," "bulls," "turnkeys," and "screws." To rebut that reputation, the CCPOA has crafted a beneficent image of prison officers that promotes two primary claims. First, prison officers work the "toughest beat in law enforcement." Second, prison officers are professionals who conduct a valuable and underappreciated public service.[109]

It is important to emphasize that I am not suggesting in this section that the CCPOA is being disingenuous. The union's members and leaders absolutely believe they enhance public safety, improve the penal system, help crime victims, etc. My point is that the union expends great resources to show people outside of the union that the CCPOA is a public service organization. In doing so, the union struggles with politicians, activists, academics, and journalists who claim the CCPOA is a greedy, self-interested organization that ultimately undermines the public good. The union's public relations efforts, therefore, are part of its politically realistic strategy. For the CCPOA, image management *is* politics.

The Toughest Beat

Since at least the early 1980s, CCPOA representatives have repeated—as if chanting a mantra—the notion that prison officers "walk the toughest beat in the state." Because of the toughness of the job, they argue, CCPOA members deserve the same prestige and compensation as other law enforcement workers. The union depicts the toughness of the prison beat in videos like *Behind the Wall: The Toughest Beat in California*; provides prison tours for journalists and legislative staff, with a requisite stop at the "weapons board" (a display of prisoner-made knives, spears, darts, and zip guns); and issues "assault alerts" to the media. It also sends pamphlets to the media and legisla-tors (e.g., *In Harm's Way: Life Inside the Toughest Beat in California*) that describe prisoners' weapons, the relatively low prisoner-to-officer ratio in California, prison overcrowding statistics, and gang activity behind the walls.

According to the CCPOA, California's prison beat is so tough because of low staffing ratios (6.46 inmates per prison officer, as compared to the national average of 4.47) and the characteristics of prisoners.[110] The union argues that only the most serious offenders serve time in state prisons, while the vast majority of convicts do time in jail, are placed on probation, or receive a combination of jail and probation. CCPOA representatives acknowledge that more than half of the convicts in state prisons have been convicted of nonviolent crimes such as drug and property crimes, but claim that statis-tics about prisoners' "commitment offense" can be misleading. One of the CCPOA's position papers, *Public Safety: Government's First Responsibility*, reads: "While it is true that just over one half of those serving time in our state prison system have a 'non-violent' commitment offense, many of the commit-ment offenses are a result of a plea bargain in which a violent or serious offense has been charged, but later dropped or reduced when the defendant agreed to plead guilty to a lesser charge or charges."[111] Moreover, commitment offense

> does not tell the offender's whole story, and it is not unreasonable to assume that the felony drug offender often engages in a lot more activity that just taking illegal drugs. On a case by case basis, judges examine all the facts to determine an appropriate sentence. If a drug felon is sent to prison, there is more going on than is reflected by the simple reference to a "commitment offense." . . . First, second and often third time drug offenders are rarely sen-tenced to prison.[112]

As described by the CCPOA, nearly all of the felons in California prisons are serious offenders who threaten public safety. In contrast, criminologist Joan Petersilia depicts California's prison population as a mixed bag of violent criminals (roughly 48%) and nonviolent recidivists with no prior sentences (jail, prison, or probation) for any violent crime (about 33%). Contrary to the CCPOA's assertion, Petersilia concludes that California's proportion of violent and serious prisoners is "quite similar to the national average."[113]

In a third argument, the CCPOA posits that the prison beat is extremely tough because convicts are committed to victimizing innocent people (citi-zens on the outside and prison officers on the inside of prison), inherently manipulative, drug-addicted, dedicated to gang activity, and untrustworthy. The following statements made by prison officers in the CCPOA's video *Hard Time: A Walk on the Toughest Beat in California* exemplify the union's depictions of prisoners in its materials:

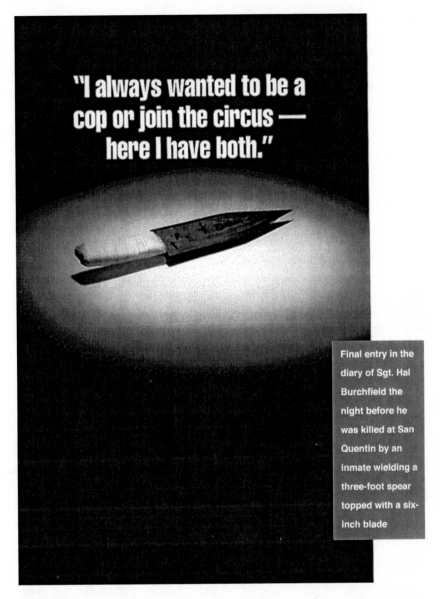

"I always wanted to be a cop or join the circus — here I have both."

Final entry in the diary of Sgt. Hal Burchfield the night before he was killed at San Quentin by an inmate wielding a three-foot spear topped with a six-inch blade

Figure 3.5.
This dramatic image from *In Harm's Way: Life Inside the Toughest Beat in California* shows how the CCPOA's public relations efforts (and, in turn, their officers' reputations) hinge on perpetuating a single view of prisons and prisoners as perpetually chaotic and inherently dangerous.

Male Officer: A lot of people have the misconception that these are people that made a mistake and came in. These guys haven't made mistakes. They intentionally injured somebody to get here.

Female Officer: One [prisoner] I can think of that sticks with me quite often is, uh, I had, uh, a man that . . . I won't even call him a man. He had raped his daughters numerous times . . . sexually molested them for years, and years, and years. Um, they even became pregnant with his children, and he killed 'em, killed the children . . . that his own daughters had become pregnant with . . . that's pretty, pretty horrific . . . This is what we deal with in here; animals like that.

Male Officer: They don't know how to work for what they, you know, want; they take what they want when they want it.

Male Officer: That's all we ever deal with, for years, is people trying to scheme us and get over on us, you know. So, that's one of the big things, they're highly manipulative. Um . . . don't trust any of 'em.[114]

As this example suggests, the CCPOA's claims to respect, professional enhancement, and resources are predicated upon a particular view of prisons and prisoners. The beat is so tough, according to the union, because prisons are circus-like institutions filled with manipulative predators. It takes a true professional to properly function in such a chaotic, ultra-violent environment. In making its case, the union contributes to popular prejudices about prisoners and promotes warehousing as the primary, if not sole, purpose of imprisonment. The "toughest beat" would not be so tough (and the union's insistence that officers are victims would not ring true) if prisons were filled people who, in general, just want to "do their time" and move on with their lives—rather than animalistic individuals programmed to cheat and harm others. The CCPOA's strategy to enhance its officers' professional image, status, and compensation depends on the public, press, and politicians believing that California prisoners are the "worst of the worst."

Professional Public Servants

The CCPOA argues that only the most professional and well-trained officers are capable of taming the "toughest beat" and promoting law-and-order behind bars. Therefore the CCPOA insists that prison officers are not thugs or hacks, but rather professional, dedicated, courageous, and skilled. The union's magazine, *Peacekeeper*, is the main vehicle the CCPOA uses to promote the professional image of prison officers (Figure 3.6). Succeeding *The Granite*, the union published the first issue of *Peacekeeper* in April 1983. The initial issue described the purpose of the new magazine:

> For over a year, we at CCPOA have been planning this magazine for a two-fold purpose. Number One, we need a document that will bring our profession more

Figure 3.6.
Cover of *Peacekeeper*, September/October 2000.

the the [sic] public eye and promulgate our needs, professionalism and thoughts to the public at large and the Legislature. Number Two, we want to better inform all [Bargaining] Unit Six personnel of all pertinent information relative to their profession.[115]

As this statement indicates, the magazine was not merely a tool for communicating with the union's quickly expanding membership. It was also created as a means for promoting the professional image of prison officers beyond the union's membership, with politicians and state officials as key targets. *Peacekeeper* was less ribald than its predecessor, *The Granite*. However, it did not shy away from attacking prison administrators, politicians, federal judges, prisoner rights groups, and other perceived enemies of prison officers and their union. In recent years the magazine (now referred to as a "digest") has become quite slick, with glossy pages and fancy graphics. In many ways, the evolution of *Peacekeeper* from a semiprofessional, somewhat edgy magazine to a professional, flashy digest parallels the transformation of the CCPOA from a small, upstart association into a large, accomplished, bureaucratic union.

In addition to promoting a professional image of prison workers, the CCPOA sponsors laws that increase professionalism among officers in California prisons and Youth Authority institutions. For example, the state has implemented CCPOA-sponsored legislation that establishes the Correctional Peace Officers Standards and Training Commission (CPOST) and mandates the 16-week basic academy for CDC and CYA (putting prison officer training on par with some police departments).[116] Additionally the CCPOA routinely advocates for better psychological screening of applicants to the Department of Corrections.

The CCPOA frames its mission not in terms of the organization or its members' pecuniary interests. Rather, the CCPOA asserts that it serves the public good in several ways. First, prison officers maintain peace in the prisons:

> Despite prison overcrowding, state budget cuts and staff shortages California's correctional peace officers are the most professional and dedicated in the nation. Safer prison design, improved training and better equipment for correctional officers have combined to stabilize prison violence since the "war years" of the 1980s, when prison violence reached its peak.[117]

The union also takes credit for reducing prison escapes in California and asserts that prison officers collectively constitute a line of defense between criminals and "law-abiding citizens."[118]

Since the early 1990s, CCPOA representatives have claimed that the union also serves the public good via promoting the interests of crime victims. In the next chapter I show that the CCPOA has fashioned crime victims as prison officers' natural constituents. The union constructed this constituency because prison officers' clients are prisoners—social pariahs. Labor scholar Paul Johnston shows that successful public sector unions build alliances with sympathetic constituents who justify the unions' demands for public resources.[119] CCPOA officials do not claim that prison officers need higher wages and better working conditions to help prisoners. Rather, they claim to need these things to better protect victims (and potential victims) from heinous criminals.

Finally, the CCPOA exhibits its commitment to the public interest with community service activities. For example, in the mid-1990s, the union created the "Thumbs Up!" child safety program, in which "officers volunteer their vacation time to photograph and fingerprint children and provide their parents with child ID cards and safety tips." According to the CCPOA, the union fingerprinted 100,000 kids between 1996 and 2006.[120] The union produced a television spot to advertise the "Thumbs Up!" program, in which adorable kids in a park raise their thumbs to the camera. As the kids frolic, a narrator says, "You do everything you can to protect them. Now, you can do one thing more with the Thumbs Up! child safety card to keep on file for emergencies. Yours free from the California Correctional Peace Officers Association. Stop by and give your kids a big thumbs up."[121]

In another outreach effort, the CCPOA funds television and print "public service announcements" (PSAs). One PSA called "Lost Child" warns parents about child abductions. The television spot depicts two middle-aged women standing in an outdoor shopping plaza. A cute little girl in a pink shirt leans against one of the women's legs. Harrowing music plays as the little girl walks away from the women. A female narrator says, "A child can slip away so quickly." The mother of the little girl frantically searches for her daughter. An intense man peers at the little girl. The man represents the "sexual predator," an evil character that is currently ubiquitous in political and popular culture.[122] The narrator continues, "You turn your head, and they can be gone. Sometimes forever. Watch your children." The man walks toward the girl. The mother runs to the girl with horror on her face and reaches the girl just before the eerie-looking man. The narrator instructs parents to "Hold them [children] close." The PSA ends as the narrator intones, "A message from the California Correctional Peace Officers Association."[123]

The CCPOA's community service activities promote the idea that the union serves the collective good by enhancing public safety, countering claims that the organization's sole objectives are to accumulate political power and enhance the material status of its officials and members. In addition, these activities promote a "culture of fear," for they bolster the notion that serious and violent offenders lurk around every corner, waiting to victimize innocent citizens (especially children).[124] They suggest that all people are vulnerable to personal attacks (e.g., abduction) and must be vigilant and prepared. In other words, the union's activities assume that we, like prison officers, are all constantly surrounded by dangerous offenders. Political discourse and popular television shows such as *COPS*, *America's Most Wanted*, and *Nancy Grace* support this assumption.[125] In a world where violent predators constantly stalk innocent bystanders, prison officers and other law enforcement workers are vital to public safety and the social good.

The CCPOA's politically realistic unionization strategy facilitated the organization's ability to take advantage of the propitious political opportunity structure that existed for the union in the 1980s and 1990s. California prison officer salaries, compared to those of officers in other states, are empirical indicators of the CCPOA's success. The average pay of California prison officers is slightly more than $73,000, which is 58% more than the national average. According to Petersilia, "it is not uncommon for California correctional officers—who are required only to be 21 years of age and have a GED or a high school diploma—to earn over $100,000 a year."[126] Figure 3.7 puts the salaries of current prison officers in historical perspective, showing the increase in pay from 1982 through 2007.

California prison officers' comparatively high current salaries are the result of the union's 2001–2006 contract negotiated with Gray Davis's administration. The independent Legislative Analyst's Office estimated "that the 2001–2006 [contract] resulted in correctional officers receiving general salary increases of about *34 percent* over this period, not including merit salary increases, overtime, and other categories of compensation. These salary increases were more than twice as much as the increases for the average state employee over the same

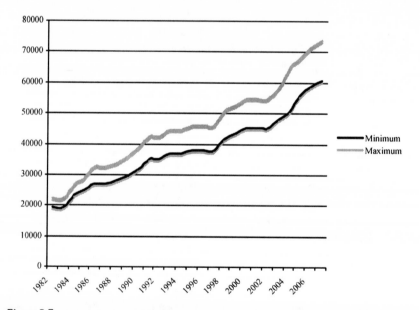

Figure 3.7.
Prison officers' yearly minimum and maximum salaries, 1982–2007.
Office of Financial Management and Economic Research, Department of Personnel Administration, "California Correctional Peace Officers Association, Unit 6, Summary of Pay Increases and MOU Terms" (Sacramento: Department of Personnel Administration, August 10, 2007).

period."[127] (Figure 3.7 illustrates the sharp spike in pay due to the 2001–2006 contract.)

The salary increases for prison officers resulted from a provision in the 2001–2006 contract called the "law enforcement comparative pay methodology." This contract stipulation pegged prison officer pay to that of California Highway Patrol (CHP) officers (which itself was linked to the salaries of police officers in five large, urban police departments); thus prison officers received substantial raises to bring their pay up to par with CHP officers.[128] This provision was extremely important to the CCPOA for both material and symbolic reasons. Along with boosting prison officers' pay, it indicated that officers inside of prisons were as worthy as officers on the street.

In addition to greatly improving prison officers' salaries, the CCPOA has won exceptional retirement benefits for its members. Since January 2006, prison officers have been able to retire as early as age 50. Retirees receive a percentage of the salary they earned at the time of their retirement. The pension amount is 3.0 multiplied by the number of years an individual worked as an officer. For example, an officer who worked 20 years receives 60% of his or her top salary, and an officer who worked 30 years receives 90%, which is the maximum an individual can receive in benefits. "Since 90% is the maximum one can earn in retirement," Petersilia explains, "working past 30 years is basically working for free."[129] Prison officers thus have no incentive to work beyond 30 years, often retiring at relatively young ages. CHP officers receive the same retirement benefits as prison officers. However, prison officers receive slightly better retirement benefits than state firefighters and far better benefits than teachers and registered nurses.[130]

Beyond salary and benefit gains, the CCPOA's early legislative record also demonstrates that the CCPOA quickly achieved political leverage. In the first six years of the CCPOA's existence (1982–1988), the legislature passed and the governor signed 88% (24 of 27) of the union's legislative proposals.[131] By the beginning of 1993, the CCPOA had 47 bills signed into law; 11 years later, that number had increased to 89.[132]

Along with legislative victories, the union has won approval from authoritative actors such as politicians, who have consecrated the union as a legitimate organization and prison officers as authentic, worthy peace officers who work "the toughest beat." For example, Governor Deukmejian gushed about prison officers in a radio address on October 12, 1985 (just months after he gave the keynote address at the CCPOA's annual convention):

Most of us have been fortunate never to have ever met a violent criminal. Imagine yourself, unarmed, locked inside a room that is jam-packed with 100 or more convicted felons. The brave men and women who staff our state prisons live this reality day in and day out . . . A correctional officer is also expected to routinely escort inmates to medical appointments, meetings with lawyers, and visits with family members. They supervise groups of dangerous, violent criminals ranging in size from 10 to 1,000 in work areas and exercise yards—again, unarmed . . . A peace officer's life is one of risk and sacrifice. California's peace officers are among the finest in the world. On behalf of all our residents, we thank you for a job well done.[133]

Approximately 23 years later, State Senator Darrell Steinberg, who became the senate president pro temp in 2008, said: "There's no question that CCPOA is a great force in California, and actually a great model of how people can come together and take an organization and make sure the voices of those who do some of the toughest work in the state get heard within the legislative and the electoral process."[134] In the remaining chapters I show just how well-heard the CCPOA has become in Sacramento and delineate many of its accomplishments, including the promotion of tough-on-crime sentencing laws, containment of prison privatization, and expansion of union authority over prison operations and management.

A subtle but powerful indicator of the CCPOA's success is the desire among other law enforcement organizations to follow its example. As the CCPOA became undeniably the most successful prison officer union in the United States, officers in other states increasingly sought to follow the CCPOA's path. To do so, they requested assistance from the California union. For example, Steve Fournier, provided consultation services to union activists in numerous states, including New York (which became an independent union in 1998), as the activists strove to establish independent unions.[135] When discussing the benefits of independence, a former president and vice president of New York's independent union, the New York State Correctional Officers and Police Benevolent Society (NYSCOPBA), echoed the earlier arguments of Don Novey and other CCPOA trailblazers. The president said, "I mean, being independent, your resources are within your state. We don't have two million dollars going to Washington, DC. That money stays here."[136] From a purely financial standpoint, the success of independent unions is difficult to dispute. According to the U.S. Bureau of Labor Statistics, four of the five states with the highest annual mean wage for prison officers are states with independent prison officer unions—California, New Jersey, Massachusetts, and New York.[137]

In addition to providing guidance to prison officers who desire to establish independent unions, the CCPOA has developed a template for political action that Don Novey and other CCPOA leaders have reportedly passed on to labor leaders in other states. On this topic, Brian Dawe, former director of Corrections USA (CUSA), a national organization that advocates for prison officers and fights prison privatization, noted:

You know, political action is just finally starting to take hold in corrections. Massachusetts didn't have a political action committee until this year. And [they've] been independent for 13 years up there . . . And then they called us, and we hooked them up with California—who helped them set up the PAC. The leader—if you want to look to anybody in corrections for political action—is California. No one knows better than Don Novey how to run that . . . Don realized right off the bat. A lot of us felt that just because we were correctional officers we deserved this, and we deserved that—rightfully or wrongly. But we learned that isn't the case. If you're going to be in the game . . . I equate it this way. If you are a correctional officer union and you don't have a political action committee, it's like playing five-card poker with three cards. You're going to win a couple of hands, but you're not going to be in the game . . . Ideally I'd like to see no money in politics. I'd like to go just on the merit of a position would win more times than not. But if you're going to . . . we don't set the rules, but we're in the game. So we've got to play by the rules.[138]

Dawe not only indicates Novey's influence outside of California, he expresses the same principle that Novey adopted decades earlier—that actors must play the political game as it is, not as it ought to be.

Along with trying to follow the CCPOA's model of political action, prison officer unions throughout the United States have mimicked the California union's public relations strategy. Unions in states as diverse as Rhode Island, Alaska, Florida, and Arizona use the "toughest beat" motto. Like the CCPOA, they contend that prison officers deserve respect and solid compensation because prison officers are professionals who work a tougher beat than other law enforcement workers. The president of Florida's independent prison officer union writes on the union's Web site:

Our brother and sister Correctional Officers walk the toughest beat in law enforcement. We do so with pride, dignity, and a desire to protect the public. The State Correctional Officers Chapter is proud of the great job Correctional Officers do in protecting the public from the criminal element. Under our watch, there are few prison escapes and the state's most violent predators are kept off the street, away from the law-abiding public.

Behind the walls, our brothers and sisters are underpaid and outnumbered while working in a dangerous environment that is overcrowded with violent felons and gang members. To make the situation even worse, prisons in Florida and nationwide are understaffed with extremely high turnover rates. Correctional Officers are routinely assaulted on the job and sometimes killed.[139]

In a recent newsletter, American Federation of State, County, and Municipal Employees (AFSCME) Council 5, which represents state prison officers in Minnesota, includes a story about members who work in the prisons titled, "We Walk the Toughest Beats."[140] The Florida and Minnesota examples illustrate that both independent unions and those affiliated with the AFL-CIO now use a public relations strategy pioneered by the CCPOA.

As well as influencing prison officer unions in other states, the CCPOA has helped shape other law enforcement advocacy groups within the Golden State. On the one hand, advocacy groups have patterned themselves on the CCPOA. For example, in a recent interview, Alan Barcelona, president of the 7,000 member California Statewide Law Enforcement Association (CSLEA), the union that represents state "protective services and public safety" workers (Bargaining Unit 7) such as fish and game wardens and state park peace officers, said plainly, "I fashioned our association after CCPOA."[141] Other groups have simply hired Novey to guide their political action operation. Since stepping down as CCPOA's president in 2002, Novey has worked as a consultant for CSLEA and the Los Angeles Police Protective League, the union that represents rank-and-file officers in the Los Angeles Police Department. When asked about his role with the police union, Novey replied, "Basically, they've asked me to help redesign and develop a smarter political action program for the future. I'm going to help them with some of the essentials of politics that are necessary for them to be above reproach . . . It's a fun project to see them grow in the political arena and help them use their money more wisely."[142]

The following chapter shows that, in addition to influencing law enforcement groups, Don Novey and the CCPOA helped develop and mold California's most powerful crime victim rights organizations. For now, it is sufficient to say that the CCPOA's politically realistic strategy has spread to other organizations within and beyond California. Whether through imitation or exportation, groups have tried to follow the CCPOA's path. It is remarkable that an organization that had no idea how to play politics just 25 years ago developed a political playbook that is being used by law enforcement and non–law enforcement groups alike. The remainder of the book demonstrates that the CCPOA has fundamentally altered the penal landscape by implementing its novel vision of labor unionization.

CHAPTER 4

Power by Proxy

The Strategic Alliance Between Prison Officers and

Crime Victims

In 1996 the California Correctional Peace Officers Association (CCPOA) distributed a public relations video, *Behind the Wall: The Toughest Beat in California*.[1] The 18-minute film was slickly produced and showed the toughness of the prison beat, highlighting the valor of the people who work it. It is frightening. Supposedly representing typical California inmates—big, black, brutish gang members armed with homemade shanks hunting their prey: prison officers—the "thin green line" of officers is the only thing standing between "us" and these predatory prisoners. After viewers have watched some ghastly examples of prison violence, former CCPOA President Don Novey summarizes the video's argument: "It's probably the most difficult and challenging job in law enforcement today."

Two sources then validate Novey's (and the film's) thesis. The first, Jan Miller, was at the time chair of the Doris Tate Crime Victims Bureau (CVB), one of the two most politically influential crime victims' groups in the state. She explains: "And the correctional officers live a very difficult life because there's not very many of them compared to the number of prisoners." The second source, Nina Salarno, deputy district attorney of Sacramento County, elaborates:

> They're inside those institutions. They're dealing with a criminal element day in and day out. It's a dangerous situation. It's a closed situation. And it's a tough situation. And getting that out to the public is very important, because I don't think people realize how awful it is inside there. I can remember walking through the institutions with the officers and listening to the inmates yell, or even spit,

or do things like that. And seeing the life that they [the prisoners] were living, kind of a luxury in there [shows prisoners kicking a soccer ball on the yard] versus these officers who are working hard to support their families, and I don't think the general public knows that.

Later in the video, Salarno emphasizes the prisoners' brutality:

It means nothing to assault an officer, to pull a weapon on an officer. It means nothing to them to go to prison. Prison is not a punishment for them anymore. They don't have any fear. It's a badge of honor to assault a police officer. It's a badge of honor to go to prison . . . And so that's making them more violent in the prisons.

The video presents Miller and Salarno as independent experts with objective views about the nature of prison officer work. In reality, however, both women are tightly connected to the CCPOA. The union literally created Miller's organization, the CVB. It also established another, related crime victims' group, Crime Victims United of California (CVUC). Nina Salarno (now Salarno-Ashford) is the daughter of CVUC's president, Harriet Salarno. Along with working as an attorney, the younger Salarno works for CVUC and, at times, the CCPOA. Put simply, Miller and Salarno are not impartial commentators—they are affiliated with and help legitimize the CCPOA.

Behind the Wall is just one small example of how the CCPOA's ongoing investment in California's two most influential crime victims' groups pays dividends. The union created these organizations principally for political (i.e., strategic) purposes. This is not to say that Novey and the union do not genuinely care for and want to assist victims and their families—they do. But the victims' groups also help the CCPOA achieve its goals from *outside of its ranks* in three main ways. First, they validate the CCPOA's argument that prison officers are uniquely skilled professionals who work the "toughest beat in the state." Second, they legitimate the CCPOA's claims that the union serves universal purposes (rather than its individual, pecuniary interests) by supporting crime victims and bolstering public safety. Third, the victims' groups provide political cover for the CCPOA by taking public positions on controversial policies related to crime and punishment, allowing the CCPOA to sidestep these issues because it fears that public officials and the media will label the union "self-interested."

While helping the CCPOA achieve *power by proxy*, the victims' groups have become major actors on the penal stage. Public officials and journalists have designated representatives of these organizations as the *voice of victims* in California, thereby marginalizing other victims' groups that promote reconciliation between offenders and convicts and prefer treatment and rehabilitation over vengeful penal sanctions. In concert with the CCPOA and other law enforcement groups, CVB and CVUC have fundamentally altered the architecture and orientation of California's penal field, thus circumscribing the state's possible approaches to crime and related social problems.

OVERVIEW OF THE "CRIME VICTIMS' MOVEMENT" IN THE UNITED STATES

In roughly the last two decades, crime victims' organizations and spokespersons have become effective, high-profile political actors.[2] The so-called crime victims' movement has successfully advocated for numerous laws that purport to advance the rights of victims. These laws seek to increase financial compensation to victims; allow victims or their representatives to make statements during criminal trials and parole hearings; protect witnesses of criminal acts from retaliation; and develop and enhance services such as counseling for victims and their loved ones. The victims' movement has also effectively pushed for legislation that stiffens penalties for perpetrators of rape, murder, domestic violence, and other serious crimes, and lengthens and intensifies parole and probation sentences.[3]

The contemporary movement for victims' rights in the United States started in the early 1970s, when feminists formed organizations to raise awareness of and strengthen laws concerning violence against women.[4] In 1974 the Law Enforcement Assistance Administration started funding crime victim services in the United States.[5] By the end of the decade, victims' advocates had established organizations like Parents of Murdered Children and Mothers Against Drunk Driving.[6] In 1981 President Reagan convened a "President's Task Force on Victims of Crime," which proposed the first constitutional amendment for victims' rights and pushed Congress to establish a federal Office for Victims of Crime to fund crime victim services.[7] The Reagan administration also instituted a National Crime Victim Rights Week in 1981. Today, all 50 states have bills of rights for victims and victim compensation programs, and 29 states have amended their constitutions to include provisions about victims' rights.[8]

Journalists, academics, politicians, and activists often refer to the thousands of groups that advocate for victims of crime as the "crime victims' movement." It is true that most crime victims' groups share common beliefs. They believe that penal institutions—police, courts, prisons, probation, and parole—and penal actors are insensitive to victims. They view the institutions as overly bureaucratic, impersonal, overburdened, and slow moving. In addition to resenting the poor treatment they receive, victims and advocates tend to believe that "the system" cares more about the accused and convicted than victims. In short, crime victims and their loved ones often feel that they suffer victimization twice: first by the perpetrators and again by the penal system.[9]

However, although crime victims' advocates share basic beliefs, no coordinated and single-minded "crime victims' movement" exists.[10] Groups that advocate on behalf of victims at the local, state, and national levels have diverse constituencies, goals, and practices. Mainstream organizations like the National Organization of Victim Assistance define victimization and victims broadly, and they serve victims of crime along with victims of natural disasters, wars, and terrorism. Other organizations advocate for reconciliation between victims and criminals and treatment for convicts. Particular organizations, which Robert Shapiro calls the "vengeance-rights lobby," promote policies that increase victim participation in the penal system, enhance compensation for victims, and implement punitive sanctions for criminals, such as "Three Strikes and You're Out" and "Megan's Law" (which intensifies surveillance of persons convicted of sex offenses).[11] They also advocate for policies that make penal institutions more austere and harsh. Penal sanctions advanced by punitive-oriented crime victims' groups, legal scholar Jonathan Simon observes, are "state-sponsored ways to reproduce a certain kind of victim voice . . . one of extremity, anger, and vengeance."[12] Even though there are many types of victims' rights groups, politicians, the media, and many victims' advocates often equate victims' rights with the vengeance-rights lobby.[13] It is generally assumed that politically conservative, vengeful crime victims' groups dominate the victims' movement because politicians have privileged and even co-opted these groups.[14] While that argument is more or less true, it misses an important fact: these groups, at least in California, have influential and well-funded supporters who provide them with organizational and financial resources and political training.

THE ROOTS OF A POWERFUL PARTNERSHIP

In the late 1980s Don Novey, CCPOA president from 1982 until 2002, and his fellow union officials decided to form alliances with crime victims' advocates. Steve Fournier, a long-time CCPOA activist and retired prison officer, explains that the relationship grew so strong that the union was seen as the "puppet master" of the victim groups:

> At one point in time—I believe it would be about 1987, '88, somewhere in that area, Don [Novey] and I were . . . driving to Salinas, to Soledad, from Sacramento. And he says, "I just don't understand what it is we're doing wrong. We've got a foot in the door politically to where people will listen to us and respond to us, but nobody on the outside understands who we are and what we do. And we can't get a break. We get bad press. We get treated badly. We get spit on by other agencies . . . Who out there is our ally?" At that point in time I simply said, "Don,

the only people out there that call us are the victims of the people that we're holding in custody. We need to embrace these folks." And of course, we went on to form the Doris Tate Crime Victims Bureau and Crime Victims United, which purely was a victims' assistance group in the beginning . . . Doris Tate goes after judges and DAs and helps victims. And they testify and lobby. And Crime Victims United is the political wing of the victims' movement. And most people have said that we're the puppet master. My exception to that is that I would rather be described as somebody that helps them find the direction. But the idea to go after the issues and the politicians is them. We just . . . I'm driving the car and they're telling me which turn to make . . . I have distanced myself from most of the victims' groups . . . because they're doing good on their own. They don't need me whispering in their ear.[15]

Nina Salarno-Ashford, the daughter of Harriet Salarno (the director and founder of CVUC), explains that, in the late 1980s, Don Novey had a clear vision of the potential payoffs an alliance between the CCPOA and victims' groups would have for both:

When we first formed this alliance between victims and correctional officers people were like—what are you talking about? Because they couldn't quite see it. But yet [Novey] could see down the road the benefits of both. And it really has formed, between Crime Victims United and CCPOA, it has formed a very strong bond that has been beneficial to the officers as well as to us.[16]

Novey and Harriet Salarno met at a 1990 parole hearing for the man who murdered Salarno's daughter, Catina, in a college dorm room in 1979. At that time, Salarno was leading a small organization called Justice for Murder Victims/Vocal Foundation in San Francisco. She facilitated support groups and lobbied state legislators (with little success) to pass victim-friendly legislation. Salarno describes her initial meeting with Novey:

[For the parole hearing of Catina's killer] . . . we organized and we had two buses going to Vacaville, filled. And cars, which we had about 300 people. We even had kids from her [Catina's] high school and her grammar school—in their parochial uniforms—saying no more crime and all that . . . And Vacaville prison didn't know what to do. They didn't know what hit them! I mean, this was never done! And we come up with our—and I planned an Italian barbeque, so we got all the requirements and permits for the barbeque. Now, Vacaville didn't know, but they didn't dare keep us out because the press was there! [Laughs] All the press! We sent press releases! I mean, everything! We had Channel 2, 4, 6! And I mean, Channel 2 even flew in with a helicopter. It was all over! Because I didn't want him to get out . . . I wanted them to know what victims go through . . .

. . . Well, this was my first introduction to CCPOA. I get off of the bus and there's a man in a black jacket with the CCPOA, and he introduced himself to me. Told me his name. And he says he's representing the president, Don Novey. I just knew vaguely what CCPOA was, and I wasn't too sure. I was very confused . . . So I invited them all to the barbeque . . . And they came to the barbeque, they met the family. They mixed with us. They were so nice . . .

. . . I didn't know how supernice they were. You know? They came. The president came down. Don Novey and all them came down . . . They were so impressed with what I did, and they came over to me and said, "You don't know how much you did." You know? To expose what victims go through and what they all do . . . And we went to go pay the caterer and they [CCPOA] picked up the bill.

. . . I was so appreciative. Well, then we got a phone call [from a representative from CCPOA] asking us if we would come up to Sacramento for a meeting. The president, Don Novey, would like to meet your entire family.[17]

Impressed with Novey's entourage and intrigued by the interest the union had shown in her small group, Salarno went to Sacramento in 1990. She met with Novey at CCPOA headquarters:

I said, "Do you want to help me?" . . . And he says, "What do you want?" And I said, "I want to be as powerful as you." You know? [Laughs] "Which I know I can't, but I would like to be. Because victims have no money. We have no membership." . . . When I told him I wanted to be that, he said—"Well, what do you mean?" And I said, "Well, Mr. Novey . . . just running a support group is not going to stop crime. We need legislators that are pro–public safety. Whether they're Democrats or Republicans. We also need a lobbyist to be able to pass good legislation. Because they [politicians] don't listen to us. They use us as a tool . . . And also, I want a foundation. I will not give up my trench work." That clinched it with Don. He said—"What do you mean by trench work?" I said, "I may come to Sacramento, but I will not give up my monthly support group, because these people need help. They all need help. They need help to know that the system is not on their side—and I want to prepare them for their trials, I want to prepare them for their paroles and everything." . . . And then I said, "I want a foundation, also—prevention for us is with children." I said, "When they [offenders] do heinous crimes you can have them. You can house them. And children is where we need to concentrate." . . . So that's what clinched it with Don. And he said, "Okay, we'll help you organize." And that's how in 1990 Crime Victims United was born.

Salarno could not have been clearer, saying outright that CVUC would not exist without Novey: "Don did it. I could not do this without CCPOA, because we didn't have the money to do it."[18]

Shortly after meeting with Salarno, Novey effectively created CVUC and CVB. CVUC's main role was political action: lobbying, endorsing and providing money to electoral candidates, and sponsoring and opposing legislation.[19] CVB's primary duty was to monitor courts to ensure that judges treated victims fairly and did not give convicts lenient sentences, and that district attorneys prosecuted serious offenders rather than negotiating plea bargains. Salarno explains key differences between CVUC and CVB:

> When he founded this in 1990 and he says, okay—Don [Novey] said— okay . . . we will form two things. We will form a political PAC and we'll form a [foundation]. Okay. One was to be called Crime Victims United of California and the other one was to be the Doris Tate [CVB], in memory of Doris Tate. She was dying . . . He told me to pick the head of that, of the Doris Tate. I said, "Well, why can't I have it all?" I remember that. You know, he was cautious. He didn't know how I was going to grow, too . . . He said, "Well, maybe someday you will have it all." And I said, "Okay."
>
> . . . So now the Doris Tate [CVB] does do some legislation . . . But they are not in Sacramento any longer. And they function out of San Diego . . . They are a fine organization. But I try to be more bipartisan. And you can see the way they endorsed and all; they were all one party [Republican]. And that's okay . . . [but] I don't want the Republicans telling us what to do and I don't want the Democrats telling us what to do.[20]

The CCPOA poured extensive financial and organizational resources into the development of CVUC and CVB. The union initially gave the organizations office space, lobbying staff, attorneys, and seed money (78% of CVB's and 84% of CVUC's initial funding).[21] According to California Secretary of State records, the union continues to financially support CVUC through its political action committees (PACs). In 2007–2008 the CCPOA contributed a total of $211,000 to CVUC's two PACs ($199,000 to CVUC's independent expenditure committee and $12,000 to its general PAC). During this period the CCPOA was the only organization that contributed money to CVUC's two PACs. The union also gave CVUC at least an additional $295,000 in "civic donations;" paid CVUC staff person Maggie Elvey $63,000; paid $8,500 to CVUC's former political director, Allen Pross; and gave $582 to Harriet Salarno for cell phone fees. In total, the CCPOA contributed more than half a million dollars ($578,882) to CVUC in 2007–2008 at the very least.[22] The CCPOA has not recently provided money to CVB through its PACs. However, it may provide money to CVB through other means. Money that the CCPOA gives CVB and other groups at fundraisers, for example, is not public information.

Birth Announcement

In 1993 the CCPOA described the formation of CVB and CVUC and characterized the "pro bono" work that it planned to do for the groups.

From *Peacekeeper*, January/February 1993

For a long time, crime victims and victim advocates have found an ally in the California Correctional Peace Officers Association (CCPOA) in Sacramento.

When victims and advocates came to Sacramento for legislative functions, CCPOA helped in many ways. It provided office space, including phones and faxes, and support to those testifying before the legislature. Now CCPOA is going even further.

On April 1, 1992, CCPOA opened a Victim Service Bureau to help victims more directly, headquartered in the Association's offices but staffed by victim advocates. The Bureau helps California victims file for compensation, completes victim impact statements, and guarantees that their rights as victims are observed.

The same month, CCPOA kicked off a Victims' Political Action Committee (PAC). The PAC is able to make political contributions and lobby—activities that most victim organizations are barred from doing because of their non-profit status, says CCPOA's Steve Fournier, who is the Administrative Officer of the new PAC.[23]

From *Peacekeeper*, March/April 1993

Of all the people who are impacted by our criminal justice system, perhaps none are [sic] more needy and yet more forgotten than the victims of violent crime. As officers in our respective systems, we see the perpetrators of crime and violence being too often afforded rights and coddling that really should be afforded the victims of these perpetrators. Therefore, the Association has authorized what is called "pro-bono" work on behalf of several victims [sic] issues. This year those issues include an outright prohibition of unsupervised conjugal visits for murderers and sex offenders and a "truth in sentencing" law for a first or second degree murder so that any good time earned would not take away from the minimum sentence imposed by the court, and would instead be considered for the purposes of parole only. Related to that, the victims would like to see an extension of the time by which parole considerations may be reviewed so that they are not subject to continually having to reappear before parole boards when their perpetrator comes up for consideration.[24]

Along with providing organizational resources to victims' groups, the CCPOA taught them how to play political "hardball."[25] Harriet Salarno asserts that Don Novey "steered us in the right direction, opened the door, and taught us what to do. He educated us."[26] She elaborates:

Well, he tells me about the games that go on. Now I can read through a lot of them, you know? He has taught us about that. He has taught us how to act when we [interview] candidates. What kinds of questions to ask. Don't talk—let them talk. You know? . . . I mean, we're very credible. We send questionnaires out. We do it with sheriffs, district attorneys, judges, all the legislators and constitutional officers. All the way up to the top. We send out the questionnaires. They fill them out . . . We set appointments for interviews in Sacramento . . . So we interview them. We have their questionnaires. We're now savvy. I know . . . if their staff filled it out, or did they fill it out? I mean, we know. It's an education. It's an education all on its own. You know? And things like that. Then we ask them all the questions. And then if we do endorse them, we campaign. If they're elected, we follow . . . we make a report card. You know, their voting record . . . So he [Novey] taught us that. He taught us about legislation. Hey, you need to do your homework [on legislation] before it comes up [in legislative committees]. Things like that. We used to go up . . . We were used as tools to go up and speak in front of the Public Safety Committee . . . Sometimes we do have to speak . . . but we've already done our homework.[27]

Novey also provided a political education to Salarno's daughter, Nina Salarno-Ashford, as Salarno-Ashford explained in an interview I conducted with her:

JP: What kinds of things have you learned from Mr. Novey?
NS-A: One of the most important things is I think everybody gets caught on party lines. And I think one of the things we've learned most from Don or working with him is that . . . it's issues, it's not people. It's not party lines. What is important is the issues. And sometimes Democrats may be better at the issue that's important versus the Republican. And you have got to be able to support who is for . . . the issue—not just the straight Republican–Democrat.
JP: Has he also helped you learn how to deal with politicians?
NS-A: Yeah. And just learning to listen, and talk. And making your way through legislation and just . . . You know, lots of times people think it's not important to attend just minor hearings. But it is always important to be there—to have your face, your name, and things like that. So a lot of that. They have helped us with the resources and the outreach, and things like that.[28]

In addition to practicing family law, Salarno-Ashford helps her mother with CVUC activities. She has also worked as a political consultant for the CCPOA.

The victims' groups feel indebted to the CCPOA; they heed advice and respond to calls for assistance from the officers' union. The victims know that their organizations would not exist (at least not in their current forms) without the CCPOA's support. In this regard, Michael Salarno, Harriet Salarno's husband, says about Don Novey: "Without his financial and emotional assistance, we could never have done this."[29] The victims' groups repay the CCPOA by working publicly on issues important to the officers and victims. Salarno-Ashford states, for example, "We go to bat for them. I mean, they protect us from the worst of the worst, and so when some of their issues come up we're the first ones to go testify or go help with them on things."[30] Maggie Elvey, the sole paid staff person for CVUC, argues that the CCPOA does not dictate CVUC's actions, however, the union does keep a close watch over CVUC's activities:

ME: The CCPOA, they don't get involved in telling you too much what to do. You know, they keep their little watch over you. Make sure you're not doing something, you know, you're not supposed to be.
JP: Like what?
ME: Well, sometimes you can get in trouble by things you say and do, and, you know, and legislators, so you have to watch your Ps and Qs.[31]

Ryan Sherman, a former lobbyist and current spokesperson for the CCPOA, makes a similar statement: "CVUC does check with CCPOA. I mean, you know, especially during candidate interviews and stuff like that, they're all, 'Well what are you guys doing? What do you think?' That doesn't mean they always follow it, but I mean if you look at their endorsements, a lot of them are very very similar."[32]

Claims about CVUC's autonomy from the CCPOA are somewhat hard to sustain when we consider CVUC's personnel. According to information obtained in September 2005, CVUC had two lobbyists, Gavin and Shari McHugh, both of whom were on the CCPOA's payroll. Peter Mitchell was a paid political consultant for both CVUC and the CCPOA. Nina Salarno-Ashford worked as a consultant for the union and CVUC. Kelli Reid, director of client services for the public relations and political consulting firm McNally Temple Associates, Inc., worked on public relations campaigns for the CCPOA and was the protocol director for CVUC and cochair of CVUC's annual crime victims' dinner. The following CCPOA officials were on CVUC's advisory board as of late 2005: Don Novey; Percy Speth, CCPOA executive secretary; and Lisa Northam, chairperson of the CCPOA's Victims' Committee and executive director of the California Correctional Crime Victims' Coalition, Inc., an organization that assists prison officers who are assaulted on duty and sues prisoners who attack officers.[33] There was less personnel crossover between the CCPOA and CVB, although, in 2005, Lance Corcoran, CCPOA vice president, was a member of CVB's advisory board.[34] In 2009 CVB (now renamed the "Crime Victims Action Alliance") listed Steve Fournier, Lance Corcoran, and Joe Bauman, CCPOA chapter president at the California Rehabilitation Center, as "advisory board members."[35]

In short, the CCPOA and victims' groups, which occupy dominant positions in the penal field, work in tandem to achieve similar goals. The victims' groups address issues that are important to the CCPOA without much, if any, pressure from their benefactor because the victims' organizations share many of the CCPOA's objectives. The union ostensibly closely watches CVUC's and CVB's actions and educates these victims' groups about media relations and political behavior because critics are eager to pounce on any misstep that the CCPOA or its allies might make.

PUBLIC CEREMONY AS SOCIAL GLUE

Representatives of the CCPOA and crime victims' groups claim that the relationship between their organizations developed out of a "natural affinity" between the victims of violent crime and rank-and-file prison officers. Don Novey explains why the CCPOA has been at the forefront of the "victims' rights movement" in California for the last 15 years: "If there is one group in California which understands the plight of these victims, it is prison officers. We have to work with the predatory element every day."[36] Lance Corcoran, CCPOA vice president, says similarly: "We are a natural fit with victims' rights groups . . . Crime victims were forgotten for many years and we feel we're a forgotten entity . . . We are victims too."[37] Harriet Salarno describes the bond between the CCPOA and CVUC: "We are aligned. Most of the candidates that they [CCPOA] like, we like—because they're public safety . . . It's common sense. It's just common sense. Sure, we differ on a few things . . . But basically we are aligned. Because it's just common sense."[38]

As described by CCPOA representatives and Harriet Salarno, the union and CVUC were destined to form an alliance. In other words, they suggest that the relationship simply evolved. This suggestion, however, is misleading. The alliance resulted from a strategic choice. Don Novey and the CCPOA chose to align with these particular crime victim advocates (and not others) to enhance the union's power and achieve its goals. That is not to say that individual prison officers and CCPOA leaders do not care about crime victims or feel satisfaction when supporting victims of crime and victims' families. Because prison officers feel unappreciated and perceive themselves as victims of abuse from managers, prisoners, the media, academics, and the courts, they greatly value the recognition they receive from crime victims' advocates, who routinely acknowledge and even celebrate the union and its members. It seems, therefore, that the emotional and psychological payoff officers and union leaders receive from supporting crime victims' groups is extremely important. Nevertheless, the CCPOA's primary motive in tying its fortune to these particular victims' groups has been political.

Since allying with these groups, the CCPOA (in concert with their victim allies) has striven to demonstrate that the alliance is "natural" rather than the product of strategic calculation. In other words, the union has attempted to manufacture affinity between it and the victims' groups. One way in which they have done this is through public ceremonies. In these ceremonies, union leaders and their crime victim allies communicate to various audiences (lawmakers, state officials, and journalists) that the ties connecting the CCPOA to groups like CVUC are organic and that the union serves the greater good through its work on behalf of victims of crime. Like the union's alliance with crime victims, these public ceremonies are, at their core, both strategic and political.[39] These enlivened gatherings place in stark relief the extreme resentment, anger, and distrust that union and crime victim activists share for institutions and groups they feel disregard and disparage them such as prison officials, academics, federal judges, and prisoners' rights advocates. These events also illuminate the CCPOA and crime victims' groups' moral clarity, determination, and mutual appreciation. By taking these public ceremonies seriously, we can better understand how these organizations think and feel about the world, their positions in it, and their commitment to changing it.

A Scene from the Field

The best example of a CCPOA-produced public ceremony is the annual "Victims' March on the Capitol." Since 1991 the union has sponsored this Sacramento event, which brings together a few dozen organizations and hundreds of individuals. Participants in the victims' march distribute and gather information; hear speeches from crime victims, politicians, and CCPOA officials; sing songs; display mementos of and mourn lost family and friends; and promote policies that ostensibly increase victims' rights while decreasing prisoners' rights.[40] The victims' march is the main public event during California's weeklong observation of "National Crime Victims' Rights Week." It draws attention from print and television journalists, politicians and their staff members, and state officials. The event is a well-attended production that provides the CCPOA and its allies a forum to communicate directly with the political establishment and indirectly with the public through the media. The following is an ethnographic account of the 2005 March.

The 16th Annual Victims' March on the Capitol
April 12, 2005

The sponsors of the victims' march could not have wished for better weather. The sun was hot, but the scorching days of summer were still a month or two away. People sitting in rows of chairs were protected from the Sacramento sun by a large, white tent in front of the steps of the state capitol. Another tent covered lines of tables on which crime victims' groups and governmental agencies had laid out materials for curious passersby to pick up. Among the 40 or so crime victims' groups at the event were CVUC, CVB, Parents of Murdered Children, Parents of Murdered Victims, Family and Friends of Murder Victims, Citizens for Law-and-Order, Citizens Against Homicide, Justice for Murdered Children, Mothers Against Drunk Driving, and Mothers Against Senseless Killings.

Posters with pictures of murder victims and their birth and death dates lined the stage in front of the capitol, as well as the walkways to the left and right of the large tents. Deep red wooden cutouts, which represented crime victims, stood motionless on the grass to the right of the tents. The crowd was diverse. Men and women of various ages, ethnicities, nationalities, and economic classes commingled, took literature from the tables, and stared at posters of victims. Some cried into sympathetic arms. Many participants wore shirts that displayed pictures of deceased family members and friends, and some constructed mini-shrines to their lost loved ones. Pain, longing, and sadness were palpable.

I perused the informational tables, grabbed literature, and talked with the volunteers. A CVUC representative handed me a flyer titled, "CVUC's Concerns with GRP 1." CVUC opposed Governor Schwarzenegger's proposed plan to reorganize the state's penal agencies and shift the focus of punishment in California from retribution and incapacitation to rehabilitation. A short paragraph on the front side of the flier explained CVUC's opposition to the governor's plan:

Rearranging the boxes on the organizational chart is, by itself, neither forward nor backward. However, the tone is ominous. In the 1960s and 1970s, we were deluded with the ideas that (1) our experts knew how to rehabilitate criminals, and (2) the same experts knew how to determine which criminals had been rehabilitated. Both suppositions were wrong, and a great many innocent people suffered from the crimes committed by the criminals released as a result.

The flier directed people at the event to take action:

The Governor's Reorganization Plan (GRP 1) will be heard on Tuesday, April 12, 2005, in the Assembly Public Safety, Room 126 on the first floor, north side of the Capitol entrance on L Street. It is URGENT that TODAY you wear your photos, take your victims' pictures, etc., and visit the hearing. Just walking thru will let the committee know that we are watching them and are concerned with GRP 1. Please read the information on the back as to what concerns CVUC has regarding GRP 1.

As CCPOA President Mike Jimenez approached the podium, one of the union's public relations representatives handed me a press release. It contained President Jimenez's prepared remarks, which included the following: "We know better than most the violent, predatory nature of these criminals—always looking for their next victim . . . We work with these criminals every day in California's prisons and youth facilities. We know the danger they pose to society." As Jimenez completed his brief opening comments, the Folsom Prison Honor Guard marched across the concrete stage and hoisted the flags of the United States and State of California. The crowd joined Jimenez in the Pledge of Allegiance. A religious invocation followed the pledge.

The event got rolling when Todd Spitzer, a handsome, young, and fiery assemblyman (R-Orange), gripped the podium and spoke with passion. He told the crowd that the penal system and legislature were ignoring the plights of victims:

> . . . You are here today because you are not getting justice . . . You tell me that as victims the court system treated you with dignity and respect; you stand up if it did so. And you stand up and you tell me if, when somebody was harmed in your family, you were treated as a victim. Or were you treated as a piece of evidence? The system talks all day long about protecting victims, but it does not today stand up for victims [loud applause].

Spitzer then told the crowd they had a duty to change the system:

> So what are we going to do about it? What responsibility do we have? All of you here today who have seen somebody convicted and sent to prison, what do you want to know? You want to know that that person stays in prison [applause and shouts of "Yeah!"]. And what do you want to know if you are here because justice hasn't found the perpetrator? You want to know that the system hasn't abandoned you . . . You have an absolute responsibility, an absolute obligation to make sure that this institution of the people [pointing to the state capitol], for the people and by the people, for the people and by *you*, creates a responsibility and accountability for those who are ruining our society by committing crimes. Stand up if you're with me on this. Stand up.

He concluded his speech by asking a series of questions. The crowd responded to each question with a resounding "Yes!"

- Are we committed to stopping crime in this state?
- Are we committed to solving unsolved murders and crime?
- Are we committed to holding parolees *in prison* so they don't continue to further victimize us?
- And are we as a society willing to say once and for all that public safety *is* our number one commitment and we'll put our money where our mouth is?

The assemblyman's energy, messages, and call and response technique fired up the crowd.

President Jimenez returned to the podium to introduce the keynote speaker, Marc Klaas. In the preceding decade, Klaas had become a minor celebrity—particularly among punitive crime victims' and law enforcement groups. In October 1993, Richard Allen Davis, then on parole abducted Klaas's 12-year-old daughter, Polly Hannah Klaas. From October until December, the press relentlessly covered the massive search for Polly. In December 1993, countless people in California and other states mourned and expressed outrage when Polly was found murdered. The media reported widely that the little girl's killer was a repeat violent offender. Polly became the face of the campaign for "Three Strikes and You're Out" in California, which, according to its proponents, was designed to incapacitate people like Davis (the following chapter provides a detailed account of the Three Strikes saga).

Marc Klaas and his father Joe Klaas became fervent proponents of Three Strikes. Joe Klaas eventually changed his position and became a vocal advocate for reforming Three Strikes. Marc Klaas, however, continues to support Three Strikes in its current form. In 1994 Marc Klaas started a nonprofit organization called KlaasKids Foundation to "give meaning to Polly's death and create a legacy in her name that will be protective of children for generations to come by pursuing the singular mission of stopping crimes against children."[41]

Klaas walked to the podium, removed his jacket, rolled up his shirtsleeves, and announced to the crowd, "It is time for us to get to work." Intense and somewhat flustered, he pushed aside his prepared remarks (or notes) and ad-libbed his address:

> This event today, ladies and gentleman, was supposed to start at 11 o'clock, but there is a very important piece of legislation that is being addressed right now. It is called GRP 1. It's the reorganization plan. Apparently Governor Schwarzenegger wants to reorganize the entire criminal justice system. He wants to start talking about rehabilitation in the same breath that we talk about punishment. Ladies and gentleman, that's what we were doing in the '60s, the '70s, in the '80s, in the early '90s, when our relatives were being slaughtered with impunity, when we were the prisoners, when the bad guys were walking the streets, and lurking in the shadows, and taking us out one by one by one. Rehabilitation doesn't work. You commit a violent crime, you've stepped over a line. You're not going to be rehabilitated, you're going to be punished.

Klaas paused as the crowd applauded loudly and shouted encouragement. He regripped the podium and continued:

> You're not going to a halfway house. You're going to be put in a 42-square-foot cell. And you're going to think about the crimes you committed, and you are going to serve a long time . . . They don't need GEDs; what they need is a slap.

They don't need a program, they don't need a law library, they don't need a weight set, they don't need TVs, they don't need a computer. What they need is ten more years. What they need to do is understand what they have done, and take the punishment like the men they will never be . . . cowards, they're the cowards they've always been and the men they will never be.

Raucous applause and shouts of "That's right!" interrupted the speaker.

. . . There's an effort in this building [points back to the capitol] right now to not have law enforcement and victims on parole boards, but to have sociologists, to have educators. You know what, we don't need sociologists to tell us what to do, we don't need educators to tell us [that prisoners] need GEDs. What we need is people like you [points to the crowd], people like me, people who have been to the bottom of the well . . . people who understand the darkness and . . . realize that the light is out here [loud applause]. Ladies and gentleman, we don't need a reorganization plan, we need stricter sentences. We don't need a reorganization plan, we need to keep bad people where they can't do harm to good people. We're the good people, they're the bad people. Keep 'em in prison. Governor Schwarzenegger understand me, read my lips: no more victims, no more crime.

The crowd gave Klaas a spirited ovation. Jimenez thanked the keynote speaker and, after another ringing round of applause for Klaas, participants hugged each other, shook hands, picked up their signs, and lined up for food and beverages supplied by the event's sponsors.

In public ceremonies like the victims' march, speakers affirm and certify the bond between the CCPOA and its aligned victims' groups. And they insist that prison officers understand crime victims' plights because they work with "the predatory element." Politicians, CCPOA activists, and crime victim representatives refer to the CCPOA as a trusted friend of victims, and describe prison officers as honorable public servants who keep convicted criminals behind bars and often suffer victimization at the hands of prisoners. In effect, the CCPOA and victims' representatives publicly validate each other's status as victims.

The messages that the presenters at public events communicate through speeches and symbols characterize two mutually exclusive moral universes divided by clear and solid symbolic boundaries.[42] As characterized in Figure 4.1, crime victims and their representatives, law-and-order public officials, prosecutors, and law enforcement workers (including prison officers) are on one side of the symbolic divide. On the other side are criminals (particularly violent criminals) and their ostensible supporters: prisoner rights' advocates, criminal defense lawyers, liberal politicians, academics, social workers, and "activist" judges.

Characteristics

Virtuous, Realistic, Innocent, and Pro-Victim	Immoral, Idealistic, Guilty, and Pro-Criminal
Crime Victims and their Representatives Prison Officers and CCPOA Prosecutors Police Officers, Parole Officers and Other Law Enforcement Workers Law-and-Order Politicians	Criminals (esp. violent criminals) Prisoners' rights Advocates Criminal Defense Attorneys "Activist" Judges Liberal Politicians Academics (esp. sociologists) Social Workers

Effects

Protect Public Safety and Honor Crime Victims	Compromise Public Safety, Help Prisoners, Dishonor Crime Victims

Figure 4.1.
Two opposing moral universes.

The CCPOA and its allies have similar goals and worldviews and favor like remedies to the "crime problem." They maintain that crime victims and their loved ones and law enforcement workers have particular and "true" knowledge about crime and punishment (as opposed to abstract academic theories) because they witness first- or secondhand the horrible effects of criminal behavior. In other words, they claim to posses "real-life expertise" (chapter 5 includes a more detailed discussion of this concept). As Marc Klaas told the audience at the victims' march, victims and their representatives are genuine experts on issues of crime and punishment and therefore should make and enforce penal policy, because they have "been to the bottom of the well" and "understand the darkness."

By portraying two well-delineated and hostilely opposed camps, the CCPOA and their allies promote a sense of belonging among their supporters and compatriots. The union and its collaborators also clearly identify "others" that threaten their interests, justifying calls for "us" to band together and fight for "our" objectives. The need to fight is paramount in the world portrayed in the public ceremonies in which the winners take all and zero-sum logic dominates. It is self-evident that armies locked in heated battle over the good of society cannot and do not understand each other or work toward similar goals. [43]

In addition to revealing problems, the groups identify relatively clear solutions. According to the CCPOA and crime victims, carping liberals develop long lists of grievances, rarely articulating convincing answers to the problems. The solutions they do provide are half-baked, ineffective, and generally harmful. Continual political action is necessary to keep California on the right path. Victims need to "make their voices heard" at legislative hearings and at ballot boxes. They need to organize and support crime victim and law enforcement organizations, and inform politicians and journalists that they support retributive punishment (not rehabilitative treatment) for violent offenders.

The CCPOA and its allies describe many examples of the positive results wrought by political action: Three Strikes and other mandatory-minimum sentencing laws, victims' rights legislation (e.g., victim impact statements), reductions of prisoners' rights and provisions, and the election of victim-friendly, pro–public safety politicians, judges, and district attorneys. By becoming political actors who advocate for victims' rights and punitive sanctions for violent offenders, crime victims and their loved ones can ease their pain, save innocent people from suffering horrible crimes, and move closer to "closure."

A Victory for the CCPOA and Its Allies

From *Peacekeeper*, December 1994

> Prisons Become Prisons Again: Inmate Rights Overturned: SB 1260 (Presley)
> Tired of 72-hour unsupervised family (conjugal) visits and quarterly care packages fueling the underground prison drug railroad? Tired of gang members getting pumped up on weights and growing in strength and intimidation that can be used on law-abiding citizens when they are released to the streets? Well SB 1260 is going to change all that. A ridiculous, convict-loving Rose Bird (California Supreme Court) decision was overturned by SB 1260. The bill grants correctional officials the legal ammo to impose "any legitimate penalogical [sic] interest" to control inmate activities, privileges, and grooming. Those privileges aren't rights any longer.
> Unfortunately, California has been jerked around by inmate attorneys since 1975, when the Inmate Bill of Rights originally passed and was subsequently signed by then-Gov. Jerry Brown. It was interpreted by the Bird Court in 1986 to require administration be no more constraining than needed to maintain "institutional security." Well, that was then and this is now. The times are a changin'. CCPOA is the source and sponsor of SB 1260 by Sen. Bob Presley that relegates inmate rights to the standard set by federal case law. As you might expect, the measure [was opposed by] the usual suspects, PRU [Prisoner Rights Union], ACLU, Friends Committee, California Attorneys for Criminal Justice. SB 1260 overturns the traditional case law relied on by inmate attorneys to define privileges as rights. The measure creates any penalogical [sic] interest as the controlling standard in regulating inmate activities (*Turner v. Safely*, U.S. Supreme Court). Issues can include: grooming standards, visiting policies, quarterly packages, weight lifting, pornography, hate literature, inmate businesses.
> Signed by the governor [Pete Wilson] September 12, 1994.[44]

The "Convict Bill of Rights" (its original name) was a major victory for prisoners and their advocates. In eliminating the bill of rights, the CCPOA and its allies provided prison staff greater latitude in controlling the minutia of convicts' lives (e.g., how they wore their hair) and made imprisonment in California more austere and harsh. In addition to limiting prisoners' already limited freedoms, the bill (along with other laws passed in 1994, such as "Three Strikes and You're Out") signaled the dominance of punitive segregation and zero-sum reasoning in California, as well as the collective power of the CCPOA and its allies in the penal and political fields (and, of course, the lack of power of their competitors). The *Peacekeeper's* assertion that "The times are a changin'" was incorrect. The times had already changed. Concern for prisoners and their rights was a thing of the past.

THE VOICE OF VICTIMS

"For too long, criminals have been given more 'rights' than victims—putting justice and public safety at risk. As *the voice for victims*, our goal is to make 'public safety' California's biggest priority."
—*Harriet Salarno, Chair, Crime Victims United of California*[45]

In CCPOA-sponsored events, leaders of the CCPOA identify certain individuals and groups as "authentic" spokespersons of crime victims. For example, during the 2003 victims' march, President Jimenez gave an award to Mike Reynolds, the architect of California's Three Strikes law, and told the crowd that Reynolds was a genuine representative of crime victims. During the 2005 victims' march, Jimenez insisted that Marc Klaas belongs to a select group of bona fide and gallant crime victim advocates, right alongside Don Novey, Harriet Salarno, and Doris Tate. In addition to naming people as spokespersons for crime victims, the CCPOA provides these individuals and their organizations with the necessary financial and organizational resources to spread their messages and recruit people to work for their cause.

Politicians and state bureaucrats delegate authority to victims' advocates who are aligned with the CCPOA by seeking out and heeding the victim advocates' advice, attending and speaking at their events (e.g., the victims' march), and appointing them to state boards and commissions. In 2004 Governor Arnold Schwarzenegger appointed Susan Fisher, former executive director of CVB and ex-president of Citizens for Law-and-Order (a small group affiliated with CVB), to the powerful Board of Prison Terms, the state agency that considers parole releases for prisoners serving nonfixed sentences (only prisoners in California with "life" sentences serve indeterminate terms). Harriet Salarno indicated in early 2004 that she encouraged Governor Schwarzenegger to appoint Fisher to the parole board:

We're working with him now with the Board of Prison Terms. We hope to get . . . Arnold to appoint a victim survivor as the commissioner of the Board of Prison

Terms. I have one in mind, very much in mind. And I am pushing her very hard. And she is from one of these organizations that I just talked to you about. She's young. She's good . . . That's Susan Fisher from the Doris Tate [Crime Victims' Bureau]. And I let it be known with Arnold that hopefully he appoints her . . . And I have told her that we will support her to get confirmed . . . She'd be an excellent commissioner.

Later, in April 2006 Governor Schwarzenegger created a cabinet position called the "Crime Victim Advocate" to "serve as California's lead advocate on state and federal policy impacting crime victims." The governor appointed Susan Fisher to the new position, thereby placing a CCPOA-aligned crime victims' advocate in his inner circle.[46]

State officials have appointed Harriet Salarno and her daughter, Nina Salarno-Ashford, to important positions. For example, in 1994 Governor Wilson named Salarno to a board overseeing the juvenile justice system in San Francisco, the city in which Salarno and her husband live.[47] In 1995 former governor Pete Wilson appointed the elder Salarno to California's Commission on Judicial Performance, a state agency that is responsible for investigating complaints of judicial misconduct and for disciplining judges. The Republican and Democratic parties have both selected Salarno as a delegate at their national conventions. In 1999 Attorney General Bill Lockyer appointed Nina Salarno-Ashford as the director of the newly created Office of Victims' Services in the California Department of Justice. As director, Salarno-Ashford was "responsible for advising the Attorney General on issues affecting crime victims, improving existing and managing new programs to benefit victims, and coordinating services between public and private programs."[48]

Journalists have also regarded CCPOA-aligned victims' advocates as legitimate spokespersons for all crime victims. Print and television reporters routinely seek statements from certain victims' advocates on important matters pertaining to prisons, sentencing laws, and victims' issues. They include the views of CVUC and CVB leaders in stories about parole reform, criminal justice bureaucracy, prison management, sentencing, and the California Youth Authority. For example, in February 2009, the *Los Angeles Times* ran an article about the Schwarzenegger administration's strategy for countering a court decision that deemed lethal injection rules illegal, thereby temporarily halting capital punishment in the state. In the article, Nina Salarno-Ashford declares, "Crime victims are going to be outraged."[49] Because the article does not quote other crime victims' advocates, it gives the impression that Salarno-Ashford speaks not just for members of CVUC, but also *for all crime victims*. This impression is false because some crime victims' organizations, such as California Crime Victims for Alternatives to the Death Penalty, expressly oppose capital punishment.

Figure 4.2.
Harriet Salarno being interviewed at the annual Victims' March on the Capitol in Sacramento, California. Author photo.

Another newspaper article further illustrates how the press designates CCPOA-allied crime victims' advocates as the legitimate voice of victims. On July 12, 2009, the *Stockton Record* published an article on prisoners and religion, echoing the age-old notion that religious devotion can transform prisoners and, ultimately, reduce recidivism. The article discusses Harriet Salarno's opinions about the topic:

> Harriet Salarno is skeptical . . . Salarno doubts that inmates can change. "If they really, truly find God and they're sincere, OK," she said. "But I'm not sure about it." Salarno . . . said she believes inmates more likely use religion to finagle the system . . . A devout Catholic, Salarno said her doubt of inmates' sincerity is fueled in part because she has yet to hear a repentant criminal offer to help a victim's family.[50]

This article is important for three key reasons. First, it is indicative of the current journalistic impulse to include the perspective of crime victims in prison-related stories that have little, if anything, to do with crime victims. It is unclear why crime victims' opinions about prisoner participation in religious activities matter. The journalist simply assumes that they do. Second, the story suggests that Salarno has expertise about prisoners' potential to change.

This expertise ostensibly derives from her experience as a mother of a murder victim. Third, as in the article on the death penalty, this piece does not include the perspective of other crime victims' advocates, suggesting that Salarno speaks for all crime victims.

Taken together, journalists, politicians, and state officials support the idea that Salarno, Klaas, and other victims' advocates with similar views are the legitimate voices of all crime victims. They do so by soliciting and publicizing these advocates' perspectives while not seeking out others with alternative perspectives. As I discuss in the conclusion of this chapter, there are crime victims' organizations in California that do not share CVUC and related groups' punitive positions on penal policy. However, they are completely over-shadowed by CCPOA-affiliated crime victims' groups.

There are four principle reasons why the media and political establishment treat CCPOA-aligned crime victims' advocates as the voice of all victims. First, these advocates have been politically active since the early 1990s. With financial backing and political direction from the CCPOA, they have lobbied politicians, made endorsements, and doled out campaign contributions for years. Moreover, they have vigorously and publicly opposed politicians, judges, district attorneys, and other state actors with whom they disagree. Unlike other victims' groups, they have extensive organizational resources (largely as the result of CCPOA's largesse) and are politically sophisticated. Second, they are convenient allies for politicians trying to show that they are tough on crime (or, at least, not soft on crime). Since the 1980s, virtually all politicians with ambitions for statewide office have sought to demonstrate their law-and-order bona fides. Obtaining an endorsement from the likes of CVB and CVUC is one way of doing so. Third, these victims fit the profile of the prototypical crime victim in public culture (although, as discussed below, this profile is in-correct): sympathetic white women and men who have lost family members to senseless violence. Finally, they tell good stories. Eschewing nuance and asserting moral certainty, they speak in terms of good and evil, right and wrong, and "us versus them." Journalists and politicians know exactly where they stand on the issues. Because Salarno, Klaas, and similarly oriented indi-viduals have been treated as the voice of *all* victims for so long, nobody questions this assumption. It is simply "common sense."

The establishment of CCPOA-allied crime victims' advocates as the voice of victims in California has truly benefited the prison officers' union. The vic-tims' groups take public positions on issues that the CCPOA sidesteps for fear that critics will label the union greedy, self-interested, or ultrapunitive. For example, not wanting to be seen as simply feathering its own nest, the CCPOA claimed in the early 1990s that it would no longer support laws that increased prison sentences for convicted criminals (the next chapter shows that the union made several extremely important exceptions to this position).[51]

Critics insist that the CCPOA's claim that it does not take stances on sentencing legislation is hypocritical, since CCPOA-aligned victims' groups often act as proxies, sponsoring and lobbying in favor of sentence-enhancement bills. Ryan Sherman, longtime CCPOA employee, acknowledges that the critics' charge is hard to deny, because the union and crime victims' groups share lobbyists:

RS: I mean for a while . . . Jeff [Thompson] was the lobbyist for CCPOA and for what was then Doris Tate Crime Victims Bureau, and so Jeff shows up in public safety committee, he's testifying for CCPOA. And the next ten sentencing bills, he goes up, "I'm Jeff Thompson, Doris Tate Crime Victims Bureau, support, support, support." So to a lot of insiders, especially [state senator Richard] Polanco, they just found that as very disingenuous.
JP: They [victims' groups] get accused of being front groups [for the CCPOA]?
RS: Exactly. Plus it wasn't just the front group, but it was the same guy.[52]

In brief, the CCPOA often does not need to take a stand on sentencing legislation—the victims' groups will do so.

On some issues, the CCPOA and victims' groups both take public positions. To have the greatest effect, the organizations combine financial, organizational, and symbolic resources, and they divide labor. The union and victims' groups do not always acknowledge their collaboration, and journalists and politicians often do not identify the nuanced ways in which the organizations work together. The campaign by CCPOA and victims' organizations to thwart parole reform in California from 2003 to 2005 exemplifies the effective ways in which these groups achieve goals and help dictate penal policy. The battle over parole reform also demonstrates that actors in the penal field, including lawmakers, must heed the demands of the CCPOA and its crime victim allies when enacting penal policy. As we see clearly in the case of parole reform, actors who ignore the wishes of the coalition risk being labeled "soft on crime," unconcerned with public safety, and insensitive to crime victims. They also risk lack of cooperation from members of the CCPOA (in this case, parole officers)—the people responsible for implementing most penal reforms.

As indicated in Table 4.1, the attempt to reform California's beleaguered parole system began in August 2003 when then governor Gray Davis and the state legislature, facing ever-swelling prison and parole populations and severe budget shortfalls, agreed during budget negotiations to reincarcerate fewer parole violators and increase and improve programs for parolees. The August 2003 decision to transform parole in California did not lead to significant changes in the parole system, however, largely because state legislators and the governor were preoccupied with the campaign to recall Governor Davis.

Parole reform received a new push in November 2003 when the independent Little Hoover Commission on California State Government Organization and

Table 4.1 CHRONOLOGY OF THE BATTLE OVER PAROLE REFORM IN CALIFORNIA (2003–2005)

Date	Event
August 2003	Governor Gray Davis and the legislature agree to reform parole in CA
November 13, 2003	Little Hoover Commission releases report on parole in CA
November 17, 2003	Arnold Schwarzenegger is sworn in as governor of CA
November 18, 2003	Schwarzenegger administration agrees to "Valdivia" lawsuit settlement
May 5, 2004	Legislators criticize delays in parole reform during legislative hearing
May 11, 2004	Government officials unveil the "New Parole Model"
February 27, 2005	*Sacramento Bee* prints criticisms of New Parole Model
March 2, 2005	Senate informational hearing on parole reform
March 8, 2005	Victims testify at Board of Prison Terms hearing
Last Week of March 2005	CVUC/CCPOA television commercial against Governor Schwarzenegger and parole reform
April 11, 2005	Schwarzenegger administration ends New Parole Model
April 11–12, 2005	CCPOA and victims celebrate victory at CVUC dinner and victims' march

Economy released a blistering report on parole in the Golden State, *Back to the Community: Safe & Sound Parole Policies*. The report concluded bluntly: "California's parole system is a billion-dollar failure." It noted that two-thirds (roughly 83,000) of California's 125,000 parolees return to prison within 18 months of their release, a rate of return more than twice the national average.[53] According to the commission, California state prisons did not prepare prisoners for their eventual release; state and local communities did not effectively employ available resources to assist parolees; and parole officers returned the vast number of parole violators to prison rather than utilizing alternative sanctions such as drug treatment or short jail sentences.[54]

On November 17, 2003, Arnold Schwarzenegger replaced Gray Davis as California's governor. The day after he was sworn into office, Schwarzenegger settled a nearly decade-old class action lawsuit against the State of California.

The lawsuit charged that the government's parole policies and practices violated convicts' and parolees' constitutional rights. The "Valdivia settlement," named after the lead plaintiff in the case, called for the state to provide offenders apprehended for violating the terms of their parole with a lawyer and a hearing within 35 days. Previously, parole violators lingered in jail or prison for months before the Board of Prison Terms reviewed their charges. The settlement also permitted parole officers to send violators to treatment programs rather than prison.[55] Schwarzenegger and the California Department of Corrections (CDC) predicted that the parole overhaul would reduce the state's prison population by 15,000 prisoners and lead to five prison closures by mid-2005.[56]

On May 5, 2004, a little more than five months after the Valdivia settlement, state lawmakers revealed in a legislative hearing that government officials had failed to implement the majority of the parole reforms mandated by the legislature in 2003 and the Valdivia settlement. Seven days after the legislative hearing, officials in the Schwarzenegger administration unveiled a "new parole model" that included

- Prerelease programs for prisoners awaiting parole;
- Risk assessment of prisoners awaiting parole;
- Coordination and concentration of community resources for parolees; and
- Alternatives to prison for parole violators, such as electronic monitoring, community-based halfway houses, and drug treatment programs.[57]

The CCPOA and crime victims' organizations lambasted the parole reforms and Governor Schwarzenegger. According to spokespersons for the union, the reforms jeopardized public safety. Chuck Alexander, CCPOA vice president, distributed a memorandum titled "New Parole Model," which communicated the union's objections to the reform proposals, to parole agents:

> As you are no doubt aware, the Department of Corrections has adopted a new leniency policy in an attempt to reduce the return of custody rate. This is an effort to save money and as being applied is a detriment to public safety. Where in the past, you may have [returned] a parolee to custody out of concern for public safety, you may now be routinely overruled by supervisory and/or management staff. Do not capitulate. If you believe continuing parole jeopardizes the public safety, stand by that, and document that . . . These recommendations are made to you in an effort to reduce and/or eliminate any liability you may face after one of these parolees creates a public outcry for some heinous crime.[58]

In effect, the memorandum encouraged parole officers to challenge, and even disregard, the state's parole directives.

The CCPOA and victims' groups were not the only critics of the new parole model. On February 27, 2005, the *Sacramento Bee* printed a scathing analysis of the parole reforms indicating that as of December 31, 2005, there were 2,529 fewer offenders in prison on parole violations (4.1% fewer) than in 2003.

> At the same time, there were 2,141 more parolees who had been incarcerated for new crimes, an increase of 13.6 percent. Corrections officials said they could not immediately determine how many of those 2,141 parolees had previously violated their parole but were allowed to remain free under the governor's new parole policy. Nor could they determine how many of them were reimprisoned . . . on homicide charges.[59]

The statistics and admission by state officials that they did not have a means of tracking parole violators' actions were damning. However, they did not have the same emotional appeal as a story about Justin Graham Corkins, also described in the *Bee* article. Corkins violated parole five times, but his parole officer did not return him to prison. Shortly after his fifth parole violation, Corkins ran over a woman with his car while under the influence of drugs and alcohol. For the CCPOA and other critics of the new parole model, Corkins' story proved that the new parole model led to victimization.

Several days after the publication of the *Bee* article, the state legislature held another hearing on parole reform. The legislators, Senator Gloria Romero in particular, chastised CDC officials for bumbling implementation of parole reform. CCPOA President Mike Jimenez declared emphatically that the new parole model threatened public safety. State senator Tom Campbell (R-Orange) snapped at Jimenez, claiming that Jimenez's opposition to the parole model was "self-interested." He suggested that the CCPOA opposed the parole reform provisions because, if implemented successfully, they would reduce the number of parole agents (and, therefore, CCPOA members). Jimenez incredulously repeated his belief that the parole model allowed dangerous felons to remain on the streets. Senator Campbell responded condescendingly by advising the union boss to take "anger management" classes. Training his glare on the senator, Jimenez growled slowly, "Don't mistake my passion for anger."[60]

Six days after the legislative hearing, representatives of three crime victims' organizations—CVUC, CVB, and Citizens for Law-and-Order—echoed Jimenez's denouncement of the new parole model during a public hearing of the Board of Prison Terms. Christine Ward, a CVB board member and rape victim, said, "Simply stated, the governor's new parole policy is placing the citizens of the State of California in greater danger. This is a very bad plan and it is very clear that the governor is not interested in public safety."[61] Responding to claims that the CCPOA orchestrated the victims' opposition to the parole reforms, the *Sacramento Bee* noted, "CCPOA officials, while acknowledging . . . their relationship with the victims' advocacy organizations, said the groups showed up on their own at [the] meeting, with no prodding from the union. 'Somebody who has been a victim of crime is pretty motivated all by themselves,' CCPOA Vice President Chuck Alexander said."[62]

The CCPOA and CVUC took their fight against parole reform to the airwaves. During the final week of March 2005, the organizations produced a television advertisement, starring Harriet Salarno and Nina Salarno-Ashford, that blasted the governor and his parole policy. The following is the text from the half-minute television spot:

Nina Salarno-Ashford: My sister Catina was murdered (gun shots and sirens in the background). Shot to death by an ex-boyfriend. No mercy, no remorse. He watched football on TV after killing her. But because of Governor Schwarzenegger's new parole policies, Catina's killer could be back on the street. The governor calls it reform. I call it dangerous.
Narrator: Over 2,500 parole violators remained free last year under the governor's plan. Over 2,000 went on to commit serious new crimes.
Harriet Salarno: You promised to stand with victims, governor. You let us down.

The tagline on the commercial read: "Paid for by Crime Victims United of California." The commercial did not mention the CCPOA, even though the union provided the funds to pay for the commercial and its airtime.[63]

Government officials had a difficult time countering the commercial's claim that the parole model jeopardized public safety. The architects of the new parole program had not set clear guidelines regarding which parole violators to leave on the streets. Consequently, "nonserious" *and* "serious" offenders remained free after violating their parole conditions. In addition, the state did not have a system for tracking new offenses committed by those parole violators who were given second and even third chances by parole agents.[64] Thus the state could not refute CVUC's statement that 2,000 of the 2,500 parole violators "went on to commit serious new crimes." In addition, the state failed to implement many of the programs meant to prevent parole violations.[65] Parole agents had to choose between giving parole violators a slap on the wrist and returning them to prison—alternative sanctions such as electronic monitoring or halfway houses were unavailable.

On Monday, April 11, 2005, the day before the victims' march, the Schwarzenegger administration issued a memorandum to the state's parole employees declaring the termination of the new parole model. Responding to reporters, a high-ranking state official stumbled around questions about the relationship between the parole model and public safety: "I don't know that it was [posing a threat to public safety] and I don't know that it wasn't.

We just want to make sure that any program we roll out increases public safety . . . if I have a program that's not increasing public safety . . . we've got to revisit it."[66] The evening that the Schwarzenegger administration announced the gutting of the parole model, Harriet Salarno, Don Novey, and their colleagues celebrated at the annual CVUC Victims' Dinner fundraiser.[67] Politicians, CCPOA activists, and crime victims' advocates continued celebrating defeat of the "new parole model" the following day at the crime victims' march.

AIDING CRIME VICTIMS AND ALTERING THE FIELD

Don Novey's choice to help transform a couple of crime victims' rights groups into powerful political actors and union allies was a brilliant strategic maneuver. Since the early 1990s, leaders of CVUC and CVB have continually advocated for the CCPOA in the realm of public opinion and the halls of the state capitol. Harriet Salarno and fellow crime victims' advocates routinely explain to legislators, journalists, and state officials that the prison officers' union is a beneficent group that stands up for victims and bolsters the public good. Moreover, they validate the union's claims that prison officers are professionals and victims who work the "toughest beat." Just as families of schoolchildren promote teachers and the California Teachers Association, crime victims' advocates endorse prison officers and the CCPOA. Lastly, the CCPOA-allied victims' groups help the union achieve policy objectives, often providing a sympathetic face to campaigns that advance the penal strategy of punitive segregation.

By facilitating the development of certain crime victims' groups, the CCPOA has not only advanced its interests, it has altered the composition of the penal field. With CCPOA's financial backing and political assistance, these groups (particularly CVUC) have become extremely powerful political players. Legislators pine for their endorsements and fear their opposition. No politician wants a crime victims' group to publicly characterize him or her as an enemy of crime victims. After all, the media, politicians, and advocacy groups continually insist that we are all potential, if not likely, victims.[68] Thus being against crime victims is tantamount to being against all "law-abiding citizens." Because of its substantial PAC operation (funded in large part by the CCPOA), CVUC can carry out campaigns to define politicians (and political aspirants) as "anti–crime victim." As dominant players in the penal field, these crime victims' groups also help determine which penal policies are imaginable. How the state responds to crime and other social trends (e.g., economic boom or crisis) depends, in part, on the positions that groups such as CVUC and CVB take— or the positions that policymakers anticipate these groups will take.

Taken together, the CCPOA has helped its allies achieve and maintain dominant positions in the penal field. As a result, politicians, journalists, and state officials treat the union's allies as the sole representatives of crime victims, ignoring (or simply not knowing) that there are other crime victims' advocates and organizations that do not share the CVUC's and CVB's punitive perspectives on criminal punishment. Groups such as California Crime Victims for Alternatives to the Death Penalty, Journey of Hope, Murder Victims' Families for Reconciliation, and California Catholic Conference (Office of Restorative Justice) maintain that harming prisoners via the death penalty or other practices and denying prisoners' basic rights does not help victims of crime, they simply produce more suffering. They also argue that encouraging prisoners to take responsibility for the harm their crimes cause through restorative justice practices and helping inmates develop the tools necessary to live crime-free lives helps victims and victims' families. These groups, in short, reject the zero-sum logic that CVUC and similar groups promote; they do not pit offenders against victims or reinforce punitive segregation.

In addition to not representing all crime victims' advocates, CCPOA-allied crime victims' groups are sociodemographically unique. The CCPOA-related advocates are primarily middle-class, white family members of murdered women and girls. As Katherine Beckett and Theodore Sasson note, however, "young men of color—especially those living in poor and urban areas—experience the highest rates of victimization, and white females report the lowest."[69] "The fact that the organized victim's rights movement is largely white and middle class," Beckett and Sasson argue, "has meant that many victims are not represented by the mainstream of the movement."[70] The CCPOA-related crime victims' advocates are also unrepresentative in terms of criminal victimization. Homicide is a unique crime. In 2007 homicide comprised 0.3% of all reported crimes in California.[71]

The "voice of victims" in California, therefore, is actually the voice of particular homicide victims (or rather, the voice of murder victims' families). It seems likely that people who have lost children to heinous murders may have particularly punitive feelings about and views on criminal punishment. That is definitely true of the leaders of the groups aligned with the CCPOA. (It is not true, however, of groups like Murder Victims' Families for Reconciliation.) Nevertheless, these particular crime victims have been the public face of the "war on crime" in California. As Jonathan Simon contends, the association of victims of violent crime with the "war on crime" is misleading, for "the war has targeted mainly crimes that are not violent and, indeed, that have no specific victims, such as violations of drug laws and laws against firearms possession by felons."[72] Simon suggests that the popular perception of the "war on crime" as a war on *violent* crime is at least partly due to the fact that victims of violent crime—such as those sponsored by the CCPOA—publicly depict it as such in commercials, media reports, voting materials, and political forums.

Although atypical, Harriet Salarno, Doris Tate, and Marc Klaas initially appealed to Don Novey and his colleagues (and continue to appeal to CCPOA's current leaders) in large part because of their specific take on victims' rights and crime and punishment more generally. Like the CCPOA's leaders, they view long sentences in austere prisons, intensive postprison supervision, and even capital punishment as the keys to both reducing crime and enhancing the well-being of crime victims and victims' kith and kin. Since joining forces in the early 1990s, the CCPOA and its allied groups have been very effective at transforming their vengeful, zero-sum take on criminal punishment into public policy, making it increasingly difficult for lawmakers and citizens to imagine that prisoners and crime victims have *any* shared interests or humanity.

CHAPTER 5

Three Strikes and the Anchor of Punitive Segregation

E ver since Don Novey became the president of the California Correctional Officers Association (CCOA) in 1980, the organization (and its successor, the CCPOA) has struggled not only to improve compensation and working conditions for prison officers, but to promote punitive segregation as the dominant penal strategy in California. As defined by David Garland, punitive segregation emphasizes "lengthy sentence terms in no frills prisons and a marked, monitored existence for those who are eventually released."[1] Rather than rehabilitation and crime prevention, punitive segregation stresses deterrence, incapacitation, and vengeance. For three decades the association's leaders have imagined themselves in a constant struggle with those who advocate for what they view as a soft, feminine perspective on punishment, which emphasizes rehabilitation, alternatives to incarceration (e.g., "community corrections"), and prisoners' rights. Against its foes, the CCOA and CCPOA have fought to remasculinize criminal punishment—that is, to make punishment swift, tough, and compassionless. The CCOA and CCPOA have sought to implement their particular view of criminal punishment in general and imprisonment in particular—a view that was marginal and somewhat taboo in the penal field from the mid-1940s through the mid-1970s.

The CCPOA has promoted punitive segregation by supporting like-minded politicians and opposing lawmakers and prospective lawmakers who do not share the union's perspective on criminal punishment, as well as by effectively creating two powerful, punitive-oriented crime victims' groups. This chapter discusses how the CCPOA also advances punitive segregation by sponsoring or supporting laws (such as "truth-in-sentencing") that lengthen prison sentences and institute prison sentences (rather than alternative sanctions) for additional classes of offenders. It discusses the CCPOA's participation in the 1994 campaign to pass California's uniquely harsh and expansive "Three Strikes and You're Out" law, which exemplifies and implements punitive segregation and provides the backbone of California's current reputation as a "tough on crime" state which is due in large part to its exceptionally tough Three Strikes law. This chapter further describes the union's efforts to defend Three Strikes once it became law, focusing particular attention on the CCPOA's role in the campaign to defeat Proposition 66, a 2004 ballot initiative to decrease the scope and effects of Three Strikes.

Although the CCPOA promotes and defends laws that characterize punitive segregation (like Three Strikes), the union is not the sole force behind these policies. Rather, it is part of a collection of organizations and individuals within the penal field, such as the California District Attorneys Association, Crime Victims United of California (CVUC), and the Doris Tate Crime Victims Bureau(CVB), that are similarly committed to punitive segregation. As a leading actor in the bloc, the CCPOA organizes and funds campaigns to promote and defend laws such as Three Strikes and establishes coalitions and develops strategies for winning those campaigns. The CCPOA's tacticians have long understood that the union can be far more effective when it works with groups who bring a variety of resources to the table than when it acts alone. The CCPOA is not just one among many participants in the law-and-order bloc. Instead, it is the *anchor* of this bloc that struggles to maintain punitive segregation as the dominant penal strategy in California.

EXCEPTIONS TO THE RULE

The CCPOA's representatives maintain that the union abstains from taking positions on sentencing policies. Former chief lobbyist, Jeff Thompson, describes the rationale for the CCPOA's policy of abstention:

> In the late '80s, early '90s . . . it became clear with all of the prison expansion and with all the growth that we could be perceived—and I think incorrectly were, anyway—as wanting to promote our own growth . . . And so we took a position in our legislative committee . . . We said we will no longer support the general 600 or so bills introduced every year to get tough on crime . . . And of course, guess who they wanted to support it? Every one of them [politicians] wanted us to support the bill. And I said . . . "First of all, I don't have unlimited staff or resources, or time. And I don't want to lobby on 600 bills. It is taking away from the agenda that our officers and board want us to pursue." It's not that we would necessarily argue with these things. But frankly, there is a good reason to lay off of them. And that's to avoid this criticism that we have a vested self-interest in supporting them. So we laid off of them. Now, we made a couple of exceptions.

And this had to do with our kind of motto of "let's do the right thing in politics." And it came down on the side of the victims.[2]

The CCPOA has made several key exceptions to its policy on sentencing laws. For example, in 1994 the union sponsored a "truth-in-sentencing" bill, which mandated that felons convicted of violent crimes serve 85% of their prison terms. Whereas the legislation did not affect the prison sentences offenders received, it affected how much of their terms they had to serve before they could be released. Thus the law affected prison sentences at the back end (rather than the front end, when judges hand down prison terms). Before Governor Pete Wilson signed the legislation in September 1994, the vast majority of prisoners could receive up to 50% off their sentence by accumulating "good time" (also called "day for day"). For every day that a prisoner behaved and worked or went to school, the state reduced his or her remaining time by a day. Critics argued that there was no truth to prison sentences, since offenders could get their terms reduced by half. They further maintained that this lack of truth reduced the deterrent effects of prison sentences, since offenders or prospective offenders knew they would not have to serve their full time. Celebrating the passage of the "truth-in-sentencing" bill, the CCPOA's Thompson wrote in the union's *Peacekeeper* magazine: "California's 50 percent off, white flower sale on crime is over! Believe it or not, the Jerry Brown-signed good time/work time credit law of 1982 gave all criminals 50 percent off their sentence. All they had to do was breathe! This mockery of justice ended with AB 2716, which goes into effect January 1, 1995."[3] This legislation simultaneously increased the length of prison terms for violent offenders and reduced government officials' ability to control the prison population, contributing to the overpopulation of the state's prisons.

In addition to the "truth-in-sentencing" law, the CCPOA sponsored other important sentencing-related bills targeting sex offenders and juveniles. For example, in 1994 the union shepherded a bill through the legislature that it called "one strike for violent sex offenders." The bill required a mandatory 25-to-life sentence for sex crimes involving force or kidnapping. About this law, which was also signed by Governor Wilson, the CCPOA commented: "Why do we have to wait for two or even three victims to suffer, especially considering most sex offenders who, when finally caught, have committed the crime numerous times already? The other point: Sex offenders rarely, if ever rehabilitate themselves. The answer: Lock 'em up (once is enough) for a long, long time."[4]

In 1994 the CCPOA also sponsored two bills concerning juvenile incarceration. The first, AB 560, reduced the age at which a minor could be tried as an adult from 16 to 14. Because of the bill, minors accused of murder are presumed unfit for juvenile court and can receive adult sentences if convicted. Jeff Thompson wrote in *Peacekeeper*: "This bill . . . targets the younger gang 'trigger men' and tries them in adult court if they commit murder. Criminals, while heartless, aren't stupid. Gangs use juveniles to carry out their kills because the system excuses them based on the arbitrary basis of chronological age. The premise of this bill is, if you can do the crime, you can do the time."[5] A related CCPOA-sponsored bill, which the union dubbed "Keep Youth Punks in Prison (Just Desserts Act)," instructed judges to send juveniles 16 and older to adult prison (rather than the California Youth Authority [CYA]) for certain violent or serious crimes.[6] Along with sponsoring its own laws concerning juvenile imprisonment, the CCPOA supported Proposition 21, the "Gang Violence and Juvenile Crime Prevention Act" of 2000.[7] Among other things, the initiative, which passed by a wide margin, mandated that juveniles 14 and older charged with murder or rape be tried in adult court; increased the number of offenses for which 16- and 17-year-olds must be sent to adult prison (rather the CYA); and increased penalties for gang-related crimes (e.g., it ordered the death penalty for gang-related murders).[8]

A Banner Year

The prison officers union had immense legislative success in 1994. The CCPOA's head lobbyist, Jeff Thompson, triumphantly described this success in the December 1994 issue of *Peacekeeper*:

California's lawmakers responded to crime issues in 1994 like no other time in the state's 143-year history.

The political pendulum, which had swung left in the 1960s (and stuck there) has swung right and gone crashing through the brick wall set up by the American Civil Liberties Union (ACLU), the Prisoners' Rights Union (PRU), California Attorneys for Criminal Justice (CACJ), the Friends Committee, and the other liberals who have dominated California for the last three decades.

. . .

Some insiders consider 1994 the premiere year for crime fighting. It was a year in which political factors and time's cosmic tumblers all fell together and opened a huge door to an incredible array of strong, conservative, common-sense laws to finally get serious with criminals.

In fact, many predict we'll never see another [year] like 1994 again. Only time will tell.

Consequently, 1994 was the best legislative program in the history of the CCPOA. In 1994, CCPOA embarked on a 10-bill package, which was almost twice our usual attempted bill load. All bills sponsored and introduced, passed, and all bills passed were signed by Gov. Wilson, which means, delightfully, that CCPOA went 10 for 10 in the Capitol this year.

Thompson accurately noted that the social and political environment was ripe for "tough on crime" legislation in 1994. The CCPOA took advantage of the window of opportunity, initiating a handful of laws that enhanced prison sentences for adults and juveniles. In doing so, the union helped solidify punitive segregation as the dominant penal strategy in California.[9]

In addition to taking positions on sentencing proposals concerning "violent" and "serious" crimes, the CCPOA has taken stances on laws dealing with "nonviolent" and "nonserious" offenses. (California's penal code determines which crimes are "violent" vs. "nonviolent" and "serious" vs. "nonserious.") For example, in 2000 the CCPOA contributed at least $150,000 to the unsuccessful campaign against Proposition 36, an initiative that diverted low-level drug offenders from prison to treatment programs in local communities. As indicated in one of the CCPOA's "Magic 13" questions in 2000, the union incorrectly claimed that Proposition 36 would "effectively decriminalize drug possession, transportation, and use by providing that any person convicted of 'non-violent drug possession offenses' shall receive probation only, by law."[10]

Taken together, the sentencing-related laws that the CCPOA has sponsored or supported (or opposed) demonstrate that the union has made important exceptions to the policy of abstention that Jeff Thompson described. The CCPOA made its most important exception in 1994 when CCPOA President Don Novey put the union's name and money behind Three Strikes.

INITIATING PUNITIVE SEGREGATION

Before presenting my analysis of the CCPOA and Three Strikes, a brief overview of the initiative process is in order. As sociologist Vanessa Barker argues, this process is extremely important to understanding contemporary criminal punishment in California, for it is a political tool that actors use to institute drastic penal laws without going through the normal legislative channels.[11]

California added the initiative, referendum, and recall to its constitution in 1911 to wrest political power from interest groups (particularly the Southern Pacific Railroad) and their bedfellows in the state house. The initiative allowed individuals or groups to initiate policy proposals without going through the legislature. The referendum permitted voters to remove elements of California law, and the recall made it possible for citizens to oust local officials, state lawmakers, and appellate court judges.[12] Californians have historically made little use of the referendum and recall. Since 1914 the voters have recalled only one statewide public official—Governor Gray Davis in 2003—and only a few referendums have qualified for the ballot in that period. But from 1911 through 1978, Californians made moderate use of the initiative process, passing 42 ballot proposals, and after 1978, use of the initiative increased greatly.[13] Between 1978 and 1996, the voters approved 40 initiatives, and between 1996 and 2002, they approved an additional 14 initiatives.[14]

The era of initiatives in the Golden State started in 1978 with Proposition 13, the "tax revolt."[15] Since the late-1970s, an entire industry has developed around the initiative process. It includes public relations specialists, pollsters, signature collectors, election consultants, and fundraisers.[16] As this industry developed, it became extremely expensive to collect the 400,000-plus signatures necessary to qualify initiatives for the ballot.[17] Sponsors of initiatives found themselves paying between $.85 and $1.50 per signature. In 2006, then, an initiative's sponsors had to pay at least $349,518 to collect 411,198 signatures (10% more than the 373,816 signatures needed to qualify an initiative for the ballot that year to cover ineligible signatures).[18] Even so, astute analyst of California politics Peter Schrag concludes, "if you spend enough money either on professional signature gatherers or send out enough direct mail appeals to well-chosen lists of voters, you can get almost anything on the ballot."[19]

The campaigns for and against ballot initiatives also tend to cost exorbitant sums.[20] For example, the campaigns in 2004 in support of and opposed to Proposition 66, an initiative to reform California's Three Strikes law, spent nearly $10.5 million collectively.[21] Largely because of its prohibitive cost, the initiative is a tool that only superrich individuals and wealthy interest groups can use to make end-runs around the legislature. Ironically, the initiative has become a tool of "the interests" whose political might the early twentieth-century Progressives had aimed to curtail.

Initiatives are an ideal means for well-heeled interest groups to make state policy and affect budgetary allocations directly. Unlike statutory proposals that go through the normal legislative process, ballot initiatives are not subject to public and professional scrutiny.[22] They force voters to choose between "yes" or "no"—there is no middle ground. Initiatives related to crime and punishment typically present voters with a choice between victims and criminals. "If voters vote 'yes' for victims rights, they are voting against criminal defendants. If they vote 'no' for victims' rights, they are apparently endorsing unsanctioned criminal violence," sociologist Barker explains.[23] The initiative process, then, is the perfect tool for "penal populists," who feel that "the people" (and the organizations that represent them), rather than penal experts and practitioners, should determine criminal punishment policies, especially sentencing laws.[24] Since the early 1970s, politicians and interest groups have employed the initiative to tap directly into and channel public

sentiment into particular penal measures. In the three decades b
no initiatives pertaining to courts, law, and order were introduce
in the three decades after 1973, 89 initiatives in this area were pro
story of Three Strikes in California demonstrates the use of the i
implement a radical law that, according to legal scholar Michael
"unthinkable" in America just decades earlier.[26]

THREE STRIKES COMES TO THE GOLDEN STATE

In 1993 the state of Washington enacted the nation's first "three strikes" law, which required life sentences for criminals convicted of three serious or violent felonies. The federal government passed a limited version of Three Strikes as part of President Clinton's 1994 Omnibus Crime Bill. By 1998, 22 states and the federal government had Three Strikes laws on the books.[27] These laws varied widely—so much so that Franklin Zimring and his colleagues questioned whether it was appropriate to lump them together under the same name.[28] As we will see, California's Three Strikes law is far more radical in both intent and effect than other laws with the same name.

The story of Three Strikes in California started in June 1992 when a parolee murdered Kimber Reynolds. In response to the murder, Kimber's father, Mike Reynolds, organized a group of men to devise a law that would incapacitate repeat offenders like Kimber's assailant.[29] The group developed a proposal that they initially called "The Street Sweeper" because, as Reynolds put it, it was "designed to get all the criminal garbage off the streets." The group eventually followed its predecessors in the state of Washington and went with the catchy, all-American name "Three Strikes and You're Out." [30]

The law that Reynolds's group developed was more complex and far-reaching than its name suggested. Actually, the bill should have been named "Two or Three Strikes and You're Out," for it mandated long prison terms for second-strikers as well as third-strikers. Under the law, individuals with a record of one "serious" or "violent" offense who committed any additional felony would receive a sentence twice as long as the current-offense term. In addition, second-strikers would have to serve 80% of their prison sentence before they would be eligible for release. The third-strike enhancement was reserved for offenders with two convictions of "serious" or "violent" crimes and a third conviction for *any* felony. Third-strikers would receive prison sentences of 25 years to life, and would not be eligible for parole until they served 80% of the quarter-century term.[31]

Reynolds recruited his state assemblyman, Bill Jones (R-Fresno), to champion the Three Strikes proposal in Sacramento. Jones then enlisted a fellow legislator from Fresno, a Democrat named Jim Costa, to cosponsor the bill. The consensus in Sacramento was that the Three Strikes bill, AB 971, had no chance of becoming law. Long-time California legislative analyst Jeff Long commented about the proposal, "[W]e didn't do any fiscal assessment [of the bill] because it didn't pass the so-called giggle test. It wasn't worth the effort, because the thing wasn't going to go anywhere, it was so patently stupid."[32]

Critics of Three Strikes thought the bill was "stupid" and draconian because the triggering strikes (both for second and third strikers) did not have to be serious or violent. For Reynolds, however, the bill jibed with his intuition about crime and criminals. He justified including nonserious and nonviolent crimes thusly: "Well, number one, if you don't know who a person is by the time they've had two 'serious or violent convictions,' I'd suggest you're a bad judge of character. The person who should get a chance is that person's next victim. The question was [how] could we get an adequate number to really sweep the criminal element off the streets?"[33] Throughout the campaign for Three Strikes, Reynolds and his cohorts described the law in terms of a zero-sum competition between crime victims and criminals. According to their logic, the law's supporters were on the side of crime victims, and its opponents were on the side of criminals. In their view, there was no room for nuance in justice.

The assembly's Public Safety Committee voted not to pass (and thereby "killed") Jones and Costa's Three Strikes legislation. Frustrated by the Sacramento establishment, Reynolds decided to put his proposal on the 1994 statewide ballot. However, he lacked the money to pay for the collection of nearly 400,000 signatures needed to qualify the initiative. In addition, he did not have sufficient public or political support for his measure. Reynolds got a glimmer of hope when the National Rifle Association (NRA) provided $40,000 to jumpstart the campaign for Three Strikes, but the NRA's initial contribution to Reynolds's campaign was still not enough to pay for the signature collections or a widespread public relations drive.[34] Reynolds's prospects were bleak.

Later that year, a heinous crime occurred in Petaluma, California that altered the fate of Three Strikes. Twelve-year-old Polly Klaas hosted a slumber party in her mother's home on the night of October 1, 1993. While she and two other girls played a board game, a burly man named Richard Allen Davis snuck into the home. Davis had been out of prison for about three months. Even though he had a long record of violent offenses, the state had paroled him after he served 8 years of his 16-year sentence. He was released early because of "good time" he accrued in prison for working and behaving well. Davis entered Polly's bedroom and told the girls that he only wanted valuables. He threatened to slit their throats if they did not cooperate, and then tied the girls' hands behind their backs, put pillow cases over their heads, and ordered them to get on the ground and count to 1,000. Davis grabbed Polly and left the scene.

On November 30, 1993, nearly two months after Polly's abduction, the police arrested Richard Allen Davis. He confessed six days later and directed the police to Polly's body. Davis got the death penalty, and Polly's abduction and murder sparked a media frenzy about repeat offenders, particularly repeat sex offenders. Conservative radio talk show hosts ridiculed lawmakers who opposed AB 971 and encouraged listeners to vent their anger about "career criminals" and spineless, "soft on crime" politicians by joining the campaign for Three Strikes. The national media fixated on the Klaas case. *People* magazine dubbed Polly "America's child."[35]

Before the Klaas abduction, Reynolds had roughly 20,000 of the 385,000 signatures he needed to qualify his initiative for the ballot. Soon after authorities found Polly's body, the campaign for Three Strikes gathered an additional 300,000-plus signatures.[36] For registered voters, supporting Reynolds's initiative was a way to avenge Polly's death and protect children from the likes of Richard Allen Davis. In short, the victimization of Polly Klaas provided a "window of opportunity" for Reynolds and his supporters.[37]

In addition to receiving backing from talk radio personalities and the public, Reynolds got the support of the Klaas family. Shortly after the police arrested Davis, Polly's father Marc and her grandfather Joe endorsed Reynolds's Three Strikes policy. The younger Klaas actively campaigned for the proposal, telling crowds: "We're running scared, folks. We have no right to be proud as a state or a country if we keep letting out these habitual offenders."[38] However, shortly after embracing the Three Strikes campaign, the elder Klaas examined the measure's fine print and found language about "serious" crimes that disturbed him. He was infuriated to learn that "nonviolent" (but "serious") crimes could trigger three-strike sentences. During a public debate on Three Strikes, Joe Klaas raged, "by punishing check bouncers the same as kidnappers and murderers, [this law] offends the memory of my granddaughter Polly."[39] After convincing his son that Reynolds's proposal was misleading, Joe and Marc Klaas publicly opposed it. In turn, they embraced an alternative measure advanced by Senator Dick Rainey, which, like Washington state's law, included only "serious" and "violent" crimes. (The younger Klaas would later reconsider, becoming a staunch supporter of Reynolds's law.)

As the drama surrounding Polly Klaas's murder unfolded, monetary assistance poured in for the Three Strikes campaign. The NRA contributed an additional $60,000 to the cause, and Michael Huffington—an extremely wealthy one-term Republican congressman from Santa Barbara who hoped to unseat California's Democratic U.S. senator, Dianne Feinstein, in 1994—gave $350,000 to the campaign. Congressman Huffington aimed to separate himself from Feinstein by taking an ultratough stance on crime. Reynolds made Huffington co-chair of the Three Strikes campaign.[40]

It was at this time that Don Novey and the CCPOA entered the fight for Three Strikes. The union contributed $100,000 to Reynolds's campaign. In the

CCPOA's *Peacekeeper*, Novey encouraged the union's membership to support Three Strikes and collect signatures for the measure.

> I suggest to you, my fellow correctional peace officers, that we deliver a Christmas present to the people of California in the form of an initiative. We now have an opportunity to put societal thugs behind bars to stay, whether for violent or serious crimes. Correctional peace officers now have that rare chance to give California citizens a break. Please get behind California's "Three Strikes and You're Out" initiative.[41] → Quote

Whereas the legislature had previously rejected Jones and Costa's Three Strikes bill, both Democrats and Republicans now jumped on Reynolds's bandwagon. Politicians had a choice of five legislative proposals that targeted repeat offenders; Reynolds's proposal was the most expansive and punitive. Governor Pete Wilson, facing reelection and hoping to outmuscle his Democratic opponent, Kathleen Brown (who had already endorsed Reynolds's initiative), swept aside the alternative proposals and publicly embraced Reynolds's legislation at Polly Klaas's memorial service. Republicans in the state senate and assembly followed their leader and backed Reynolds's version of Three Strikes. Mimicking President Clinton and other "New Democrats" in Washington, DC, California Democrats took positions on crime that were equally, if not more, punitive than those of their Republican counterparts.[42] When Bill Jones reintroduced Reynolds's Three Strikes bill in March 1994, Democrats stepped aside with full knowledge that 80% of the public supported Jones and Costa's bill.[43]

Because the state legislature passed Jones's Three Strikes bill, Reynolds did not have to go the initiative route, but he pursued the initiative anyway in order to keep politicians from tinkering with the law. The governor and two-thirds of both the assembly and the senate would have to approve any amendments to an initiative version of Three Strikes—while they could more easily make changes to it if it was implemented only through the regular legislative process. When asked why he submitted signatures for Proposition 184 even though the legislature had passed an identical law, Reynolds said, "We don't want anyone to squirm out of it. We want this puppy screwed, glued, and tattooed."[44] Reynolds submitted 840,000 signed petitions and qualified the initiative, now called Proposition 184, for the November 1994 ballot. According to Proposition 184's sponsors, the voters had a choice between supporting "violent felons" (although the law targeted both violent and nonviolent felons) and supporting crime victims, as expressed in the official 1994 General Election Ballot Pamphlet:

> 815,000 California voters signed petitions to place 3 Strikes and You're Out on the ballot. We did it because soft-on-crime judges, politicians, defense lawyers,

and probation officers care more about violent felons than they do victims. They spend all their time looking for loopholes to get rapists, child molesters, and murderers out on probation, early parole, or off the hook altogether. Well, this time it's victims first.[45]

When asked to choose between repeat "violent felons" and "victims," 72% of the electorate selected the latter. Now only a two-thirds vote of the assembly and senate (along with the governor's signature) or a new ballot initiative could change or eliminate California's new Three Strikes law.

THE CCPOA DEFENDS "ITS" LAW

Once Don Novey provided seed money to Reynolds, the CCPOA fully embraced Three Strikes. Reflecting on the 1994 election, Novey wrote in *Peacekeeper*: "[Mike] Reynolds sought the assistance of CCPOA and we jumped on board— we were determined to help him rid our neighborhoods of violent felons. Three Strikes and You're Out became *our* initiative."[46] The CCPOA also wrote in 1995:

> California lawmakers owe the voters the obligation to stay on course with a "Three Strikes" policy. We believe that there is some "sharpening" of the legal language needed to help it from being overturned on some technical points. However, the spirit of "Three Strikes" needs to be followed and pro-tected.[47]

The CCPOA and related organizations have been the foremost protectors of Three Strikes since its passage in 1994. They have lobbied intensely against and have helped quash bills that would amend Reynolds's law. Reports obtained from the Secretary of State's office show that the CCPOA lobbied to defeat the seven bills proposed to reform Three Strikes between 1995 and 2003 (see Table 5.1). The reports also document that the CCPOA's chief lob-byist Jeff Thompson, while simultaneously representing the union, lobbied against three of the bills on behalf of the Doris Tate Crime Victims Bureau. Thompson also lobbied against two others for CVUC while another CCPOA lobbyist, Gavin McHugh, lobbied on CVUC's behalf against an additional bill.[48] In short, these reports show that CCPOA lobbyists opposed six of the seven Three Strikes reform bills on behalf of the union and an allied crime victims' group (the CCPOA lobbied against all seven).

In tandem with its lobbying efforts, the CCPOA communicates to legis-lators that protecting Three Strikes is one of its top priorities. For example, after the voters approved Proposition 184, the CCPOA added the following question to the "Magic 13" list of questions it asks potential endorsees: "Do

Table 5.1 LEGISLATION TO AMEND "THREE STRIKES AND YOU'RE OUT" IN CALIFORNIA, 1995–2003

Year	Bill No.	Author	Intent	Result
1996	SB 2089	Marks	All Strikes = Serious/Violent	Failed
1996	AB 1444	Kuehl	All Strikes = Serious/Violent	Failed
1997	SB 1317	Lee	All Strikes = Serious/Violent	Failed
1999	SB 79	Hayden	All Strikes = Serious/Violent	Failed
2000	AB 2447	Wright	All Strikes = Serious/Violent	Failed
2002	AB 1790	Goldberg	All Strikes = Serious/Violent	Failed
2003	AB 112	Goldberg	All Strikes = Serious/Violent	Failed

you favor or oppose legislation that changes the 'three strikes' law?" By asking this question of political hopefuls, the union expresses its commitment to Three Strikes as well as its expectation that politicians it supports with endorsements and financial contributions will oppose or remain neutral on legislation that weakens or eliminates Three Strikes.

Former state assemblywoman Jackie Goldberg, sponsor of three unsuccessful bills to reform Three Strikes, argues that certain legislators (including critics of Three Strikes) will not support legislation to reform the law because they fear political opposition from the CCPOA and other interest groups:

> The people who want to keep [Three Strikes] are extremely well organized and make major contributions to elected officials. So what has happened is you have an enormous amount of [political] intimidation. People who are in assembly races know that they're term-limited [to two terms], know that they may want to run in a senate race a few years from now, and know that certain groups like police and prison guard unions, district attorneys, and crime victims' organizations will pay for [or against] campaigns.[49]

Because two-thirds of both houses of the legislature must approve reforms to Three Strikes, proponents of Reynolds's law need only convince a handful of lawmakers who support reforms to vote against their preference or abstain. The CCPOA and allied groups make backing reforms, which are unlikely to pass and get a governor's signature (Governors Wilson, Davis, and Schwarzenegger all support Three Strikes in its original form) a politically risky endeavor. In sum, the union and related groups obstruct the reformation (or elimination) of Three Strikes via the legislative process. They also obstruct attempts to reform the law via ballot initiative.

After Three Strikes had been law for several years, Jim Benson, a political moderate who had dabbled in local and statewide politics, contacted Sam Clauder, a consultant who previously worked on several initiative campaigns, including the campaigns for Proposition 36, the initiative to place drug offenders in treatment programs rather than prison, and Proposition 184. In 1994 both Benson and Clauder strongly supported Proposition 184. However, they became disillusioned with the policy when they heard stories about offenders who received very long prison sentences for nonviolent, and in some cases victimless, crimes. Therefore they sought to place a proposition on the ballot that would narrow the law's scope.

Aware of Joe Klaas's opposition to Reynolds's Three Strikes law, Clauder asked the elder Klaas to help him and Benson raise money for the initiative campaign. Unlike his son Marc, who had since become a staunch advocate of Three Strikes, Joe Klaas remained intensely opposed to Reynolds's law and gladly joined Clauder and Benson. In 2003 Benson, who assumed responsibility for the campaign's daily operations, sent out fundraising letters and emails signed by Joe Klaas and the actor Ed Asner. The three men were elated when they unexpectedly received a check for $300,000 from Jerry Keenan, a very wealthy owner of a Sacramento auto insurance firm. With Keenan's donation in hand, the group aimed to qualify their initiative, which would become Proposition 66, for the 2004 statewide ballot.[50]

Jerry Keenan had a personal reason for backing the campaign for Proposition 66. In 1999 Keenan's 21-year-old son, Richard, had flipped his car after smoking marijuana and drinking beer. Two of his passengers died in the wreck. Richard Keenan pleaded guilty to two counts of vehicular manslaughter and one count of "causing great bodily injury," a strikeable offense. Jerry Keenan was shocked that his son now had a strike on his record. "When Richard was linked to Three Strikes, it opened my eyes," he said. "Something was horribly wrong if a three-strikes law could affect someone like Richard."[51]

Similar to the alternative Three Strikes measures that the state legislature considered in 1994 (e.g., Senator Rainey's bill, which Marc and Joe Klaas had both supported), Proposition 66 would require that all strikes be "violent" or "serious." The initiative would eliminate the "any felony" provision of Reynolds's law. In addition, Proposition 66 would reduce the number of felonies that qualified as strikes. The initiative would require the state to resentence offenders serving indeterminate life sentences under Three Strikes if their third strike was "nonviolent" or "nonserious" as defined by the proposition. The initiative would also mandate that the state try eligible offenses in separate trials in order for each offense to be counted as a strike (Reynolds's law allowed a defendant to receive multiple strikes in a single trial). Finally, Proposition 66 would increase prison sentences for offenders convicted of sexual crimes against children under the age of 14.[52] The sexual crimes provision was a transparent effort to forestall accusations that the proposition was "soft on crime."

Even though opponents of Proposition 66 disliked all of the initiative's provisions, with the possible exception of that relating to sex offenders, they most fervently criticized the ones that reduced the number of serious or violent offenses and mandated resentencing incarcerated "strikers." The opponents locked in on one of the offenses that would no longer be considered serious or violent: "unintentional infliction of significant personal injury while committing a felony offense." The "No on 66" campaign quickly publicized that Richard Keenan, son of Proposition 66's financial backer, was convicted of inflicting great bodily harm on a friend when he wrecked his car while under the influence of marijuana and alcohol—a "strikeable" offense under Reynolds's law. Because it was retroactive, Proposition 66 would remove Richard Keenan's "strike." The reform measure—or at least one of its provisions—seemed like a clear-cut attempt to get a rich man's son out of prison.

The CCPOA established an organization to defeat Proposition 66. The union hired Nina Salarno-Ashford, daughter of the president of CVUC, Harriet Salarno, to organize a coalition of law enforcement and victims' groups (Californians United for Public Safety [CUPS]) opposed to Proposition 66.[53] CUPS established a PAC called "Californians United for Public Safety, Independent Expenditure Committee" (CUPS-IEC). CUPS would serve as the organizational base for the anti-66 campaign.

Selective Members of Californians United for Public Safety[54]

Law Enforcement Organizations
California Correctional Peace Officers Association
California Coalition of Law Enforcement Associations
Peace Officers Research Association of California
California State Sheriffs Association
California Police Chiefs Association
California Firefighters Association
California Association of Deputy Attorneys General
California Narcotic Officers Association
Association of Los Angeles Deputy Sheriffs
State Coalition of Probation Organizations

Crime Victim Organizations
Mothers Against Drunk Driving

Crime Victims United of California
Citizens Against Homicide
Family and Friends of Murdered Victims
Justice for Murder Victims
Doris Tate Crime Victims Bureau
Parents of Murdered Children
Mothers Against Gang Violence
Victims of Violent Crime

Crime Victim Advocates
Mike Reynolds, author of Three Strikes
Marc Klaas, KlaasKids Foundation
LaWanda Hawkins, president, Justice for Murdered Children
Marcella Leach, executive director, Justice for Homicide Victims

On April 20, 2004, I attended the CCPOA's annual Victims' March on the Capitol, essentially a celebration of Three Strikes and a rally against Proposition 66. In his opening remarks, CCPOA President Mike Jimenez said,

Today we are gathered to renew our faith in the most progressive and aggressive Three Strikes law in the nation. I want to let you know today that we will not forget. We're going to stand strong behind Three Strikes. And we believe that we *are* targeting the appropriate criminal element—those individuals who have made conscious choices to make careers of crime. We believe that Three Strikes is working.

Later in the event, Nina Salarno-Ashford presented a plaque to Mike Reynolds that read,

In memory of Kimber. In tribute to Mike Reynolds on behalf of the People of California. Thank you for Three Strikes and You're Out, a loving father's memorial to his lost daughter. Your courage and perseverance has spared countless families that heartache you have endured. We will never forget all you've done. Presented April 20th, 2004—Victims' March on the Capitol.

Reynolds accepted the plaque and made a few sardonic remarks. "I'm really not prepared to make any speech, but I will just make a couple of comments," he said. "Ten years ago we made a really amazing discovery: the leading cause of crime is criminals. And the leading source of criminals is our prison system. My daddy used to tell me everybody's got to be somewhere. And I think we all know where criminals need to be. Thank you."[55]

As of mid-October 2004, the CCPOA had spent approximately $245,650 on the "No on 66" campaign—$199,000 of which went into CUPS-IEC.[56] With funds from the CCPOA and several other contributors, CUPS conducted a relatively minor public relations campaign against Proposition 66.[57] For example, on September 21, 2004, the coalition launched its "Felon a Day" campaign against Proposition 66. The press release for the campaign read,

> "Every day between now and the election, we'll be releasing at least one mug shot and rap sheet of a felon who will be released early by Proposition 66," said campaign spokesperson Cam Sanchez, president of the California Police Chiefs Association. "These are very dangerous people—serial child molesters, rapists, murders [sic] and career criminals with long histories of serious crime," said Sanchez. "They and thousands more like them will be back on the street if Proposition 66 becomes law."[58]

Californians United for Public Safety also sent out press releases announcing that major law enforcement officials and organizations opposed Proposition 66.

Even though CUPS's efforts received media attention, they did not change public opinion, which favored reforming Three Strikes. As shown in Table 5.2, 65% of likely voters supported Proposition 66 on October 13, just over two weeks before the election. As it began to appear that Joe Klaas and other critics of Three Strikes would celebrate on election night, CUPS received a major infusion of cash for a full-scale media campaign. During the last week of October 2004, Henry T. Nicholas III, founder of Broadcom Corp. and an Orange County billionaire, contributed $1.9 million to the "No on 66" campaign. Nicholas would chip in an additional $1.6 million to the anti-Proposition 66 efforts, for a total $3.5 million.[59]

Nicholas's family background sheds light on why he helped finance the opposition to Proposition 66. In 1983 Nicholas's sister was murdered by her ex-boyfriend. In response to the murder, Marcella Nicholas Leach, Henry's mother, cofounded Justice for Homicide Victims and later became vice chair of CVUC. In 2005 Leach received the U.S. Department of Justice's prestigious National Crime Victims' Rights Week Award.[60] Newspaper reporters referred to the murder of Nicholas's sister, but they did not discuss Nicholas's connection, via his mother, to CVUC. Thus the newspapers suggested that Nicholas was a rich, bereaved brother who unexpectedly rescued the "No on 66" campaign, rather than a rich, bereaved brother who was related (literally) to CVUC and, by extension, the CCPOA.[61]

Right after Nicholas pledged to help bankroll a media blitz against Proposition 66, former Governor Pete Wilson pulled Governor Arnold Schwarzenegger headfirst into the fight against the initiative. Wilson convinced Schwarzenegger to put money and effort into defeating Proposition 66.[62] The *Los Angeles Times* reported, "On Oct. 22, the day after Wilson's call, Schwarzenegger made 'No on 66' the top priority of his ballot measure campaigning. On Oct. 23, the governor spent the afternoon making TV advertisements opposing the initiative in a Los Angeles studio. He also converted TV time he had bought to fight two gambling measures into time for 'No on 66' ads."[63]

Governor Schwarzenegger's "California Recovery Team," a fund he developed to pay for ballot initiatives, contributed more than $2 million to the fight against Proposition 66. The CCPOA added $500,000 to the cause (in addition to the $245,650 it had already spent).[64] The union paid the advertising firm McNally Temple Associates to develop a couple of anti-Proposition 66 commercials. However, CUPS previously did not have enough money to buy time on television and radio. Now the "No on 66" coalition tapped into its new financial windfall to air the anti-Proposition 66 advertisements throughout California.[65]

The coalition produced three television commercials and three radio spots. The first television commercial, "He Raped Me," features a white, middle-aged rape victim. As eerie, tense music plays in the background, the woman says, "He had a knife at my throat and said he was going to kill me. Then he raped me." A mug shot of the rapist flashes on screen. A white man, his head hangs listlessly to the side, making him appear drunk or perhaps brain damaged. The woman continues, "He killed two women. Now Prop. 66 will set him free." The camera peers into the woman's eyes and then pans over mug shots of convicts (the same mug shots used in the "Felon a Day" campaign; see Figure 5.1). The narrator says, "Proposition 66 creates a loophole that will release 26,000 dangerous felons." The advertisement cuts to David Paulson, a member of the California District Attorneys Association, who stands in front of what appears to be a courthouse. He says, "These aren't petty offenders. They're career criminals with

Figure 5.1.
A still from a "No on 66" commercial, which warned that the proposition would release a flood of violent criminals onto the streets. Mug shots of offenders were used to instill fear and literally put a face on the proposal.

long histories of serious crime." Standing on a grassy knoll with kids playing behind him, Marc Klaas continues where Paulson leaves off: "Murderers, rapists, and some very dangerous child molesters." The narrator says, as pictures of California governors appear on the screen, "Opposed by California's last five governors and every DA in the state, Republican and Democrat." As the advertisement concludes, the collage of mug shots reappears with a large red "No on 66" stamped across it. The narrator warns, "Protect your family. No on 66."[66]

The two other commercials feature a man who is very comfortable in front of the camera, Governor Arnold Schwarzenegger. In "Early Release," the governor stands in front of a black backdrop and says sternly, "Under Proposition 66, 26,000 dangerous criminals will be released from prison." As he utters the words "dangerous criminals," he moves in front of seven oversized black-and-white mug shots of convicted felons (the same "Felon a Day" mug shots). The governor continues, "Child molesters. Rapists. Murderers. Keep them off the streets and out of your neighborhood. Vote no on 66. Keep them behind bars." As the governor intones the last sentence, prison bars slam in front of the mug shots. The second commercial featuring Governor Schwarzenegger, "Criminals," is nearly identical to "Early Release." Even though the arrangement of words in the two advertisements varies, both commercials communicate a powerful message via a charismatic and (at that time) popular man. Schwarzenegger all but promises Proposition 66 will release extremely dangerous and violent criminals, and those predators will come to your neighborhood and victimize your family.

The radio spots express the same messages (albeit more concisely) as the television ads. Two of the radio spots feature Jerry Brown, former liberal democratic governor of California and (in 2004) mayor of Oakland, California. Mayor Brown explained his opposition to Proposition 66 in a television interview: "I've joined the campaign—because we in Oakland do have a lot of crimes, and the last thing we need is some of the most dangerous people coming back into the community after we all thought they'd been locked up for the rest of their lives." He continued,

> The ones that Proposition 66 deals with are the worst of the worst, and in most cases, they're coming back [to prison] anyway. So everybody is saved all the grief of having to go through another victimization, maybe another murder, another burglary, another robbery, and have them then convicted and go back into prison. It just keeps them there. Because they've proven by their behavior that that is their M.O.—their modus operandi is a criminal act.[67]

As mayor of Oakland, Brown had set his sights on the attorney general's office. He worked to befriend law enforcement organizations in Sacramento, including his former foe, the CCPOA. As was shown in chapter 2, Don Novey and the other founders of the CCPOA had once detested Brown; as governor,

Brown's support for the anti-death penalty Bird Court had infuriated them. And the union's leaders continued their disdain for Brown at least until the late 1990s, including him on a list of enemies sent to CCPOA members in 1999.[68]

But Brown's efforts to defeat Proposition 66 helped rehabilitate his relationship with the CCPOA. Voters in the Bay Area and other regions of the state received recorded telephone messages in which Brown encouraged them to oppose Proposition 66. Brown also opposed Proposition 66 in newspaper and television interviews and stumped against the initiative with former California governors. Along with ex-governor Gray Davis, Brown demonstrated bipartisan opposition to Proposition 66. The "No on 66" campaign could honestly claim that even liberals like Jerry Brown (the architect of the Rose Bird court) opposed the measure to reform Three Strikes. Brown's new "tough on crime" persona and law-and-order stances (most importantly, his actions against Proposition 66), have won him praise from powerful law enforcement and crime victims' organizations. For example, the California Police Chiefs Association and the CCPOA (once vehemently opposed to all that Brown stood for) endorsed Brown in his successful race for California attorney general in 2006. The CCPOA also endorsed Brown in his winning bid for governor in 2010.

The various anti-Proposition 66 advertisements (including the "Felon a Day" press releases) expressed consistent and powerful messages. They aimed to frighten voters with warnings of a flood of violent criminals that would drown "your neighborhood," victimize "your families," and terrorize "your children." The anti-Proposition 66 campaign's main advertisement, "He Raped Me," spotlighted a white, maternal crime victim. Her appearance implicitly suggested that Proposition 66 threatened the personal safety of everybody—including (or especially) white, middle-class and working-class families and children.[69]

The advertisements also employed the image of the "sexual predator," which has been prevalent in politics and the media in the United States since at least 1990.[70] Popular television shows often use the term "sexual predator" and comment on the most sensational details of high-profile sex-related crimes. As Jonathan Simon writes, terms like predator and prey invoke "non-human forms of danger." "Sexual predators" are "state-defined 'monsters'" that are constructed as inherently evil, voracious, and unredeemable—they "can be neither altered or eliminated but only managed" (hence the ubiquity of sex offender registries and notification laws).[71] Marc Klaas appears in "He Raped Me" not because he is an expert on crime and punishment, but because he connects Proposition 66 to Polly Klaas's abduction and murder. Moreover, for viewers with good memories, Klaas invokes the image of Polly's abductor and murderer, Richard Allen Davis—the personification of the sexually violent "career criminal" who is irredeemably programmed to victimize.

The "Yes on 66" team seemed caught off guard by the late infusion of cash into the "No on 66" campaign and the corresponding media blitz.[72] However, proponents of the initiative launched a public relations counteroffensive, funded with money from Jerry Keenan and billionaires George Soros, John Sperling, and Peter Lewis.[73] "Yes on 66" produced an advertisement called "Joe," which starred Joe Klaas. With a look of grandfatherly sincerity, Klaas said into the camera,

> I helped lead the fight for a Three Strikes law because of a personal tragedy in my family. That law has put a lot of dangerous people in prison. But there was a flaw in the law. We're putting people away for life when their third strike is a nonviolent crime, like stealing aspirin—and we're paying a million dollars to incarcerate each one. That's not what we voted for. Proposition 66 fixes the flaw in the law.

The proponents of Proposition 66 spent approximately $3,508,415 for the production and airing of the television advertisement.[74]

Whereas the anti-Proposition 66 commercials warned of impending doom, the pro-Proposition 66 advertisement targeted technical problems with Three Strikes ("a flaw in the law") and deemed the law unjust, expensive, and misleading ("That's not what we voted for"). The "Argument in Favor of Proposition" in the ballot summary used similar logic to persuade voters. It announced, "PROPOSITION 66 IS NOT ABOUT GETTING SOFT ON CRIME, IT'S ABOUT GETTING SMART ON CRIME."[75] The ballot argument (but not the television advertisement) also played the "sex offender" card. One of the argument's four bullet points read, "Protect our children by stopping child molesters with a '1 Strike' sentence." The ballot argument was somewhat confusing because it suggested that Three Strikes was too tough on some criminals, but not tough enough on others (namely, "child molesters").

Taken together, the "Yes on 66" campaign claimed that California needed a more nuanced, less expensive Three Strikes law. It attempted to reason with voters and appeal to their sense of fairness.[76] The "Yes on 66" campaign's arguments, in other words, were academic, technical, and rational. The "No on 66" campaign's messages were primarily emotional; they targeted voters' guts rather than their minds. Advertisements against the measure did not discuss cost-effectiveness, fairness, or the relative "smartness" of tinkering with Three Strikes. The commercials' harrowing music, scary images, and simple yet powerful messages communicated that Proposition 66 would create chaos, destroy communities, and lessen personal safety.

The "No on 66" strategy sought to capture the public imagination and generate negative feelings among the electorate. Contemporary political strategists (including those who worked on the campaign against Proposition 66) routinely frame penal policies to stir up voters' fears and anxieties not just

Table 5.2 TREND OF VOTER PREFERENCE REGARDING
PROPOSITION 66 (AMONG LIKELY VOTERS)

Date (2004)	Yes	No	Undecided
May	76%	14%	10%
June	76%	14%	10%
August	69%	19%	12%
October 13	65%	18%	17%
October 21–27	55%	33%	12%

The Field Poll, "Large Majority Supports Easing of Three Strikes Law," Release No. 2121 (San Francisco: Field Research Corporation, June 10, 2004); The Field Poll, "Late-Breaking Surge of No Votes on Prop. 66," Release No. 2146 (San Francisco: Field Research Corporation, October 30, 2004).

about crime, but also an assortment of other issues such as family stability, economic security, access to quality education, availability of health care, demographic diversity, and international developments (e.g., terrorism and the "war on terror").[77] If voters feel a penal policy will intensify disorder and insecurity in their lives, they are apt to oppose it—regardless if the policy is "smart" or not.[78] Understanding this political reality, the "No on 66" campaign assured voters that the initiative would cause major disorder to families and communities.

The strategy against the initiative worked. Table 5.2 shows that a large majority of likely voters favored Proposition 66 until late October 2004. Support for Proposition 66 quickly fell as the public campaign against the measure, which featured authoritative people such as Governor Schwarzenegger insisting that the initiative would create mass chaos, gained steam. Support for Proposition 66 continued to fall in the final days leading up to the election. The initiative enjoyed an early lead on election night; however, the lead dropped precipitously, and Proposition 66 failed 53% to 47%. It appears that voters supported reforming an extremely costly and, according to Proposition 66's proponents, broken law until they repeatedly heard that such reform would cause entropy in a social world marked by rapid, major changes, making their lives dangerous and unmanageable.

On April 10, 2005, nearly six months after the defeat of Proposition 66, I attended the annual CVUC fundraising dinner. The program featured keynote speaker Nancy Grace, former prosecutor and star of "Court TV," a sensationalist, melodramatic television show in which Grace comments on high-profile criminal cases and heaps scorn on "sexual predators." During the dinner, CVUC and CCPOA representatives honored their allies in the state legislature, celebrated their recent achievements, and articulated their future goals. In addition to cheering the recent demise of Governor Schwarzenegger's attempt at parole reform (see chapter 4), the attendees rejoiced about Proposition 66's defeat and vowed to keep protecting Mike Reynolds's Three Strikes law from all challengers.[79]

Nina Salarno-Ashford handed out framed "No on 66" bumper stickers to prominent people who opposed Proposition 66, such as CCPOA President Mike Jimenez and Orange County Sheriff Mike Corona. The people at the event excitedly awaited the arrival of Henry Nicholas III, who was to arrive in Sacramento by private airplane. Salarno-Ashford announced that she would eventually replace her mother, Harriet Salarno, as the leader of CVUC, and said that she hoped Nicholas would serve alongside her. Harriet Salarno and Marcella Leach cheered and smiled widely at the prospect of their children taking the reigns of CVUC. Henry Nicholas III did not arrive at the event. Nonetheless, the speakers emphatically praised him in his absence.

In addition to celebrating Henry Nicholas III, CVUC representatives and other speakers lauded Don Novey for spearheading the campaign against Proposition 66. At Novey's behest, Nina Salarno-Ashford had organized CUPS, which served as the organizational base for the "No on 66" campaign. The CCPOA pushed along an ailing "No on 66" operation when other individuals and organizations that opposed the initiative (including Governor Schwarzenegger) were missing in action.[80] Along with contributing nearly $855,000 to defeat the initiative, the CCPOA brought together various like-minded organizations (and their resources) to oppose Proposition 66 with one voice—a voice that ardently insisted that Californians' personal safety hinged on the survival of Three Strikes.[81] Moreover, the CCPOA, with the assistance of talented public relations professionals, developed images and arguments that attempted to frighten the electorate into voting against Proposition 66 and counter the technical arguments made by the proponents of the initiative.

Although the CCPOA played a very important part in the campaign to defeat Proposition 66, the union was by no means solely responsible for the initiative's defeat. This point brings us to a central argument of this chapter. The CCPOA is part of a bloc within the penal field that struggles to maintain punitive segregation as the leading penal strategy in California. As used here, a bloc is an association of actors with similar interests who work toward shared goals. Blocs are not formal organizations with membership roles (although they may become formal organizations). Actors in a bloc do not always work together to accomplish particular tasks (such as passing a piece of legislation); however, their collective efforts advance the actors' shared interests and worldviews. Crime victims groups, law enforcement associations, and the state's association of prosecutors are also key actors in the bloc. As shown in the story of Proposition 66, past and present politicians participate in the bloc as financiers and public spokespersons. The story also provides support for the claim that the CCPOA is the anchor of the bloc rather than simply one participant among many. To win campaigns concerning penal laws, the CCPOA contributes hundreds of thousands (and sometimes millions) of dollars, organizes like-minded groups and individuals, and develops strategies. In short, the CCPOA is not the sole reason that California continues to have the country's most stringent Three Strikes law, as critics sometimes suggest. Rather, it is an essential actor in a bloc that helped pass Proposition 184 in 1994 and factored centrally in the campaign to defend Reynolds's law against changes a decade later.

THE IMPORTANCE OF THREE STRIKES

The CCPOA and similarly positioned actors vigorously defend Three Strikes because of what it does and what it represents. As noted previously, Reynolds and his compatriots designed Three Strikes to have the utmost effect—to "get all the criminal garbage off the streets." The law promised to neutralize violent and nonviolent criminals by locking them behind bars. As anticipated, the law has caught numerous people in its expansive net. Between 1994 and 2004 approximately 87,500 people received "sentence enhancements" under Three Strikes. Of those, 80,000 were "second-strikers" and 7,500 were "third-strikers." On December 3, 2004, there were almost 43,000 prisoners serving time under the Three Strikes law—about 26% of California's total prison population (about half of the second-strikers apparently completed their sentences between 1994 and 2004).[82] As of 2004, 14 of the 22 states with three-strikes laws had fewer than 100 people incarcerated under these laws. Only California, Florida, and Georgia imprisoned 400 or more third-strikers. California had a total population of about 35 million and a Three Strikes population (including second-strikers) of about 43,000. The other 22 states with three-strikes laws had a total population of roughly 112 million and a combined three-strikes population of 10,624.[83]

A recent report by the California State Auditor shows that California's Three Strikes population remained stable between 2004 and 2009. As of April 2009, 43,000 of the state's 171,500 prisoners (roughly 25%) were sentenced under the law.[84] Of this total, 8,500 were serving sentences of 25-to-life.[85] The report estimates that "striker" inmates serve, on average, sentences that are nine years longer than nonstrikers. The state will pay approximately $19.2 billion in additional costs because of the striker population's extended sentences. Remarkably, the current convictions (i.e., the convictions that triggered the Three Strikes law) of more than half of the total striker population (23,099 of 43,000) were nonserious and nonviolent.[86] Approximately 3,700 prisoners are serving sentences of 25-to-life for nonserious and nonviolent offenses.[87] Three Strikes continues to greatly affect the prison population and state coffers.

In the eyes of the CCPOA and related groups, the passage of Three Strikes represented positive penal reform for several reasons. First, The law greatly reduced judicial authority and increased prosecutorial discretion. The prosecutor decides whether or not to charge a person under Three Strikes, and the law (not the judge) determines the sentence for a person convicted under it.[88] The architects of this policy privileged prosecutorial over judicial discretion because district attorneys represent victims and typically equate success with guilty verdicts. Moreover, they felt that judges typically sided with defendants and convicts over victims. Therefore they were determined to deny judges the power to water down Three Strikes during the sentencing phase of trials.[89]

Second, for the CCPOA and its allies, Three Strikes was a victory over "liberal" policymakers who, before the 1990s, spurned "tough" approaches to crime control and, in the words of the union, made incarceration in California "the ultimate welfare program." Reflecting on 1994 and Three Strikes, the CCPOA wrote in 1995, "Many of us would argue that California has finally come to its senses and is prioritizing crime fighting the way it's been ignored throughout most of the 60's and 70's and halfway through the 80's." The union added, "True reform is happening presently which is to repeal the liberal policies of the 60's and 70's and get tough with the criminal element."[90] Reynolds and his coauthors expressed the same idea on the dust cover of their book about Three Strikes:

> It is the story of one family's heartbreak, of behind-the-scenes political maneuvering by soft-on-crime, liberal politicians in an effort to eviscerate the law, and it's the story of the ultimate victory by a majority of Californians who, in a reversal of decades of citizen neglect, defied the crime "experts" and voted for common sense and justice.

Three Strikes, in short, exemplifies Reynolds, Novey, Salarno, and their colleagues' ultramasculine views about criminal punishment. Unlike allegedly soft, effeminate crime control strategies that claim to treat convicts and help them integrate back into society, Three Strikes is a tough law with a tough name that eliminates ("strikes out") criminals from society.[91]

Third, Three Strikes exemplifies the CCPOA and its partners' beliefs about penal expertise. They claim that "crime experts"—academics, policy wonks, and penal professionals—do not understand the truth about crime and criminals, for the "experts" have intellectual rather than direct, experiential knowledge about the nature of criminals, the pain that criminals cause their victims, and the fear lawbreakers instill in "law-abiding citizens." As explained in chapter 4, CCPOA representatives insist that traditional experts empathize with criminals and depict offenders as victims of socialization, societal neglect, and lack of opportunities. In addition, the experts espouse ill-conceived, anachronistic, and ultimately dangerous notions of "rehabilitation." The CCPOA argues that traditional experts advocate a "political philosophy that absolves [criminals] of responsibility for their actions, makes excuses for their behavior and assumes responsibility to change them." According to the union, this "philosophy" is "a dismal failure," for "the *criminal* is responsible for his own choices."[92] If academics and other purported authorities had direct contact with criminals and victims, they would not "make excuses for" offenders; they would see that felonious behavior is evidence of weak moral judgment or just plain evil.

According to the CCPOA, law enforcement officers (including prison officers), crime victims, and prosecutors are the true penal experts because they have direct (or nearly direct) experience with crime. They claim to intuitively understand the nature of criminals and what "works" to prevent crime because of their "real-life" experiences working with criminals (in the case of law enforcement and prosecutors). Thus, the CCPOA asserts, "our practical day-to-day, year-in, year-out experience with the criminal element supports our positions."[93] Victims of crime and their family members claim to understand crime and punishment because of their pain. Victims' kin have expertise because of the *secondary pain* they experience when family members are murdered, raped, or otherwise victimized. The loss or violation of a loved one produces "truth"—authentic knowledge. Recall Marc Klaas's claim that crime victims (and their family members) see the light after being at the "bottom of the well." In an essay written in 2001, Nina Salarno-Ashford similarly explained that her experience as the sister of a murder victim provides her unique insight into the value of the death penalty, which, she maintains, gives victims' families an "overwhelming sense of peace" through the "elimination of evil and execution of the killer."[94] The CCPOA and its allies contend that their perspectives on crime and punishment are "common sense" derived from closely watching criminals inside and outside of prisons and from feeling (directly or indirectly) the pain caused by criminals.

Finally, Three Strikes' emphasis on incapacitation resonates with their belief that "prisons work." In a 1995 pamphlet, the CCPOA addressed the argument that prisons are ineffective:

> Our response is to ask the following question: How many robberies, rapes, and drive-by shootings have you heard of being perpetrated by suspects while in prison? None. Can't happen. On the contrary, prisons do work. No crimes are committed upon the public when the criminal is locked up. Without incarceration there is no public safety. Prisons work just fine. They incapacitate the convicted criminal.[95]

Both Reynolds and the CCPOA support incapacitation because they believe that the vast majority of criminals are unredeemable. On this topic, the

CCPOA writes, "The criminal pretends to change and the system pretends to believe them [sic] but they remain 'predators' of people, situations, and institutions. They take whatever they can, anyway [sic] they can."[96] CCPOA representatives routinely refer to offenders as "the criminal element." In doing so, they suggest that offenders are an undifferentiated mass of criminogenic beings—rather than individuals with unique histories who commit crimes (but are not inherently criminal). Mandatory-minimum sentences such as Three Strikes likewise treat classes of criminals the same—they all get long prison sentences and no mercy.

In sum, Three Strikes validates and helps implement the CCPOA and its allies' particular view of penal common sense. The defeat of Proposition 66 affirmed the "tough on crime" values and "strict father" morality embodied in Reynolds's law. For its supporters, Three Strikes signals that California privileges victims over defendants and prisoners. It indicates that "punitive segregation" remains the dominant (albeit continually challenged) crime control strategy in California. Three Strikes also affirms the social status and "public worth" of the CCPOA and its allies, which felt unappreciated and disregarded during the rehabilitation era.[97] The law, then, is a symbol of the groups' collective success and a totemic emblem that represents the groups. The CCPOA and other actors in the dominant bloc within the penal field passionately fend off attacks on Three Strikes because those attacks are affronts to a larger set of values, self-perceptions, and worldviews.

CHAPTER 6

Monopolizing the Beat: The Fight Against Prison Privatization

At the same time that the California Correctional Peace Officers Association (CCPOA) was struggling to pass and protect Three Strikes, it was battling on other fronts. One of its main foes was the private imprisonment lobby. In the mid-1990s, conditions in California seemed ripe for private prison entrepreneurs. The penitentiaries were dangerously overcrowded, government reports and legislators documented mismanagement and scandals behind bars, and the state's recidivism rate was steadily high. As lawmakers criticized the bloated and dysfunctional prison system, Democrats and Republicans alike considered privatization a viable option, cheaper and more efficient than state prisons. They also maintained that private prisons would give public prisons some competition, forcing the state facilities to function more effectively. In 1996 Charles Thomas, a sociologist who advocates on behalf of for-profit penal facilities and has served as a member of boards of directors for private prison corporations, predicted that California would embrace the effort: "Even a pretty solid dam can only hold back a finite amount of water. In my judgment, the dam is about to break in California."[1] Marvin Weibe, vice president of private prison company Cornell Corrections, said in 1996 that, in California, "Privatization is inevitable."[2]

Writing in 1993, criminologist David Shichor suggested that private prison corporations would gain lucrative contracts in California and other states through political action. Resistance to the growing private prison lobby was, he thought, unlikely:

> These features of corporate political activity should be seen in light of the fact that there are no comparable PACs or lobbying organizations dedicated for the sole purpose of representing inmates . . . Thus, there may not be a balance

between the corporate private prison lobby's influence and organizations that are likely to be concerned with prisoners' rights.[3]

As Shichor foresaw, the political opposition to private prison corporations, at least in California, would not come from prisoner rights' organizations; it would come primarily from labor unions and their allies.

In the Golden State, the CCPOA served (and still serves) as a political counterweight to private prison corporations. The union opposes privatization because private prisons, which do not use union labor, threaten the job security of prison officers and, potentially, the strength of the CCPOA itself. Moreover, the union's leaders believe that imprisonment is properly a state function that should not be contracted out to for-profit companies, which are foremost responsible to shareholders rather than state officials and taxpayers. Put simply, the union opposes privatization for both material and ideological reasons. Activist-scholar Christian Parenti credits the CCPOA for its efforts against for-profit incarceration: "In their fight against privatization the guards defend not only their own interests but inadvertently the larger agenda of public accountability and democratic control over state functions. As bad as public prisons are, private one [sic] are worse, both in fact and principle."[4] Criminologist Michael Jacobson, former commissioner of New York City's Department of Corrections and current president of the Vera Institute of Justice, argues that private prison companies' lack of success in California is "testimony to the clout of the CCPOA."[5]

Whereas scholars agree that the CCPOA impedes prison privatization in California, they do not explain how or to what extent the union achieves this goal. This chapter discusses how, since the mid-1990s, the CCPOA has fought prison privatization on several fronts. In addition to sponsoring and opposing legislation, the union's lobbyists and officials inform lawmakers about what the CCPOA sees as the evils of private prisons. Allies in the legislative and executive branches of government then use the CCPOA's information to oppose expansion of prison privatization. The union's allies in Sacramento, including former governor Gray Davis, have blocked privatization moves through the budgetary process, ostensibly on behalf of the union. In addition, the CCPOA explicitly and implicitly threatens the political future of lawmakers and would-be lawmakers who support the expansion of for-profit facilities in California. Political figures (and aspiring ones) must reckon with the specter of the CCPOA when considering backing private incarceration.

In these ways, the CCPOA serves as an organizational barrier to prison privatization in California. However, it is not the only such obstacle. Other state worker labor unions and the American Civil Liberties Union (ACLU) also oppose privatizing prisons. The California Department of Corrections (CDC) typically supports contracting out low-level offenders, however, it does not support legislative proposals for large-scale privatization, which would threaten to reduce the agency's authority and resources.[6] Taken together, a temporary alliance between the CCPOA and the CDC (labor and management)—with assistance from other labor unions, the ACLU, and legislators— has kept the government from operating medium- and maximum-security adult prisons in California. (As I describe later in the chapter, the union and its allies have not stopped the government from housing state convicts in prisons in other states.) In doing so, they have maintained the state's virtual monopoly on incarceration.

INTRODUCTION OF PRIVATE PRISONS TO CALIFORNIA

Scholars, politicians, and journalists tend to describe "public" and "private" incarceration as mutually exclusive categories. They typically depict incarceration as a public (county, state, or federal) enterprise in which the private sector periodically participates to make a profit. The public/private split is misleading (at least in Anglo-American countries), for the private sector has been involved with incarceration and other forms of criminal punishment for centuries. For example, the private sector participated extensively in the transportation of prisoners, the convict lease system, and the development of modern prisons. Legal scholar Malcolm Feeley states, "many—perhaps most—new forms of punishment in modern Anglo-American jurisdictions have their origins in proposals of private entrepreneurs."[7]

The current debate over public versus private incarceration started in the 1980s when entrepreneurs established businesses to profit from building and operating prisons in the United States and other countries. The largest private prison company, Corrections Corporation of America (CCA), started in 1983 and obtained its first contract to manage a prison in 1984. In 1985 Florida's legislature authorized the state to establish contracts with companies for the management of prisons. In 1987 Texas awarded two 500-bed facility management contracts to CCA and two 500-bed contracts to CCA's main competitor, Wackenhut Corrections Corporation (Wackenhut is now called the Geo Group Inc.). During the 1990s, the number of private prisons increased rapidly. In 1990 there were roughly 15,000 private prison beds in the United States.[8] Just nine years later the number of beds had skyrocketed to more than 140,000.[9] In 1999 private facilities housed approximately 69,000 state and federal prisoners, about 5.3% of the country's total prison population. In 2006 the number of state and federal prisoners housed in private facilities was nearly 112,000, more than 7% of the U.S. prison population.[10] Further, private imprisonment has expanded worldwide, taking hold in Australia, England, Scotland, South Africa, Surinam, and New Zealand.[11]

The large private prison companies—Wackenhut and CCA—did not enter the market in California until the mid-1990s, for reasons I explain later. However, the private sector has always been involved in imprisonment in the Golden State. In fact, the state's first prison was a privately owned 268-ton ship called the *Waban*. In 1852, as the *Waban* became overcrowded and offenders escaped with increasing frequency, the state used convict labor to erect San Quentin State Prison.[12] For decades the state has contracted with private vendors to design and construct penal facilities; provide medical, management, and treatment services; and operate prisoner work programs.[13] California houses more than half of all juvenile offenders in private community-based facilities. These private institutions serve as alternatives to the state's youth authority facilities, which are essentially prisons for juveniles.[14]

California did not house adult state prisoners in private facilities until the mid-1980s (with the exception of the *Waban*). At that time, officials in the CDC wanted the state to incarcerate parole violators—a growing sector of the prison population—in alternative settings and reserve prison beds for felons convicted of new crimes. In 1986 CDC representatives signed an agreement with Eclectic Communications (which later changed its name to Cornell Corrections)—a private company with a focus on social work that operated drug treatment facilities in California—to own and manage a community correctional facility (CCF) in the northern California town of La Honda. The facility, called Hidden Valley Ranch, would house parole violators with short sentences who otherwise would do time in state prison.

The CDC's contract with Eclectic Communications raises two questions: Was the agreement legal? And what was the CCPOA's response? CDC officials and their lawyers figured that the deal with the private company was legal because California's government code permits the directors of state agencies to establish contracts with the private sector to provide "services" as long as the contracts save the state money and do not displace civil service employees (state workers).[15] Article VII of the California Constitution, a holdover from the Progressive era, also forbids replacing civil service workers with private employees. CDC officials believed that CCFs would produce cost savings for the state and would not displace state workers (namely, prison officers) because CCFs did not exist previously—they were new facilities ("services") that were, according to the CDC, qualitatively different from prisons.[16]

The state's contract with the private company caught the CCPOA off guard. In fact, the union did not learn of the deal until Hidden Valley Ranch was operational. It is important to remember that, in 1986, the CCPOA was still in its infancy—it was still learning the political game and establishing its political operation. The state's contract with Eclectic Communications marked a turning point for the CCPOA regarding privatization; a union representative said plainly: "CCPOA has vigorously opposed the concept of private prisons since 1986, when it first learned of the contract between CDC and Eclectic Communications, Inc., for the operation of Hidden Valley Ranch in La Honda, California."[17]

Whereas the CCPOA opposed the private CCFs (which it called "prisons"), the union did not object to all forms of private incarceration in California. For example, in 1987 the CCPOA wrote, "We have no problem with the contracting out of facilities to handle illegal aliens awaiting deportation or lightweight juveniles" (a reference to private juvenile halls). It continued, "While CCPOA can tolerate the use of private vendors in some of the small half-way house operations (even though we have problems with the security of these operations), for a host of good reasons we are vehemently opposed to turning over the protection of the public to 'business'." The union concluded, "At best, the CCPOA sees only a very limited role for the private sector in the handling of our prison and youth authority."[18]

The CCPOA stridently opposed the private CCFs because the facilities resembled "prisons" and employed nonstate employees. In other words, the union now viewed privatization as a "turf issue."[19] The handful of private facilities did not endanger the job security of state prison officers. However, the prospect of large-scale prison privatization threatened officers' (or at least union officials') perception of future job security. They worried that the private CCFs would open the door for genuine private prisons (both adult and youth) in California.

In addition, prison privatization threatened officers' professional identities. The CCPOA promoted the notion that only professional "correctional peace officers" could manage the "toughest beat." Security employees who worked in the private facilities did not have peace officer status, received relatively little training, and earned low wages in contrast to state prison officers. The private companies suggested that custody staff worked rather uncomplicated jobs and therefore did not need extensive training or deserve higher compensation. CCPOA officials took offense to the private companies' implicit statement about the value of custody staff. They asserted that a solid divide separated the "professional peace officer" who worked in public penal facilities from the "rent-a-cop" who worked in the "prisons for profit."[20]

The CCPOA tried to stop the state from contracting with private companies by filing a lawsuit in superior court.[21] The union claimed that a CCF was "not much different than a minimum security prison," and therefore did not constitute a new state function (or service), as the CDC claimed. The CCPOA further argued that the "state [was] unlawfully giving jobs to non-civil service workers, in violation of the state constitution and Civil Service Act."[22] The superior court did not take action on the CCPOA's lawsuit because the union abandoned the case. Neither legal documents nor CCPOA sources explain why the union dropped the lawsuit, but the most probable explanation is that the CCPOA's lawyers were uncertain about the strength of their case. In order to win the lawsuit, the union needed to demonstrate that the CCFs replicated current prison services. Even though the CCFs had some characteristics of state prisons (e.g., secure perimeters), they also had qualities of halfway houses and treatment facilities. If the court had decided that the CCFs were new services (and therefore did not displace current state employees), the state would have gained additional legal authority to house convicts in private facilities.[23]

After the CCPOA abandoned its lawsuit against the state, the CDC granted contracts to several companies to operate private CCFs. In the 1990s government officials also gave contracts to counties to run CCFs, as local politicians saw the CCFs as opportunities for revenue.[24] Whereas initially the state sent only parole violators to the CCFs, it gradually transferred low-level prisoners with short sentences to these private facilities in order to clear space in the state prisons for more serious offenders.[25] In 1997 California had 12 CCFs that operated under contracts with either private businesses or local governments, housing approximately 4,000 state prisoners.[26] In 2005 California still had 12 CCFs—6 were private and 6 were county facilities. One of the 12 CCFs housed female offenders. Together, the facilities had capacity for 4,733 prisoners.[27]

During the 1980s and first half of the 1990s, neither state officials nor politicians officially proposed to privatize adult prisons in California—surprising because, during that period, privatization companies such as CCA and Wackenhut rapidly expanded and California's prison population grew exponentially. There are three primary reasons for the lack of political attention to prison privatization. First, the large private prison corporations, particularly CCA, simply did not lobby for medium- and maximum-security prisons in California until the mid-1990s. They concentrated their efforts in southern states such as Tennessee, Texas, and Florida. Moreover, the companies established lucrative deals with the federal government and administrations in other countries. Second, California was still building prisons approved during Governor Deukmejian's tenure. Finally, prison privatization would have required support from influential democratic legislators, whose party held substantial majorities in the assembly and senate until the mid-1990s. Democrats in the state legislature were largely allied with California's increasingly influential public workers' unions, and support for large-scale privatization of state services would have undermined that alliance.

In 1994 several factors coalesced to produce a "window of opportunity" for private prison companies in California. First, Governor Wilson, elected in 1990 and reelected in 1994, promoted privatization as a means of shrinking state government. Moreover, Governor Wilson had a hostile relationship with state workers' unions (the CCPOA was an exception) and wanted the legislature to reform civil service laws to facilitate privatization.[28] Second, the "Republican Revolution" of 1994 ushered in the first Republican majority in the state assembly in 25 years.[29]

A third factor was California's prison overcrowding dilemma. In 1995 California's prison population was 135,000 and its housing capacity was 116,500

(142,000 when including "nonpermanent housing" such as gymnasiums, day-rooms, and other areas that were not designed for long-term housing). The CDC predicted that by mid-1998, all available housing spaces would be occupied and that the total prison population of California would exceed 300,000 by mid-2005—a 126% increase.[30] California's newly implemented "Three Strikes and You're Out" law contributed to policymakers' fears that the system would soon overflow with felons. As the prison population increased, voters and legislators refused to fund enough prisons to alleviate the persistent over-crowding. Whereas California authorized 16 new facilities during Governor Deukmejian's tenure, it approved only 5 new ones during the Wilson and Davis administrations (1991–2003).

A final factor opening this window of opportunity for private prison companies was fear that California's ever-expanding corrections budget was taking away funding from vital public services. From 1983–1984 until 1994–1995, spending for corrections increased by 14% per year; in terms of spending, it was the fastest growing program in the state. By the time voters approved Three Strikes in 1994, corrections accounted for about 7% of the state's total $54.7 billion budget and fears about its price tag were intensifying.[31]

Legislators and other critics charged that even though the state allocated billions of dollars for corrections, the prisons were mismanaged, scandal-ridden, and ineffective at preparing prisoners for life on the outside.[32] Several high-profile incidents in which prison officers were accused of abusing their charges, sometimes with tacit support of their superiors, provided ammunition for the CDC's critics (chapter 7 describes these incidents). These detractors also cited California's high recidivism rate, which hovered around 60%, as clear evidence that the prisons were mere warehouses. Leading lawmakers viewed the CDC as broken beyond repair and looked for alternative means of confining and reforming state prisoners.

THE POLITICS OF PRISON PRIVATIZATION

As legislators and state officials scrambled to ease the state's prison over-crowding crisis, for-profit companies sought approval to operate private prisons in the Golden State. Representatives for CCA recruited Senate Minority Leader Rob Hurtt, a conservative Republican from Orange County, to champion their cause in the legislature. Hurtt then asked Senator Dan Boatwright (D-Concord), a notoriously pugnacious, centrist Democrat who had previously worked as a deputy district attorney, to work with him on the private prison issue. Boatwright held leadership positions on two prison-related committees in the senate: he was chair of the Joint Legislative Committee on Prison Construction and Operations (the "Prison Committee") and vice-chair of the Senate Committee on Public Safety. Boatwright's positions on these committees provided him with considerable authority over legislation concerning the prison system.

A self-described fiscal conservative, Senator Boatwright felt that the state's prison construction binge would eventually bankrupt the state. He thought the CDC mismanaged its finances and wasted taxpayer dollars and viewed the CCPOA as a meddlesome organization that increased bureaucratic inefficiency and obstructed sensible penal reform.[33] Boatwright opposed all of the proposals for prison construction that came through his Prison Committee and Public Safety Committee—and all such proposals *had* to go through one or both.[34] He wanted the state and the private sector to develop creative, cost-effective ways to house California's ever-expanding prison population. For these reasons, Senator Hurtt hoped Boatwright would see privatization as a valid alternative to the expansion of state prisons.

Boatwright was unfamiliar with private prisons, so, before agreeing to work with Hurtt and CCA, he appointed a staffer, Bernie Orozco, to examine existing models of privatization in other states and brief him on the findings. Upon completing his survey, Orozco drafted a bill based on Florida's model. In 1993 Florida's legislature created a new governmental agency, the Florida Correctional Privatization Commission, and vested the commission (rather than the state's Department of Corrections) with the responsibility of contracting with private prison companies and overseeing their management and operations.[35] Orozco's proposal called for the creation of a nine-member panel with similar responsibilities as those of Florida's private prison commission. California's privatization agency would have authority to contract for five facilities between 1996 and 2002. Senators Hurtt and Boatwright agreed to move forward on Orozco's proposal. The resulting legislation, SB 2156, the "California Correctional Facilities Privatization Commission Act of 1996," essentially sought to create a parallel private prison system that would compete with the existing public system.[36]

While the senate deliberated on SB 2156, unorthodox alliances developed to advocate for and against the legislation. The pro-SB 2156 side included representatives of CCA and other private prison companies, conservative Republicans, and Democrats who were staunch critics of the prison bureaucracy. The anti-SB 2156 contingent consisted primarily of the CCPOA and other unions (including independent law enforcement unions and the American Federation of Labor and Congress of Industrial Organizations [AFL-CIO]), prisoners' rights and civil rights organizations (such as the ACLU), and democratic legislators who were pro-union and antiprivatization.

Governor Wilson did not take an official position on SB 2156. His silence, however, signaled that he was, at best, ambivalent about the bill (even though he had advocated for privatizing government services and SB 2156 was a Republican bill). The three most logical explanations for Wilson's unwillingness to support SB 2156 were that CDC officials (who are in the executive branch) did not want to give authority over prison construction and man-agement to an autonomous commission; that Wilson's administration feared that private prisons would perform worse than the already low-performing public prisons; and that one of the governor's most generous supporters (and the only union that supported him), the CCPOA, vigor-ously opposed the bill.[37] To ease overcrowding, Wilson proposed building 15 new state prisons, which would vastly beef up (rather than shrink) the state's prison system. The CCPOA, in a position paper titled *Meeting the Challenge of Affordable Prisons*, similarly proposed that the state build its way out of the prison-overcrowding problem. The union wanted the state to con-struct "mega prisons," which would "cluster three or four smaller prisons at the same site" and house approximately 13,500 prisoners each. The "mega prisons," the CCPOA explained, would "dramatically reduce construction and operating costs by consolidating infrastructure, logistics and other expenses."[38]

To make matters worse for SB 2156's proponents, the leader of the senate, Bill Lockyer (D-Hayward), did not support the legislation. Senator Lockyer did not back SB 2156 because he had his own plan for relieving prison overcrowd-ing, which did not include privatization of prisons.[39] In addition, he did not want to upset organized labor, for he relied on the unions for campaign con-tributions. As explained in chapter 3, leaders of the two main parties in state government are responsible for raising and distributing money to electoral candidates. If Lockyer had lost union support, it could have devastated his party's fundraising for future elections.

Figure 6.1 shows the composition of the fight over SB 2156. The private prison companies, relatively minor players in both the penal and political fields, had allies in the legislature, including two prominent Democrats, Boat-wright and Senator Richard Polanco (D-Los Angeles), but they did not have support from the governor or the leader of the senate. The pro-SB 2156 side had incorrectly predicted that Governor Wilson would join the temporary alli-ance and level the playing field. Instead, the private companies and their legis-lative supporters faced a powerful alliance comprised of the CDC, legislators, public sector unions (most importantly, the CCPOA), defense attorneys' groups, and civil rights organizations.

The composition of the fight over SB 2156 does not fully explain the out-come of the bill. Another essential factor was lobbying by the anti-SB 2156 side, particularly the CCPOA. The union insisted that private prisons, in pur-suit of cost savings and profits, cut corners on staff training, standards, and compensation, as well as safety equipment and processes. In addition, the union maintained that private prisons were accountable to shareholders, not to the state and taxpayers. Even though lawmakers and state bureaucrats would have limited authority over private prison operations, the state would remain legally responsible for prisoners. The union's representatives, in short,

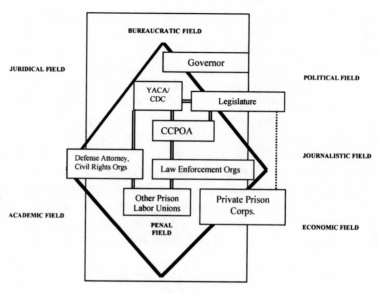

Figure 6.1.
Composition of fight over the Private Prison Commission
Dashed single line connects proponents of SB 2156; double line connects opponents.

sought to convince lawmakers that private prisons were both fiscal and legal risks.[40]

The senate came within two votes of passing SB 2156. The bill's near success was due to bipartisan lobbying from Democrats Boatwright and Polanco and Republican Hurtt. Rather than address prison overcrowding through privatization, the legislature approved Wilson's plan to build more state prisons—a plan that the CCPOA endorsed. Discussing the legislative fight over SB 2156, Boatwright said, "There is no reason not to pass the bill except that it is still opposed by the correctional peace officers of the state of California."[41] The CCPOA's chief lobbyist, Jeff Thompson, similarly contended that the union killed the legislation. But even though the CCPOA spearheaded the efforts against SB 2156, the union's efforts do not fully account for the legislative defeat. The CDC's opposition, Wilson's silence, a temporary alliance of state workers' unions, and pressure from civil rights groups were also important reasons for the defeat of SB 2156.

When Senator Boatwright's tenure in the senate ended in 1996, his democratic colleague Senator Polanco continued the push for private prisons. Like Boatwright, Polanco reasoned that private prisons were cheaper and more effective than state prisons. At a minimum, he thought, the private facilities would provide competition that would force the state facilities to shape up, and they would serve as yardsticks by which to evaluate the public prisons. He shared Boatwright's view of the CCPOA as a bully that decreased the prison system's efficiency and effectiveness.[42] Polanco wanted the state to allow private companies to build and operate minimum- and maximum-security penal facilities in California. However, he concluded that wide-ranging prison privatization was not, at that time, feasible in the Golden State.[43] The composition of the penal field made extensive prison privatization impracticable.

Understanding that the game was stacked against him and other supporters of large-scale prison privatization, Polanco took an incremental approach. The senator's chief consultant on prison issues, Gwynnae Byrd, explains:

> We were always trying to be creative about some way of allowing privates to come into the fold, you know . . . Give them some piece of the action . . . Polanco soon realized we're not going to get a maximum-security [private prison], so let's take that off the table and let's work with other pieces of this and see where we can go and who, you know, what population would be acceptable [to house in private prisons].[44]

Byrd and her boss figured that minimum-security female prisoners would be one such acceptable population.

In February 1997 Senator Polanco introduced SB 818, the "Nonviolent, Nonserious Women Offenders Alternative Sentencing Act," which would *require* the state to transfer to private community correctional facilities all female prisoners with nonviolent and nonserious convictions and no more than 18 months left to serve.[45] The bill also mandated that the state convert a prison for females into a prison for males after transferring the female inmates to the private facilities. Polanco explained why SB 818 focused on women (rather than both men and women): "Here I thought, maybe members could be more receptive to women inmates than men because the perception is that they're not as violent."[46]

Polanco and Byrd argued that the legislation would help women by taking them out of large state prisons that offered few programs and services and placing them in small private facilities that would provide ample rehabilitative opportunities. "The purpose of this bill," wrote the senator, "is to house women more cost-effectively while providing treatment and other services that address the life circumstances that brought women into the criminal justice system."[47] Strategically, they did not include all female prisoners; rather, they selected only females convicted of "nonviolent" and "nonserious" crimes. They reasoned that contracting out these women would save money by reserving expensive state beds for hardened male criminals.[48]

As framed by Senator Polanco and his staff, SB 818 looked like a rather small measure to assist female prisoners who committed relatively minor felonies and

lingered in increasingly overcrowded state prisons that lacked the means for prisoner self-improvement. Even though Polanco and his staff believed that the bill
would help women, their main goal was to give private prisons a "piece of the action," as Byrd explained. The piece was not as small as the bill's proponents indicated—because of the large number of female prisoners who were incarcerated
for drug offenses, roughly 74% of the total female prison population in California
qualified as "nonviolent" and "nonserious" offenders.[49]

Polanco's strategy was successful in the senate largely because he had support from two influential legislative caucuses. Agreeing with the senator's argument that SB 818 would help women, the Women's Legislative Caucus
endorsed the bill. The Latino Caucus, which Polanco led, also supported the
legislation.[50] Neither the CDC nor Governor Wilson took positions on SB 818
while the bill was in the senate. On the anti-SB 818 side, the CCPOA lobbied
only tepidly against SB 818 in the senate, but geared up for a full-fledged fight
in the assembly.

The battle over SB 818 was indeed much fiercer in the assembly. Several
influential organizations joined the CCPOA to defeat SB 818. As was the case
during the fight over the Private Prison Commission, state workers' unions
and the central council of the AFL-CIO, the ACLU, and two politically influential law enforcement organizations (Peace Officers Research Association of
California and the Los Angeles Deputy Sheriffs) opposed SB 818. Of equal, if
not more importance, the CDC now registered opposition to the bill. Since the
CDC was part of the executive branch, the agency's opposition signaled that
Governor Wilson did not support the bill. When SB 818 was in the assembly,
the composition of the fight paralleled the shape of the battle over SB 2156
(see Figure 6.1).

As with SB 2156, the CCPOA led the lobbying efforts against SB 818. The
union tried to expose Senator Polanco's main motivation—to incrementally
expand privatization in California. Its lobbyists argued that contracting out
female prisoners would not help women, as Polanco insisted. Rather, it would
place women offenders in untested institutions that were prone to riots,
escapes, and other disturbances. The union's lobbyists provided politicians
and staffers with stories of recent, major scandals in private facilities.[51] The
ACLU supported the CCPOA's arguments about the potential dangers of
prison privatization (particularly their lack of accountability and transpar-
ency), and law enforcement organizations backed the union's argument that
SB 818 threatened public safety.[52]

During the floor debate over SB 818 in the assembly, two of the CCPOA's
legislative allies, Assemblymen Jim Battin (R-La Quinta) and Rod Pacheco
(R-Riverside), echoed the union's arguments against the bill. Wielding charts
that the CCPOA produced, Battin exclaimed, "This bill is very ingeniously
written to benefit privateers who have chosen to use state government to
make a lot of money . . . I'm not willing to put my family's safety at risk by

contracting out any element of law enforcement." Pacheco asked sarcastically if legislators wanted "the Department of Corrections to house prisoners—or the Mattel Corporation [which makes toys for children]." Assemblywoman Helen Thomson (D-Woodland) repeated the CCPOA's contention that SB 818 would harm rather than help female prisoners. "SB 818 is a bad experiment, and like so many bad experiments, it uses women as its first guinea pigs," she proclaimed.[53]

Whereas SB 2156 only fell a couple of votes short of passage, SB 818 suffered a decisive defeat in the assembly. Once again, the CCPOA took credit for killing the legislation. Senator Polanco and lobbyists for the private prison companies also claimed that the CCPOA killed the bill, unintentionally reinforcing the "specter of the CCPOA."[54] The CCPOA undeniably contributed to SB 818's decisive defeat. However, the union was not solely responsible for the bill's fate. Polanco and his staff, in concert with lobbyists for private penal facilities, made persuasive cases for SB 818, leading some legislators to privately support the law.[55] However, they were incapable of getting votes for the bill because legislators calculated the bill's opposition. The CCPOA and other law enforcement groups, AFL-CIO, ACLU, and CDC all opposed it. Potential responses from the retributive CCPOA and other organizations simply made supporting the legislation too politically costly.

MEANWHILE, IN THE DESERT . . .

After the assembly defeated SB 818, CCA took another tack. Essentially, it tried to make an end-run around the legislature by building a $100 million maximum-security prison in California *on speculation* (i.e., without first having a contract to receive prisoners). CCA sited the prison in California City, a small town located approximately two hours south of Los Angeles in a barren stretch of the Mojave Desert. CCA officials assumed that once the facility was operational, the CDC would send state convicts to the prison to alleviate overcrowding. On this point, David Myers, then president of CCA, asserted: "If we build it, they will come."[56]

The CCA's bold move raised immediate questions: most obviously, could the state legally house prisoners in the private facility? CCA officials anticipated that the CCPOA would file a lawsuit to stop the state from sending prisoners to their facility. However, the company believed that the courts would approve the private prison because of the CDC's history of contracting out for private services (including CCFs). Moreover, the company claimed that the private prison would not displace current civil service employees, since the state could not fill its existing prison jobs (and was spending vast amounts on overtime). CCA argued, in brief, that it would create new jobs without displacing old ones.

Company officials framed their work-around as a selfless gesture to the state of California—rather than a straightforward attempt to spurn legislation and turn a profit. "We're willing to make the investment. We understand the growing need for secure prison beds in California," Myers said.[57] CCA also argued that the private prison would boost California City's emaciated economy by providing tax revenue and at least 500 jobs. Senator Polanco, CCA's foremost proponent in the state legislature, agreed that the private prison would be a boon for the state: "Recidivism is high, and rehabilitation is nearly nonexistent. Our escalating corrections budget is taking funds away from higher education and other programs. Let's save some money."[58]

Obviously the CCPOA opposed the speculative endeavor, as well as the contention that the prison would be a benefit to the state and California City. For example, the union's spokesperson, Lance Corcoran, said when asked about CCA's prisons: "We call them dungeons for dollars because their allegiance is to stockholders, not to the public . . . Private prisons look good up front, but what do you think will happen to quality and costs when pressure from stockholders builds over time?"[59] Then CCPOA President Don Novey said about the CCA's Dave Myers: "This guy's full of bull. Public safety should not be for profit. It's just kind of stupid."[60]

Along with publicly ridiculing CCA, CCPOA officials privately pressured the Wilson administration not to send prisoners to the desert lockup. As he had throughout the legislative battles over prison privatization, Governor Wilson did not formally take a position on the issue. Toward the end of Wilson's governorship, the prison population stabilized, reducing the state's need to send prisoners to private facilities. When he left office in 1999, the CCA facility remained empty. His successor, Gray Davis, was a steadfast supporter of public worker unions and a close ally of the CCPOA. As I describe later, Davis allegedly promised to help the CCPOA rid the Golden State of private penal facilities.

Unable to obtain state prisoners, CCA turned to the federal government for help. In 2001 the Bureau of Prisons inked a lucrative three-year deal (with seven one-year options) with CCA. The compact guaranteed the company, which was facing serious financial and public image problems, $68.7 million a year in revenue, amounting to roughly one-quarter of CCA's annual earnings at that time.[61] Put simply, the federal government bailed CCA out of the potentially dire situation they created by building the California City prison on speculation.

ZEROING OUT THE CCFs

At the beginning of the new millennium, California remained free of medium- and maximum-security private prisons housing state convicts. However, the

Golden State still had nine minimum-security private CCFs that collectively held approximately 2,000 prisoners. Sticking to its zero-tolerance policy on private prisons, the CCPOA wanted Governor Gray Davis's help in eliminating the CCFs.

A friend to the union, Davis attempted to use the budget process to get rid of the remaining private CCFs. (The flowchart in Figure 6.2 summarizes the major steps of the state's budget process.) In his budget plan for 2002–2003, Davis proposed that the state not renew contracts for five of the private CCFs when they expired on July 20, 2002. (The four other CCFs would shut their doors when their contracts ended in 2007.) The governor argued that closing the CCFs would shave roughly $5.1 million off of the state's $20 billion deficit. The Legislative Analyst's Office, however, estimated the savings at only $2.8 million and cautioned that the closures would contribute to California's perpetual prison overcrowding problems.[62]

The governor called for closing facilities operated by Cornell Corporations, Wackenhut, Alternative Programs Inc. (API), and Management Training Corporation (MTC). Lobbyists for the companies tried to persuade the Davis administration and leading legislators that their facilities saved the state money, reduced recidivism, and helped their communities. However, their utilitarian arguments and cost-benefit analyses did not have the desired effects. Numerous legislators agreed with the companies' representatives; however, they refused to oppose the governor (and the CCPOA) on what they viewed as a relatively minor issue.[63]

Still committed to prison privatization, Senator Polanco vowed to fight for the CCFs during legislative proceedings on the budget. Polanco was the chair of the Budget Subcommittee on Corrections. As illustrated in Figure 6.2, budget committees like Polanco's can delete or restore funding for items in the governor's budget. However, the governor can use line-item veto authority to delete funding that subcommittees restore. As chair of the Democrat-controlled corrections committee, Polanco could reinstitute the funding for the private facilities.

Even though Polanco pledged to lobby for the CCFs, the private prison companies feared that Governor Davis would eliminate funding for their facilities with his veto power. In order to save their contracts, they had to get the governor to change his mind. API, MTC, and Wackenhut stuck with their strategy of face-to-face lobbying and letter writing, in hopes that the Davis administration would see the value of their facilities and change its position. Cornell Corrections, however, switched from persuasion to confrontation.[64]

Cornell diverged from the other companies by publicly questioning the motives behind Davis's proposal to close the private CCFs. The company believed that the governor eliminated the contracts as a favor to the CCPOA, noting that the union had contributed more than $2.5 million to Davis's campaign for governor and had given him a check for an additional $252,000 shortly

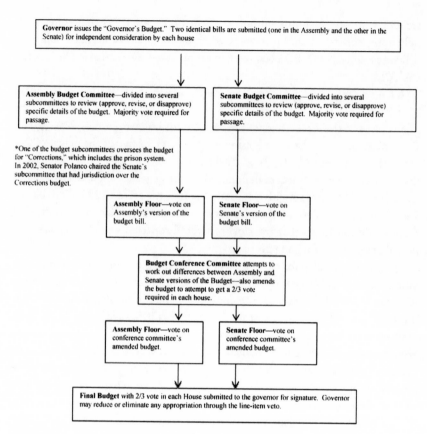

Governor issues the "Governor's Budget." Two identical bills are submitted (one in the Assembly and the other in the Senate) for independent consideration by each house

Assembly Budget Committee—divided into several subcommittees to review (approve, revise, or disapprove) specific details of the budget. Majority vote required for passage.

Senate Budget Committee—divided into several subcommittees to review (approve, revise, or disapprove) specific details of the budget. Majority vote required for passage.

*One of the budget subcommittees oversees the budget for "Corrections," which includes the prison system. In 2002, Senator Polanco chaired the Senate's subcommittee that had jurisdiction over the Corrections budget.

Assembly Floor—vote on Assembly's version of the budget bill.

Senate Floor—vote on Senate's version of the budget bill.

Budget Conference Committee attempts to work out differences between Assembly and Senate versions of the Budget—also amends the budget to attempt to get a 2/3 vote required in each house.

Assembly Floor—vote on conference committee's amended budget.

Senate Floor—vote on conference committee's amended budget.

Final Budget with 2/3 vote in each House submitted to the governor for signature. Governor may reduce or eliminate any appropriation through the line-item veto.

Figure 6.2.

after he announced his budget and the private prison closures. Cornell representatives charged that Davis's move to shutter the CCFs was hard evidence of quid pro quo.

In late January 2002, a lobbyist for Cornell obtained information that seemed to support their charge. The union's head lobbyist, Jeff Thompson, recorded a message on the CCPOA's 5150 hotline, which provides updates on political issues that are of interest to the union. The hotline is set up to inform union members, but anybody with the hotline number (which, at the time, was available on CCPOA's Web site) can call it. Thompson said in the message,

> As many of our members are aware, the whole concept of privatization has been a thorn in our side as far as professional development of the correctional peace officer series . . . So the controversial elements of privatization are being rejected by Governor Davis's latest budget. The CCF contracts are gone for the 2002–2003 fiscal year, and that move is much appreciated. *It does follow through with*

Figure 6.3.
A still from "Blood Money," which accuses then-governor Gray Davis of eliminating private prisons as payback to the CCPOA. Video by RF Communications.

promises made by Governor Davis in past years on this subject matter, so the governor is a man of his word in that regard.[65]

Cornell's lobbyist recorded the message.[66]

To help with the campaign for the CCFs, Cornell hired a seasoned political consultant named Don Fields. Fields made a half-hour video called *Blood Money: The Killing of Two Award-Winning Programs*, which highlighted the rehabilitation programs in Cornell's CCFs, community support for the facilities, and Governor Davis's relationship with the CCPOA (Figure 6.3). The video began with an audio clip of Jeff Thompson's 5150 hotline message, which said the governor was "a man of his word" for eliminating the contracts of the private CCFs. The video's narrator then stated the film's thesis:

Political payoff or a terrible mistake? This is a story about the governor's decision to give the state prison guards a billion dollar pay raise and to kill two award-winning private community correctional programs. Unless the governor changes his mind, these two minimum-security prisons will cease to exist June 14th.[67]

Cornell spent $70,000 to produce and air the video in cities that Davis needed to win in his upcoming bid for reelection. Stephen Green, spokesperson for the Youth and Adult Correctional Agency, responded to the video, "They can't win the fiscal argument, so they're stooping to these mudslinging tactics. They are spending a lot of money in what is a totally futile and self-destructive effort to try to keep their contract."[68]

Major newspapers in California covered Cornell's fight with the Davis administration. Without exception, the newspapers echoed Cornell's argument regarding the governor's apparent quid pro quo deals with the CCPOA. In an editorial titled "A Big Prison Paycheck," the *San Francisco Chronicle* wrote, "This brand of flagrant deal-making is public policy at its worst. Davis has rejected leadership for policy gain." The *San Diego Union-Tribune* editorialized, "all but the most naïve will know the governor was simply paying back the public prison guards' union for its generous contributions to his reelection campaign." Further, the *Los Angeles Times* steamed, "With record budget deficits threatening the state, there is growing evidence that private prisons, for some uses, are cost effective. How can politicians ignore this alternative? The answer remains what it has been for years: Follow the political clout and the campaign money."[69]

As the media echoed the private prison companies' critical view of Davis's relationship with the CCPOA, Senator Polanco tried to restore funding for the private CCFs through the budget process. In addition to saving the private facilities, Polanco did not want the senate to approve funding for a new maximum-security prison in central California. Conversely, killing the private facilities and obtaining resources for the new prison were two of the CCPOA's primary budgetary priorities. The chair of the senate's main budget committee, Senator Steve Peace, had final say over the two budget items. Peace had to decide between upsetting one of his colleagues—who was also the senate majority leader—or a powerful advocacy group that was one of his long-time supporters. Unsure of Peace's positions on the two budget items, Polanco cut a deal with him. He agreed to drop his opposition to the new prison if Peace supported retaining funding for the private CCFs. Peace reluctantly accepted the deal, apparently figuring that the new prison was more important to the CCPOA and CDC than were the private CCFs. Plus, Davis could use his veto authority to deny financial support for the CCFs, but the governor would not be able to *restore* funding for the new prison.

Since Davis could still eliminate the funding for the CCFs, Cornell continued its public relations campaign against the governor and the CCPOA. Cornell's lobbyist produced a lay analysis of the CCPOA's 2001–2006 contract, documenting the compact's apparently exorbitant costs and transfers of managerial functions to the CCPOA and charging that legislators had approved the contract without reading or understanding its provisions.[70] Cornell's lobbyist provided his analysis of the contract to Senator Polanco's staff.[71] Shortly thereafter, Polanco convened a public hearing on the contract, which led to more press coverage of the ties between the governor and the prison officers' union.[72]

The private company's claims about Davis's alleged pay-to-play relationship with the CCPOA became part of a more general story regarding the ties between Davis's fundraising and policies. Critics of the governor accused him of approving a $95 million deal with the software company Oracle Corporation as payback for a $25,000 donation. The media reported that Davis opposed legislation sponsored by the California Teachers Association because the union refused a request to cough up $1 million for his reelection campaign.[73] And Davis's detractors suggested that the governor responded slowly and ineffectively to California's electricity crisis in 2001 and 2002 (which produced exorbitant energy costs and rolling blackouts throughout the state) because of campaign contributions he had received from energy producers.[74]

With the 2002 election scheduled for November, the Davis administration wanted the quid pro quo accusations to go away. Therefore Davis agreed to reinstate funding for the private CCFs with one condition: Cornell had to stop its public relations campaign against him.[75] In other words, Davis changed his mind for political reasons—not because he suddenly valued the CCFs. Ironically, Cornell succeeded in this fight by employing two of the CCPOA's favorite tactics: confrontation and ridicule. With help from reporters, editorialists, and legislators (particularly Senator Polanco), Cornell turned the senate's relatively insignificant decision to close the private CCFs into "news."

CCPOA officials were upset with Davis over the CCFs and the negative press that Cornell had stirred up about their contract and relationship with Davis. The fact that legislators and the governor approved funding for California's thirty-third prison (called "Delano II" because it would be the second prison in Delano County) was not enough to assuage the union's leaders. The CCPOA expressed its anger by lashing out at Phil Wyman, a Republican assemblyman from the rural town of Tehachapi, about 120 miles northeast of Los Angeles. In 2002 Wyman ran for reelection to the state assembly. A political newcomer named Sharon Runner was Wyman's main competitor in the Republican primary, and the CCPOA spent $260,000 dollars helping her defeat Wyman. It was an enormous amount for a primary in this district.[76] The CCPOA spent the vast majority of the money on attack ads against the incumbent. Runner won by more than ten percentage points.

The CCPOA targeted Wyman because he had advocated for private prisons. For example, he backed CCA's speculation scheme in the Mojave Desert because he believed that the prison would help revive the economy of California City (in his district). Further, Wyman criticized Davis for removing funding for the CCFs, saying: "Quite obviously, it is a political payback from the governor."[77] Regardless of whether or not the CCPOA was responsible for Wyman's defeat, the tactic communicated a clear message to sitting and aspiring politicians: support private prisons and the CCPOA may come after you. The union knew that the media would publicize its actions against Wyman, thereby helping warn current and future politicians about the dangers of opposing the CCPOA. For example, a 2002 article in the *Sacramento Bee* read:

> With 28,000 members paying $59 a month in dues, Novey and his board have ample cash to throw into all types of political races. It's known throughout California that if CCPOA has strong enough feelings about a race, it's going to spend money trying to get its ally elected and its foe defeated. Ask anyone who supported Assemblyman Phil Wyman, the outgoing Republican incumbent from Tehachapi. Wyman, a big supporter of the private prisons Novey's union opposes in large part because his members can't work in them, lost to Sharon Runner in the primary after CCPOA spent $260,000 on her behalf.[78]

The union made an example of Wyman; it attacked him to fuel the "specter of the CCPOA" and strike fear into would-be political antagonists. The CCPOA was less concerned about Wyman (or Runner, for that matter) than with lawmakers who would read or hear rumors about the private prison supporter's reelection defeat.

Lobbyists for private prison companies contend that the CCPOA's tactic works. Rodney Blonien, a lobbyist for Geo Group Inc. (formerly Wackenhut), says, "You go visit a legislator to talk about privatization, and when they hear [the union] is opposed you get this look like, 'Why are you even talking to me?'"[79] Mark Nobili, a lobbyist for Cornell, maintains that the Wyman saga often comes up in his discussions with lawmakers:

> I talked to [names legislator] about a privatization issue . . . And he said that exact thing to me. He's like . . . "I'm never going to get involved with private issues." And I said, "Yeah, but here's the deal" . . . And he's like, "No. They [the CCPOA] dumped 200,000 some-odd dollars into Wyman's race; I don't need that." And that was it.[80]

Clearly, spending $260,000 to help defeat Wyman paid off handsomely: the CCPOA helped remove a proponent of privatization from office and erected a large caution sign for any lawmaker who might consider embracing for-profit prisons in California.

AN ORGANIZATIONAL OBSTACLE TO PRIVATIZATION IN CALIFORNIA

Criminologist David Schicor's prediction that prison privatization would spread like wildfire because of the lack of a political counterbalance to the well-heeled private prison lobby has not panned out in California, largely because of the CCPOA. It is important to note that Shichor published his article in 1993, before the private companies tried to gain a foothold in California; hence Shichor was not privy to the CCPOA's intensive efforts against privatization in the mid to late 1990s and early 2000s. Moreover, privatization was expanding rapidly in the early 1990s, as Shichor indicated. However, it did so in states that lacked strong prison officer and other state workers' unions. The states in which prison privatization took off—Florida, Tennessee, and Texas—are "right-to-work" states; workers in these states do not have to join a union or pay dues or an agency fee as a condition of their employment. Unions in states with right-to-work laws tend to be weaker than unions in states without the laws.[81] Without strong unions to provide a political counterweight, the private prison companies were able to establish firm footholds in the right-to-work states. Only then did they move to gain a share of the carceral market in states with formidable public sector unions (like California).

The CCPOA, we have seen, uses multiple tactics to oppose prison privatization in California. It fights against pro-private prison legislation using intensive lobbying and the formation of alliances with other unions, law enforcement groups, and even traditional foes like the ACLU. In addition, the union encourages and ostensibly makes deals with lawmakers to act as the union's proxy in Sacramento and oppose prison privatization. The CCPOA informs electoral candidates about its zero-tolerance policy on private prisons during the "Magic 13" interview process, and implicitly—if not explicitly—requests that the candidates uphold that policy. The union also forcefully opposes legislators who support privatization, as shown in the Wyman example. Lawmakers understand that supporting private prisons in California may bring down the wrath of the "powerful prison guards' union."

Although the CCPOA is a major impediment to prison privatization in California, it is not the *sole* reason why private prison companies have had little success in the Golden State. Other state workers' unions oppose privatizing prisons too. Legislators are reluctant to support privatization proposals that offend unions, especially those (like the CCPOA) that are major campaign contributors. Democrats are timid about backing privatization because large unions are among their biggest financial benefactors. Because of democratic domination in both houses of state government, private prison companies must get backing from Democrats in order to achieve legislative victories. California's civil service laws also impede prison privatization (as well as other forms of "contracting out" that threaten state workers' jobs), limiting the types of public services that private companies may perform.

If the CCPOA's action is one among several reasons for private prison companies' lack of success in California, why do scholars and activists give the union so much credit? A couple of things account for this misperception. First, the CCPOA is the loudest and most active opponent of private prisons in the Golden State. CCPOA lobbyists testify against all prison privatization proposals—not only in Sacramento, but also in local counties that consider approving private penal facilities.[82] Moreover, the union routinely portrays itself as the public's protector against the evil "privateers." It produces the perception that it will go to any lengths to defeat private prisons—including dumping hundreds of thousands of dollars into a seemingly inconsequential primary election. The CCPOA generates an aura of omnipotence and ubiquity that leads people to argue that the union is responsible for keeping private prisons out of California. By continually describing the CCPOA's power and giving the union sole credit for containing prison privatization in California, the media, lawmakers, and lobbyists paradoxically enhance the CCPOA's political clout. The union's strategists hope that the specter of the CCPOA causes politicians and state bureaucrats to think twice before embracing prison privatization. As I have said before, although CCPOA officials complain that detractors refer to the organization as the "powerful prison guards' union," they skillfully craft this image for political reasons. As long as politicians fear reprisals from the union, private prison companies will remain marginal actors in the penal field, and the state and CCPOA will retain their veritable monopoly on imprisonment.

POSTSCRIPT: PRIVATIZATION BY OTHER MEANS

In recent years, private prison companies seemingly realized that the obstacles to building and running large adult prisons in the Golden State were too large to get around. Thus they took another route to obtain contracts to house California prisoners. They worked with former governor Schwarzenegger, who refused to accept campaign contributions from state workers' unions (but did take money from private prison companies), to get the state to ship California prisoners to private prisons in other states.[83]

In October 2006 the Schwarzenegger administration declared a "Prison Overcrowding State of Emergency," arguing that extreme overcrowding in the state's prisons created conditions of "extreme peril" for the safety of officers and prisoners.[84] The governor and his legal staff argued that the declaration gave them authority to transfer California prisoners to private facilities in other states. The CCPOA and State Employees International Union (SEIU) filed a lawsuit to block the transfers. The unions argued that the administration illegally declared the state of emergency and violated the state constitution, which forbids the government from contracting out services that civil service employees conduct. According to the California Constitution, the state may only contract out for services that civil servants are unable to adequately perform, or if the services "are of such an urgent, temporary, or occasional nature that the delay incumbent in their implementation under civil service would frustrate their very purpose."[85]

The superior court sided with the CCPOA and SEIU on both counts and ordered the administration not to send prisoners to private prisons in other states. The governor's office and private prison companies appealed the judge's decision, and, in June 2008, an appellate court overturned the ruling, arguing that the law permitted exceptions to civil service protections in cases of dire emergency. In effect, the court ruled that shipping prisoners out of state was justifiable because the perilous overcrowding in California's prison and jails (which also were overflowing) was a genuine crisis. With legal backing, the government exported, between November 2006 and June 2008, approximately 3,900 state prisoners to private facilities in Mississippi, Tennessee, Oklahoma, and Arizona.[86]

The Schwarzenegger administration was able to increase, at least temporarily, prison privatization in California (or rather, send California prisoners to private prisons) because it did not need legislative approval. By going around the legislature, the governor did not have to fight the CCPOA and its allies (i.e., other unions, the ACLU, and politicians). The governor viewed his own end-run around the legislature as a major achievement. In a public relations report titled "Prison Reforms: Achieving Results," the Schwarzenegger administration touted its shipment of state prisoners to private prisons elsewhere as a success: "To date these transfers have provided much-needed breathing room in overcrowded prisons . . . CDCR has now signed contracts for 8,132 out-of-state beds, meeting its goal."[87]

Ironically, Schwarzenegger's audacious move to ship state prisoners to private facilities supports the main argument of this chapter. The administration knew sending prisoners to private prisons in other states was the only way that it could give the private prison companies a "piece of the action," to quote Gwynnae Byrd once again. In fact, the governor proposed transferring state prisoners to private facilities within California before deciding to contract with out-of-state private facilities. Specifically, he proposed sending minimum-security female prisoners to private CCFs and housing technical parole violators in local reentry facilities rather than state prisons.[88] The proposal (which was part of a package of proposals to alleviate prison overcrowding) died in the legislature.[89] After the proposal's failure, the administration moved forward with the state of emergency declaration. The governor had to go around the legislature to send state prisoners to private facilities because of lawmakers' unwillingness to support prison privatization within the Golden State, which, I have argued, is testament to the influence of organizations—particularly the CCPOA—in the capitol and penal field.

CHAPTER 7

Who Rules the Beat? The Battle Over Managerial Rights

I n 1978 the U.S. Department of Justice (DOJ) published two reports on the growing trend of prison officer unionization. The first report, "Prison Employee Unionism: Its Impact on Correctional Administration and Programs," claimed that an upsurge of labor activism—including strikes, slowdowns, and lawsuits—had jolted prison managers and state officials throughout the nation. "Just ten years ago," the report explained, "such activities on the part of correctional employees were virtually nonexistent." It continued, "That correctional officers from New York and California would sue their superiors in federal court over decisions on budgeting, hiring, and promotion is a remarkable development in agencies which have traditionally been paramilitary in their administrative procedures." Further, the report marveled, "Even more remarkable is the increase in job actions by correctional employees in such states as Ohio and New Jersey, where strikes by public employees are illegal."[1] Because the paramilitary organization of prisons had historically provided extensive authority to management and limited the power of rank-and-file workers, penitentiary officials expected total allegiance from their subordinates.[2] To them, the prison labor unrest at the close of the 1970s seemed like mutiny.

In addition to feeling betrayed as officers unionized, prison officials worried that union contracts would reduce their discretion and capacity to meet critical objectives: "Correctional administrators frequently see these collective bargaining agreements as an erosion of managerial prerogatives. A complaint commonly heard is that the correctional administrator's ability to operate a safe and effective institution has been impaired by a collective bargaining agreement."[3] The second of the DOJ's reports, "Prison Employee Unionism: Management Guide for Correctional Administrators," agreed: "The emergence of correction workers' unions . . . has provided direct and indirect power to narrow management discretion and to influence the policies and programs of correctional institutions."[4]

When the DOJ released the twin reports, Don Novey and his fellow union activists at Folsom Prison were strategizing to take over the California Correctional Officers Association (CCOA), in large part to fight against what they viewed as management's unlimited, arbitrary, and often malicious authority. The Folsom officers thought that administrators inside the prisons and officials at headquarters in Sacramento discounted line officers' concerns and punished rank-and-file workers—particularly union activists and other officers who did not toe the managerial line. The pugnacious leaders of the CCOA, who retained their positions when the CCOA became the California Correctional Peace Officers Association (CCPOA) in 1982, saw the penologists and professional (credentialed) managers who filled the supervisory ranks in the California Department of Corrections (CDC) in the decades following World War II as callous and condescending toward custody staff. They also claimed that administrators routinely implemented demoralizing policies that put officers in harm's way. True to their roots, the CCPOA's leaders have worked for nearly three decades to shift managerial rights and discretion from "the suits" to the workers.

Critics of the union maintain that the CCPOA has more than reached this goal. They argue, in fact, that the CCPOA has turned the tables on management and now rules the beat. For example, the Corrections Independent Review Panel (CIRP), a commission chaired by former governor George Deukmejian and charged with auditing the prison system, concluded in 2004:

> Recognizing that there must be a balance between management's obligation to direct the activities of the department in order to achieve operational goals and a union's obligation to ensure that its members receive just wages and work in a safe and fair environment, it is clear that the pendulum has shifted too far to the union's side . . . the union has been granted authority over traditional management rights. Those concessions have undermined the ability of corrections management to direct and control the activities of the department.[5]

Likewise, prominent criminologist Joan Petersilia wrote, "[The CCPOA's] bargaining efforts . . . have radically changed management's ability to control the day-to-day running of prisons."[6] And speaking to the *Los Angeles Times* in 2007, then-leader of the California Department of Corrections and Rehabilitation (CDCR) James Tilton said flatly: "I need some of my management rights back."[7]

This chapter discusses the obvious and subtler ways in which the CCPOA has shifted authority in the state's penal institutions from managers to workers. It shows that the union's ability to wrest authority from the bosses is the product of its organizational capacity and strategies, its alliances with legislators and state officials, and the impotence of California's penal agencies. The CCPOA contributes to—but is not solely responsible for—the penal agencies' instability. Indeed, as numerous governmental reports and independent studies attest, these agencies have been all but inept since the 1980s (before the union had much power). Nevertheless, because the union and management confront each other as enemies in a battle and work at cross-purposes, each contributes to the further dysfunction of the Golden State's enormous prison system.

THE RULES OF THE GAME

A primary purpose of the CCPOA is to enhance its members' autonomy and control over workplace decisions. Union negotiators have won contract provisions (the "rules of the game") that redefine employee–employer relations, shifting authority from managers to workers. These rule changes have *decreased managers' discretion* in various areas, including overtime allocation, job transfers, and job assignments. The most expansive and controversial of the contract provisions that narrow managerial discretion concerns "post-and-bid."

Post and Bid

One of the most constant and caustic criticisms that CCPOA members made about their bosses during the 1980s and 1990s was that their superiors used discretion over job assignments to reward their friends. Writing in the June 1985 issue of *Peacekeeper*, a prison officer asserted:

> I have been employed by the Department of Corrections for approximately 3 years, 6 months . . . I have seen many injustices and favoritisms when it comes to shift and job assignments . . . There are many officers who are given job assignments, not based on merit or seniority, but instead, they are "on the leg," dating a sergeant or a lieutenant, or even related to a sergeant. Not only do these people get preferential treatment of [sic] jobs, but also shift [assignments] and of course most of the officers I am referring to also have weekends off . . . post-by-seniority would help keep down favoritism, nepotism, and "leg handling." I also believe it would have a positive effect on morale and would be a small reward for the officers who have put a few years into the Department of Corrections.[8]

In addition to their accusations of nepotism, officers argued that their bosses punished rank-and-file workers who challenged the status quo with undesirable posts, shifts, and days off. Arguing that they wanted to limit favoritism and retribution, the CCPOA lobbied for "post-and-bid," a procedure that allocates positions by seniority rather than managerial discretion. Under post-and-bid, each prison posts its available jobs. Officers then bid for job assignments, and management allocates the assignments to the most senior bidders (regardless of factors such as physical fitness, skill level, or dependability).

During negotiations over the CCPOA's 1992–1995 contract, the Wilson administration agreed to a post-and-bid pilot project at three prisons. In the pilot program, 60% of the "Correctional Officer" job assignments at the three facilities would be filled by seniority. Management would retain discretion over the other 40% of positions and the local CCPOA chapter and prison managers would collectively decide which posts would be included in the union's 60% and management's 40%. The contract also called for expanding the pilot program to three additional facilities in 1995. The CCPOA's 1998–1999 labor agreement, also approved by Governor Wilson, expanded the post-and-bid system to all of the state's prisons. However, the agreement did not include large classifications of workers, including all apprentices (officers with less than two years on the job), transportation officers, correctional counselors, and medical technical assistants (hybrid nurses and prison officers). Moreover, the agreement included a "10% rule" that allowed management to remove and reassign workers who did not "possess the knowledge, skills, aptitude, or ability to perform at an acceptable standard in the [position] to which the employee had bid."[9] Although they could reassign these workers, managers would have to give the workers another of their chosen posts, a stipulation that further limited the number of positions over which managers had discretion.[10]

The union's 1999–2001 contract, agreed to by Gray Davis, expanded post-and-bid from 60/40 to 70/30 throughout the prison system, making 70 of every 100 prison positions nondiscretionary. Although the percentage of bid positions increased, the 10% rule and exclusions of large classifications of union members remained.[11] The CCPOA's 2001–2006 contract, also approved by the Davis administration, expanded post-and-bid beyond rank-and-file correctional officers to include medical technical assistants and correctional counselors in both adult and youth prisons.[12]

While managers retain discretion over a limited number of rank-and-file positions, the union has achieved a uniquely extensive and inflexible post-and-bid system. Neither the California Highway Patrol nor the state's five largest police agencies have post-and-bid.[13] Other state prison systems do use seniority in assigning jobs, however, their rules are less rigid than those in the California system. For example, in New York, prison officials have wide latitude to reassign officers to fill vacancies or implement new programs (in California, managers can only reassign 10% of officers).[14] Because of the expansiveness and rigidity of post-and-bid in the Golden State, managers argue that they cannot place the most skilled workers in the most challenging and vital positions. Warden Miller (a pseudonym, as discussed in note 15) scoffs:

> Well, what happens then is [that] staff control where they work. You do not always end up with the staff—the best staff—in the best position to do the best job. You have staff who have the most seniority getting those jobs that are the more kickback, second watch, weekends-off jobs. Where they may not be your most energetic, personable, professional staff. They're not people you would fire, but they're not the folks you want at the front gate. But post-and-bid takes away from you your ability to put the best person at the front gate.[15]

Petersilia argues that managers "frequently attribute their inability to implement new policies to these post-and-bid rules, which limit their ability to bring in staff who share their reform ideas."[16] In brief, administrators lament that post-and-bid limits their capacity to manage facilities and implement reforms by removing their discretion over job assignments.

Personnel Investigations

In addition to negotiating contract provisions that decrease managerial authority in job placement, the CCPOA has won contract terms that, on the one hand, limit administrators' capacity to monitor and sanction rank-and-file workers, and, on the other hand, increase workers "rights." The union insists that these measures are necessary to protect officers from the "management team." As a prime example, I describe controversial and influential provisions concerning personnel investigations.

A major impetus for the creation of the CCOA, and later the CCPOA, was prison officers' perception that management used the adverse action process to instill fear in and obtain compliance from rank-and-file workers. To support claims that management maliciously harasses its officers, CCPOA representatives point to adverse action statistics ("adverse action" is a term used in labor relations that means disciplinary action). For example, former union president Don Novey said during a legislative hearing in 1998: "In my 28 years in this system, we have had an aggressive management style . . . that has led up to 45% of the State Personnel Board's [adverse action] caseload [for all state employees]."[17] Union leaders maintain that the large percentage of adverse actions exemplifies the hostility of administrators and internal affairs investigators toward prison officers. Of course, the hefty percentage could also reflect high levels of misconduct by CCPOA members rather than managerial vindictiveness.

Insisting that it was imperative to protect officers from hostile managers and overzealous, undertrained investigators, the CCPOA won two contract provisions that empower the targets of investigations while limiting the authority of investigators. Both of these provisions *exceed* the protections guaranteed by the "Peace Officer Bill of Rights" (POBR), the industry standard of due process protections for law enforcement workers.[18] The POBR provides protections to all certified peace officers (including prison officers, highway patrol officers, and police officers) regarding political activity, investigations and interrogations, union and legal representation, and adverse actions. The law pertains only to investigations that may lead to formal disciplinary action (e.g., firing, suspension, written reprimand, demotion, or punitive transfer); it does not relate to criminal investigations.

The first contract provision, Section 9.09, requires management to immediately provide officers with grievances filed by prisoners if the complaints could lead to disciplinary action. The provision stipulates that the grievances, including any written, audiotaped, or videotaped statements, be provided to officers when they are filed, even if the officer has not yet been interviewed about the incident.[19] Critics of this policy argue that providing the complaints to officers before they are interviewed compromises investigations, as the accused and his or her union representative can develop alibis before the interview. Because the contract also requires that subjects of investigations receive at least 24-hour notification before an interview, officers and their representatives have time to coordinate with potential witnesses and other subjects of the investigation.[20] Further, critics argue that turning over complaints to officers makes prisoners vulnerable to retaliation.[21]

The second provision, known as "Side Letter 12," stipulates that *witnesses* involved in departmental investigations have the right to bring a union representative to interviews.[22] Critics make three principle arguments against this provision. First, witnesses feel that they *must* obtain union representation, because if they do not, CCPOA representatives and other officers will suspect that they have something to hide or, even worse, are "rats." Second, witnesses who do bring a union representative to an interview are reluctant to make damning comments against fellow workers for fear that the union representative will inform coworkers of the witnesses' statements. Third, the same CCPOA representative may attend both the interviews of witnesses and the interrogations of subjects, allowing the union representative to coordinate testimony between the witnesses and subjects.

Critics of the contract provisions charge that these stipulations, as used by the CCPOA, promote a "code of silence" among officers. The strongest proponent of this perspective has been John Hagar, a "special master" appointed by U.S. District Judge Thelton Henderson to monitor the implementation of court orders resulting from a 1995 class-action lawsuit. In that case, Henderson ruled, among other things, that prison staff at Pelican Bay Prison commonly used excessive force against prisoners with implicit permission from their superiors. In reports to Henderson, Hagar wrote about the CCPOA's contract provisions: "The [contract] places inmate victims in immediate jeopardy whenever they report the abuse of force. It also serves to prevent timely and cost-effective investigations and provides the CCPOA with the ideal instrument to enforce the code of silence."[23] He added that Section 9.09 and Side Letter 12 "can be utilized by CCPOA representatives to ensure a strict code of silence concerning inmate abuse cases." Further,

> Correctional officers who meet with investigators do so under the watchful eye of their CCPOA representatives. Correctional officers who meet with an investigator without their CCPOA representation are readily identified by the CCPOA, and can be subjected to shunning and other misconduct by the correctional officers under investigation.[24]

Hagar concluded bluntly, "the current [contract] between the CDC and CCPOA renders fair investigations into the abuse of force *almost impossible*."[25]

In response to criticisms, CCPOA officials argue that their contract provisions are necessary and do not hinder fair and efficient investigations. For example, they claim that Section 9.09 is necessary to protect officers from baseless complaints and manipulative inmates:

> A correctional peace officer's authority is constantly challenged and manipulated by inmates. One frequent inmate tactic is to falsely accuse and attack the credibility of a correctional peace officer. A correctional peace officer needs credibility and integrity to maintain his or her authority with the inmates. It is crucial that a correctional peace officer know who may be trying to manipulate or undermine his authority *at the time* for at least two reasons. First, the correctional peace officer must be in a position to defend him or herself against the accusations while the matter can be recalled. Secondly, the correctional peace officer must take precautionary measures to prevent any perception of retaliation against the inmate accuser.[26]

About the issue of retaliation against complainants, Chuck Alexander, CCPOA vice president, exclaims:

> [If] you're going to make an allegation against me, let me respond to it. And if it's such an egregious issue, move the inmate. I mean, if that's the concern—that I'm going to go sneak over there in the middle of the night, open his door and kill him—fucking move him. Put him on a bus, move him, and then say, "Okay, here's the issue." But no, they just make these scurrilous accusations that, "Oh, the only reason you want [the complaint] is so you can go get the inmate and . . ." Bullshit. That's not the case whatsoever.[27]

Instead, union leaders contend that management really dislikes Section 9.09 because the provision reduces the bosses' capacity to railroad officers.

Officials of CCPOA also defend Side Letter 12, the provision that allows witnesses to have union representation during investigations. Union activists fought for Side Letter 12 because they believed a very thin line separated witnesses from subjects of investigations. Witnesses, they feel, need union representation during investigative interviews because managers routinely manipulate witnesses and turn them into subjects. CCPOA President Jimenez alleges:

> [Investigators] used to bring people in as witnesses to investigations and then ask them questions like "What'd you do?" "What'd you know?" "How did you get there?" Not what did you see, not along that line of questioning. There were examples, very specific examples, and we had notice letters of people being witnesses who ultimately had adverse action taken against them.[28]

Jimenez argues that officers who witness staff misbehavior are reluctant to report it because they fear becoming subjects of investigations: "[Officers] don't trust the investigative process. [They] have watched an investigation get turned on somebody that tried to do the right thing . . . That's the way it's done. That's the way it's been done."[29]

Whether or not the CCPOA's contract provisions are justified, they undeniably cut into management's traditional authority over personnel investigations. Prison administrators think that the policies make it extremely difficult to investigate and sanction rogue officers, facilitating lawlessness inside prisons. Union activists assert, to the contrary, that the contract provisions merely level the playing field and protect officers' due process rights.

Spotlight on Corcoran and the Specter of the CCPOA

The CCPOA's contract provisions about personnel investigations received intense criticism as a handful of scandals erupted at the now-infamous Corcoran prison. Media outlets pounced on sensational allegations of abuses behind the walls while the CCPOA used its contractual rights to rally behind officers and its political capital to oust a district attorney and kill a reform bill. As the Corcoran scandals unfolded, the specter of the CCPOA loomed large.

The most notorious of these scandals became known as "Gladiator Days." In the mid-1990s, the media reported that prison officers at the Central Valley facility had allegedly organized fights between rival gang

(continued)

members in small, confined exercise yards. The officers, the stories maintained, placed wagers on the fights, but shot the prisoners ("gladiators") with lethal ammunition if the fighters refused to quit battling. The "Gladiator Days" allegedly left at least one prisoner dead.[30]

A second scandal, deemed the "Calipatria Bus Incident," involved a group of officers who reportedly brutalized a busload of African American prisoners who were transferred from the prison in Calipatria to Corcoran. The officers, it was said, had erroneously believed that the prisoners had assaulted staff back at Calipatria.[31] Another story, "Ninja Day," concerned Corcoran's emergency response team. The team reportedly conducted a mock fire drill as an excuse to don black hoods and gloves, beat up prisoners, and trash their cells.[32] And finally, a fourth scandal concerned several officers and a prisoner nicknamed the "Booty Bandit." Reports accused officers of locking Eddie Dillard, a prisoner who had allegedly kicked a female officer, in a cell with a prisoner named Wayne Robertson, aka the "Booty Bandit." Robertson was described as "a big, beefed up prison enforcer who boasted in official reports that he raped unruly inmates as a favor to Corcoran staff."[33] Officers reportedly allowed (if not encouraged) Robertson to repeatedly sexually assault Dillard.

Multiple agencies investigated the reports of abuse at the prison. CDC investigators, the local district attorney, and the state attorney general looked into possible criminal conduct by staff, and the Federal Bureau of Investigation (FBI) investigated reports concerning the violation of prisoners' constitutional rights.

Investigators publicly blamed the CCPOA for obstructing their inquiries at Corcoran. For example, a state investigator asserted: "The union and the governor's office ran the investigation. We would try to question a witness, and the union was there blocking us. The [union] even told us how many interviews we could do, and our bosses in Sacramento backed them. This was no independent inquiry, it was a sham."[34] Others involved with the investigations, especially the local district attorney, shared this frustration about witness interviews, which, due to Side Letter 12, included union representatives on hand for observation. State investigators and the district attorney insisted that the presence of the CCPOA in the interviews discouraged witnesses from disclosing important information for fear of looking like "snitches" in front of union representatives. Moreover, those charged with getting to the bottom of the salacious Corcoran stories claimed that the union routinely interrupted and ultimately thwarted their investigations.[35]

Actions the CCPOA took outside of Corcoran strengthened the notion that the CCPOA protected its officers from detection and punishment. At the conclusion of the Corcoran investigations, the federal government tried eight officers for their reported involvement in the "Gladiator Days" incident, and California's attorney general tried four officers for their alleged participation in the "Booty Bandit" affair. Juries in both trials acquitted the officers. Defense attorneys, prisoners' rights advocates, and journalists claimed that the CCPOA was partly responsible for what they viewed as an egregious injustice.[36] Even before the trials began, these critics accused the union of biasing the jury. For example, *Los Angeles Times* reporter Mark Arax wrote:

> In recent weeks, the union has launched a media campaign targeting residents in Hanford and surrounding farm communities, airing radio and TV ads that feature menacing inmates with tattoos and harried guards walking "the toughest beat in the state."
>
> Union officials say the commercial spots are designed to "get our message out" and aren't intended to influence jurors in the state trial or an upcoming federal prosecution of eight Corcoran officers accused of staging inmate fights in a ritual known as "gladiator days."
>
> But prosecutors and prisoner rights groups say the timing and target of the ads are no accident. Kings County is home to Corcoran and two other state prisons, as well as hundreds of smaller fruit farms and big cotton spreads. Correctional officers and farmers in Wrangler jeans and Chevy trucks dominate the landscape.[37]

After the juries rendered verdicts in both cases, an article in the *San Diego Union-Tribune* read:

> Prosecutors in both cases faced the daunting task of trying prison guards in California's Central Valley. Jurors in the state's rural heartland tend to be sympathetic to guards because prisons provide as many as 10,000 jobs.
>
> The state's powerful prison guard union ran television and radio commercials before and during both trials, describing inmates as violent predators and Corcoran State Prison as the "toughest beat in the state."[38]

Many felt that it was obvious that the CCPOA's media campaign had tainted the juries.

Further fueling the accusations that the CCPOA was obstructing the detection and punishment of rogue officers at Corcoran, the union worked to unseat Donald Strickland, the district attorney of Kings County (home to Corcoran prison). *Los Angeles Times* reporters Marx Arax and Mark Gladstone described the action: "Last month, Strickland was defeated by a challenger who had the union's financial backing.

(continued)

The union blanketed the county with a last-minute, $27,000 mailer that accused Strickland of being in league with prison gangs."[39] Referencing Arax and Gladstone's reporting, the Sacramento Bee editorialized, "Kings County District Attorney Donald Strickland, who did pursue a brutality case against one Corcoran officer, was defeated in his re-election bid last month by an opponent who had the guard union's financial backing. How chilling is that?"[40] CCPOA officials argued that they contributed to Strickland's defeat because the district attorney did not prosecute prisoners who assaulted officers.[41] Regardless of the union's motivation for targeting Strickland, the action sent an unmistakable message: district attorneys who investigate and prosecute officers risk union retaliation.

This message was reinforced by the CCPOA's involvement in another district attorney election in 1998. Around the same time that the union contributed to Strickland's defeat, it spent approximately $18,000 to unseat Del Norte District Attorney Bill Cornell.[42] Pelican Bay State Prison is in Del Norte County, and Cornell had investigated prison officers accused of orchestrating violence against prisoners there. The CCPOA made the same argument for targeting Cornell that it used to justify going after Strickland—that he did not prosecute prisoners who reportedly assaulted staff. Unlike Strickland, Cornell withstood the attacks and won reelection. Nevertheless, the CCPOA's action was a success: it warned district attorneys with prisons in their jurisdictions that they should prosecute all prisoners accused of assaulting staff and be very careful when deciding to investigate and punish officers.

Finally, the specter of the CCPOA was reinforced in 1999 by the union's opposition to SB 451, which called for transferring authority for investigating and prosecuting officers accused of criminal misconduct (like those at Corcoran) from district attorneys to the California Attorney General. The change was proposed because local district attorneys, particularly those in small counties, did not have the resources to investigate and prosecute complex cases, and because, clearly, the CCPOA could intimidate district attorneys, especially those in counties that had prisons. Attorney General Bill Lockyer intended to establish an independent unit within the attorney general's office for investigating and prosecuting prison employees.

The bill passed in the senate, but died in the Assembly Public Safety Committee; it did not even make it to the assembly floor for a vote. The CCPOA lobbied vigorously against the measure, claiming that the legislation was "unnecessary." The bill's quick death in the assembly infuriated Attorney General Lockyer, who told the Los Angeles Times:

The CCPOA torpedoed this thing. One of the assemblymen who voted against it, Jim Battin, pulled me aside and said, "Bill, sorry, but I'm whoring for the CCPOA." At least he was honest. The others who voted against it were either stupid or disingenuous. Frankly, I'm pretty outraged, because I really believe it was an important reform for this state.

Lockyer added, "It's no secret that the CCPOA's involvement in politics has intimidated some D.A.'s, and they lack the resources so it becomes easy to rationalize not going forward with a criminal case against a correctional officer."[43] Assemblyman Battin, who had received $105,000 from the CCPOA in the previous four years, denied that he admitted to killing the bill on CCPOA's behalf. The attorney general later retracted his statement about Battin and apologized publicly to the assemblyman. Lockyer's retraction, however, did not weaken the perception that the CCPOA had protected rogue officers through political maneuvering.

Taken together, the CCPOA's involvement in the Corcoran investigations and their aftermath strengthened the feeling among investigators, prison managers, and state officials (as well as newspaper editorial boards) that the union's contract provided the organization with too much authority over employee investigations, thereby eviscerating the bosses' capacity to detect wrongdoing and discipline officers. The CCPOA's actions related to the "Gladiator Days" and "Booty Bandit" trials, along with its opposition to the district attorneys and SB 451, exacerbated the growing perception that the union could and would go to any lengths to protect its members—even those who reportedly brutalized their charges. Whereas the union's efforts to defend officers ingratiated the CCPOA to members, they fueled critics' belief that the CCPOA promotes a "code of silence" that prohibits officers from informing on each other, as well as the notion that the union allows officers to act with impunity, contributing to lawlessness behind the walls.

Thus far I have described contract provisions that reduce managers' traditional rights. I now turn to provisions that allow the CCPOA and its members to contest and ultimately shape prison policies, procedures, and programs. The first of these provisions, Section 27.01, known as the "entire agreement" clause, stipulates that prison administrators must negotiate with the CCPOA regarding any workplace changes in a broad set of circumstances.[44] Prison officials must notify the CCPOA of proposed changes affecting its members at least 30 days before implementing them, and the union then decides if it wishes to convene negotiations. Agreements reached through these negotiations then become part of the CCPOA's contract, but if the union and state officials do not come to an agreement, the union may take the issue to binding arbitration. If wardens or prison officials in Sacramento implement policies that affect CCPOA members' working conditions or routines without informing and negotiating with the union, workers or the union can file grievances. In fact, a large percentage of the CCPOA's grievances concern Section 27.01. In 2006, for example, 300 of the 488 grievances filed by the CCPOA accused management of violating Section 27.01.[45]

The "entire agreement" provision is extremely important to the CCPOA because it mandates that management cannot unilaterally implement work-related changes without union support. Managers and state officials argue that the provision gives the CCPOA undue power over prison operations and reduces managerial flexibility. They insist that they cannot implement policies, programs, or services without approval from the union. For example, administrators at North Kern State Prison instructed officers to conduct additional visual checks on prisoners in solitary confinement in order to prevent suicides. Because management did not inform the CCPOA about the change, the union filed a grievance.[46] By challenging managerial actions (even something as basic as increasing surveillance of prisoners), the CCPOA creates additional work for administrators and potentially stalls or even stops procedural and policy changes.

Requiring the CCPOA's approval for operational alterations makes managers reluctant to innovate, argues David Glib, director of the Department of Personnel Administration: "I can't tell you how many times they [managers] may not act at all, just because it would be so difficult . . . It's such a hammer out there that it forces us down a path that fundamentally we cannot manage, or it's very difficult to manage, without the union's concurrence one way or another."[47] State officials also oppose the "entire agreement" clause (or, more accurately, the CCPOA's use of the clause) because of the large number of time-consuming arbitration cases that the union files as the result of failed negotiations with the state.[48]

Managers feel that the CCPOA uses the grievance and arbitration process to harass them and affect prison operations. The union's contract stipulates the types of grievances and outlines the grievance process from the initial filing through binding arbitration. CCPOA members can file three types of grievances. The first, "contract grievances," are disputes regarding the interpretation, application, or enforcement of the contract's provisions. The second, "policy grievances," are complaints concerning issues not covered in the CCPOA's contract. The third, "health and safety grievances," include disputes over working conditions that potentially endanger workers. As detailed in Figure 7.1, the grievance and arbitration process includes up to five steps, starting with an informal discussion and moving through binding arbitration.

The CCPOA—or, more precisely, union members and representatives at certain prisons—have a reputation for bombarding uncooperative wardens with grievances. Warden Miller insists that an ever-flowing stream of grievances made life extremely difficult for managers at his institution:

[My] supervisors would say, "We can't do our jobs." You can't work with a staff person. You can't say anything to a staff person. Everything became so grievable. Even if it wasn't grievable. They'd file a grievance, anyway. Because they believe everything that happened to them, they had a right to grieve it. Rather than those things that were clearly defined in the contract as grievable. You could file a grievance on anything. I mean people began to grieve you [if] you looked at [them] wrong. People began to grieve [because they] didn't like your tone of voice ... They would become formalized grievances that would go to headquarters.[49]

Although neither the state nor the union keeps comprehensive data on local grievances, the Department of Personnel Administration maintains data on Level 4 complaints filed by all state workers. Because Level 4 is the final step before arbitration, these data indicate unions' respective propensity for exhausting the grievance and arbitration process. Figure 7.2 presents data on Level 4 grievances by bargaining unit per year from 1997 through 2006. It shows the percentage of the total number of complaints filed each year for 5 bargaining units (none of the other 16 bargaining units or "excluded employees"—that is,

1. *Informal Discussion*: An employee or union representative discusses the grievance with a supervisor. If the issue is resolved to the satisfaction of both parties, the grievance process ends. If it is not adequately resolved, the process moves to step 2.

⇩

2. *Formal Appeal*: The employee or union files a formal written grievance with the "appointing authority" (prison warden, CYA superintendent, or parole region administrator). This is the final level of appeal for health and safety grievances. If the appointing authority does not resolve a policy grievance or contract grievance to the employee or union's satisfaction, the process moves to step 3a or 3b.

⇩

3a. *Formal Appeal Two*: The employee or union files a formal written grievance with the Director of the CDC or CYA. This is the final level of appeal for policy grievances. If the Director does not resolve a contract grievance to the employee or union's satisfaction, the process moves to step four.

OR

3b. *Mini-Arbitration*: The CCPOA may appeal grievances concerning particular contract provisions to mini-arbitration. In this case, the state and union choose an impartial arbitrator from a mutually agreed-upon list of arbitrators. The arbitrator adjudicates the grievance at the local facility (he or she typically reviews multiple grievances at a time). After analyzing evidence from both parties, the arbitrator makes a final and binding decision. The arbitrator cannot "add to, delete, or alter any provisions" of the contract: he or she may only make rulings concerning the application of the contract. The mini-arbitration process was implemented to expedite the grievance and arbitration process and decrease the perpetual backlog of traditional arbitration cases.

⇩

4. *Formal Appeal Three*: The employee or union files a formal written contract grievance with the Department of Personnel Administration. If the DPA does not resolve the grievance to the employee or union's satisfaction, the process may move to step five.

⇩

5. *Arbitration*: If unsatisfied with DPA's response to a contract grievance, the CCPOA may request arbitration. The process is similar to mini-arbitration; however, the arbitrator reviews one level-five grievance at a time, and the proceedings take place in Sacramento. Additionally, level-five arbitration involves contract provisions that cannot be included in mini-arbitrations.

Figure 7.1.
The grievance and arbitration process.
Agreement Between State of California and California Correctional Peace Officers Association, July 1, 2001 through July 2, 2006, at §6.01–6.15.

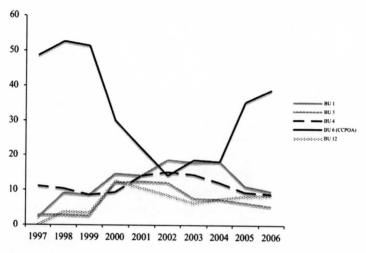

Figure 7.2.
Percentage of total Level 4 grievances per year, by bargaining unit (1997–2006).
Information provided by the Department of Personnel Administration, Labor Relations.

workers without collective bargaining rights—filed more than 10% of Level 4 grievances in any of the nine years). The graph indicates that the CCPOA (Bargaining Unit 6) filed a disproportionate number of Level 4 grievances from 1997 through 2000. From 2001 until 2004, the percentage for the CCPOA dropped, likely because of the implementation of the "mini-arbitration" process (step 3b in Figure 7.1) as part of the CCPOA's 1998–1999 contract. Mini-arbitration allowed the CCPOA to arbitrate many contract issues without a third formal appeal (step 4). But from 2004 until 2006, the CCPOA's percentage of grievances jumped again, likely due to the efforts of the Schwarzenegger administration to eliminate or redefine key provisions of CCPOA's contract (chapter 8 describes the battle between Schwarzenegger and the CCPOA over the union's contract).

The CCPOA's large percentage of Level 4 grievances cannot be pinned just on the union's size. Although Bargaining Unit 6 is one of the larger units, with 14% of the state's workforce, it is not the largest unit. Rather, the CCPOA's confrontational style of unionism and acrimonious relations with management primarily account for Bargaining Unit 6's disproportionate number of high-level grievances.[50]

Taken together, the data indicate that the CCPOA uses the grievance/arbitration process as a weapon in the battle over managerial rights—ironic, because the process was developed in the 1930s to facilitate "industrial peace" in private industries marked by wildcat strikes and work slowdowns.[51] In a context where strikes and slowdowns are illegal, flooding management with grievances is an effective alternative. Managers who refuse to implement contract provisions and governmental policies as the union deems appropriate risk drowning in tidal waves of grievances. The CCPOA's hyperactive use of the grievance/arbitration process encourages managers to take the path of least resistance and bend to the CCPOA's will. As Warden Miller suggested, it also contributes to managers' frustration and their impression that the union *really* runs the prisons.

CONFIRMATION OF THE SPECTER

Legislators, editorialists, and state agencies routinely criticize prison managers for buckling to CCPOA demands. But we have seen that administrators acquiesce to the CCPOA, at least in part, to avoid floods of grievances. Another reason for their apparent submission is that managers believe that politicians and state officials unfairly help the union at their expense. Managers cite many examples to demonstrate that politicians and state officials stifle administrative discretion and authority on behalf of the CCPOA. Here I describe one prototypical example of the union's perceived power: warden confirmations.

From the mid-1940s until 2005, the governor appointed wardens and the upper house of the legislature, the senate, confirmed them. Because of the CCPOA's strong ties with high-ranking politicians, it was assumed that the union influenced the selection of agency-level and institutional-level administrators. Managers and would-be managers feared upsetting the union because they believed that the CCPOA could derail their careers.

It was the 1944 Prison Reorganization Act, which created the Department of Corrections (see chapter 2), that gave the governor authority to appoint prison wardens and the senate the authority to confirm the governors' appointments (it gave the senate the same authority in other major appointments, such as the director of the CDC and the superintendent of the California Youth Authority [CYA]).[52] In 2005, California's legislature, with prodding from the Schwarzenegger administration, removed the senate's confirmation authority. Thus the senate no longer has the authority to confirm or reject the governor's warden appointments. A major impetus for this change was the CCPOA's reported ability to affect the confirmation process.

As practiced before 2005, the confirmation process provided opportunities for groups like the CCPOA to affect the selection of wardens. After receiving an appointment, the appointee served as an "interim warden" for up to one year. During the interim period, the Senate Rules Committee vetted the appointee. Committee staff members visited the prison and interviewed workers, prisoners, and community members. Before voting on the interim warden's appointment, the Rules Committee held a public hearing in which legislators questioned the candidate and various parties made statements in support of or in opposition to the appointee. If the Rules Committee voted to confirm the interim warden, the full senate then voted on the appointee; typically the senate rubber-stamped the Rules Committee's vote (after all, the chairperson of the Rules Committee is the senate leader). If the Rules Committee voted down the candidate, his or her candidacy was effectively dead.

Journalists, state officials, legislators, prisoners' rights activists, and lawyers asserted that the CCPOA influenced, if not dictated, who became warden in California. For example, former governor George Deukmejian wrote in a 2004 editorial about the mismanagement of the prison system: "To compound the problem [of managerial dysfunction], each warden must be confirmed by the Senate, and the confirmation usually is not approved if there is an objection from the California Correctional Officers Association [sic], the employees union."[53]

Suspicion about the CCPOA's ability to shoot down warden appointments was most intense during Gray Davis's tenure (1999–2003). As detailed in chapter 3, the CCPOA spent millions on Davis's two gubernatorial campaigns. Critics charged that Davis, in return, gave the union considerable authority over appointments, including wardens. The perception that the CCPOA had "veto power" over warden selections intensified during the late 1990s and early 2000s because of the union's connections in the Rules Committee. During this period, John Burton was the senate pro tem and chairperson of the Rules Committee. Also discussed in chapter 3, the CCPOA made large contributions to Burton and enjoyed good relations with him.

In this period, Ryan Sherman, a long-time CCPOA staff member, left his job with the union to work for state senator and Rules Committee member Gloria Romero (D-Los Angeles). Media reports noted that the former union staffer "worked on warden confirmations" for Senator Romero and implied that he influenced warden confirmations on behalf of the CCPOA. For example, an article in the *San Francisco Chronicle* stated:

> During Sherman's stint with Romero, the committee confirmed 21 wardens. Critics of the state's prison system have long complained that the union has used its political clout to greatly influence who becomes a warden. Both Sherman and Romero insist that while he was working for the senator, his loyalties were for her. "He worked for me, not the union," Romero said. State records show that wasn't always true. According to state records, Sherman, who runs a separate political consulting firm, was paid $500 from the union while working for Romero. The union also spent $600 to fly him to a conference.[54]

Regardless of whether or not Sherman served the CCPOA's interests while working for Senator Romero, reports that he worked on warden confirmations *enhanced the perception* that the CCPOA was influencing the confirmation process.

Spokespersons for CCPOA deny that the union controlled the confirmation process. Responding to a question on this topic, CCPOA official Lance

Corcoran exclaimed: "I wish to God we had veto power. It is very hard to take out a warden . . . We don't have that kind of communication with the governor . . . It's not like we've got a Batphone to his office."[55] Craig Brown, the CCPOA's head lobbyist in the late 1990s, also denies that the union controlled the confirmation process; rather, he claims, the union simply helped vet appointees:

> We help do the screening that the administration should have done. In other words, when we go after a warden with facts and arguments, we're usually right. And if the administration would have known it, they wouldn't have appointed that person. They just don't do their homework sometimes. Their due diligence isn't as due . . . come on, we [union members] live with these people [wardens]. We know what they do. Give us a break.

As described by Brown, the union's participation in the confirmation process was innocuous and informational.

Critics of the union and the confirmation process contend that the CCPOA's influence was far more insidious *in practice*; appointees believed that CCPOA's "input" carried great weight, if not determined their fate. Warden Miller describes the confirmation process from a manager's point of view. When the Rules Committee staff visited interim wardens' facilities,

> they [brought] with them . . . any letters or any issues that had been brought forth to the committee regarding you. And so they . . . show up . . . with all these lists of complaints by the union, and you had to make those issues . . . you had to explain them in a satisfactory manner to the staff committee so that they could go back . . . and give the Senate Rules Committee a favorable report on you.[56]

According to Miller, if the interim warden failed to adequately address the CCPOA's issues, the appointee faced a difficult confirmation hearing and possible rejection.

The widespread belief that the officers' union influences, if not controls, the warden confirmation process is an example of the specter of the CCPOA in action. Clearly the union did not block all of the wardens that it opposed. Nevertheless, there was consensus that that union *could* block warden and other confirmations. For example, when asked about the CCPOA's role in the confirmation process, Brian Parry, a longtime CDC administrator, described the following incident:

> My number two for a number of years got assigned to be the warden at Corcoran State Prison. He was there for six months and his appointment was pulled, saying that . . . the legislature would never approve it or something. And he was

the investigator [of an officer at Pelican Bay State Prison]. Just my gut-level feeling is he didn't get that job because the union interfered with the appointment, or that the union was going to oppose him in whatever venue they do that. Whether they do that over at the legislature or they were going to show up at his appointment hearing and have one guy after another say he was a rotten investigator, he was a rotten person . . . And that's just guts. No way to prove that. If I could, I would have made an issue of it. But that's just a feeling I have.[57]

Roderick Hickman, former secretary of the CDCR, maintains that he and Governor Schwarzenegger advocated for ending the senate's role in warden confirmations in 2005 to reduce what they viewed as the CCPOA's undue influence "at the local level"—that is within the prisons. To be blunt, the state changed the warden confirmation process in large part (if not solely) to reduce the union's reported power over prison administrators, as exercised through its proxies in the legislature.[58]

In sum, whether or not the CCPOA actually had the power to derail a person's appointment was less important than people's fear that the union *could* derail the process. It was precisely because of this apprehension that people with aspirations for high-level management positions in the prison system felt they needed to consider the CCPOA's perspective before making significant managerial decisions. Warden Miller maintained that interim wardens routinely made concessions to the local union "so that the union would not oppose them during confirmation."[59] Sensing that the union had unbridled access to politicians and state officials, managers felt outgunned and powerless. Warden Miller captured this powerlessness when talking about the CCPOA's access to legislators:

I knew of the relationship between the union and [my local senator]. I had to move mountains to get him to come on a tour of the prison, so I could show him that everybody—all the staff—in the prison weren't being mistreated [as the CCPOA contended] . . . He was always at [the CCPOA's] luncheons. He was at their local union meetings. Things I could never get invited to—he was there. But I had to move mountains to get him to come meet with me. And so the political influence, then—all [the senator] had to do was stand up in one of those committees and say something about [me]. My career and all of it could be lost . . . And so that is why the union and their money has the ability to affect in such small ways . . . We used to be given direction that when the [CDC] was advocating the support of a piece of legislation we were to go out and meet with our local legislators and explain the legislation to them, and give them the department's perspective. Well, if you can't even get a meeting with [the legislators], or the union has just taken them to Hawaii to explain the legislation— who do you think . . . whose side are [the politicians] voting on?[60] . . . That was the perspective of [prison managers]. And like I used to say, *perspective is everything. It may or may not be real, but my perspective is my reality. And that's all I got. You can tell me it's wrong—but it's mine. And so people operate with those realities. It may be a distorted one, but that's what they live by every day. And when you see things that seem to support that perspective you have no way and reason to disbelieve it.*[61]

According to prison managers, the warden confirmation process was part of a more general problem: the CCPOA's use of proxies (particularly legislators) to limit managerial authority and discretion. The perception of managers that politicians and state officials tilt the game in favor of the CCPOA demoralizes them, makes them reluctant to take positions that could potentially upset the union, and enhances their feeling that the CCPOA rules the beat.

Pushing out the Secretary

Prison managers and state officials not only worry about the CCPOA's reputed ability to influence appointments and confirmations. They also fear the union's ability to make their lives difficult and even push them out of their jobs. This fear was reinforced by the CCPOA's persistent, furious campaign against Roderick Hickman. On October 7, 2003, California voters recalled Governor Davis and selected Arnold Schwarzenegger to succeed him. Upon taking office, Schwarzenegger appointed Hickman—a Democrat and former prison officer—as secretary of the Youth and Adult Correctional Agency (YACA) (a cabinet position). With instructions from the governor, who had painted the CCPOA as a poisonous "special interest" during the recall campaign, Secretary Hickman erected a firewall between the union and prison officials, eliminating the open-door policy that the CCPOA reportedly enjoyed during Davis's governorship. In an interview with the *Los Angeles Times*, Secretary Hickman emphasized the administration's stance vis-à-vis the CCPOA: "We're heading in a new direction . . . [The CCPOA] can get on the train or get left at the station."[62] Hickman also angered the union by arguing that a pervasive "code of silence" corrupted staff in the adult and youth prisons. CCPOA representatives insisted that Hickman erroneously characterized all officers as corrupt.

In response, CCPOA activists attempted to humiliate the secretary. For instance, they put a picture of a smiling Hickman on milk cartons. Above the picture, they wrote in large block letters "MISSING." A description of the "missing" state official read:

(*continued*)

Last seen running for cover after promising to clean up the mess at CDC, leaving line officers and department personnel to twist in the wind. Often found hiding under his desk in classic duck-and-cover fetal position.
If found, please return to active duty—or early retirement.
REWARD—10,000 Rodney Bucks.

"Rodney Bucks" were fake money the CCPOA made up to mock Hickman (Figure 7.3). The bucks featured Hickman's profile, deemed the secretary incompetent ("not worth a buck") because of simplistic cost-cutting measures he had outlined in several memoranda, and suggested that Hickman had sold out rank-and-file officers for personal gain.

The CCPOA's allies in the legislature participated in the campaign against Hickman. Nobody was more helpful to the union at this time than assemblyman and CCPOA member Rudy Bermúdez. For example, on January 10, 2005, a prisoner at the Correctional Institution for Men, Chino (CIM) fatally stabbed prison officer Manuel A. Gonzalez. CCPOA Vice President Lance Corcoran blamed Secretary Hickman for the murder, saying, "I'm sticking all of it on him." Union President Mike Jimenez echoed Corcoran, "He's the one calling the shots," referring to Hickman. "When you get to the institutional level, the message is being sent to us that there's a green light on staff. If an inmate complains on anything we do, it's immediately investigated. If we complain, it's malfeasance. They're making us the bad guys, and this is something that is being handed down from the top."[63] CCPOA representatives claimed that state officials not only gave prisoners a "green light" to assault staff, the officials also failed to equip officer Gonzalez with a protective vest—even though vests were stored in a locker on prison grounds. In essence, the union argued that prison administrators and their bosses in Sacramento

Figure 7.3.
The "Rodney Buck." CCPOA, 2004.

were personally responsible for the first murder of a California prison officer in nearly two decades.

Assemblyman Bermúdez also blamed Hickman. "I believe there is a tremendous problem in the Department of Corrections," Bermúdez said. "When you put correctional officers below the criminals that they are protecting us from, it places parole agents and correctional officers in harm's way."[64] Bermúdez and CCPOA leaders insisted that prison officials accept responsibility for Gonzalez's murder and terminate the managers who failed to equip Gonzales with a protective vest. On February 10, 2005, Bermúdez held a press conference about Gonzalez's murder. The assemblyman stood at a podium with about a half-dozen CCPOA officials behind him. A picture of Manuel Gonzales was propped to the right of the podium. With news cameras rolling, Bermúdez held up a protective vest and said deliberately, "This was in a locker." After a healthy pause, he continued while pointing to the picture of Gonzalez, "And that man died because of it." Again facing the cameras, he went on, "I have two questions for the Department of Corrections and agency secretary Hickman. Who's responsible? And I want to know when they're going to be terminated."[65]

In February 2006, Assemblyman Bermúdez, several of his legislative colleagues, and the CCPOA again attacked Secretary Hickman and his staff when news surfaced that parole officers—with orders from their superiors—temporarily housed sex offenders in motels that were located near schools. The temporary housing scheme violated a recently implemented law that forbid sex offenders from living within one-half mile of schools. State officials claimed that regional administrators authorized the scheme out of necessity (i.e., lack of housing elsewhere). Bermúdez lambasted state authorities for passing the buck: "They're trying to end this at the regional level, but this goes a lot further, a lot higher. This goes straight to the cabinet" (i.e., to Hickman).[66]

On February 23, 2006, Bermúdez convened an "in-district" hearing to "get to the bottom" of the sex offender housing issue. Bermúdez noted with irritation that Secretary Hickman and several other high-level prison officials were absent, even though he had requested their attendance. The hearing was a public spectacle designed to demonstrate that Secretary Hickman and his policies jeopardized public safety (particularly the safety of innocent children) on behalf of social pariahs, "high-risk sex offenders." Dramatizing the danger of housing sex offenders near schools, Bermúdez said it was like "putting the fox in charge of the henhouse." He continued, "If a child goes down the hallway to get ice in one of the motels, what if he is lured into the parolee's room?"[67]

(continued)

On February 28, 2006, Hickman submitted his letter of resignation to Governor Schwarzenegger. The secretary resigned because of constant pressure from "interest groups" (by which he meant the CCPOA), the press, and legislators. In addition, he wrote that he no longer felt that he had the unqualified support of the governor and his staff. Hickman claimed that Schwarzenegger's chief of staff, Susan Kennedy (who previously worked as deputy chief of staff for Governor Gray Davis), dealt with the CCPOA behind his back to quell harsh opposition from the union as the 2006 gubernatorial election approached.[68] He thought that the governor's staff was more interested in appeasing "special interests" than reforming the prison system.[69] (Hickman's successor, Jeanne Woodford, also says that she resigned because the Schwarzenegger administration negotiated with the CCPOA behind her back.)[70] When questioned about his resignation several years later, Hickman said simply: "The biggest problem that I had was the relationship I had with the union."[71]

After Hickman's abrupt resignation, CCPOA officials celebrated, informing the membership: "We have won this battle but there's still a war to win. Secretary Hickman is gone, but his policies and protégés remain. Those policies and personalities are no less dangerous absent Rod Hickman."[72] In virulently opposing Hickman, the CCPOA reinforced its image as a union that is willing to go to war with "the bosses," even a member of the governor's cabinet. Moreover, it showed, once again, that it had the necessary connections in the legislature to make life incredibly difficult for prison managers. In doing so, the union reinforced managers' perception that, with the help of politicians, it could and would take them out if it so desired.

THE BIGGEST BALL ON THE TABLE

Thus far I have described examples that typify the CCPOA's success at reducing managers' rights and enhancing the authority of the union and rank-and-file workers. I have argued that the union's ability to decrease managers' rights and obtain control over aspects of prison operations is a function of the CCPOA's strategies, personnel, and relationships. However, this is only a partial argument. To understand the CCPOA's achievements in this area, we must address the union's main competition in the imprisonment field: the state's penal bureaucracies. Steve White, California Superior Court judge and former director of the Office of Inspector General, a state agency that investigates misconduct in the prison system, eloquently explained while testifying in a legislative hearing about staff misconduct in California's prisons in 2004:

[The Youth and Adult Correctional Agency is] an immense organic entity, and there's no center to it. It has no leadership. It has no structure that stands on principle. It has an organization that doesn't work except in ad hoc and informal and let's-make-it-go-aways that have been largely managed on local levels—that is to say, in the respective prisons—by virtue of collaboration between the wardens and the CCPOA. To a lesser extent, it has managed—to the extent that word even applies—at the headquarters level, also in collaboration with the CCPOA.

The CCPOA has come in for a great deal of criticism [during this hearing], much of it well deserved. But having said that, I'm mindful of this: the CCPOA has a mission of its own, and it has a fairly narrow scope. The department has a very large mission. It's statutory and constitutional. It's a very wide scope. The CCPOA has managed, through its leadership talents, its ability to amass political monies, and its sheer competence—they know what they're doing—to move the department off its larger comprehensive role and refocus the department on CCPOA's turf. They're on CCPOA's agenda. CCPOA drives it. And I think that a metaphor you could look to would be a billiard table. There's a ball on that table that's the legislature, and there's a ball on that table that's the administration. That administration includes the governor's office and YACA, and it includes the Department of Corrections and CYA, and so forth. And there's another ball on the table [the CCPOA], and it beats those other balls back and forth across the felt. It does that on a pretty regular basis.[73]

In this section I describe the organizational weakness of the state's penal agencies. A large body of social scientific literature delineates determinants of "strong" state agencies—that is, those with a "center," to use Judge White's term. Strong agencies have sufficient *administrative capacity*, the ability to achieve clearly defined goals given limitations in resources and challenges from social groups, other agencies, and legislators.[74] Agencies that lack adequate administrative capacity (such as California's penal bureaucracies) have great difficulty fending off competitors. Therefore competitors (in this case the CCPOA) can more easily accomplish their goals, often at the expense of the state agencies. And, as Judge White poignantly expressed, that is exactly what has occurred in California.

Purposes and Goals

Effective bureaucracies have clear and relatively consistent functions and aims; they focus their attention and resources on mastering a select number of interrelated tasks and reaching specific markers. Moreover, having clear aims allows an agency's leaders to communicate to personnel and outside observers (e.g., politicians, the media, and public) the organization's purpose. Ideally, then, the agency and its leaders are evaluated according to their ability to meet the specified tasks. Consistency is important because bureaucratic organizations, as sociologists Kietrich Rueschemeyer and Peter Evans argue, "are geared to do certain things relatively well and, *as organizations*, cannot easily switch to or expand into other fields of action."[75] Bureaucratic organizations typically fail at tasks for which they were not initially charged; hence the U.S. military is good at fighting wars but ineffective at nation building, as seen so clearly in Afghanistan and Iraq.

State officials (e.g., the director of the prison system) and institution-level managers (e.g., wardens) routinely express deep frustration about having to continually shift gears because of pressure from the governor's office, politicians, and the courts, and indirect pressure from the media. On this topic, Brian Parry, former CDC deputy director, says,

> We get caught between a judge and the legislature. The judge tells us to do something, and the legislature says, "We don't care what the judge says, we passed a law, and you're not getting any money." We get caught in a cross [fire] . . . It's such a goofy system. You have the governor and the legislature, and they don't get along. The departments get caught in the middle . . . It forces the department to respond one way . . . our ability to change [directions] is very laborious . . . And politicians blackmail the department [by withholding funds until certain changes are made].[76]

Judicial decisions, changes in laws, and directives from politicians routinely multiply managers' responsibilities and, at times, lead to incompatible objectives.

In addition to juggling conflicting aims of incarceration, prison officials must manage the incredible growth of California's penal system. The prison boom of the 1980s and 1990s created major managerial problems for the leaders of YACA and its respective departments, and it continues to produce enormous challenges for officials in the CDCR. (Recall that the 2005 "Prison Reorganization" bill changed YACA to the CDCR.) Rather than work toward long-term goals (such as reducing recidivism, developing effective relationships between managers and employees, grooming future leaders, and coordinating the CDCR's departments), managers obsessively focus nearly all of their attention and resources on housing and caring for the ever-expanding (and often physically or mentally ill, chemically dependent, and gang-involved) prison and parole populations. While testifying at a 1998 legislative hearing on the scandals at Corcoran prison, former CDC director James Gomez explained that nonstop growth of the prison population handcuffed and greatly frustrated managers. When Gomez was asked to make recommendations to avoid future prison scandals, he stated:

I think the best recommendation I could give you, once again, goes back to let this system settle down. Stop the growth. Let them [managers] go out and spend the time reviewing policies and procedures and communicating.

They spend all their time on trying to manage growth. You have to understand that the Department of Corrections, 120,000 inmates a year come in; 110,000 leave, and they have a net 10,000 gain.

. . .

They need to have an opportunity to settle down as a department and go out and do policy and procedure reviews, do monitoring reviews. Get back into the basics of, of running the prison system, not just going from adding this 5,000 beds to this 3,000 beds, to that 7,000 beds, to hiring this 3,500 staff or that 4,000 staff.

And so, I think part of that is, is to give them an opportunity to, to level off and manage the department better, where everything is not focused on growth and lawsuits.[77]

The state's inability to manage the already overwhelming, but steadily increasing prison population leads to other problems, such as lawsuits, which add new, diverse challenges to managers' already long to-do lists.

In brief, California's prison system has (since at least the mid-1960s) developed an acute case of multiple personality disorder. It has numerous responsibilities and objectives, each of which tends to conflict with another. In addition to running more than 30 gang-infested, racially polarized, and perpetually overcrowded prisons and an assortment of camps, the CDCR operates gigantic medical, mental health, and education systems. Politicians, jurists, and state officials continually force prison officials to work toward certain (and not other) goals in specific ways. The state prison agencies' lack of clear and consistent goals limits their administrative capacity. Moreover, it handicaps managers in battles with the CCPOA, which, as Judge White noted, actually has clearly articulated, constant goals. Whereas the state organizations must simultaneously focus attention and resources on numerous disconnected pursuits, the CCPOA concentrates on a relatively small number of interrelated objectives. The union's sharp focus is one of its great advantages in the battle over managerial rights.

Organizational Structure and Resources

In addition to clear and relatively circumscribed goals, an archetypically strong state agency has as organizational structure with an "unambiguous location of decision making and channels of authority," as well as policies and procedures that facilitate coordination throughout the agency, minimize duplication, and encourage innovation.[78] In other words, a strong, effective bureaucracy is a well-oiled machine with an undisputed leader (or team of leaders) that sets policy and monitors the agency's progress. It also has information technology (IT) that allows the timely and efficacious gathering and sharing of data and proficient technical and administrative employees who "utilize information and forecasting to plan and to execute plans in rationalized form."[79]

During its 40-plus-year existence, YACA's leadership failed to develop an effective organizational structure. In 2004 the CIRP, an independent blue-ribbon commission, characterized YACA's organizational structure:

> To a significant extent, the problems of California's Correctional system grow out of its structure. The Secretary of the Youth and Adult Correctional Agency, for example, has no control over line operations. Instead, the state's 32 prison wardens and eight juvenile institution superintendents each operate indepen-dently, with little consistency in procedures and minimal help from headquar-ters. Lines of responsibility are blurred by layers of bureaucracy between managers and functions. Accountability is absent, as is transparency for the public into the system's inner workings. Clear, uniform policies governing the system's most vital functions—fiscal matters, personnel and training, internal affairs, information technology, and health care—are equally lacking. Boards, commissions, and other entities that have evolved over decades perform dupli-cate and overlapping functions. And the system's organizational structure has not kept up with the massive growth of inmate population or with the vast geo-graphical spread of the institutions.[80]

And more than *25 years* ago, political scientist John Dilulio addressed the CDC's organizational dysfunction:

> As one official expressed it, the 1980s will be the decade in which CDC replaces its "ridiculous, crazy quilt, asinine" operations with a "professional management system," grounded in techniques such as management by objectives (MBO): "There has been no attempt to bring contemporary management principles to this department—until now!"[81]

Clearly the official was mistakenly optimistic about the CDC's capacity to de-velop a more rational and effective organizational structure.

The prison bureaucracy's lack of IT contributes greatly to its organizational confusion and ineptitude. On this topic, the Independent Review Panel con-cluded, "The Department of Corrections is technologically antiquated. The equipment and systems are old and cannot communicate with each other. [IT] staffing is too low and budgetary allocations are dismal. Most important, there is a lack of uniformity and training."[82] Insufficient data management makes it extremely difficult for the prison system to manage personnel expen-ditures related to overtime, sick leave, and workers compensation.[83] It also frustrates efforts to classify and process the logjam of prisoners who enter the system on a daily basis.

Leadership

Solid leadership is an extremely important element of administrative capacity. After all, experienced, qualified leaders are needed to construct and maintain a binding organizational culture; frame and disseminate the agency's mission; establish budgets, review spending, and procure funds; recruit and promote skilled personnel; and ensure that the bureaucratic machinery functions smoothly. To develop effective leaders, state agencies and other bureaucratic organizations must establish hiring and promotion plans that fill leadership positions with skilled managers, adequately train new administrators, and provide job descriptions that clearly delineate managers' responsibilities. According to the Independent Review Panel mentioned previously, California's prison system lacks these mechanisms for effective leadership:

> The state's correctional system has not developed a cadre of leaders who can manage the department . . . Wardens do not systematically receive training and experience needed before they are appointed, and in fact, *there is no job description for the warden assignment.* Supervisors and mid-management personnel also do not receive proper training and there is no succession plan to ensure that experienced employees rise upward through the organization.[84]

The Legislative Analyst's Office wrote in 1997–1998, "Because the prison system has grown so rapidly in recent years, many mid-level correctional managers—correctional sergeants and lieutenants—have been promoted quickly through the ranks, gaining relatively little managerial experience."[85] Although the incredible growth of the prison system helps explain the plethora of inexperienced managers, it does not account for the lack of planning, training, and job descriptions.

Management turnover is another factor in the shortage of consistent, qualified leadership in the prison system. Figure 7.4 shows that the CDC had steady leadership for approximately the first 17 years of its existence. Since then, the department's directors have come and gone every few years. There also has been extensive turnover at the top in the CYA, as shown in Figure 7.5. Widespread leadership turnover is problematic, political scientist Daniel Carpenter argues:

> Although many agencies suffer from too little turnover and the rigidity that may result from stasis, high turnover is usually more damaging . . . Officials with longer tenure, rising to authority within their bureaus (with experience at many different

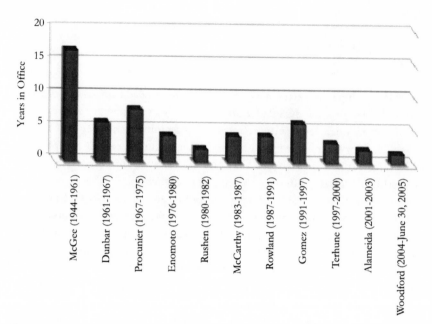

Figure 7.4.
Department of Corrections directors, 1944–2005.

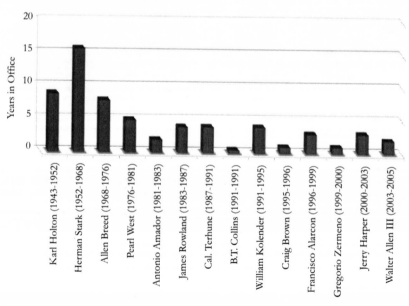

Figure 7.5.
California Youth Authority secretaries, 1943–2005.

levels), possess enhanced leadership skills and the ability to solve organizational dilemmas. Longer-tenured officials possess a better sense of the history of their programs and are better able to make comparisons over time. In other words, bureaus with lower turnover rates are usually better equipped to learn.[86]

A report on the youth prison system makes a similar argument: "This rapid change in agency leadership means that directors have a short time to learn the agency and a short time to make any change. Staff see directors come and go. New ideas flower and die. The agency remains the same." It later contends that the turnover has "allowed institutions to become Balkanized. Practices are inconsistent and policy is not always followed."[87] In short, the lack of stable leadership in the CDC and CYA has contributed to the departments' lack of administrative capacity and tendency to flounder.

Carpenter alludes to the problem of rigidity and stasis in state agencies. Stasis is typically associated with limited turnover, but the CDC and CYA suffer from these problems even with their extensive turnover. In court documents filed in *Plata v. Davis*, a class action lawsuit about medical care in the adult prison system, Judge Thelton Henderson argued that the prison management had a "deeply entrenched bureaucratic mind-set":

> This mind-set is a classic example of what the sociologist Thorstein Veblen terms "trained incapacity." State officials have become so inured to erecting barriers to problems that appear to threaten the bureaucracy (or that at least appear to require the bureaucracy to bend or flex) that the officials have trained themselves into a condition of becoming incapable of recognizing, and acting in response, to true crisis.[88]

Here insularity, rather than turnover, is the problem: officials in the prison system are products of that bureaucracy. Many of these managers are former officers who have moved up the ranks or bureaucrats from other (similarly dysfunctional) state agencies. Just as troubling, these leaders tend not to look beyond the borders of California for fresh ideas; they continually recycle worn-out, ineffective strategies.

In sum, because of its lack of administrative capacity, the prison system failed to meet critical objectives. Consequently a federal judge took over the CDC's medical system, forced CYA officials to overhaul the entire youth prison system, and have threatened to release tens of thousands of prisoners to alleviate unconstitutional conditions in the state's adult prisons. Since the mid-1980s, legislative committees and independent governmental bodies (e.g., the California State Auditor and Officer of Inspector General) have found that prison officials routinely mismanage their resources, leading to outrageous cost overruns and budgetary shortfalls. Further, reports show that both the adult and youth prison systems fail miserably in their attempts to provide meaningful educational, vocational, and treatment programs to offenders, thereby contributing to the state's perpetually high recidivism rate.[89] And the problems have evidently continued since the reorganization of the prison bureaucracy in 2005. A 2009 report by the Bureau of State Audits describes overspending, out-of-control staff overtime (particularly among prison officers), a continued dearth of up-to-date IT, and insufficient processes for evaluating inmate programs.[90] With the exception of preventing prisoner escapes, the state's prison agencies have botched all of their essential tasks, leading to near-constant criticism and a crisis of legitimacy.

Unequal Competition: A Case in Point

Because California's prison agencies lack administrative capacity, managers simply cannot compete with the union and its representatives. Personnel investigations illustrate this claim. The CCPOA allocates extensive resources to employ skilled lawyers and field agents to assist any union members under investigation for alleged misconduct. Along with a cadre of staff dedicated to representing its members, the CCPOA maintains effective lines of communication between CCPOA headquarters, regional field offices, lawyers, and local representatives to coordinate the representation of members during investigations and discipline hearings. At any moment, the union can call up its Spartan-like force, which relishes in vigorously defending CCPOA's members.

The state, on the other hand, has a weak investigative apparatus. Many of its investigators lack training and experience, and its legal staff is overworked, overextended, and often inexperienced. Moreover, the agencies lack sufficient IT capacity to effectively manage staff investigations and discipline. A 1997 report by the Legislative Analyst's Office (LAO) summarized the CDC's system for investigating and disciplining staff:

> Based upon our discussions with the CDC and outside experts on internal affairs issues, we do not believe that the CDC has an effective and efficient program in place to deter personnel misconduct, to investigate misconduct when it does occur, or to discipline those who violate departmental personnel policies or the law. The CDC's internal affairs operations, in our view, are fragmented, duplicative, and ineffective.[91]

As the LAO indicated, the state is incapable of systematically identifying staff misconduct. Furthermore, when the state does find wrongdoing, it often fails to mete out appropriate punishment in due time. In a particularly damning report, the Office of the Inspector General showed that the State Personnel Board, the state agency that oversees adverse action cases in the CDC and other governmental departments, overturned at least 40% of adverse action cases filed against prison staff because the CDC failed to discipline officers within the one-year statute of limitations.[92]

Personnel investigations are prime examples of how the CCPOA's influence over the prison beat is due in part to the state penal agencies' own lack of administrative capacity. Personnel investigations are also indicative of other CCPOA–management confrontations. For example, the union typically outguns the state in meet-and-confer deliberations required under Section 27.01 of CCPOA's contract and in grievance and arbitration procedures. Again, contract provisions—what I have called the "rules of the game"—provide the CCPOA with opportunities to influence managerial decisions, and in some cases, gain the upper hand in battles with the bosses. But, ultimately, the state's penal agencies are simply no match for the CCPOA; it is like an amateur sporting team trying to compete with a professional squad.

A Vicious, Dysfunctional Cycle

Clearly the 1978 DOJ reports on prison officer unionization were prophetic. The CCPOA has undeniably reduced the authority that facility-level managers (like wardens) and state officials have over traditional administrative duties while enhancing workers' influence in California's adult and youth penal institutions. Through contract negotiations and legislative feats, the CCPOA has *formally* limited administrative authority over sacrosanct administrative functions. Moreover, the union has reduced managerial discretion in employee investigations and discipline and has greatly expanded the scope of issues subject to grievance and arbitration, thereby fueling the number of employee complaints and draining management's resources.

The CCPOA has also *informally* abridged administrative power through its hyperactive use of the grievance and arbitration process. By filing and encouraging members to file numerous grievances (and taking many of those grievances through the entire arbitration process), the union saps management's resources and encourages administrators to make concessions to the union and rank-and-file workers so as to avoid being buried in formal complaints. The union has also cut into management's authority by influencing (and, just as importantly, appearing to influence) the processes for appointing and confirming wardens and other administrators. The CCPOA has created the perception that it can kill an appointee's confirmation, which strikes fear into would-be administrators and appointees, causing them to continually consider the union's position before making decisions.

The CCPOA's authority inside the prisons is due to the union's resources and tactical acumen. Characteristics of the CCPOA tell only half the story, however. The union's power in this area is also a result of the weakness of its main competitors in the imprisonment field: the state's penal agencies. In other words, we can only understand the CCPOA's authority over prison operations and management *in relation* to the instability and ineffectiveness of the CDCR and YACA before it. It is also important to recognize that both the CCPOA's power inside the prisons and the penal agencies' weakness are related to the politicization of the penal and imprisonment fields in the last several decades. Politicians' involvement in major and minor prison-related issues allows advocacy groups like the CCPOA to indirectly affect these issues through legislative proxies. Further, legislators' continual demands decrease prison administrators' authority and autonomy. Politicians also weaken prison management by routinely passing laws that increase the prison population while not providing for sufficient space to house that population. As we have seen, prison administrators must focus their energies primarily on dealing with overcrowding rather than on other essential tasks such as running effective rehabilitation programs or improving labor relations. In short, politicization of the penal and imprisonment fields helps account for the nature, shape, and outcome of the battle over the beat.

Although the CCPOA has altered the balance of power between workers and managers, the union does not control prison operations, as some critics suggest. There are two primary reasons for the perception that the CCPOA runs the prisons. First, CCPOA representatives routinely exaggerate the union's authority over managerial affairs. Doing so, they highlight the union's clout and achievements and pump up the specter of the CCPOA so that prison managers understand that the union can and will "take them out," or at least make their lives miserable. Ironically, negative publicity about the union's ostensible power behind the walls is due, in part, to the CCPOA's chest pounding. Because they have seemingly worked hard to gain their reputation, it looks disingenuous when CCPOA leaders claim that the union is the victim of detractors who describe the organization as omnipotent (the "powerful prison guards union").

The second reason for the exaggerated perception of CCPOA's control over prison operations is due to the traditional, paramilitary organization of prisons. Following the classical military model, prisons (like police departments) in the United States were

> designed to accommodate a distribution of official discretion that gave those at the top the greatest and broadest decision-making authority and closely limited discretion at the lowest organizational levels. In the military, after all, the generals and their commander-in-chief make all the great decisions . . . Meanwhile, soldiers are limited to doing and dying, rather than wondering why.[93]

By shifting authority from the bosses to the workers, the CCPOA has destabilized the paramilitary foundation of California prisons. It has disoriented and greatly frustrated prison officials (especially those who remember when managers had greater control over their workforce), making them feel like the union stole the keys to the prisons.

Critics who claim that the CCPOA rules the beat often suggest that the union is responsible for the prison system's deep dysfunction. This assertion is clearly false. As discussed earlier, managerial problems have plagued the penal agencies since at least the mid-1970s, but the union has only been a formidable force in Sacramento and behind the walls for about 20 years. It is conceivable, if not probable, that the penal agencies would have major managerial problems even without interference from the CCPOA. Nevertheless, since the union amassed significant political power and organizational strength, it has further weakened these already relatively weak state agencies.

Currently both the CCPOA and CDCR are jointly responsible for the managerial problems in the prison system. Because the union and management confront each other as enemies, they work at cross-purposes and blame each other for mismanagement. Warden Miller claims that rank-and-file workers and management used to feel that they were on the same side:

> We used to really feel—I'll speak personally; it's personal, but it's conversations I've had over the last several years, many years before I retired—that the family, the feeling of family in the Department of Corrections was lost. You were just a member . . . I mean, people felt like a big team. And I think—I believe—all of that has been lost.[94]

The warden's reflections may romanticize employee–employer relations in earlier years. Nonetheless, they suggest that workers and managers today *do not* act like they are on the same team or have joint responsibility for prison operations. Because management and the union continue to face off rather than cooperate, their respective "victories" are Pyrrhic, producing nothing but deadlock, overspending, slow or aborted policy implementation, shoddy programs, misconduct, and endless red tape—the very problems that judges, journalists, academics, and politicians point to when they call for ousting prison officials and reversing the CCPOA's achievements.

CHAPTER 8

Changing of the Guard: A New Direction for the CCPOA and California?

On March 24, 2007, the *Los Angeles Times* ran a story titled, "Prison Guards Union Shows its Softer Side." The article asked, "Is one of California's most feared unions now playing nice?" As evidence of the California Correctional Peace Officers Association's (CCPOA's) niceness, the article noted, "Union officials have opened up the organization to academics, pushed for new spending on alternatives to incarceration, and begun regular meetings with other unions." Moreover, "the union has convened a working group of inmate advocates, defense attorneys, and politicians who support the kinds of shorter sentences that were long anathema to the union. Their goal: creating a sentencing reform bill that, with the union's sway over legislators, could pass the Legislature this year." State senator Gloria Romero reinforced the notion that the CCPOA had remade itself. "The union is still the 800-pound gorilla in the prisons, but this is not your father's union," she stated. "They are taking the prison crisis and reshaping not only the prison system in California but also reshaping themselves. The gorilla has moved."[1]

THE CCPOA TODAY

The *Los Angeles Times* article about the CCPOA's "softer side" indicated that the union had become increasingly open to and respectful toward new ideas and groups. Throughout Don Novey's tenure as president of the union, the CCPOA kept its enemies (both imagined and real) far away, refusing to even acknowledge potential common ground with other groups, particularly those that advocated for "prisoners' rights." At the same time, these supposed enemies disdained the CCPOA. In the years since Mike Jimenez replaced Don Novey as the CCPOA's president, the union's leaders have met and formed relationships with historical foes—including prisoners' rights lawyers and reform-oriented academics. The main topic of these meetings has been California's prison overcrowding crisis and the resulting threats of federal receivership.

Another apparent indicator of the gorilla's movement was a policy report that the union produced and distributed to state legislators in early 2007.[2] The report promoted "behaviorally-based risk assessment procedures" to determine whether parolees needed intense, lengthy supervision or alternative sanctions such as day reporting (regular check-ins at designated centers). In other words, the CCPOA suggested that the state end its one-size-fits-all approach to parole. The report also offered several sentencing-related proposals. It recommended that the state and counties work together to "develop plans for building facilities to house appropriate inmates who have less than 180 days left on their sentences and could benefit from placement in local programs. These facilities should be located to maximize success of intensive rehabilitation efforts—in conjunction with community and job-placement organizations."[3]

The report went on to suggest that the state knock 30 days off select prisoners' sentences: "Inmates with no convictions for serious, violent, or sex offenses and who have not been issued serious rules violations in the prior 12 months would receive a 30 day 'good behavior credit,' but would be subject to a higher level of supervision by the parole officer during the initial release period."[4] The union also recommended the formation of a sentencing commission—surprising since the CCPOA had opposed similar proposals in previous years.[5] The sentencing commission would review sentencing policies and determine "whether the state can establish appropriate guidelines for *nonviolent offenders*;" conduct "careful fiscal analysis of the cost, infrastructure, and staffing implications of proposed changes to criminal laws;" and "develop a plan for changing state sentencing to place appropriate offenders in less costly alternatives to state prisons—such as state jails or group homes." The proposed commission would not have any authority to implement its recommended sentencing policies, and the CCPOA did not specify who might serve on the commission.[6]

President Jimenez's rhetoric about prison and sentencing reform also signaled a possible change of philosophy in the union. In April 2007 Jimenez spoke at the California Democratic Party's state convention in San Diego. Sporting a small ponytail, beard, and scholarly eyeglasses, Jimenez did not look like a stereotypical leader of a conservative law enforcement union. And, given the CCPOA's long-established commitment to tough-on-crime ideas and policies, Jimenez's comments seemed as disconcerting as his physical appearance. He told the friendly crowd:

> I had a prepared statement that I'd been working on for a couple of weeks. But things changed for me earlier this week [when the legislature passed AB 900, Schwarzenegger's plan to reduce prison overcrowding]. And on Thursday I became very disappointed in what was going on in California. On Thursday there was a decision made to increase the *prison-industrial complex* in California. This is not done with my support or the support of the men and women that work inside the prisons in California . . .
>
> On Thursday I was extremely disappointed, but today I want to let you know I am not deterred and I am not dissuaded. We are going to change what's going on in California . . . Thursday did not signify an end to anything. Thursday signified a new beginning, a new fight. And today I'm going to carry on from that beginning. To borrow from Martin Luther King, Jr., as well, today I have a dream. I have a dream that the bricks and mortar that were planned to build new prisons will instead be used to build new schools. Today I have a dream that not one of these cells will ever be occupied by the child of a person in this room today. Today I have a dream that an ounce of prevention will be embraced instead of a pound of cure by the California legislature and this administration . . .
>
> I'm going to stand with you until we win this battle, and until we put money in schools and *quit putting money in prisons*, and we use our good senses.[7]

It was remarkable that Jimenez used the term "prison-industrial complex" to criticize Schwarzenegger's prison-building plan. The prison-industrial complex (PIC) has become a buzzword for the inherently destructive nature and consequences of incarceration and to suggest that individuals and groups profit (financially and politically) from America's prison binge. The slogan spread with the publication of a December 1998 article in *Atlantic Monthly* by Eric Schlosser, "The Prison-Industrial Complex."[8] It is doubtful that Jimenez knew the etymology of this phrase. Nonetheless, his use of it was remarkable, not only because of its association with prison abolitionists, but also because advocates of the PIC perspective claim that prison officer unions in general and the CCPOA in particular profit from and fuel the "prison-industrial complex." The term is often used to condemn groups like the CCPOA.

Questions about Jimenez's ideological orientation intensified with the publication of an article in the liberal magazine *Mother Jones* titled "Taming of the Screws."[9] In the article, Jimenez described the penal system as "assembly-line justice" and, drawing on the notion that prisons are "crime schools," contended that the state should not imprison low-level offenders because these convicts "get worse" behind bars. Jimenez advocated crime prevention and suggested that California's prison sentences were too long:

We plan to fail . . . You can put all the police officers you want on the street, but if we don't give those kids hope of a future, of a life, of an ability to make something of themselves, they don't care about life. Nobody's willing to forgive anymore. And we are willing to lock people up for unreasonable periods of time.[10]

Although CCPOA officials have long recognized the need for better crime prevention programs, they have never—at least to my knowledge—argued that prison sentences are too long. Moreover, CCPOA spokespersons have not encouraged the public or politicians to "forgive" criminals. Rather, they have traditionally argued that crime is a personal, rational choice, and the state must punish offenders swiftly and harshly to achieve individual and general deterrence. To forgive is to excuse, the union argued in the past. But Jimenez's remarks in *Mother Jones* further indicated a potential ideological reversal for the CCPOA. The fact that Jimenez even agreed to an interview with *Mother Jones* at all signaled a change; his predecessor, Don Novey, never would have spoken to such a liberal magazine.

In spring 2008 Jimenez attempted to back up his rhetoric with action when he hired a parolee, Raul Gomez, to work in the CCPOA's legislative office in downtown Sacramento. Jimenez explains his decision to hire Gomez:

> I met Raul while attending [sic] Latino Legislative Caucus policy summit on juvenile justice in Los Angeles in May of this year. I was very impressed by Raul and the progress he demonstrated with his positive attitude. His words indicated maturity, with a willingness to accept responsibility for his decisions that resulted in his incarceration. He shared life experiences with me and other attendees that humbled me . . . I felt it was important that policymakers, in the department [of corrections] and the legislature, hear what he had to say.[11]

By hiring Gomez, Jimenez intended to "lead by example and demonstrate that the men and women of CCPOA are committed to improving the California adult and juvenile systems of incarceration."[12] For Jimenez, employing Gomez—and thereby aiding a parolee's postincarceration transition—was putting his money where his mouth was.

What explains the CCPOA's apparent shift of direction? The foregoing paragraphs allude to a key factor: change of leadership. After 20 years as the union's president, Don Novey resigned in 2002. Novey's successor, Mike Jimenez, was not a prison officer during the CCPOA's early, formative years. Moreover, he entered the prison system after the "war years" (the period of extreme violence inside the prisons) and the "Era of Treatment." Therefore he was not (and is not) as committed to his predecessor's narrow "lock'em up" views on crime and punishment or his animosity toward "liberal" ideas and people or anything related to "prisoners' rights."[13] On this topic, Chuck Alexander, CCPOA vice president, says, "The prior regime [of CCPOA leaders] grew up in the era of lock them up and throw away the key, warehouse type prisons. The current regime—while we came into the system at the tail end of that, I think we look at things with a different eye."[14]

After he stepped down as union president, Novey continued to work for the CCPOA as a paid political consultant. However, the relationship between Novey and other long-time union leaders such as Steve Fournier and Tommy Marich (see chapter 2) with Jimenez and the new generation of leaders deteriorated. At the end of 2009, the CCPOA fired Novey from his position as political consultant because of intense disagreements over policy (e.g., Novey and other old-timers had openly castigated Jimenez for his pro-rehabilitation rhetoric and for hiring a parolee), strategy regarding contract negotiations and elections, and general leadership of the union. In response to his firing, Novey publicly lashed out at Jimenez. The *Sacramento Bee* posted emails Novey had sent to Jimenez after learning of his dismissal. In one of the emails, Novey wrote: "Jimenez, it's fine to go after me, but your Stalin like attacks on the membership and inability to focus on the concerns of the troops disappoints me." He continued, "Jimenez get a life and return to the institution . . . I consider your action unfortunate and displaying poor leadership skills."[15] Novey's dismissal signaled the official (and likely final) break between the old and new leadership of the CCPOA.

The union also seemingly shifted course because Jimenez had personal experiences that forced him to reevaluate his ideas about crime and punishment. The article in *Mother Jones* explained that one of Jimenez's two sons, Joshua, "got into drugs, went to a boot camp in Utah . . . was charged with a string of

Figure 8.1.
The new generation of CCPOA leaders. Jimenez and Alexander testify at a legislative hearing in 2008. The California Channel.

low-end felonies, dropped out of high school, and told his father he had nothing to look forward to in life." In response, Jimenez claimed to have realized, "there are lot of Joshuas who don't even know their dads. They get involved with the criminal justice system. It's a terrible reality. I realized there are a lot of kids in there who shouldn't be."[16] About his reaction to Joshua's experiences, Jimenez told the *Los Angeles Times*, "I've been humbled . . . I gotta believe in redemption. I gotta believe that you can convert."[17]

The CCPOA's apparent changes were not solely due to its leaders' biographies and experiences. They were also reactions to changes in the penal and bureaucratic fields. The election of Arnold Schwarzenegger as governor significantly changed both fields. As previously noted, Schwarzenegger strongly opposed the CCPOA during the campaign to recall Governor Davis and after he took office. He and his staff (particularly Roderick Hickman) maintained that the CCPOA promoted a "code of silence," handcuffed prison managers, and obstructed reform. (The Corrections Independent Review Panel, chaired by George Deukmejian, made similar arguments; see chapter 7.) It is important to note that sentencing and prison reforms were imperative at this time because of incredible budgetary shortfalls and the threat that federal judges would place the prison system in federal receivership or mandate the release of thousands of prisoners to relieve pressure in California's unconstitutionally overcrowded prisons.

In September 2007, after months of contentious, fruitless contract negotiations with the CCPOA, the Schwarzenegger administration imposed a "last, best, and final" contract offer on the union. The offer, which went into effect when the CCPOA unsurprisingly rejected it, eliminated or weakened provisions in the union's previous contracts that the administration felt gave the CCPOA too much authority inside the prisons (post-and-bid, the grievance and arbitration process, and the "entire agreement" clause all took hits).[18] It also eliminated the CCPOA's pay raise formula (the "law enforcement methodology") that had linked the union's raises to those of the California Highway Patrol (CHP). Through his rhetoric and actions, Schwarzenegger firmly positioned the CCPOA as an enemy of reform that was unworthy of its past achievements. In response, the CCPOA lashed out against the governor and his staff, going so far as to threaten to fund a campaign to recall him from office. The CCPOA also attempted to show that it was an agent (not an enemy) of reform that was committed to helping ease the state's overcrowding crisis—and therefore was deserving of a new contract that reinstituted the provisions the administration had deleted or watered down.

As the contract fight was going on, the CCPOA also received intense criticism from U.S. District Court Judge Thelton Henderson and his "special master," John Hagar. Henderson and Hagar had argued that the CCPOA fueled the "code of silence" and promoted lawlessness in the prisons. When the union went after Secretary Hickman, the judge and special master, like Schwarzenegger, insisted that the CCPOA was an enemy of prison reform. They argued that the union targeted Hickman because he had implemented important policies and practices to enhance personnel investigations and ensure officers found guilty of harming prisoners or committing other misdeeds were disciplined. After Hickman's resignation, Hagar wrote to Henderson:

> Understanding that a lack of support from the Governor's office would mean an end to prison reform, and realizing that a return of the Davis era practice of allowing the CCPOA to over-rule decisions of the CDCR Secretary would render his efforts to end the code of silence impossible, Mr. Hickman made the decision to resign as CDCR Secretary.[19]

Once again, the CCPOA appeared as a principal obstacle to fixing the state's badly broken prison system.

Criticism of the CCPOA in this period came from a third source: newspaper editorial boards. Editorial writers for the *Sacramento Bee, Los Angeles Times,* and *San Francisco Chronicle* repeated and supported criticisms of the CCPOA coming out of Governor Schwarzenegger's office and Judge Henderson's chambers. As a whole, editorials in these newspapers between 2002 and 2006 depicted the CCPOA as a self-interested and immoral organization that used "pay-to-play" tactics to inappropriately, though legally, control politicians and state agencies, corrupt prison management, fuel prison expansion, and obstruct efforts at rational penal reform.[20] Moreover, the editorials encouraged Schwarzenegger and other policymakers to take on the CCPOA and push through large-scale changes to the penal system. After Secretary Hickman cited CCPOA influence in the Schwarzenegger administration as a main reason for his resignation, the *Sacramento Bee* editorialized:

> As noted here Sunday, Schwarzenegger once seemed interested in a comprehensive approach toward prison reform . . . He seemed willing to confront the California Correctional Peace Officers Association, the powerful union that effectively controls the prison system and opposes any attempt to alter sentencing guidelines to improve parole procedures. But Schwarzenegger now has the aura of a scared politician, one who doesn't want the CCPOA and its affiliates to get in the way of his re-election chances.[21]

Combined with Hagar and Henderson's reports and Schwarzenegger's comments (as well as those of the Corrections Independent Review Panel [CIRP] he authorized), the newspaper commentaries forcefully refuted the CCPOA's claim that the union enhances the public good and benefits taxpayers.

It was in the context of this harsh criticism from dominant agents in the penal and neighboring fields that the CCPOA seemed to change its tune. By portraying the union as a cooperative, progressive organization, CCPOA activists tried to strip its critics of ammunition, a particularly important task because of the CCPOA's efforts to land a new contract. In a letter to the CCPOA's members in which Jimenez explained his decision to hire parolee Raul Gomez (a decision that had infuriated outspoken union members), Jimenez connected the union's newfound spirit of reform to its battle for a new contract. "By leading by example, we can continue to be respected and credible participants in the reform of the prison system *as we strengthen our position in our push for a just and proper [contract]*," Jimenez wrote. He further explained:

> I have heard those of you whom have voiced an opinion loud and clear. Many of you are unhappy with my decision. But I can't implore you enough to stop and consider before you get on a keyboard and write to a blog or website, that the people we are all charged with supervising are the brothers and sisters, the nephews and nieces, the children and grandchildren of people from all walks of life . . . Calling parolees thugs, scumbags, convicts, or any of a host of other derogatory names in a public forum doesn't endear our profession to anyone. Nor does the frequently expressed opinion calling for the wholesale dismissal of the approximately 325,000 human beings we are charged with supervising as unredeemable and unworthy of a future. *These people who are quick to opine give no reason whatsoever to provide better benefits, pay or working conditions for those of us who remain to be heard.*

As indicated in Jimenez's letter, the CCPOA's apparent change of direction was, in large part, an attempt to deflect criticism from the media, federal courts, and Schwarzenegger's administration. By presenting the CCPOA as an agent of reform, Jimenez hoped he would be in a better position to get his members a new, generous contract.

Contrary to the CCPOA's burst of reform rhetoric in 2006 and 2007, the union has acted in ways that suggest it has not loosened its commitment to punitive segregation or stopped acting as the anchor of the law-and-order power bloc in the penal field. The CCPOA's actions related to three initiatives on the November 2008 statewide ballot support this claim. Its fervent opposition to a recent legislative proposal that called for, among other things, the creation of a potentially effective sentencing commission backs this argument.

The first initiative, Proposition 5 (the "Nonviolent Offender Rehabilitation Act"), proposed to increase the types of drug offenders that could be diverted from prison to treatment and to allocate nearly $400 million annually for chemical dependency treatment for juveniles and adults. Proposition 5 also proposed to reduce the length of parole for "nonviolent, low-risk parolees" from three years to one year and to divert parolees who violate the terms of their parole or commit misdemeanor offenses from prison, which would greatly decrease California's prison population. In addition, the measure sought to expand rehabilitation inside prisons by mandating individualized treatment for all prisoners 90 days before release and giving the parole board the authority to increase "good time" credits for nonviolent prisoners who participate in rehabilitation programs. To institutionalize rehabilitation, the measure mandated the creation of new positions (such as the Secretary of Rehabilitation and Parole) and new state bureaucracies (the Treatment Diversion Oversight and Accountability Commission and the Parole Reform Oversight and Accountability Board). In short, Proposition 5 called for fundamental transformations of California's penal system. Although CCPOA President Jimenez had been calling for wholesale changes to the state's approach to punishing offenders (particularly "nonviolent" and "nonserious" offenders), the union effectively bankrolled the successful "No on 5" campaign, spending $1,825,000 to defeat the initiative.

Whereas Proposition 5 sought to reverse the Golden State's commitment to punitive segregation, the other two initiatives, Propositions 6 and 9, sought to reaffirm that commitment. Proposition 6, the "Safe Neighborhoods Act," was a prototypical "tough-on-crime" initiative that mandated massive spending increases for law enforcement and ramped up penalties for gang members (and their associates) and methamphetamine users and dealers. It also expanded the conditions under which juveniles could be tried as adults and sent to prison. According to the Legislative Analyst's Office, Proposition 6 would cost at least $365 million per year.[22] The voters defeated this initiative, likely because of its exorbitant price tag.

Proposition 9, the "Crime Victims' Bill of Rights," proposed to amend the state constitution and various state laws to expand the "rights" of victims. For example, victims would have the right to be notified of and participate in (and therefore potentially influence) *all public criminal proceedings*, including those pertaining to postarrest release, plea bargains, sentencing, and parole. Along with enhancing victims' rights, the initiative authorized several major changes to the parole process. For instance, it would increase the period between parole hearings for prisoners with "life" sentences from 1 to 15 years—the parole board would have the authority to shorten periods between hearings if "clear and convincing evidence" demonstrated that a prisoner would be fit for parole before 15 years. (Recall that after serving a specified length of time in prison, prisoners with "life" sentences are eligible for parole. Prisoners with "natural life" sentences—life without the possibility of parole—are not eligible for parole.) Proposition 9 also proposed denying state-appointed counsel for parolees charged with violating the terms of their parole (it made exceptions for indigent parole violators).

A little discussed, but extremely important, provision in Proposition 9 prohibited early release of prisoners to reduce overcrowding and ordered state and local governments to allocate sufficient funds so that jail and prison inmates served their entire sentences behind bars (this provision contradicted the CCPOA's "Blueprint," which supported early release for selective prisoners). Mike Reynolds, the "grandfather" of California's "Three Strikes and You're Out" law, helped write Proposition 9, and Crime Victims United of California (CVUC) and other punitive crime victims' organizations lobbied for the initiative (CVUC President Harriet Salarno signed the ballot argument in favor of the initiative). Faced with a choice of voting for or against victims of crime, Californians approved Proposition 9.

The CCPOA endorsed both Propositions 6 and 9, arguing that the initiatives would help victims and enhance public safety. (The CCPOA contributed at least $85,000 to Proposition 9. Whereas the union bankrolled the opposition to Proposition 5, Henry T. Nicholas III, the son of CVUC Vice President Marcella Leach, primarily financed Propositions 6 and 9.) The union's positions on these measures undeniably contradicted Jimenez's comments about "reform," for they epitomized the very ideas and practices that the CCPOA president insisted were counterproductive and corrosive.

At the end of August 2009, the CCPOA opposed a legislative proposal to establish a sentencing commission in California. The proposal was part of a bill to reduce the state's corrections budget. Although the CCPOA opposed other elements of the legislation, I focus here on its position on the sentencing commission because, I argue, this position is very instructive on the topic at hand: the CCPOA's current approach to criminal punishment. The proposed commission had the potential to create real change. For one thing, it had "teeth." Sentencing guidelines developed by the commission would become law unless the legislature passed a bill with a majority vote and the governor's signature to reject the guidelines. In other words, the legislature would have to take or leave the guidelines. It could not tweak them. For another thing, staunch advocates of the penal status quo would not dominate the membership of the commission. The commission's 13 voting members would include 2 academic experts, 1 legal scholar, 3 judges, and 2 public defenders. It would also include one district attorney, one sheriff, one chief of police, and one chief probation officer. The proposal also included three *nonvoting* members: a crime victim, an ex-offender, and a mental health or substance abuse expert (law enforcement groups were apoplectic about the inclusion of an ex-offender on the commission).

In expressing opposition to the sentencing commission, the CCPOA claimed that the body's purpose was to "reduce criminal sentences in order to lower prison population levels and reduce costs."[23] The proposal did not state this as the commission's purpose. However, it seems that the union deemed this as the goal for three reasons. The first two I have already discussed: the commission's membership and its authority to implement guidelines unless the Democrat-dominated legislature rejected them. The third reason concerns the language in the legislative proposal. The bill specified that the commission would "render sentences in all cases within a range of severity proportionate to the gravity of offenses, the harms done to crime victims, and the blameworthiness of the offenders."[24] Guided by this mandate, the commission would likely reduce punishments that it considered too harsh for certain crimes (it could also increase sanctions that it viewed as too lenient).

The legislation stipulated that "sentencing rules shall reflect the principle that incarceration is appropriate for those who commit a violent offense or offenders who have a record indicating a pattern of regular or increasingly serious criminal offense." The CCPOA and other opponents of the sentencing commission seemed to interpret this statement to mean that the commission's guidelines would permit the state to only incarcerate "violent" and "serious" felons. The commission, therefore, would mandate alternative sanctions for *all* "nonviolent" and "nonserious" offenders, greatly reducing the number of people sent to prison. This translation seems rather narrow, for "nonviolent" and "nonserious" offenders could exhibit a "pattern of regular and increasingly serious criminal conduct" and therefore would ostensibly receive prison terms. Nevertheless, it is likely that the commission would recommend sanctions other than prison for many nonviolent, nonserious offenses (another provision of the bill expressly directed the commission to "encourage the use of intermediate sanctions consistent with the protection of public safety").[25] After all, a major impetus for the sentencing commission proposal (and a main reason why Governor Schwarzenegger supported it) was to show the federal court—which had just ruled that California had to decrease its prison population by 40,000 offenders within two years—that it was serious about reducing prison overcrowding in the short *and* long terms. The sentencing commission would be charged with achieving this goal rationally and responsibly—that is, without risking public safety. If the CCPOA truly wanted to reduce the state's reliance on incarceration (particularly for nonviolent and nonserious offenders) and, to quote President Jimenez, "quit putting money in prisons," then it would have supported (or at least not opposed) the sentencing commission proposal.

As a result of vigorous opposition from the CCPOA and other law enforcement groups, a small group of Democratic assembly members who were facing reelection or seeking election to higher office objected to the sentencing commission proposal (along with all Republicans in the assembly). The group of Democrats feared that the union and other groups would tar them as "soft on crime," hindering their political advancement. The speaker of the assembly dropped the proposal.

In all, it appears that the CCPOA has changed in only one key way. The organization is undeniably more open than it was under its iconic front man Don Novey. The union's leaders now regularly meet with people and groups that their predecessors viewed as enemies—including public interest lawyers, academics (even criminologists and sociologists), and prison reform activists.

As they have formed relationships with former foes, CCPOA officials (particularly President Jimenez) have changed their rhetoric, making statements that their predecessors would consider soft-headed, liberal nonsense.

Although the CCPOA's rhetoric has changed, its actions have not followed suit. Not only does the CCPOA continue to support California's commitment to punitive segregation, it also continues to back groups that aggressively reinforce the penal status quo. CVUC, for instance, remains so punitive that it recently argued against a cost-savings measure that would allow early parole for critically ill prisoners. Harriet Salarno of CVUC maintained the measure was "unfair to the victims" and was "playing games with public safety."[26] The victims' group also opposed the establishment of a specialized court in San Diego that is meant to help (not just punish) veterans who commit crimes when they return to civilian life. CVUC did not explain its position to the court.[27] In opposing the medical release proposal and veterans' court, CVUC reveals a persistently rigid, knee-jerk punitiveness.

Simply put, the union's recent actions contradict President Jimenez's rhetoric, making the organization seem disingenuous. Its reform language seems like a practical response to harsh criticism from authoritative actors in the penal and neighboring fields, including the governor, Judge Henderson, and newspaper editorialists, who charge that the union is a major obstacle to curtailing the massive overcrowding crisis. The tactic of posing as an agent of reform is consistent with the union's politically realistic disposition—the CCPOA is playing the political game as it is today. And because of the state's economic meltdown and mandates from the federal court to draw down the prison population, staunchly opposing sentencing and prison reform would be reckless.

My use of hesitant words like "seems" and "appears" when discussing the CCPOA's current approach to criminal punishment is purposeful. The CCPOA's leaders only began to verbally support sentencing and prison reform a few years ago. Therefore it is too soon to say unequivocally that the CCPOA will not be an agent of change—even though indicators thus far suggest that it will not. It is true that, as leaders of a large organization with a punitive culture, the CCPOA's officials understand that they cannot move too quickly regarding reform or they will be voted out of office. The union leaders' rhetorical shifts, then, may be attempts to slowly get the membership behind them before taking bold action on policies. But whether the divide between the CCPOA's rhetoric and action is just a politically realistic tactic to defend the union against criticism and win a new contract or a legitimate sign of change is unknowable at this point. So far it is only clear that the union's new generation of leaders is far less isolationist and narrowly ideological than the previous generation. Therefore there is at least the possibility that President Jimenez and his colleagues will find common ground with reformers and work to loosen the Golden State's stubborn attachment to the policies and ideas that initially fueled, and now reinforce, the state's truly remarkable penal crisis.

Although the California legislature failed to institute a sentencing commission, it did pass legislation to draw down the prison population as federally mandated. (If the government had failed to do so, judges had threatened to place the entire prison system in federal receivership and hold the system's leaders in contempt of court.) The legislation has three principal components that, as of 2010, affect prisoners and ex-prisoners. The first permits the state to cut time from the sentences of "low-risk," "nonviolent" prisoners with a record of good behavior who work on firefighter crews, earn a high school degree or trade school certificate, or complete a chemical dependency program. Prisoners will earn six weeks of "good time" for each program they complete. The state estimated that 1,500 prisoners would leave prison early in 2010 because of this portion of the law.

The second component provides "day-for-day" credits to prisoners "whether they are on a waiting list for a full-time assignment, participating in programs, or undergoing reception center processing, so long as the inmate is discipline-free during that time."[28] Prisoners used to receive one day off their sentence for every three days served, but now receive one day off their sentence for each day they are behind bars.

The third element of the law eliminates parole supervision for select "low-risk" ex-prisoners (police retain the authority to search the ex-prisoners without a warrant). These low-risk former offenders cannot be returned to prison for "technical violations," such as failing a drug test. The government expected that approximately 5,000 ex-prisoners would be eligible for the new parole (or, rather, nonparole) program in 2010 and that the extremely large proportion of prison admissions that are technical parole violators would shrink dramatically (recall that more than half of the people admitted to California prisons each year are technical violators).[29]

The policy changes enacted under the law may be short-lived. In February 2010, CVUC filed a lawsuit against the Schwarzenegger administration for implementing the changes. The CCPOA-aligned group argued that the law violates constitutional provisions enacted under Proposition 9 ("Marcy's Law"), which, among other things, disallow early release of prisoners because of overcrowding.[30] If CVUC's lawsuit is successful, the government will have to find another way to reduce the prison population or risk federal receivership.

Because the federal judges did not mandate *how* the state should create space in the prisons (only that it must), it created an object of struggle within the penal field. The CCPOA, CVUC, the governer, legislators, and other agents in the field have been battling over how to reduce the population since the judges issued their order. It was only because law enforcement groups and crime victims' organizations, in concert with their allies in the legislature, killed other proposals to shrink the prison population that the state settled on the stopgap measure of the "early release program" in the first place. Now there is an intense struggle over this policy—just as there will be if the state has to come up with an alternative.

The state's response to the judges' mandate has largely been shaped by the composition and orientation of the penal field. The authority of the CCPOA, other law enforcement groups, crime victims' organizations, and "tough-on-crime" politicians makes it extremely difficult to enact policy changes that would loosen the state's commitment to punitive segregation and seriously shrink the prison population. The recent reforms, for example, do nothing to fix the state's penal code, a complex, incomprehensible mess that lacks an overarching philosophy or purpose, gives judges little room to consider important mitigating and aggravating factors when imposing sentences, and requires long, often-disproportionate prison sentences while disregarding alternative sanctions that might cost less and better serve offenders, victims, and taxpayers. Without fundamental changes, California's prisons will soon overflow again, leading to further, and likely more drastic, actions by the federal judges. For those concerned with significantly altering the existing penal conditions in California and other states, the main practical lesson of this book is that long-term, major transformation requires changing the composition and culture—the prevailing norms, values, and assumptions—of the penal field.

Composition

To change the composition of the field means to alter the relationships between the positions of agents in the field. The game fundamentally changes when subordinate players gain power and challenge the dominant agents and when new agents obtain positions in the field (as we saw in chapter 4 with the creation of CVUC and similar groups). An array of actors in and around the penal field opposes punitive segregation for professional, ethical, scientific, practical, and even political reasons. Table 8.1 provides a short, and by no means exhaustive, list of organizations that have either opposed policies that promote punitive segregation or supported policies designed to undermine the penal status quo. These agents occupy subordinate positions in the penal field. There are two main reasons for their marginal status. First, dominant agents, including the CCPOA and its allies, have fought against these challengers, promoting policies that limit their authority and routinely castigating them as enemies of the collective good. Second, with rare exceptions, the competitors have not skillfully played the political game (when they have played it at all). Their marginal status is at least partly self-imposed. Individuals and groups who oppose punitive segregation tend to act as if moral and rational scientific arguments alone will convince lawmakers and voters to support policy reform (see chapter 5 and the campaign for Proposition 66, the ballot initiative to reform Three Strikes).

An alternative perspective—espoused by Saul Alinsky and applied by the CCPOA—suggests that solid arguments (no matter how ethically, legally, or scientifically sound) are not the motor force of social change: *power is*. Alinsky defines power as the "ability, whether physical, mental, or moral, to act."[31] Individuals and groups use power to make others listen to them and, ultimately, to act in particular ways. Alinsky argues, "You don't communicate with anyone purely on rational facts or ethics of an issue . . . It is only when the other party is concerned or feels threatened that he will listen—in the arena of action, a threat or a crisis becomes almost a precondition to communication."[32] Ethical and logical arguments are far more persuasive when backed by force (or the perception of force), a lesson the CCPOA learned very well. We have seen that lawmakers and state bureaucrats sometimes (if not oftentimes) agree with challengers in the penal field who promote policies that diverge from the law-and-order status quo. But they do not take up the challengers' cause—and in some cases actively oppose the challengers' proposals—because they fear powerful promoters of the status quo.

To compete with the dominant actors in the penal field and make policymakers listen, the challengers would need to play the political game as it exists, not as they wish it to be. One strategy would be for the challengers to form an oppositional bloc. As we have seen in earlier chapters, a bloc is not a formal organization or a fleeting alliance. Rather, it is a group of individuals and agents who combine resources in pursuit of a particular goal or set of goals. The actors listed in Table 8.1 have periodically joined forces to support or oppose particular policy proposals (e.g., Proposition 66); however, they have not consistently acted as a bloc. To do so would require them to combine resources and acquire the *means of political production*: political action committees (PACs), full-time lobbyists, and media/political consultants. Of course, these political tools are expensive. However, financiers such as George Soros have shown a willingness to spend millions to change the penal status quo. Moreover, the labor unions and professional groups listed in Table 8.1 could contribute substantial money to reform campaigns. In short, there are sources of financing for reform efforts; yet, nobody is currently responsible for collecting and using the funds to develop the requisite political machinery.

Developing political tools is not, itself, an end. The bloc would need to skillfully use the tools to gain power and change the penal field. This would require proficient organizers to produce and execute game plans. As described earlier, the success of campaigns that promote punitive segregation are partly (if not largely) due to the efforts of Don Novey and other proficient political organizers. Alinsky and the CCPOA are instructive on potential strategies. First, organizations in the bloc could oppose lawmakers and state bureaucrats who

Table 8.1 CHALLENGERS IN THE PENAL FIELD

CRIME VICTIM
- 1000 Mothers to Prevent Violence
- California Crime Victims for Alternatives to the Death Penalty
- Journey of Hope
- Murder Victims' Families for Reconciliation

FAITH-BASED
- American Friends Service Committee
- California Catholic Conference (Office of Restorative Justice)
- California Council of Churches (California Church IMPACT)
- Faith Communities for Families and Children
- Los Angeles Council of Churches
- Lutheran Office of Public Policy–California
- Office of Restorative Justice of the Archdioceses of Los Angeles
- Progressive Jewish Alliance

LEGAL/CIVIL LIBERTIES
- American Civil Liberties Union
- California Attorneys for Criminal Justice
- National Lawyers Guild
- Prison Law Office
- Youth Law Center

ADVOCACY
- Californians United for a Responsible Budget
- Center on Juvenile and Criminal Justice
- Critical Resistence
- Drug Policy Alliance
- Equal Justice Society
- League of Women Voters of California
- National Association for the Advancement of Colored People
- National Council on Crime and Delinquency
- Taxpayers for Improving Public Safety

PROFESSIONAL ASSOCIATIONS
- American Psychiatric Association
- California Public Defenders Association
- California Council of Community Mental Health Agencies
- California Faculty Association
- California Professional Firefighters
- National Association of Social Workers, California Chapter
- National Alliance on Mental Illness
- National Black Police Association
- Law Enforcement Against Prohibition

LABOR UNIONS
- AFSCME, Local 2620 (Health and Social Services Professional Employees)
- California Federation of Teachers
- California Labor Federation, AFL-CIO
- California Nurses Association
- California Teachers Association
- SEIU California State Labor Council

promote punitive segregation—they could punish lawmakers who advance their careers by being "tough on crime." For example, they could organize campaigns featuring crime victim advocates, religious leaders, and current or retired criminal justice professionals (e.g., judges, police chiefs, district attorneys, and department of corrections officials) arguing that a lawmaker or prospective politician supports costly, unreasonable policies that drain public resources from education and crime prevention programs. The challengers could further contend that, by supporting such policies, politicians (or would-be politicians) harm children, victims of crime, and the collective good.[33] Alternatively or additionally, they could highlight relationships between politicians and unpopular advocacy groups, suggesting that by supporting "tough-on-crime" policies, the politicians demonstrate that they are more committed to their contributors than their constituencies. (Recall from chapter 6 that Cornell Corporation successfully used this tactic to force then governor Davis not to eliminate several minimum-security private prisons.) Taking another page from the playbook of CCPOA and its allies, the crime victims' groups in Table 8.1 (or new, explicitly political crime victims' groups in the mold of CVUC) could formally oppose political candidates who differ with their views on how to help victims. In brief, the agents in the bloc could increase their power through confrontation, which Alinsky insists, forces powerful actors to *respect* less powerful actors (see chapter 3). Eventually politicians and would-be politicians may perceive that the consequences of flexing their "tough-on-crime" muscles outweighs or at least equals the benefits of doing so.

In addition to enhancing power through confrontation, the agents in the bloc could extend their influence through promoting and rewarding like-minded electoral candidates. Since the mid-twentieth century, politicians and elected state officials have been very influential actors in California's penal field. Organizations such as the CCPOA have endorsed and funded politicians who share their view of crime and punishment, and they have rewarded sitting lawmakers who take positions on penal matters that the organizations support. The groups in the oppositional bloc could follow the CCPOA's lead by supporting—through campaign contributions, endorsements, independent expenditures, and voter drives—electoral candidates who are committed to an alternative, progressive approach to crime control. Once in office, the policymakers could serve as proxies for the organizations, advocating for policies that reduce the prison population and promote public safety and victims' well-being. Thus the groups could change the shape of the penal field by combining resources and forming a forceful, oppositional bloc, pushing politicians who oppose their interests out of the field and bringing lawmakers who support their goals into the field.

The empowerment of currently marginal or minimally powerful agents does not mean that the presently dominant CCPOA and CCPOA-supported victims' groups should not have voices—even strong voices—in debates about penal policies and priorities. These groups correctly claim expertise based on their concrete experiences. For example, Harriet Salarno and other leaders of crime victims' groups have important insights about the terrible ways that penal institutions and personnel often treat victims of crime and their families. They also have expertise about the services and protections that victims need and deserve. CCPOA leaders and members have extensive knowledge about the daily operations of prisons and the parole system, as well as prison officers' needs and desires (in terms of training, equipment, material compensation, and respect). Prison officers and parole agents, after all, are the frontline workers, the "street-level bureaucrats," who see how policies and programs play out "on the ground."

The CCPOA and its allies are important agents in the penal field, but their "real-life expertise" does not necessarily make them experts about sentencing policy, the needs of offenders and ex-offenders, or the best ways to help prisoners and former prisoners live crime-free lives. Changing the penal field does not mean denying that the currently dominant agents in the field lack expertise, it means that we accept that they are not the *only* legitimate and relevant experts. It also means, however, that agents with other forms of expertise (based, for example, on conducting rigorous scholarly research, working with and providing services to offenders and ex-offenders, or adjudicating cases) must become authoritative agents—and assert their expertise—in the penal field.

Culture

I have tried to detail throughout this book that prevailing penal practices and priorities in California reflect and reaffirm certain common-sense notions about crime, punishment, and related issues, such as the role and efficacy (or lack thereof) of government. I have also attempted to demonstrate that the CCPOA and its allies have worked to solidify these conceptions throughout the last few decades. Undeniably, the media and politicians have also hardened penal common sense. To fundamentally transform California's approach to crime control, oppositional groups and individuals need to challenge dominant assumptions in the penal field that underlie the penal status quo and develop and disseminate an alternative vision of criminal punishment.

This counterperspective would disrupt ideas that currently go unchallenged in Sacramento and in many popular discussions about crime and punishment. For example, it would challenge the idea that punitive crime victims' representatives are the sole "voice of victims." Groups like the CVUC represent a particularly retributive brand of "crime victims' rights," one that assumes that policies that help prisoners automatically harm crime victims, and vice versa. Other crime victims' groups do not share this assumption. They claim that harming prisoners via the death penalty and denying prisoners basic rights do not help victims of crime—they simply create more suffering and resentment. They claim that encouraging prisoners to take responsibility for the harm their crimes cause through restorative justice practices and helping inmates develop the tools necessary to live crime-free lives helps victims and victims' families. Because virtually all agents in the penal field fear offending crime victims, they do not question the representativeness of groups like CVUC. In order to break the penal status quo, contenders in the field will need to provide an alternative view of crime victims' rights, for "law-and-order" policies are generally justified in the name of "victims of crime."[34] Moreover, they will need to impel journalists and politicians to solicit opinions about penal issues from alternative crime victims' advocates. Only then can these advocates advance an alternative perspective on helping victims and enhancing public safety.

This counterperspective will also need to challenge the notion that "prison works." For several decades now, policymakers have assumed that hyperincarceration reduces crime and helps victims. The prison boom undoubtedly contributed to reductions in crime over the last 15 years (principally through incapacitation), however, American crime rates fell primarily because of factors unrelated to imprisonment (e.g., demographic and economic shifts and changes in policing strategies and technology).[35] Researchers have shown that hyperincarceration does not "work" as well as its proponents claim.

An alternative narrative should not only highlight incarceration's limited pay off, it must also emphasize the consequences of the prison boom—including the financial costs, so-called collateral damage caused to families and communities, and massive growth of dysfunctional governmental institutions. It should include the fact that hyperincarceration is criminogenic—that is, the overwhelming majority of people who leave prison are generally less prepared to "make it" on the outside than when they entered prison, so they are more likely to reoffend. Furthermore, it should present viable alternative responses to crime that hold offenders accountable for their actions *and* improve society—for example, working on public works projects, paying restitution, etc.—without draining state coffers. It should also include public health approaches to crimes such as drug use, which are more effective than penal responses, as shown in other countries.[36] The counterperspective should ask if and how "prison works" (and for whom does it work). Moreover, it should ask: "Are there alternative responses to crime that may work better than imprisonment?" These same questions could and should be asked about other sanctions, such as the death penalty and parole.[37]

Changing the penal status quo requires challenging the taken-for-granted notion that offenders are foreign "others" that are less than human and fundamentally different than "us." Terms such as "career criminals," "juvenile superpredators," and "sexual predators" exemplify this notion. Popular rhetoric that dehumanizes and demonizes socially constructed groups of offenders *justifies* "tough-on-crime" policies such as Three Strikes, Megan's Law, Jessica's Law, life without the possibility of parole for juvenile offenders, and the death penalty, which presume that some categories of people are inherently dangerous, immutable, and quasi- or nonhuman.[38] Harsh punishment and intensive supervision are necessary to protect the public if throngs of monstrous criminals stalk the citizenry. By incapacitating criminals deemed innately violent, prison undoubtedly "works." In addition to justifying punitive segregation, dehumanization and demonization fuel it.[39]

A major reason that this denial of humanity persists is that prisoners are hidden from the public. Hence advocacy groups, politicians, the media, and academics shape the dominant representations of convicts. These representations are typically of manipulative, brooding, and dangerous predators who literally thirst for blood. Challengers in the penal field can counter the tendency to dehumanize prisoners by creating opportunities for prisoners to tell their stories and voice their concerns. In addition, challengers can fight against the "media ban" in California and other states that forbids journalists from conducting face-to-face interviews with prisoners.[40] The California Department of Corrections and Rehabilitation (CDCR) and victims' groups including CVUC are the main proponents of California's media ban. The CDCR claims that media interviews threaten institutional security. It is conceivable, if not probable, that the CDCR also fears media scrutiny. The crime victims' groups profess to support the ban because of fear that prisoners may profit from their crimes by becoming celebrities.

Taken together, transformation of the penal field requires refuting the depersonalization and demonization of offenders—processes that facilitate warlike policies, which strive to eliminate entire groups of people through banishment behind bars or capital punishment, and obstruct efforts to provide meaningful services and programs to prisoners and former prisoners. It also requires denying that prisoners comprise an undifferentiated mass that is defined solely by their degraded legal status and place of residence. Prisoners are individuals with often complex subjectivities, histories, and concerns. Challengers can alter prevailing penal "common sense" by confronting efforts to dehumanize offenders and by helping to produce new spaces—and strengthen those that already exist—in which prisoners can speak for themselves. Allowing the dominant agents in the penal field to continue to shape our collective view of "the prisoner" will undoubtedly frustrate efforts to change the penal status quo.

Speaking Out

The Prison University Project (PUP) and the Prison Creative Arts Project (PCAP) are excellent examples of existing programs that promote

(continued)

prisoner expression within and beyond the walls. The PUP runs a college program at San Quentin prison in California. (Disclaimer: I volunteered with the PUP in the late 1990s.) It also publishes an annual journal of prisoners' writings and artwork, hosts creative performances, and organizes symposia about current events, allowing prisoners to dialogue with people involved in the public policy arena (see Figure 8.2). The PUP helps prisoners develop and improve skills to analyze and communicate effectively about events and issues inside and outside of the prison, and it

Figure 8.2.
A prisoner at San Quentin speaks during the inaugural "Day of Peace Celebration" in April 2007. The event was organized by a group of men at San Quentin with support from the Prison University Project. Photo by Heather Rowley.

provides opportunities for challenging dominant representations of prisons and prisoners.

The PCAP has operated in Michigan's adult and juvenile penal institutions for more than 20 years. The program seeks to "make possible the spaces in which the voices and visions of the incarcerated can be expressed." It facilitates workshops on creative writing and the visual and performing arts, organizes exhibitions of prisoner art and produces performances (including 210 plays in 22 prisons), and helps prisoner-artists develop portfolios of their art and creative writing.[41] The founder of PCAP, Buzz Alexander, emphasizes the value of connecting prisoners and nonprisoners through artistic expression: "Among our main goals is to break stereotypes and to foster a dialogue between those who are incarcerated and the community . . . Art is a tool to connect and to understand on many levels the hearts and minds of those living in Michigan prisons as well as our own."[42]

Altering the penal field will be a gradual process. Fields typically change over time rather than through immediate rupture. We saw that the triumph of "law-and-order" did not simply occur in 1976 with the end of indeterminate sentencing. Rather, it unfolded over several decades.[43] Transformation of the penal field depends, in part, on macrolevel developments. After all, the penal field is embedded in society and thus societal trends affect what occurs inside the field. For example, economic decline provides opportunities for challengers: the state simply cannot afford continued prison expansion. At the same time, economic decline fuels anxiety among the populace, particularly those in the lower and middle classes. Incumbents in the field can tap into and stir up this anxiety by highlighting the alleged chaos they claim alternative penal policies would produce. Ethnic and racial division also permeates the penal field, as dominant agents in the field arouse racial prejudice and fear through explicit and coded racialized images and language. Because these social factors permeate and condition the struggles in the penal field, transformation of the field depends, in part, on the amelioration of deep inequalities and divisions that mark contemporary California, and the United States more generally.

Gradual transformation of the penal field can make policies, practices, appointments, ideas, and sentiments that are currently unthinkable thinkable. It is important to remember that practices we now take for granted, such as Three Strikes and juvenile transfer to adult court, were politically unthinkable a half-century ago.[44] Before the 1980s it was also unthinkable that private companies would own and operate maximum-security prisons in much of the

United States. With the transformation of the penal field, it may become thinkable that a governor will appoint a crime victim advocate who believes it is possible to help victims without creating undo suffering for prisoners. It may become thinkable that if the state creates a sentencing commission, government officials might appoint commissioners who believe that prison does not work for all or even most felons; who believe that alternative sanctions are appropriate for many offenders; and who believe that the commission need not simply replicate the relations and priorities that characterize the penal field today. It may become thinkable that the state will make a real commitment to preparing prisoners for life on the outside and to helping ex-prisoners once they leave prison. It may become thinkable that we come to view prisoners as individuals who commit felonious and sometimes downright evil acts rather than as felonious, evil, semi- or nonhumans. Finally, in a transformed penal field, it may become thinkable that the ever-expanding prison system will actually contract and that the "toughest beat" might no longer be so tough for offenders, prison personnel, or communities.

APPROACHING PUNISHMENT WITHIN AND BEYOND CALIFORNIA

Ultimately the story of the CCPOA is uniquely Californian. The state's incredible prison boom, collective bargaining laws, and political traditions and institutions facilitated the union's ascent and influence on penal policies and priorities. Employing its distinctive politically realistic unionization strategy, the CCPOA took advantage of the propitious political and cultural environment in the 1980s and 1990s, achieving great successes for correctional workers and greatly affecting the scope and characteristics of incarceration and related penal practices. A *collateral consequence* of hyperimprisonment in California, then, was the expansion of an organization—the CCPOA—that, along with its allies (some of whom it helped create), has made it extremely difficult to implement large-scale sentencing and prison reforms. Although prison officer unions in states like Rhode Island and New York are political actors, none has been as central to its state's recent penal history as the CCPOA has been in the Golden State.

But while the specific story of the CCPOA is distinctively Californian, the analytical perspective used to explain that story is not. Through my study of the CCPOA, I have tried to show that analyzing the relationship between the penal field (and its subfields) and interest groups (broadly conceived) helps us better comprehend why agents make certain moves (and not others). The actions that interest groups and other organizations take—and taking no action is, in fact, taking an action—are shaped by the actions or anticipated actions of others in the field. It is for this reason that the specter of the CCPOA is such a powerful force and effective weapon in the struggle over penal outcomes. One's position in the field partially determines the possible moves that the player can make. The dominant orientation of the field also circumscribes possible actions available to agents in the field. Analysis of this sort helps us move beyond frameworks that explain practice as just the product of narrow material interests or ideological commitments. Agents within and beyond California who battle over criminal justice matters take (or do not take) policy positions, form coalitions (or got it alone), and make public pronouncements (or remain silent), in large part because of their positions in the penal field.

In addition to furthering our understanding of the moves players make, analyses of the relationship between actors and the penal field provides a much richer view of organizations' effects on criminal punishment than do studies that focus solely on sponsoring and opposing legislation, lobbying, giving campaign contributions, making public statements, and participating in legislative hearings. By focusing squarely on the relationship between actors and fields, we can better understand *how* prison officers' unions, prosecutors' associations, crime victims' groups, criminal justice agencies, prisoners' rights organizations, and other agents alter (however slightly) the architecture and orientation of the social space in which battles over penal options occur. Put simply, this type of analysis enhances our understanding of how collective actors both directly *and* indirectly affect penal outcomes.

The effect of actors like the CCPOA on the penal field matters because the field shapes what is possible and impossible concerning criminal punishment. As explained in the first chapter, fields are like prisms—they refract macro-level trends. The set of relations and principles that constitute the penal field thus determines how jurisdictions respond to these trends. Because states have varying penal fields, they may not react to these social trends in the same ways. In order to understand why one state (or county or the federal government) responds to structural trends in a particular manner, we must comprehend the composition and culture of its own penal field. In addition, the shape and orientation of the penal field affects which actors are able to take advantage of available political and legal processes (e.g., the warden selection or ballot initiative process), as well as how these actors employ such tools. In other words, the penal field helps determine why and how legal and political institutions affect penal outcomes.

I have argued throughout this book that understanding the contours and underlying principles of the penal field helps us answer concrete empirical questions such as why California voters defeated Proposition 66 (the initiative to reform Three Strikes) in 2004 or why the Golden State has not embraced widespread prison privatization in the face of mounting budget deficits and extreme prison overcrowding. I maintain that scholars can use this analytical approach to understand particular empirical questions about penal policies and priorities in other locales. For instance, it could be employed to understand why prison privatization bloomed in some states rather than others, why "three strikes" laws in other states are far less expansive and punitive than in California, or why several states (unlike California) have established sentencing commissions that limit prison overcrowding while promoting equity in sentencing.

The analytical perspective advanced here also leads to clear predictions about state-level penal variation more generally. Based on this approach, we would expect that criminal punishment regimes vary between states because of differences in states' respective penal fields. For example, because California is much more punitive than Minnesota, we would expect that the two states' penal fields differ considerably.[45] More precisely, we would predict that traditional criminal justice experts such as social scientists, penal professionals (e.g., judges and leaders of the department of corrections), and state bureaucrats have more authority in Minnesota than in California. We would also expect that punitive interest groups have less penal capital in the North Star State than the Golden State. It is also likely that Minnesota's penal field is more autonomous than California's, therefore, politicians and other outsiders have comparatively limited power to shape sentencing and related policies.

Along with dissimilarity in the architecture of the two fields, we would expect variation in the fields' respective cultures or orientations. For example, we would predict that zero-sum reasoning; dehumanizing images of and rhetoric about offenders; and the proposition that "prison works" are less prevalent and powerful in Minnesota than in California. We would further anticipate that Minnesota is more committed to rehabilitation, community sanctions, and cost-effective use of state resources than California. It is likely that dominant agents in Minnesota's penal field would take pride in supporting sensible, technically rational criminal punishment goals and policies—i.e., being "smart on crime" (not simply "tough on crime").

Taken together, it is assumed that social structural factors and political and legal institutions do not sufficiently explain why California is far more punitive than Minnesota. The *shape of struggle* over penal policies and priorities in these two states must differ is consequential ways. Of course, only systematic comparative research can determine the validity of these hypotheses.

This analytical perspective can be used to increase our knowledge of national and subnational penal variation, helping us comprehend why jurisdictions (local, state, or national) choose different penal paths, even when dealing with similar levels of crime and political and economic forces. I want to be very clear that I am not arguing for agent-centered analyses of punishment that exclude larger social structural factors. Instead, I claim that social structural analyses that ignore the battles between actors to shape criminal punishment are *incomplete*—as are analyses that focus on actors without attention to key macrolevel factors such as the economy, race and ethnic relations, crime, and demographics. By seriously examining the struggles over penal policies and practices that take place in and around the penal field, we can better understand why criminal punishment is so tough in some places and not so tough in others. Thus comprehending the contours and prevailing principles of the penal field is a necessary step toward rectifying the incredible, enduring, and destructive "correctional crisis" within and beyond California.

METHODOLOGICAL APPENDIX

This study began inadvertently in 2001 while I was conducting research on higher education in prisons. I scheduled an interview with Richard Polanco, a California state senator, to discuss a bill he had recently authored that contained a minor provision about college behind bars. The senator stood me up. Sensing my frustration, his scheduler sent me to talk with Gwynnae Byrd, Polanco's chief consultant on prison issues. Polanco was the senate majority leader (second in command in the upper house of California's legislature) and chair of the Joint Legislative Committee on Prison Operations and Construction (the "Prison Committee"), the legislative body charged with overseeing the prison system. It was Byrd, however, who supervised the Prison Committee's day-to-day operations.

Byrd and I had a lively discussion about prison education and a host of related issues. At several points she complained that she did not have sufficient assistance. Being an excited and opportunistic graduate student, I offered free labor—with the condition that I could observe the Prison Committee's activities. Looking at me a bit quizzically, Byrd accepted the free help. I viewed the "volunteership" as an opportunity to witness firsthand the "politics of punishment"—the undefined subject of my then-emerging dissertation project. I wanted to understand how California transformed from a national leader in progressive incarceration during the decades following World War II to a national trailblazer in punitive segregation in the 1980s and 1990s. More specifically, I wanted to comprehend how and why the state enacted certain penal policies and discounted others.

Throughout most of 2001 and into 2002, I rode the train from Oakland to Sacramento (about 78 miles) once or twice a week (when the legislature was in session) to help the Prison Committee and conduct exploratory research. When I was not studying issues, sorting mail, or doing other tasks, I sketched out—albeit in piecemeal fashion—the structure of the political and bureaucratic games, particularly those related to criminal punishment. I jotted down the relevant actors who competed against each other over bills, budget allocations, and administrative actions. I chronicled the resources groups and individuals employed to achieve their aims and noted the relationships between the actors in the arenas in which penal decisions were hammered out. As I watched tussles over penal issues play out, one group was omnipresent: the California Correctional Peace Officers Association (CCPOA). Even when CCPOA representatives were not physically present, they were there in spirit. Politicians, legislative staff ("staffers"), state bureaucrats, and prisoners' rights activists continually talked about the union and wondered about its positions.

For example, I attended a meeting with California Department of Corrections (CDC) officials, staffers, and attorneys who represented prisoners. The subject of the gathering was a "violence control program" that the CDC developed to reduce violence in the state's super-maximum-security prisons. After a couple of hours, the group agreed on changes to the proposed program. But before adjourning, a staffer asked a CDC official if he had discussed the program with the CCPOA. When the official said that he had not, several people dropped their heads to their chests. A few people chuckled to express the apparent futility of the meeting. The official assured the group that he would check with the union immediately. As we left the room, Byrd wondered why the CDC wasted our time. Like many others in Sacramento, she believed that the CCPOA had an up or down vote on prison-related policies. Without the union's buy-in, she felt, the violence control program would never see the light of day. This example played out time and again during my tenure in the legislature.

Before volunteering with the Prison Committee, I had heard of the CCPOA; however, I knew very little about the group. My ignorance about the CCPOA flummoxed Byrd and other staffers, for they saw the union as omnipotent and ubiquitous. From their perspective, the CCPOA determined the Golden State's penal policies and priorities. Thus the initial objective of this study was to get at the root of this "common-sense" view of the CCPOA. I wanted to know the extent and character of the union's power. In other words, I set about studying if the CCPOA was, in fact, omnipotent and ubiquitous. And if it was not all-powerful and everywhere, why did people think it was? Moreover, I sought to understand how this undeniably successful labor group became a formidable political player. Was the widespread perception about the CCPOA's dominating influence on penal policymaking accurate? What direct and indirect effects did the union have on the scope, shape, and trajectory of criminal punishment in California? In short, this study developed organically out of my experiences in the legislature.[1]

I employed three interrelated methods to answer these questions (and others that arose during the research process). The first method was semistructured, in-depth interviews. I conducted 58 open-ended, taped interviews. The vast majority of these interviews were face to face; the rest were conducted on the telephone. I also did at least 40 additional informal (non-taped, nonstructured) telephone interviews, most of which addressed specific questions and were relatively short (generally between 10 and 30 minutes). Interviewees included current and former CCPOA members and employees. I conducted formal follow-up interviews and had informal conversations with several union activists and staff that allowed me to investigate and, on occasion, reconcile contradictory accounts, dig deeper about particular subjects, and ask questions about topics that surfaced after the initial interviews. The interviews with CCPOA-affiliated individuals helped me chronicle and explain the union's development from the late 1950s until 2010 and provided crucial data on the CCPOA's goals, strategies, and achievements.

It is important to note that I did not interview former CCPOA president Don Novey. After several unsuccessful attempts to contact Novey, I received a phone call from him. At the end of the call he told me that he would not participate in the study. Based on his questions, it was clear that he distrusted me because of my work with the Prison Committee that Senator Polanco chaired. As discussed in chapter 3, Polanco was a harsh critic of the union. I learned during interviews with other people affiliated with the CCPOA that Novey viewed me as a "prisoners' rights activist."

Although unfortunate, Novey's refusal to participate in my study was understandable because of his and the union's longtime distrust of academics (particularly sociologists), antipathy toward Polanco, and zero-sum vision of the world, in which individuals and groups are either pro-victim/pro-law enforcement or pro-prisoner. I explain in chapter 8 that the new generation of leadership in CCPOA is less ideological and more open than Novey's generation of leadership. The current leaders believe that engaging critics may lead to less negative and more nuanced representations of the CCPOA—and that pushing away possible detractors reinforces perceptions of the union as an insulated, ideologically rigid, and intolerant organization. It is primarily because of this strategy of engagement (which clearly differentiates the old and new leadership) that President Mike Jimenez and other current leaders permitted me to interview them and attend CCPOA events.

In addition to people associated with the CCPOA, I interviewed individuals who routinely interacted with the union: legislators, legislative staffers, former employees of the CDC, journalists, lobbyists, representatives of other state workers' unions, lawyers involved in prison litigation, leaders of prisoners' rights organizations, and representatives of crime victims' groups. These interviews helped me construct general maps of the penal and imprisonment fields, locate the CCPOA within those fields, and flesh out the CCPOA's historical trajectory. They also facilitated my understanding of the various forms and effects of the CCPOA's power.

Along with interviews, I conducted archival research. The documents that I collected fit into four general categories. The first were materials produced by the CCPOA and its predecessor (the California Correctional Officers Association [CCOA]), including complete sets of the union's two primary newsletters: *The Granite* (1978–1981) and *Peacekeeper* (1983–2009). I also gathered CCPOA public relations videos and pamphlets, policy tracts, labor contracts, analyses of legislation, and memoranda. The second category consisted of empirical indicators of political action and activity—specifically, campaign contribution records and reports of lobbying expenses. As I describe in chapter 3, campaign contributions and lobbying help advocacy groups gain access to politicians and state bureaucrats. These data provided indicators of the CCPOA's political resources relative to other actors in the penal, imprisonment, and political fields. The third category of materials included reports and other documentation from the legislature (e.g., legislative analyses of bills) and state agencies involved in labor and criminal punishment (e.g., CDC and Department of Personnel Administration). Finally, I gathered electronic and print newspaper articles, which provided glimpses into particular incidents involving the CCPOA and the struggles between the union and the staffs of major newspapers in California (particularly editorialists).

The third type of research I conducted was direct observation. With the exception of my work in the senate in 2001–2002, I did not engage in participant observation. After ending my volunteership in the legislature, I attended numerous public and private events; however, I always did so as a note-taking sociologist rather than as a participant. I observed legislative events, such as press conferences and hearings on bills, issues, and the state budget. I also observed CCPOA's community service events, rallies that the union sponsored (e.g., the annual Victims' March on the Capitol), fundraisers for crime victims' groups, and a national convention for crime victims' advocates. Finally, I attended three of CCPOA's annual conventions.

While attending these events, I saw the CCPOA "in action." I witnessed how the union framed its interests during public hearings and debates, as well as how it presented crime, punishment, the nature and function of unions, and numerous other issues. I also observed how CCPOA officials promoted the union to the membership and how they socialized activists (e.g., during workshops at the CCPOA conventions). While attending union functions, I observed CCPOA activists speaking and acting much more candidly than when they performed in public. These events provided momentary views of the union (or rather its most active members and leaders) when they were "backstage" and out of the bright lights.

By conducting these three interrelated types of research, I was able to retrace the CCPOA's historical trajectory and elucidate its worldview, goals, and strategies; outline the development of the penal and imprisonment fields; and situate the union within those fields. Moreover, my mixed-method approach unearthed the CCPOA and its allies' implicit and explicit effects on criminal punishment. Official documents, such as legislative analyses and campaign finance documents, indicated the organizations' involvement and potential effects on policies, electoral races, and the like, but only interviews and direct observation provided insights into the subtle ways in which the union influences people and agencies. I witnessed the "specter of the CCPOA," seeing firsthand how it affected lawmakers and other actors. In short, it was my fieldwork in Sacramento that allowed me to see, feel, and describe the aura of the CCPOA—the invisible yet palpable social phenomenon that initially inspired this study—and nearly a decade of research, analysis, and writing has helped me make sense of it.

APPENDIX A:
CCPOA COMMITTEES[1]

Bylaws: Interprets, recommends, analyzes, and researches proposals and amendments to existing bylaws and standard operating procedures.

Correctional Counselor: Reviews statewide correctional counselor issues and reviews grievances relevant to correctional counselor issues.

Credentials: Oversees elections/ballots within the CCPOA and enforces the union's rules under the bylaws and standard operating procedures.

Executive Legal Defense: Works with the Executive Council on legal defense issues.

Federal Political Action: Develops the issues to be addressed by federal electoral candidates seeking the CCPOA's endorsement. It determines which candidates receive the CCPOA's endorsement.

Finance: Oversees the finances of the CCPOA.

Hearing: Administers hearings regarding disciplinary actions against CCPOA members.

Job Action: Assists and oversees pickets and other demonstrations.

Labor: Prepares and distributes materials and data to the board of directors to assist the chapters in representing their members in all forms of labor issues.

Legislative: Assesses and determines the CCPOA's legislative goals.

Membership: Oversees programs to increase and benefit the membership of the CCPOA. It manages the CCPOA's Scholarship Foundation, and recommends financial awards to the families of slain prison officers.

Negotiation: Conducts contract negotiations with the State of California.

Path: Monitors issues related to blood-borne pathogens and infectious diseases that concern CCPOA members.

Political Action: Develops the issues to be addressed by statewide electoral candidates seeking the CCPOA's endorsement. It determines which candidates receive CCPOA's endorsement.

Prison Review and Construction: Monitors and makes recommendations related to the planning and construction of adult and juvenile prisons.

Public Relations: Seeks to improve the public image of prison officers and the CCPOA.

Supervisory: Conducts meet-and-discuss sessions with state officials on behalf of supervisors.

Victims: Updates the board of directors on activities and issues of the victims' associations that the CCPOA supports.

APPENDIX B:
POLITICAL ACTION COMMITTEES

Local (LOPAC): The CCPOA executive council encourages local chapters to form PACs. Local chapters submit proposals to endorse and provide campaign money to candidates for local offices (e.g., district attorneys, judges, and sheriffs). The statewide PAC must approve all local endorsements and campaign contributions.

Federal (Fed-PAC): Endorses and provides campaign contributions to candidates for federal office.

Independent Expenditures (IE-PAC): Independent expenditures are payments made on behalf of candidates. They must not be coordinated with candidates' campaigns. IE-PAC funds activities on behalf of candidates in statewide elections (e.g., television and radio ads) and contributes money to political parties and campaigns for or against ballot initiatives.

Issues: Funds legal services, public relations, political consultants, polling, and campaigns for and against ballot initiatives.

Governor's Cup Invitational Golf Tournament (sponsored by the CCPOA): Makes campaign contributions to gubernatorial candidates.

Native American Peace Officers (NAPO): A joint PAC comprised of the CCPOA and several Native American tribes that have gambling interests. The NAPO PAC funds campaign contributions and independent expenditures.

Northern Alliance of Law Enforcement (NALE): Established in 1999, NALE is a joint PAC of law enforcement organizations and is sponsored by the California Union of Security Employees (CAUSE) and the CCPOA. It contributes money to statewide and local candidates.

Crime Victims United: A joint PAC of Crime Victims United of California (CVUC) and the CCPOA. It contributes money to local and statewide candidates (see chapter 4).

NOTES

CHAPTER 1

1. John Irwin, *Prisons in Turmoil* (Boston: Little, Brown and Company, 1980), chap. 2.
2. John Conrad, "Foreword," in Richard McGee, *Prisons and Politics* (Lexington, MA: Lexington Books, 1981), x.
3. Jonathan Simon, *Governing Through Crime: How the War on Crime Transformed American Democracy and Created a Culture of Fear* (New York: Oxford University Press, 2007), 151; McGee, *Prisons and Politics*; Eric Cummins, *The Rise and Fall of California's Radical Prison Movement* (Palo Alto, CA: Stanford University Press, 1994), 274.
4. California Department of Corrections and Rehabilitation, *Facts and Figures*, http://www.cdcr.ca.gov/Divisions_Boards/Adult_Operations/Facts_and_Figures.html (accessed March 9, 2009).
5. California Department of Corrections and Rehabilitation, *California Prisoners and Parolees: 2007* (Sacramento: CDCR, 2008), 32.
6. Franklin Zimring, Gordon Hawkins, and Sam Kamin, *Punishment and Democracy: Three Strikes and You're Out in California* (New York: Oxford University Press, 2001), 17. California has 38 million residents, compared to approximately 147 million for France and Germany.
7. Joan Petersilia, *Understanding California Corrections* (Berkeley: California Policy Research Center, May 2006), 1; California Department of Corrections and Rehabilitation, *Facts and Figures*.
8. Ruth Wilson Gilmore, *Golden Gulag: Prison, Surplus, Crisis, and Opposition in Globalizing California* (Berkeley: University of California Press, 2007), 10; California Department of Corrections and Rehabilitation, *Facts and Figures*.
9. Craig Haney, "Mental Health Issues in Long-Term Solitary and 'Supermax' Confinement," *Crime and Delinquency* 49, no. 1 (2003): 124–156; Lorna Rhodes, *Total Confinement: Madness and Reason in the Maximum Security Prison* (Berkeley: University of California Press, 2004).
10. Little Hoover Commission, *Putting Violence Behind Bars: Redefining the Role of California's Prisons* (Sacramento, January 18, 1994).
11. John Irwin, *The Warehouse Prison: Disposal of the New Dangerous Class* (Los Angeles: Roxbury Publishing, 2005).
12. I use the term "prison officer" rather than "prison guard" or "correctional officer" for analytical reasons. This term is specific because prison officers in California work in *prisons* and are certified peace *officers*. They do not guard prisons from those who want to break out their crime partners, as did the earliest "prison guards" in California. Moreover, the state employs these workers to maintain institutional order, not to correct prisoners.

13. Petersilia, *Understanding California Corrections*, 21.

14. See, for example, Center for Juvenile and Criminal Justice, *California Prisons* (San Francisco, 2002, report).

15. Carol Williams, "Justice Kennedy Laments the State of Prisons in California, U.S.," *Los Angeles Times* (February 4, 2004), http://latimes.com/news/local/la-me-kennedy4-2010feb04,0,1430237.story (accessed February 12, 2010).

16. Jill Stewart, "Correctional Action Plan," *Sacramento News & Review* (April 15, 2004), http://www.newsreview.com/sacramento/Content?oid=28637 (accessed June 5, 2004).

17. "State Prisons' Revolving Door: An Education in Brutality" (February 19, 2004), B12; "State Prisons' Revolving Door: Rein in the Guards' Raises" (March 10, 2004), B12; "State Prisons' Revolving Door: Put Muscle Behind Reform" (April 15, 2004), B14; "State Prisons' Revolving Door: A Starting Point for Reform" (July 2, 2004), B12.

18. Journalistic and activist writings on the CCPOA, overall, are moralistic and focus on blaming and shaming, which obstructs systematic, nuanced analysis ("The Cunning of Imperialist Reason" in Loïc Wacquant (ed.), *Pierre Bourdieu and Democratic Politics* [Cambridge: Polity Press, 2005], 182). For a prototypical example of accusatory writings on the CCPOA, see Dan Pens, "The California Prison Guards' Union: A Potent Political Interest Group," in Daniel Burton-Rose (ed.), *The Celling of America: An Inside Look at the U.S. Prison Industry* (Maine: Common Courage Press, 1998), 134–139. Scholarly writings on the CCPOA are not so moralistic; however, they point to but do not untangle the relationship between penality and the union. See, for example, Katherine Beckett, *Making Crime Pay: Law and Order in Contemporary Politics* (New York: Oxford University Press, 1997), 100; Michael Jacobson, *Downsizing Prisons: How to Reduce Crime and End Mass Incarceration* (New York: New York University Press, 2006), 67–68; and Zimring et al., *Punishment and Democracy*, 223.

19. Nelson Lichtenstein, *State of the Union: A Century of American Labor* (Princeton, NJ: Princeton University Press, 2002).

20. Mary Bosworth insightfully notes that many studies analyze California prisons and remark on the state's penal problems. "Yet, notwithstanding the frequency with which the 'Golden State' is the site of academic inquiry, it has rarely been acknowledged or explored as significant in its own right," Bosworth writes ("Review of *Golden Gulag* and *The Prison and the Gallows*," *British Journal of Criminology* 47, no. 5 [2007]: 834–837). There are two recent exceptions. Gilmore's *Golden Gulag* ties California's trajectory to changes in the state's political economy. Vanessa Barker's study, *The Politics of Imprisonment: How the Democratic Process Shapes the Way America Punishes Offenders* (New York: Oxford University Press, 2009), argues that state political institutions and traditions shape penal outcomes.

21. Jacobson, *Downsizing Prisons*, 87–91.

22. Lydia Chàvez, *The Color Bind: California's Battle to End Affirmative Action* (Berkeley: University of California Press, 1998); Isaac Martin, *The Permanent Tax Revolt: How the Property Tax Transformed American Politics* (Palo Alto, CA: Stanford University Press, 2008); Peter Schrag, *Paradise Lost: California's Experience: America's Future* (Berkeley: University of California Press, 1999); Peter Schrag, *California: America's High-Stakes Experiment* (Berkeley: University of California Press, 2006).

23. Irwin, *Prisons in Turmoil*; Chrysanthi S. Leon, "Compulsion and Control: Sex Crime and Criminal Justice Policy in California, 1930–2007" (PhD dissertation,

University of California, Berkeley, 2004); Candace McCoy, *Politics and Plea Bargaining: Victims' Rights in California* (Philadelphia: University of Pennsylvania Press, 1993); Zimring et al., *Punishment and Democracy*.

24. Stanley Aronowitz, *From the Ashes of Old* (New York: Basic Books, 1998); Paul Johnston, *Success While Others Fail* (Ithaca, NY: ILR, 1994); Steven Lopez, *Reorganizing the Rust Belt* (Berkeley: University of California Press, 2004).

25. Johnston, *Success While Others Fail*, 11–14.

26. William J. Sabol, Heather C. West, and Matthew Cooper, *Prisoners in 2008*, NCJ 228417 (Washington, DC:, Bureau of Justice Statistics, 2009).

27. Pew Center on the States, *One in 100: Behind Bars in America 2008* (Washington, DC: Pew Center on the States, 2008).

28. Bruce Western, *Punishment and Inequality in America* (New York: Russell Sage Foundation, 2006), 16.

29. Jacobson, *Downsizing Prisons*; Western, *Punishment and Inequality*.

30. Francis A. Allen, *Decline of the Rehabilitative Ideal: Penal Policy and Social Purpose* (New Haven, CT: Yale University Press, 1981); David Garland, *The Culture of Control: Crime and Social Order in Contemporary Society* (Chicago: University of Chicago Press, 2001).

31. Malcolm Feeley and Jonathan Simon, "The New Penology: Notes on the Emerging Strategy of Corrections and its Implications," *Criminology* 30, no. 4 (1992): 449–474.

32. Irwin, *The Warehouse Prison*; Mona Lynch, *Sunbelt Justice: Arizona and the Transformation of American Punishment* (Palo Alto, CA: Stanford University Press, 2010), 3; James E. Robertson, "Houses of the Dead: Warehouse Prisons, Paradigm Change, and the Supreme Court," *Houston Law Review* 34 (1997): 1003–1063. A 2004 Bureau of Justice Statistics report noted, "Over three-fourths of the States spent 96% or more of prison funds on current operations such as salaries, wages, benefits, supplies, maintenance, and contractual services" (James J. Stephan, *State Prison Expenditures, 2001*, NCJ 202949 [Washington, DC: Bureau of Justice Statistics, 2004]).

33. The Sentencing Project, "Incarceration and Crime: A Complex Relationship" (Washington, DC: The Sentencing Project, 2005).

34. Beckett, *Making Crime Pay*. See also Katherine Beckett and Theodore Sasson, *The Politics of Injustice: Crime and Punishment in America* (Thousand Oaks, CA: Pine Forge Press, 2000); Dario Melossi, "Gazette of Morality and Social Whip: Punishment, Hegemony, and the Case of the USA, 1972–1992," *Social & Legal Studies* 2 (1993): 259–279.

35. On the relationship between American's punitive turn and "late modernity," see Garland, *The Culture of Control*; Jock Young, *The Exclusive Society: Social Exclusion, Crime and Difference in Late Modernity* (New York: Sage, 1999). International comparative studies show that the legal and political institutions of the United States allow public sentiment and political opportunism to directly shape penal outcomes. Unlike the United States, countries like England and Germany have institutional arrangements (e.g., professional commissions and governmental agencies) that insulate critical penal decisions from popular emotional outbursts and political opportunism while investing significant authority in the hands of "experts" such as legal scholars and state bureaucrats. Differences in political and legal institutions, then, help explain why the United States has more punitive penal policies and a much higher rate of incarceration than other Western industrial democracies. Marie Gottschalk, *The Prison and the Gallows: The Politics of Mass Incarceration in America* (New York: Cambridge University Press, 2006);

Joachim Savelsberg, "Knowledge, Domination, and Criminal Punishment," *The American Journal of Sociology* 99, no. 4 (1994): 911–943; John Sutton, "Imprisonment and Social Classification in Five Common-Law Democracies, 1955–1985," *The American Journal of Sociology* 106, no. 2 (2000): 350–386; James Q. Whitman, *Harsh Justice: Criminal Punishment and the Widening Divide between America and Europe* (New York: Oxford University Press, 2003); Zimring et al., *Punishment and Democracy*.

36. Loïc Wacquant, "Deadly Symbiosis: When Ghetto and Prison Meet and Merge," *Punishment & Society* 3, no. 1 (2001): 95–133); Donald Braman, *Doing Time on the Outside: Incarceration and Family Life in Urban America* (Ann Arbor: University of Michigan Press, 2007), chaps. 3 and 4; Michael Tonry, *Malign Neglect: Race, Crime, and Punishment in America* (New York: Oxford University Press, 1996); Elijah Anderson, *Code of the Street: Decency, Violence, and the Moral Life of the Inner City* (New York: W.W. Norton & Company, 1999).

37. Franklin Zimring and Gordon Hawkins noted extensive state-level variation in imprisonment nearly twenty years ago: "There is in fact more diversity in rates of imprisonment among the cross section of American states than one finds when a comparison is drawn across the whole of Western Europe" (*The Scale of Imprisonment* [Chicago: University of Chicago Press, 1991], 150). Other indicators of state-level variation in punitiveness include imprisonment risk, length of prison terms, parole revocation rates, spending on punishment, and punitive policies. See, respectively, Natasha Frost, "The Mismeasure of Punishment: Alternative Measures of Punitiveness and Their (Substantial) Consequences," *Punishment & Society* 10, no. 3 (2008): 277–300; Jacobson, *Downsizing Prisons*; David Jacobs and Ronald Helms, "Collective Outbursts, Politics, and Punitive Resources: Toward a Political Sociology of Spending on Social Control," *Social Forces* 77, no. 4 (1999): 1497–1523); Zimring et al., *Punishment and Democracy*.

38. Barker, *The Politics of Imprisonment*; Gilmore, *Golden Gulag*; Lynch, *Sunbelt Justice*; Robert Perkinson, *Texas Tough: The Rise of America's Prison Empire* (New York: Metropolitan Books, 2010).

39. I use the terms "interest group" and "advocacy group" interchangeably. Following Clive Thomas and Ronald J. Hrbrenar, I define interest group as "an association of individuals or organizations or a public or private institution that, on the basis of one or more shared concerns, attempts to influence pubic policy in its favor" (quoted in Lisa Miller, *The Perils of Federalism* [New York: Oxford University Press, 2008], 22). This definition includes single-issue organizations (e.g., Mothers Against Drunk Driving and Families Against Mandatory Minimums), labor unions, professional associations, government agencies (e.g., Department of Corrections), law firms and associations (e.g., Prison Law Office), religious groups, private sector businesses and lobby organizations, and civil liberties groups (Miller, *The Perils of Federalism*, 23–25).

40. "The New Politics of Criminal Justice: Of 'Three Strikes,' Truth-in-Sentencing, and Megan's Laws," *Perspectives on Crime and Justice: 1999–2000*, Lecture Series 4 (Washington, DC: National Institute of Justice, March 2001), 8.

41. Michael Campbell, "Agents of Change: Law Enforcement, Prisons, and Politics in Texas and California" (PhD dissertation, University of California, Irvine, 2009); Lynch, *Sunbelt Justice*; Miller, *Perils of Federalism*; Perkinson, *Texas Tough*; Heather Schoenfeld, "The Politics of Prison Growth: From Chain Gangs to Work Release Centers and Supermax Prisons, Florida, 1955–2000" (PhD dissertation, Northwestern University, 2009). Political scientist Lisa Miller also shows that single-issue lobbies

and criminal justice actors are important actors in shaping penal outcomes at the federal level (*Perils of Freedom*, chapter 3); see also Gottschalk, *Prison and the Gallows*.

42. Bourdieu's perspective focuses attention on the *relations* between relatively bounded social environments or microcosms (what he calls *fields*) and agents (individuals, groups, and organizations). I employ Bourdieu's theoretical framework because it directs our attention to the assorted ways in which fields and agents continually shape each other in a recursive or dialectical manner. Moreover, Bourdieu contends that fields are objective structures with their own internal logic, and they refract economic, political, and cultural national and international trends as well as external events (e.g., wars), helping us understand why such trends and events have varying effects across geographical regions and over time. Bourdieu's insistence that fields are objective structures with *magnetic force* distinguishes his notion of field from kindred concepts such as "policy domain" or "policy environment." (For an overview of the use of these related concepts see Frank R. Baumgartner and Beth L. Leech, *Basic Interests: The Importance of Groups in Politics and in Political Sciences* [Princeton, NJ: Princeton University Press, 1998].) In short, Bourdieu offers a midrange analytical strategy that pushes the researcher to examine how particular fields (rather than "society," "state," "nation," etc.) shape social phenomena. It also encourages us to investigate how agents within and outside of fields affect the composition and orientation of fields. In doing so, it provides an opportunity for a richer understanding of the effects interest groups and other actors have on public policy. For a concise yet thorough overview of Bourdieu's sociological perspective, see Pierre Bourdieu and Loïc Wacquant, *An Invitation to Reflexive Sociology* (Chicago: University of Chicago Press, 1992).

43. The metaphor of a sporting field is not meant to suggest that the penal field is an actual physical space. Unlike a sporting field, there is no place that we can point to that is the penal field. The penal field is an invisible structure; nevertheless, agents in the penal field (like those on a sporting field) are subject to its rules and regularities and affected by the movements of other agents in the field.

44. The bureaucratic field is the social space of state bureaucracies and actors (bureaucrats) responsible for implementing governmental policies. The bureaucracies (e.g., department of education, department of corrections, etc.) are in the executive branch and under the direction of the governor—although the legislature allocates funding for the bureaucracies through the budget process. On the concept of the bureaucratic field, see Pierre Bourdieu, *Practical Reason* (Palo Alto, CA: Stanford University Press, 1998), chap. 3 ("Rethinking the State: Genesis and Structure of the Bureaucratic Field").

45. I use the terms "agents," "actors," and "players" synonymously.

46. Pierre Bourdieu, *Sociology in Question* (New York: Sage, 1995), 73. On the tendency of subordinate agents to challenge and dominant agents to preserve the distribution of capital (and thus the structure of the field), see Bourdieu and Wacquant, *An Invitation to Reflexive Sociology*, 108–109, and Pierre Bourdieu, *Language and Symbolic Power* (Cambridge, MA: Harvard University Press, 1999), chap. 5.

47. Bourdieu explains that the actions available to a player in a field, as well as the actions the player takes, are affected by the player's *habitus*, socially constituted "schemes of perception, appreciation, and action" (Pierre Bourdieu, *Pascalian Meditations* [Palo Alto, CA: Stanford University Press, 1997], 138). Therefore Bourdieu is not a strict structuralist, for a player's position in the social structure (or field) does not solely determine the players' actions.

48. I adopted the concept "punitive segregation" from David Garland ("The Culture of High Crime Societies: Some Preconditions of Recent 'Law and Order' Policies," *British Journal of Criminology* 40 [2000]: 347–375), 350.

49. Bourdieu and Wacquant, *Invitation to Reflexive Sociology*, 17.

CHAPTER 2

1. Interview, Steve Fournier, August 11, 2004.

2. Interview, Larry Corby, March 12, 2004.

3. Interview, Tommy Marich, July 7, 2004. Don Novey, the first president of the CCPOA, also refers to the CCOA as "just a good old boys club" (John Hurst, "The Big House that Don Novey Built," *Los Angeles Times*, February 6, 1994, 16).

4. Shelly Bookspan, *A Germ of Goodness: The California State Prison System, 1851–1944* (Lincoln: University of Nebraska Press, 1991); Heather Jane McCarty, "From Con-Boss to Gang Lord: The Transformation of Social Relations in California Prisons, 1943–1983" (PhD dissertation, University of California, Berkeley, 2004).

5. John Irwin, *Prisons In Turmoil* (Boston: Little, Brown and Company, 1980), chap. 1.

6. Bookspan, *A Germ of Goodness*, 119.

7. For discussions of the history and defining features of the rehabilitative ideal, see Francis Allen, *The Decline of the Rehabilitative Ideal: Penal Policy and Social Purpose* (New Haven, CT: Yale University Press, 1981); and Francis Cullen and Karen Gilbert, *Reaffirming Rehabilitation* (Cincinnati, OH: Anderson Publishing, 1982).

8. Bookspan, *A Germ of Goodness*, 112.

9. For detailed discussions of "con bosses" and their function in the "inmate society" in the first half of the twentieth century, see McCarty, "From Con-Boss," chap. 2; Donald Clemmer, *The Prison Community* (New York: Rinehart, 1958); and Gresham Sykes, *The Society of Captives: A Study of a Maximum Security Prison* (Princeton, NJ: Princeton University Press, 1971). Con bosses were integral to the informal system of "mutual accommodations," in which powerful prisoners received favors from prison staff for helping to keep the peace in prisons. Favors provided for con bosses included cushy jobs, contraband, and permission to roam freely inside the prisons (and in some cases, outside of the prisons).

10. McCarty, "From Con-Boss," 19.

11. Bookspan, *A Germ of Goodness*, 116.

12. McCarty, "From Con-Boss," 20–21.

13. McGee was director of the CDC from 1944 until 1961. In 1961 the state established the Youth and Adult Correctional Agency (YACA), an umbrella agency that included the CDC, California Youth Authority, and Adult Authority. McGee served as the secretary of YACA from 1961 until 1967. On McGee's efforts to create bureaucratic rationalization in the state's prison and parole systems, see Jonathan Simon, *Poor Discipline: Parole and the Social Control of the Underclass, 1890–1990* (Chicago: University of Chicago Press, 1993), chapter 3.

14. Bookspan, *A Germ of Goodness*, 116.

15. John Dilulio, *Governing Prisons* (New York: Free Press, 1987), 189.

16. McCarty, "From Con-Boss"; Richard McGee, *Prisons and Politics* (Lexington, MA: Lexington Books, 1981); Jonathan Simon, *Poor Discipline*. Between 1944 and 1957, the Adult Authority was an autonomous agency with control over parole policy. The California Department of Corrections gained authority over parole policy in 1957 (Simon, *Poor Discipline*, 74). About the prominence of experts and research in parole policy, Simon concludes, "No other correctional program had

ever committed itself to the kind of research effort that was made during the 1950s and 1960s in California (p. 94).

17. Irwin, *Prisons in Turmoil*.
18. California Department of Corrections, *Biennial Report 1959–1960* (Sacramento: CDC, 1961), 20.
19. Irwin, *Prisons in Turmoil*. Numerous prison officers did participate in one rehabilitative activity: group counseling. When the CDC administrators had difficulty recruiting "free staff" to facilitate group therapy sessions, they had prison officers lead the sessions. McCarty writes, "The use of custody staff as counselors in the group therapy program became so commonplace that in October of 1957 the specifications for Correctional Officer, Sergeant, Captain and Lieutenant were revised to include under the typical tasks job description the following language: 'May participate as leaders in group counseling of inmates'" (McCarty, "From Con-Boss," 69).
20. California Department of Corrections, *Management Survey* (Sacramento: CDC, 1972), 37.
21. California Department of Corrections, *Management Survey*, 39, 105.
22. Theodore Davidson, *Chicano Prisoners: The Key to San Quentin* (New York: Holt, Rinehart, and Winston, 1974), 29.
23. Irwin, *Prisons in Turmoil*, 131–132. Erving Goffman and David Rothman, respectively, discuss the seemingly inherent tensions that exist between treatment and custody functions, as well as between treatment and custody personnel. Erving Goffman, *Asylums* (New York: Anchor Books, 1961); David Rothman, *Conscience and Convenience* (New York: Aldine de Gruyter, 2002).
24. John Irwin, *Rogue* (unpublished memoir), 270–271.
25. Davidson, *Chicano Prisoners*, chap. 3; McCarty, "From Con-Boss"; Irwin, *Prisons in Turmoil*; Erik Olin Wright, *The Politics of Punishment* (New York: Harper & Row, 1973).
26. Joan Petersilia, *When Prisoners Come Home* (New York: Oxford University Press, 2003), 262–263.
27. Irwin argues that rehabilitation programs (particularly education programs) produced a politicized "prison intelligentsia." Prisoner-students explored big ideas and "serious literature," which helped them become critical thinkers and "see through things," including the foundational premise of the 1950s "medical model" of rehabilitation, which concluded that convicts were socially and psychologically "sick." The prison intellectuals "contributed heavily to the great disillusionment with and the eventual dismantling of the rehabilitative ideal" (Irwin, *Rogue*, 63–65). In his autobiography, Malcolm X describes his transformation in prison from street hood to a "prison intellectual" (Alex Haley and Malcolm X, *The Autobiography of Malcolm X* [New York: Ballantine Books, 1973]).
28. Cummins, *The Rise and Fall of California's Radical Prison Movement* (Palo Alto, CA: Stanford University Press, 1994), 24.
29. Irwin, *Prisons in Turmoil*, 69–70.
30. James Jacobs, "The Prisoners' Rights Movement and Its Impacts," *New Perspectives and Imprisonment* (New York: Cornell University Press, 1983), 37.
31. Malcolm Feeley and Edward Rubin, *Judicial Policy Making and the Modern State* (New York: Cambridge University Press, 1998), 13.
32. Feeley and Rubin, *Judicial Policy Making*, 13.
33. Irwin, *Prisons in Turmoil*, 70–72.
34. Ibid., 134, 183–184.
35. Cummins, *The Rise and Fall*, 164, emphasis added.

36. Ibid., 165.
37. Ibid., 168.
38. Ibid., 178.
39. Ibid., 209.
40. Ibid., 226.
41. The BGF became one of the four main prison gangs in California. The other three were the white supremacist Aryan Brotherhood and two Mexican gangs: the Mexican Mafia and the Nuestra Familia. Obviously the growth of prison gangs greatly threatened officers' safety and peace of mind. The growing influence of the gangs undoubtedly contributed to officers' desire for a union, which ideally would enhance officers' safety and collective authority behind bars (Christian Parenti, *Lockdown America: Police and Prisons in the Age of Crisis* [New York: Verso, 1999], 198; McCarty, "From Con-Boss," chap. 5).
42. Joint Legislative Committee on Prison Construction and Operations, *Violence at Folsom Prison: Causes, Possible Solutions* (Sacramento, 1985), A-12.
43. McCarty, "From Con-Boss," 229. Violence against staff occurred in other states too. For example, in the wake of George Jackson's death, prisoners at Attica State Prison in New York took over the institution between September 9 and 13, 1971. During the revolt, 11 prison staff and 32 prisoners were killed (Tom Wicker, *A Time to Die: The Attica Prison Revolt* [Lincoln: University of Nebraska Press, 1994]).
44. Irwin, *Prisons in Turmoil*, 133–134, emphasis added.
45. Cummins, *The Rise and Fall*, 130.
46. Ibid., 190.
47. Ibid.
48. Robert Montilla, *Prison Employee Unionism: Management Guide for Correctional Administrators* (Washington, DC: U.S. Department of Justice, January 1978), 7. On page 8, Montilla defines "meet and confer" as "a formalized process whereby correctional administrators and union representatives meet to discuss employee working conditions, benefits, organizational and operational procedures, and other matters affecting employees. A meeting agenda is prepared and minutes are maintained. In addition to the communications value of such meetings, management is expected to make some affirmative response to union requests. However, there is no procedure to resolve disputes by involvement of third parties, and no contracts result from this process."
49. Jessica Mitford, *Kind and Unusual Punishment* (New York: Vintage Books, 1974), 218.
50. McCarty, "From Con-Boss," 230.
51. Tim Findley, "Prison To Let Some Insiders In," *San Francisco Chronicle*, August 26, 1971, 1.
52. *Los Angeles Times*, "13 Guards Quit San Quentin in Wake of Killings," August 30, 1971, 3.
53. Tim Findley, "The Bitter Guards," *San Francisco Chronicle*, August 30, 1971, 18.
54. *San Francisco Chronicle*, "Guards' Proposal on Rebel Convicts," September 20, 1971, 5.
55. Cummins, *The Rise and Fall*, 231.
56. Mitford, *Kind and Unusual Punishment*, 218. In 1972 the California Supreme Court ruled that the death penalty violated the state constitution, which forbids cruel and unusual punishment. The California legislature reinstated the death penalty in 1977, with modifications to pass muster with the state's Supreme Court.
57. Cummins, *The Rise and Fall*, 256.
58. Ibid.

59. McCarty, "From Con-Boss," 277–278.
60. Cummins, *The Rise and Fall*, 256.
61. Ibid.
62. Starting in the 1960s and continuing through today, "law and order" has indicated a preference for punitive segregation. There are many ways to conceive of and achieve "law and order." The advocates of "law and order," however, argue that severe penal sanctions for crime are needed to uphold the law and produce public order. As used in this book, "law and order" refers to the particularly punitive approach to crime control that the CCPOA and its allies have promoted. I also use the terms "tough on crime" and "punitive segregation" as shorthand for this approach.
63. McCarty, "From Con-Boss," 292.
64. Ibid., 294.
65. Ibid., 296.
66. Ibid., 293.
67. Cummins, *The Rise and Fall*, 249.
68. Allen, *Decline of the Rehabilitative Ideal*.
69. American Friends Service Committee, *Struggle for Justice* (Philadelphia: American Friends Service Committee, 1971).
70. The report found that "38 percent of the correctional officers have been physically assaulted at least once during their career. In one institution the assault rate was nearly 50 percent. Of the 38 percent, almost one-third had been the victims of 3 to 5 assaults with battery, 7 percent had sustained 6 to 10 assaults with battery, and 8 percent had 11 to more than 20 assaults with battery" (Joint Legislative Audit Committee, *An Operational Audit of California Correctional Institutions* [Sacramento: Office of the Auditor General, March 14, 1977], 7).
71. California was not the first state to provide these rights to public employees. Twenty-four other states had laws on the books that provided state workers collective bargaining rights (Montilla, *Management Guide*, 7).
72. Bookspan, *A Germ of Goodness*, 33.
73. Edward Bunker, *Education of a Felon* (New York: St. Martin's Press, 2000), 248. Historian Shelly Bookspan describes Folsom's early history in similar terms (*A Germ of Goodness*, chap. 2).
74. Ray Johnson (with Mona McCormick), *Too Dangerous to be at Large* (New York: The New York Times Book Co., 1975), 77.
75. Dilulio, *Governing Prisons*, 138.
76. Numerous prison officers referred to the "Folsom Way" during my field research. A former long-time warden of a state prison in California who asked to remain anonymous told me that it is common knowledge in the CDC that "There's the CDC way, the corrections way, and the Folsom way."
77. Senate Rules Committee, hearing transcript (Sacramento: California Senate, February 20, 1985).
78. Interview, Steve Fournier, August 11, 2004.
79. Joint Legislative Audit Committee, *An Operational Audit*.
80. Jane Chapman and coauthors write, "In 1974, the [California] Department of Corrections initiated a carefully developed, step-by-step plan to open all 'posts' in male institutions to women officers, thus providing them with the breadth of work experience necessary to qualify for promotion 'up-through-the-ranks'" (*Women Employed in Corrections* [Washington, DC: Government Printing Office, 1983], 4).
81. Laura Mecoy, "Sex Abuse at Folsom Prison, Women Charge," *Sacramento Bee*, February 21, 1985, A1.

82. Barbara Owen, *The Reproduction of Social Control: A Study of Prison Workers at San Quentin* (New York: Praeger, 1988), 61.

83. Ibid., 65.

84. In her study of San Quentin, Owen wrote: "Many female officers report a steady amount of harassment from both the prisoners and the staff" (*Reproduction of Social Control*, 65). In the early to mid-1980s, the CDC and legislature conducted five separate investigations at Folsom in response to allegations made by female officers regarding sexual harassment (Laura Mecoy, "Folsom Prison Gets 5th Sex-Bias Probe, Senate Committee Latest to Investigate," *Sacramento Bee*, February 28, 1985, A16).

85. See Catherine Mackinnon's classic, *Sexual Harassment of Working Women: A Case of Sex Discrimination* (New Haven, CT: Yale University Press, 1979); Susan Martin and Nancy Jurik, *Doing Justice, Doing Gender* (Thousand Oaks, CA: Sage, 1996).

86. Loïc Wacquant correctly argues that transformations in welfare and penality in the last three to four decades signify and fuel retrenchment from the prototypically feminine New Deal state to the prototypically masculine neoliberal state (*Punishing the Poor: The Neoliberal Government of Social Insecurity* [Durham, NC: Duke University Press, 2009]). I argue that the CCPOA and other agents in California have factored centrally in this remasculinizing of the state.

87. Interview, Steve Fournier, August 11, 2004.

88. Folsom chapter of the California Correctional Officers Association (Folsom CCOA), *The Granite* 1, no. 22 (January/February 1981), 4.

89. *San Francisco Chronicle*, "Prison Guard Suit Cites Racial Ruling," September 18, 1976, 2.

90. *The Granite* 1, no. 4 (April 1979), 15.

91. *The Granite* 1, no. 8 (September/October 1979), 20–21.

92. Labor historian Nelson Lichtenstein notes that affirmative action disrupted existing seniority systems, which upset many workers. "Seniority was part of the moral economy of the work regime; it represented the most important 'property' interest a worker held in his job" (*State of the Union: A Century of American Labor* [Princeton, NJ: Princeton University Press, 2002], 206). Like workers in other industries, prison officers believed that they could move up the occupational ladder by accruing years on the job. Because affirmative action reportedly disrupted the seniority system, workers felt that this one sure way of career advancement no longer existed.

93. John Dilulio characterizes 1975–1983 as a period of "organizational drift" in the CDC. Jiro Enomoto and Ruth Rushen, the CDC directors in that period, "were correctional neophytes who lacked their predecessor's [Raymond Procunier] charisma and failed to develop any compensating levers of executive leadership" (Dilulio, *Governing Prisons*, 133).

94. *The Granite* 1, no. 11 (January 1980), 22.

95. *The Granite* 1, no. 25 (August 1981), 9.

96. During my fieldwork, CCPOA activists consistently complained that prison officials, policymakers, and academics with advanced educational credentials discounted and looked down upon them. This feeling at least partially accounts for the CCPOA's anti-intellectualism and antipathy toward academics.

97. *The Granite* 1, no. 12 (February 1980), 8.

98. *The Granite* 1, no. 13 (March 1980), 8.

99. *The Granite* 1, no. 20 (October/November 1980), 19.

100. Interview, Jeff Thompson, July 1, 2004.

101. *The Granite* 1, no. 23 (May 1981), 3.
102. Ibid., 13.
103. Interview, Larry Corby, March 12, 2004.
104. Interview, Jeff Thompson, July 1, 2004.
105. *The Granite* 1, no. 22 (January/February 1981), 23, original in all caps.
106. *The Granite* 1, no. 15 (May 1980), 19.
107. *The Granite* 1, no. 17 (July 1980), 14–15.
108. Interview, Steve Fournier, August 11, 2004.
109. *The Granite*, 1, no. 22 (January/February 1981).
110. Interview, Larry Corby, March 12, 2004.
111. Interview, Jeff Thompson, July 1, 2004.
112. Interview, Steve Fournier, August 11, 2004.

CHAPTER 3

1. For a clear and thorough discussion of "political opportunity structure" and social movement theory, see Doug McAdam, John McCarthy, and Mayer Zald (eds.), *Comparative Perspectives on Social Movements: Political Opportunities, Mobilizing Structures, and Cultural Framings* (New York: Cambridge University Press, 1996).
2. CCPOA leaders do not describe their strategy as "politically realistic," nor do they identify these three tenets as the heart of their strategy. I distilled the concept of "politically realistic unionism" and isolated the three tenets to characterize the essence of the union's strategy.
3. Eric Cummins, *The Rise and Fall of California's Radical Prison Movement* (Palo Alto, CA: Stanford University Press, 1994), 253. In 1976 the California Legislature changed Penal Code Section 1170 to make punishment the purpose of imprisonment.
4. Cummins, *The Rise and the Fall*, chaps. 9 and 10.
5. Candace McCoy, *Politics and Plea Bargaining: Victims' Rights in California* (Philadelphia: University of Pennsylvania Press, 1993), 24.
6. Ibid., 24–25.
7. Ibid., 22. Individual crime victims (and friends and families of crime victims) and small, politically inconsequential victims' rights groups participated in the campaign for Proposition 8; however, they did not spearhead the measure or contribute significantly to its passage. Punitive-oriented crime victims' organizations did not become significant political players in California until the 1990s.
8. Heather Jane McCarty, "From Con-Boss to Gang Lord: The Transformation of Social Relations in California Prisons, 1943–1983" (PhD dissertation, University of California, Berkeley, 2004), 324.
9. Joan Petersilia, "Crime and Punishment in California: Full Cells, Empty Pockets, and Questionable Benefits," in *Urban America: Policy Choices for Los Angeles and the Nation*, eds. James Steinberg, David Lyon, and Mary Vaiana (Santa Monica, CA: Rand, 1992), 157–205.
10. California Department of Corrections, *Newscam* 13, no. 3 (May 1981), 3.
11. McCarty, "From Con-Boss," 327–328.
12. Ibid., 324.
13. Ibid.
14. Richard Simpson, *Jailhouse Blues: Hard Time for County Taxpayers: A Study of Rising County Costs of Incarceration* (Sacramento: California Counties Foundation, 1991); Petersilia, "Crime and Punishment in California," 5–6.
15. Petersilia, "Crime and Punishment in California;" Franklin Zimring and Gordon Hawkins, *Prison Population and Criminal Justice Policy in California* (Berkeley, CA: Institute of Governmental Studies, 1992).

16. Zimring and Hawkins, *Prison Population and Criminal Justice Policy in California*.
17. California Department of Corrections, *Newscam* 9, no. 6 (November–December 1981), 2. A report by the independent, nonpartisan Little Hoover Commission noted, "Judges in 1975 sentenced 5 percent of the felony offenders to state prison; in 1992 they were sending 22 percent. The courts in 1975 sentenced 40 percent of felony convictions to probation with a jail term first; by 1992 the figure had risen to 61 percent" (Little Hoover Commission, *Putting Violence Behind Bars: Redefining the Role of California's Prisons*, Report #124 [Sacramento: Little Hoover Commission, January 1994], http://www.lhc.ca.gov/lhcdir/124rp.html [accessed April 10, 2006]).
18. Center for Juvenile and Criminal Justice, "California Prisons" (San Francisco: Center for Juvenile and Criminal Justice, May 17, 2002), II-4.
19. Legislative Analyst's Office, *Correctional Officer Pay, Benefits, and Labor Relations* (Sacramento: Legislative Analyst's Office, February 7, 2008), 4.
20. Center for Juvenile and Criminal Justice, "California Prisons," II-3. CCPOA officials announced at the union's 2006 membership convention that the organization's budget was $26 million for 2006.
21. Field notes, CCPOA 2004 Convention, August 31, 2004.
22. California Statewide Law Enforcement Association, "CSLEA Government Affairs Staff & Consultants," http://www.cslea.com/govt_staff.asp (accessed July 3, 2009).
23. Interview, Joe Bauman, July 3, 2009.
24. *The Reproduction of Social Control: A Study of Prison Workers at San Quentin* (New York: Praeger, 1988), 56.
25. Interview, Jeff Thompson, July 1, 2004.
26. The strength of public workers' unions "rests chiefly on political-organizational resources: first, legal rights, organizational status, and established procedures; second, strategic alliances within the shifting political universe of the public agency, including clients, constituents, and other participants in that political universe; third, forms of voice that can help mobilize new organizations, build or prevent alliances, and, by framing and appealing to 'the public interest,' put a potent political edge on the workers' demands" (Paul Johnston, *Success While Others Fail: Social Movement Unionism and the Public Workplace* [Ithaca, NY: ILR Press, 1994], 11).
27. Saul Alinsky, *Rules for Radicals: A Pragmatic Primer for Realistic Radicals* (New York: Vintage Books, 1971), 12.
28. Frank Baumgartner and Beth Leech, *Basic Instincts: The Importance of Groups in Politics and in Political Science* (Princeton, NJ: Princeton University Press, 1998), 52–53.
29. I learned of the link between the CCPOA's politics and Alinsky during back-to-back seminars at CCPOA's 2004 membership convention in Reno, Nevada. The seminars were called "Police, Power, and Organization" and "Politics and Confrontation." Ronald G. DeLord led both of the seminars. DeLord, a former police officer, is president of the Combined Law Enforcement Associations of Texas (CLEAT). CLEAT is a 15,000-member statewide police labor organization that "provides legal assistance, labor relations, political action, insurance programs and legislative representation to its members." He is also "the president and co-founder of the *Police and Fire Labor Institute*. The institute provides leadership training to police and fire labor officials. Their philosophy is Saul Alinsky's, 'Change comes from power, and power comes from organization'" (Ronald G. DeLord, "Police, Power, and Organization" [seminar packet, August 30, 2004], 1).

DeLord is also the coauthor of several books, including *Police Association Power, Politics and Confrontation: A Guide for the Successful Police Labor Leader* (Springfield, IL: Charles C. Thomas, 1997). I should note that CCPOA leaders did not indicate to me that Alinsky influenced them. This is not important for my analysis—I am simply arguing that the union's strategy reflects Alinsky's core principles about politics.

30. Dan Morain, "Guards Union Spreads Its Wealth," *Los Angeles Times*, May 20, 2004, A1.
31. California Far Political Practices Commission, "Big Money Talks" (Sacramento: California Fair Political Practices Commission, March 2010), 41.
32. Jenifer Warren, "When He Speaks, They Listen," *Los Angeles Times*, August 21, 2000, A1.
33. Morain, "Guards Union Spreads Its Wealth," A1.
34. In 2003 the Pechanga Band of Lucieno Indians was the "largest spender on state politics" (Morain, "Guards Union Spreads Its Wealth," A1).
35. California Far Political Practices Commission, "Big Money Talks," 42.
36. Baumgartner and Leech, *Basic Interests*, chap. 2.
37. Bruce Cain and Thad Kousser, *Adapting to Term Limits: Recent Experiences and New Directions* (San Francisco: Public Policy Institute of California, 2004), 17.
38. Craig Brown started working for the CCPOA in 1999.
39. The federal government forbids ex-government officials from lobbying their former agencies, but California allows former officials, such as Brown, to lobby their ex-employer (Teresa Watanabe, "Official Launched Lobbying Career When He Quit State Prison Post," *San Jose Mercury News*, November 16, 1987, A1).
40. California Far Political Practices Commission, "Big Money Talks," 41.
41. Stephen Green, "The Changing of the Guard," *Sacramento Bee*, March 6, 1989, A1.
42. Between 2000 and 2010, the California Teachers Association was the biggest contributor among advocacy groups to the California Democratic Party, giving the political organization more than $6.5 million (California Far Political Practices Commission, "Big Money Talks," 12).
43. CCPOA, *Constitution, Bylaws and Standard Operating Procedures* (Sacramento: CCPOA, August 2004), 4–5.
44. In the 1997–1998 and 1999–2000 election cycles, about two-thirds of the CCPOA's money went to Democrats, who held (and still hold) large majorities in both houses, and about one-third went to Republicans (Common Cause, "Investment Patterns of the Top Ten Contributors" [Washington, DC: Common Cause, 2002]).
45. California Far Political Practices Commission, "Big Money Talks," 41.
46. Interview, Steve Fournier, August 11, 2004.
47. Interview, Jeff Thompson, July 1, 2004.
48. Morain, "Guards Union Spreads Its Wealth," A1.
49. CCPOA, "Win, Lose, or Draw—The Important Thing Is To Be a Player," *Peacekeeper* 11, no. 1 (January/February 1993), 17.
50. Interview, Jeff Thompson, July 1, 2004.
51. Andy Furillo, "Support of Guards Pivotal, Lucrative," *Sacramento Bee*, August 6, 2006, http://www.sacbee.com/content/politics/story/14289443p-15116918c.html (accessed August 8, 2006).
52. California redraws its political districts every ten years. In 1980 and 2000 the state legislature redrew the districts. In 1990 the California Supreme Court redrew the districts because the legislature and governor could not reach an

agreement. Predictably, incumbent legislators redrew the boundaries to benefit themselves and their respective political party, therefore the vast majority of districts were "safe" (noncompetitive). In the 2004 election, not a single assembly or senate seat changed parties. The political districts that the court redrew were far more competitive than those composed by politicians (Common Cause, "Designer Districts: Safe Seats Tailor Made for Incumbents" [Washington, DC: Common Cause, April 2005]).

53. California Secretary of State, "General Election—November 7, 2006," http://www.vote.ss.ca.gov/Returns/stasm/all.htm (accessed November 8, 2006); CCPOA, "CCPOA Legislative Endorsements 2006," http://www.ccpoanet.org (accessed November 8, 2006).

54. Interview, Jeff Thompson, July 1, 2004.

55. John Hurst, "The Big House that Don Novey Built," *Los Angeles Times*, February 6, 1994, 16.

56. Fair Political Practices Commission, "State Contribution Limits (History and Amounts)" (Sacramento: Fair Political Practices Commission, October 2008). Every two years the Fair Political Practices Commission adjusts the limits on contributions. In 2009 PACs could contribute $7,800 for legislative races, $12,900 for statewide offices, and $25,900 for governor (Fair Political Practices Commission, "California Contribution Limits" [Sacramento: Fair Political Practices Commission, January 12, 2009]).

57. Charles H. Bell, "California Campaign Finance and Lobbying Regulation," http://www.bmhlaw.com/lawsum.htm (accessed November 20, 2006); Fair Political Practices Commission, "Gift and Contribution Limits Adjusted," http://www.fppc.ca.gov/index.htm (accessed November 20, 2006).

58. Interview, Jeff Thompson, July 1, 2004.

59. For example, former U.S. senator and presidential candidate Bill Bradley calls the CCPOA the "pioneer of the IE in California" (Bill Bradley, "Bill Bradley's New West Notes," http://billbradley.pajamasmedia.com [accessed November 26, 2006]).

60. Fox Butterfield, "Political Gains by Prison Guards," *New York Times*, November 7, 1995, A1.

61. Interview, Jeff Thompson, July 1, 2004.

62. Warren, "When He Speaks," A1.

63. Anonymous (Letter to the Editor), "Governor Deukmejian Speaks at CCPOA Convention," *Peacekeeper* 3, no. 11 (November 1985), 21.

64. *Sacramento Bee*, "Rivals Race Against Crime," October 2, 1990, A1.

65. *Sacramento Bee* columnist Dan Walters astutely noted that the CCPOA's endorsement allowed Wilson to play "the union card": "With the endorsement came nearly a million dollars in campaign contributions, offsetting the massive financing that other unions were pouring into the campaign of Wilson's Democratic foe, Dianne Feinstein" ("Wilson Weighs Hardball Play," *Sacramento Bee*, August 26, 1992, A3).

66. Political pundits argued that the CCPOA's media campaign was key to Wilson's victory. For example, John Jacobs editorialized in the *Sacramento Bee*: "As the 1990 governor's race headed into its final weeks, the late Otto Bos, a top political aide to Pete Wilson, told Don Novey that Wilson needed a victory margin of 8 percent to 10 percent in the Central Valley to defeat Democrat Dianne Feinstein. Novey, president of the California Correctional Peace Officers Association—already on its way to becoming a powerful public employee union—swung into action, pouring almost $1 million into paid television and radio ads in the Central Valley on Wilson's behalf.

Wilson won the Central Valley by some 16 percent, while defeating Feinstein by only 3.5 percent statewide" (John Jacobs, "Lungren's Bad Omens in Poll and CCPOA Media Campaign," *Sacramento Bee*, October 13, 1998, B7).

67. *Sacramento Bee*, "Independent Ads Help Wilson," October 26, 1990, A3.
68. Butterfield, "Political Gains by Prison Guards," A1.
69. Warren, "When He Speaks," A1.
70. Stephen Green, "State Union Says 'Skip Our Pay Hike,'" *Sacramento Bee*, April 25, 1991, A3.
71. Stephen Green, "New Union Tries to Enlist State's Prison Officers," *Sacramento Bee*, November 8, 1991, A3.
72. Andy Furillo, "Prison Officers Union on a Roll: Gains Big Raise, Court Victories," *Sacramento Bee*, October 12, 1998, A1.
73. John Irwin, *Lifers: Seeking Redemption in Prison* (New York: Routledge, 2009), 6–7.
74. Dan Smith, "Davis Pulling Away from Lungren," *Sacramento Bee*, October 30, 1998, A1.
75. Jenifer Warren, "Master of Capitol Arts Retires as Union Chief," *Los Angeles Times*, August 4, 2002, A6.
76. Phoebe Wall Howard, "GOP's Ad Attacks Prison Guard Union's Credibility," *Fresno Bee*, October 29, 1998, A1.
77. Furillo, "Prison Officers' Union on a Roll," *Sacramento Bee*, October 12, 1998, A1.
78. The CCPOA contributed more than $1 million to Davis's relatively easy reelection campaign against Republican Bill Simon (Warren, "Master of Capitol Arts," A6). California Secretary of State records indicate that the NAPO PAC contributed at least $512,140 to Gray Davis's reelection campaign.
79. Mark Martin and Pamela Podger, "Prison Guards' Clout Difficult to Challenge," *San Francisco Chronicle*, February 2, 2004, A1.
80. Warren, "When He Speaks," A1.
81. Kevin Yamamura, "Report Links Money to Key Legislation," *Sacramento Bee*, March 19, 2002, A3.
82. These figures do not include contributions the CCPOA made to "Democratic Leadership in the Senate" and "Democratic Leadership in the Assembly," which were de facto contributions to Burton and Brown, respectively.
83. Cain and Kousser, *Adapting to Term Limits*, chap. 4.
84. Morain, "Guards Union Spreads Its Wealth," A1.
85. In an exposé on the CCPOA, Pamela MacLean writes: "The union even supplies its own candidates in some elections, supporting the candidacy of chapter president Kelly Breshears in 2001 for city council in Blythe (located between Ironwood State Prison and Chuckawalla Valley State Prison) and correctional officer Gary Grimm—a former Blythe councilmember—for the local school board. Breshears lost; Grimm won" (Pamela MacLean, "The Strong Arm of the Law: A Small Union of California Prison Guards Wields Enormous Political Power," *California Lawyer* 22, no. 11 [November 2002], 25–29).
86. California Secretary of State, Campaign Finance Records (Sacramento: Secretary of State), http://cal-acess.sos.ca.gov (accessed December 16, 2006).
87. Center for Juvenile and Criminal Justice, "California Prisons," III-3.
88. California Secretary of State, Campaign Finance Records (accessed December 16, 2006).
89. Field Notes, CCPOA 2004 Membership Convention, August 31, 2004.

90. The Center for Juvenile and Criminal Justice reports that the CCPOA spent at least $108,000 on district attorney races from 1996 to 2000 ("California Prisons," III-9).
91. MacLean, "Strong Arm of the Law," 25–29.
92. CCPOA, "Political Action Works! But You Be The Boss," *Peacekeeper* 5, no. 10 (October 1987), 5, emphasis added.
93. Martin and Podger, "Prison Guards' Clout," A1.
94. Interview, Jackie Speier, May 5, 2006.
95. Ronald DeLord, "Police, Power, and Organization," 21
96. Alinsky, *Rules for Radicals*, 127, emphasis in original.
97. Interview, Jeff Thompson, July 1, 2004.
98. Morain, "Guards Union Spreads Its Wealth," A1.
99. In *Rules of the Sociological Method* (New York: Free Press, 1982, 59), Emile Durkheim defines "social facts" as "every way of acting, fixed or not, capable of exercising on the individual an influence, or an external constraint." The specter of the CCPOA is not a material thing that we can see, touch, and precisely describe. However, the image of the specter has real effects (acts as an "external restraint") and is therefore a "social fact." Even though they cannot see the specter, politicians can feel it.
100. Center for Juvenile and Criminal Justice, "California Prisons," II-3.
101. Cosmo Garvin, "On Guards," *Sacramento News & Review*, October 7, 1999, 3.
102. John Seeley, "Fire in the Belly: The Hasty Departure of Richard Polanco," *LA Weekly*, March 16, 2001, 24.
103. Seeley, "Fire in the Belly."
104. Warren, "When He Speaks," A1.
105. Interview, Ryan Sherman, June 11, 2004.
106. Interview, Jackie Speier, May 5, 2006.
107. Johnston, *Success While Other Fail*, 209.
108. Alinsky, *Rules for Radicals*, 43–44.
109. I showed in the previous chapter that Richard McGee and his coworkers in the California Department of Corrections propagated the image of the professional "correctional officer." The CCPOA built upon this image of the correctional officer—it did not create it.
110. Joan Petersilia, *Understanding California Corrections* (Berkeley: California Policy Research Center, 2006), 22.
111. CCPOA, "Public Safety: Government's First Responsibility," position paper (Sacramento: CCPOA, 2003), 5.
112. CCPOA, "In Harm's Way," pamphlet (Sacramento: CCPOA, 2003), 5.
113. Petersilia, *Understanding California Corrections*, 56.
114. CCPOA, *Hard Time*, video (Sacramento: CCPOA, 2003).
115. CCPOA, "Hello," *Peacekeeper* 1, no. 1 (April 1983), 4.
116. Established in 1984, CPOST is a joint management–employee commission that establishes job-training standards for custodial staff and ensures implementation of those standards. As part of his reorganization of the state's prison bureaucracy in 2005, Governor Arnold Schwarzenegger abolished CPOST and placed responsibility for officer training with a new agency, the Corrections Standards Authority.
117. CCPOA, "In Harm's Way," 11.
118. Ibid, 11.
119. Johnston, *Success While Others Fail*, 81–84.
120. CCPOA, "Governor, why hurt the kids?" flyer (Sacramento: CCPOA, 2006).

121. CCPOA, "Thumbs Up," television advertisement, http://www.ccpoa.tv/ (accessed December 1, 2006).
122. Jonathan Simon, "Megan's Law: Crime and Democracy in Late Modern America," *Law & Social Inquiry* 25, no. 4 (October 2000), 1111–1150; Loïc Wacquant, *Punishing the Poor: The New Government of Social Insecurity* (Durham, NC: Duke University Press. 2007), chap. 7.
123. CCPOA, "Lost Child," television advertisement, http://www.ccpoa.tv/ (accessed December 1, 2006).
124. Barry Glassner, *The Culture of Fear: Why Americans are Afraid of the Wrong Things* (New York: Basic Books, 1999).
125. Ted Chiricos, Kathy Padgett, and Marc Gertz, "Fear, TV News, and the Reality of Crime," *Criminology* 38, no. 3 (2000), 755–785; Sarah Eschholz, Ted Chiricos, and Marc Gertz, "Television and Fear of Crime: Program Types, Audience Traits, and the Mediating Effect of Perceived Neighborhood Racial Composition," *Social Problems* 50, no. 3 (December 2003), 395–415; Ronald Weitzer and Charis Kubrin, "Breaking News: How Local TV News and Real-World Conditions Affect Fear of Crime," *Justice Quarterly* 21, no. 3 (September 2004), 497–520.
126. Petersilia, *Understanding California Corrections*, 21. In 2005, 2,386 (approximately one out of ten) prison officers earned more than $100,000. See Steve Schmidt, "Prison Guards Lock Up Bundle in OT Pay," *San Diego Union-Tribune*, February 28, 2006, A1.
127. Legislative Analyst's Office, *Correctional Officer Pay, Benefits, and Labor Relations* (Sacramento: Legislative Analyst's Office, February 7, 2008), 9, emphasis added. Fitness pay is a prime example of the "other compensation" that prison officers receive in addition to their base salaries. Prison officers "get a bonus of $65 to $130 per pay period for simply completing a physical fitness exam, regardless of their physical shape. The [California Highway Patrol], on the other hand, requires employees to meet certain physical requirements to earn the bonus. As a result, all 33,000 CCPOA members are receiving fitness pay, in essence making it part of their income instead of being a performance-based bonus" (Petersilia, *Understanding California Corrections*, 24).
128. Legislative Analyst's Office, *Correctional Officer Pay, Benefits, and Labor Relations*, 8.
129. Petersilia, *Understanding California Corrections*, 23.
130. Ibid., 24.
131. CCPOA, "The Connection Between Politics and Prisons: A Commentary," *Peacekeeper* 6, no. 8 (March 1988), 8.
132. CCPOA, "CCPOA's Legislative Successes (as of October 2004)" (Sacramento: CCPOA, n.d.).
133. CCPOA, "Governor Deukmejian Praises The CPO," *Peacekeeper* 3, no. 11 (November 1985), 28.
134. Steve Weiss, "In a Company of Heroes," *Peacekeeper* 26, no. 2 (2009), 28.
135. Interview, Steve Fournier, July 11, 2004.
136. Interview, Carl Canterbury and Rich Harcrow, September 19, 2002.
137. Bureau of Labor Statistics, *Occupational Employment and Wages, May 2008* ("Correctional Officers and Jailers), http://www.stats.bls.gov/oes/current/oes333012.htm (accessed June 29, 2009).
138. Interview, Brian Dawe, June 8, 2004.
139. The Florida Police Benevolent Association, State Correctional Officers Chapter, "Message from the President," http://www.scopba.org/welcome.htm (accessed July 2, 2009).

140. American Federation of State, County, and Municipal Employees (Council 5, Minnesota), "We Walk the Toughest Beats," *Stepping Up* 4, no. 3 (May/June 2009), 1.

141. Jon Ortiz, "Fiscal Changes Hit Prison Officers Union Hard," *Sacramento Bee*, June 28, 2009, A1.

142. Ron Kaye, "LAPD's Union Takes Hard-Line Approach to Tough Times," *NBC Los Angeles News*, http://www.nbclosangeles.com/news/local/_LAPDs_Union_Hard-line_Approach_to_Tough_Times.html (accessed July 2, 2009).

CHAPTER 4

1. CCPOA, *Behind the Wall: The Toughest Beat in California*, video (Sacramento: CCPOA, 1996).

2. Jonathan Simon, *Governing Through Crime* (New York: Oxford University Press, 2007), 24.

3. Robert Elias, *Victims Still: The Political Manipulation of Crime Victims* (Newbury Park, CA: Sage, 1993); Marlene Young, "The Victims Movement: A Confluence of Forces," unpublished manuscript (Washington, DC: National Organization for Victim Assistance, 1997).

4. Marlene Young, "The Victims Movement," 1.

5. Bruce Shapiro, "Victims & Vengeance: Why the Victims' Rights Amendment is a Bad Idea," *Nation* 11, no. 19 (1997), 13.

6. Young, "The Victims Movement," 2.

7. Shapiro, "Victims and Vengeance," 13.

8. Young, "The Victims Movement," 3.

9. Joel Best, "Victimization and the Victim Industry," *Society* 34, no. 4 (1997), 13; Robert Elias, *The Politics of Victimization: Victims, Victimology, and Human Rights* (New York: Oxford University Press, 1986); Norval Morris, *The Future of Imprisonment* (Chicago, IL: University of Chicago Press, 1974), 55–56.

10. Best, "Victimization and the Victim Industry," 13; Katherine Beckett and Theodore Sasson, *The Politics of Injustice: Crime and Punishment in America* (Thousand Oaks, CA: Sage, 2004), 140.

11. Shapiro, "Victims and Vengeance," 13.

12. Simon, *Governing Through Crime*, 106.

13. Elias, *Victims Still*, chap. 4.

14. Ibid., chap. 6.

15. Interview, Steve Fournier, August 11, 2004.

16. Interview, Nina Salarno-Ashford, March 24, 2004.

17. Interview, Harriet Salarno, February 17, 2004.

18. Ibid.

19. CVUC also developed a charitable foundation, which CVUC describes on its Web site as a "public benefit corporation formed to provide assistance and support to individual victims of criminal activities and their families. Children are one of our highest priorities. We also support and assist other non-profit organizations' activities and programs that support law enforcement and the prosecution of criminals. Crime Victims United's main goal is to protect victims. With the help of our supporters, we have been able to institute and fund the 'Teddy Bear Project' and the 'Literacy Project.' Each of these programs is geared toward children. The Teddy Bear Project is a program dedicated to assisting in the adoptions of at-risk youths. The Literacy Project provides reading and educational materials to underprivileged

children in California" (Crime Victims United of California, "Charitable Foundation," http://www.cvucf.org/about.html [accessed September 1, 2005]).

20. Interview, Harriet Salarno, February 17, 2004.
21. Shapiro, "Victimization and the Victim Industry," 13–14.
22. California Secretary of State, "Campaign Finance," http://cal-access.sos.ca.gov/campaign/ (accessed January 10–11, 2009).
23. CCPOA, "Little Pieces, The 'PAC' for Victims," *Peacekeeper* 11, no. 1 (January/February 1993), 47.
24. CCPOA, "Doris Tate Crime Victims Bureau," *Peacekeeper* 11, no. 2 (March/April 1993), 20.
25. Jenifer Warren, "Victims' Rights Group Blasts Prison Rehab Plan," *Los Angeles Times*, April 1, 2005, B7.
26. Center for Juvenile and Criminal Justice, "California Prisons" (San Francisco: Center for Juvenile and Criminal Justice, May 17, 2002), III-13.
27. Interview, Harriet Salarno, February 17, 2004.
28. Interview, Nina Salarno-Ashford, March 24, 2004.
29. Pamela MacLean, "The Strong Arm of the Law: A Small Union of California Prison Guards Wields Enormous Political Power," *California Lawyer* 22, no. 11 (November 2002), 25–29.
30. Interview, Nina Salarno-Ashford, March 24, 2004.
31. Interview, Maggie Elvey, January 14, 2004.
32. Interview, Ryan Sherman, June 11, 2004.
33. Crime Victims United of California, "Contact Us," http://www.aquahost.com/cvuc/contact.html (accessed September 1, 2005).
34. Crime Victims Bureau, "Management Team," http://www.doristate.com/membership.htm (accessed September 1, 2005).
35. Crime Victims Action Alliance, "CVAA Board of Directors," http://www.cvactionalliance.com/Board%20of%20Directors.html (accessed July 16, 2009). The Doris Tate Crime Victims Bureau changed its name to the Crime Victims Action Alliance. The organization explains: "In late 2006, early 2007, the [CVB] went through a re-organization and decided to also change their name to better reflect the work that the organization does—and Crime Victims Action Alliance was born. During that same time the Foundation went through a reorganization and became the Crime Victims Assistance Network (iCAN) Foundation" (Crime Victims Action Alliance, "Our History," http://www.cvactionalliance.com/History.html [accessed July 16, 2009]).
36. Fox Butterfield, "Political Gains by Prison Guards," *New York Times*, November 7, 1995, A1.
37. Pamela MacLean, "Strong Arm of the Law," 25–29.
38. Interview, Harriet Salarno, February 17, 2004.
39. I elaborate this argument and extend existing theories about the political uses of public gatherings in the article "Manufacturing Affinity: The Fortification and Expression of Ties between Prison Officers and Crime Victims" (*Journal of Contemporary Ethnography* 37, no. 6 [2008], 745–777).
40. The CCPOA and victims' groups gather together and nurture their symbolic bond in other events, such as the annual CVUC "victims' dinner" fundraiser; CCPOA's annual convention, in which Harriet Salarno and other leaders of crime victims' groups participate; and episodic rallies for or against specific issues (e.g., initiatives to reform sentencing laws) and people (e.g., judges).

41. Marc Klaas, "Our Story," KlaasKids Foundation, http://www.klaaskids.org/pg-ourstory.htm (accessed June 2, 2010).

42. Michèle Lamont and Virág Molnár define "symbolic boundaries" as "conceptual distinctions made by social actors to categorize objects, people, practices, and event time and space . . . Symbolic boundaries . . . separate people into groups and generate feelings of similarity [and difference] and group membership . . . They are an essential medium through which people acquire status and monopolize resources." Symbolic boundaries reinforce material divisions between groupings of individuals ("The Study of Boundaries in the Social Sciences," *Annual Review of Sociology* 28 [2002], 168).

43. Scholars note that interest groups, politicians, and media pundits increasingly define penal policy in terms of a zero-sum game between prisoners and crime victims (c.f. David Garland, *The Culture of Control: Crime and Social Order in Contemporary Society* [Chicago: University of Chicago Press, 2001]; Franklin Zimring, Gordon Hawkins, and Sam Kamin, *Punishment and Democracy: Three Strikes and You're Out in California* [New York: Oxford University Press, 2001] et al., *Punishment and Democracy*; Joshua Page, "Eliminating the Enemy: The Import of Denying Higher Education to Prisoners in Clinton's America," *Punishment and Society* 6, no. 4 [2004], 357–378). The logic of zero-sum is so entrenched today that a relatively recent scholarly book on "victims and victims' rights" states on its cover: "Defendants vs. Victims' Rights" (Sara Faherty, *Victims and Victims' Rights* [Philadelphia, PA: Chelsea House Publishers, 1999]). Before even opening the book, readers get the impression that the rights of defendants and the rights of victims are mutually exclusive and antagonistically opposed to one another.

44. CCPOA, "Prisons Become Prisons Again: Inmate Rights Overturned: SB 1260 (Presley)," *Peacekeeper* 12, no. 5 (December 1994), 33.

45. CVUC, "Crime Victims United of California," http://www.crimevictimsunited.com/ (accessed February 24, 2010), emphasis added.

46. Office of the Governor, "Press Release: Gov. Schwarzenegger Sponsors Crime Victims Bill of Rights and Announces New Crime Victim Advocate" (June 27, 2006), http://gov.ca.gov/index.php?/press-release/1102/ (accessed July 16, 2009).

47. Shapiro, "Victims & Vengeance," 16.

48. Office of the Attorney General, "News Release: Attorney General Names New Leadership Team to State Crime and Violence Prevention Center" (April 27, 1999), http://www.ag.ca.gov/newsalerts/release.php?id=490&span=1&endMonth=12&endYear=2007&month=0&span=1&year=1999 (accessed July 16, 2009).

49. Carol Williams and Maura Dolan, "Schwarzenegger Changes Strategy in Execution Debate," *Los Angeles Times*, February 24, 2009, B1.

50. Scott Smith, "An Appeal to the Divine," *Stockton Record* (on-line), July 12, 2009, http://www.recordnet.com/apps/pbcs.dll/article?AID=/20090712/A_SPECIAL0266/307129969 (accessed September 28, 2010).

51. CCPOA, "Public Safety: Government's First Responsibility: Perspectives on the Debate Concerning Criminals, Prisons and Proposals for Improved Criminal Justice," policy paper (Sacramento: CCPOA, 2003).

52. Interview, Ryan Sherman, June 11, 2004.

53. In comparison, California released nearly 12,000 parolees from prison in 1980, 2,995 of whom returned to prison (Little Hoover Commission, *Back to the Community: Safe & Sound Parole Policies* [Sacramento: Little Hoover Commission on California State Government Organization and Economy, 2003]).

54. In 2001 approximately 58% of all prison admissions were technical parole violators (i.e., parolees who violated the terms of the parole but were not convicted of
new crimes) (Michael Jacobson, *Downsizing Prisons* [New York: New York University Press, 2005], p. 146). Three representatives of crime victims' groups testified
at the commission's public hearings on parole. Harriet Salarno and Nina Salarno-
Ashford spoke on behalf of CVUC and Susan Fisher testified for CVB. No other
crime victims' advocates testified at the hearings (Little Hoover Commission,
Back to the Community).

55. Harriet Chiang, "State to Revamp Parole System: Lawsuit Settlement Seeks to
Reduce Inmate Population," *San Francisco Chronicle*, November 19, 2003, A1.

56. Don Thompson, "California Prison System Plans Sweeping Parole Changes," *Associated Press* (November 12, 2003), http://legacy.signonsandiego.com/news/
state/20031112-2027-ca-parolechanges.html (accessed November 20, 2003).

57. Andy Furillo, "Hearing Slams Parole Overhaul," *Sacramento Bee*, March 3, 2005,
A3.

58. Chuck Alexander, "New Parole Model," memorandum (Sacramento: CCPOA,
March 18, 2004). Petersilia suggests that Alexander's (and parole agents') concerns about lawsuits are not unfounded: "One important implication of an increasingly litigious society, larger caseloads, and the reduction in the quality of
client supervision is the increased potential for lawsuits arising from negligent
supervision by a parole officer of her clients. Lawsuits of this type stem from allegations of nonperformance and improper performance of official responsibilities."
Threats of lawsuits affect parole officers' "desire to take chances on an offender
who is relapsing, although it is now recognized that frequent relapses are a part of
the journey towards recovery" (Joan Petersilia, *When Prisoners Come Home: Parole
and Prisoner Reentry* [New York: Oxford University Press, 2003], 85–86).

59. Andy Furillo, "Parolee Arrest Pattern Changes," *Sacramento Bee*, February 27,
2005, A1.

60. Furillo, "Hearing Slams Parole Overhaul," A3.

61. Andy Furillo, "Victim Advocates Decry Parole Reform," *Sacramento Bee*, March 9,
2005, A3.

62. Ibid.

63. Andy Furillo, "Parole Overhaul Scrapped," *Sacramento Bee*, April 12, 2005, A1.

64. Warren, "Victims' Rights Group Blasts Prison Rehab Plan," B7.

65. Mark Martin, "Delay in Parole Reform Cuts into Savings—Promise of $109 Mil-
lion Trim in Corrections Budget Fades as Prison Population Soars," *San Francisco
Chronicle*, May 5, 2005, B3.

66. Furillo, "Parole Overhaul Scrapped," A1.

67. Field notes, CVUC victims' dinner, April 11, 2005.

68. On this topic, Jonathan Simon writes: "For more than three decades, the making
of crime laws has offered itself as explicitly as the subject for expressing the
common interest of the American people. We are crime victims. We are the loved
ones of crime victims. Above all, we are those who live in fear that we or those
we care for will be victimized by crime. Although few of us recognize this as a
primary identity, our social practices and the way our lawmakers make laws for
us testify to that. By writing laws that implicitly and increasingly explicitly say
that we are victims and potential victims, lawmakers have defined the crime victim as an idealized political subject, the model subject, whose circumstances and
experiences have come to stand for the general good" (*Governing Through Crime*,
109–110).

69. Beckett and Sasson, *The Politics of Injustice*, 77. See also Donald Braman, *Doing Time on the Outside: Incarceration and Family Life in Urban America* (Ann Arbor: University of Michigan Press, 2007), 103–104.

70. Beckett and Sasson, *The Politics of Injustice*, 148.

71. California Department of Justice, *Crime in California: 2007* (Sacramento: California Department of Justice, December 2008), vi.

72. Simon, *Governing Through Crime*, 76.

CHAPTER 5

1. David Garland, "The Culture of High Crime Societies: Some Preconditions of Recent 'Law and Order' Policies," *British Journal of Criminology* 40 (2000), 350.

2. Interview, Jeff Thompson, July 1, 2004.

3. Jeff Thompson, "Truth in Sentencing: AB 2716 (Katz)," *Peacekeeper* 12, no. 5 (December 1994), 30.

4. Jeff Thompson, "One Strike for Violent Sex Offenders: SBX 26 (Bergeson)," *Peacekeeper* 12, no. 5 (December 1994), 31–32.

5. Jeff Thompson, "14 Years Old? If You Kill, You're Old Enough!: AB 560 (Peace)," *Peacekeeper* 12, no. 5 (December 1994), 28.

6. *Sacramento Bee*, "Capitol Digest," August 9, 1994, A4. The crimes included were murder or voluntary manslaughter; mayhem; rape; sodomy by force, violence, duress, menace, or fear of bodily harm; oral copulation by force, violence, duress, menace, or fear of bodily harm; lewd acts with a child under the age of 14; any felony punishable by death or imprisonment for life; any felony in which great bodily injury is proved; any robbery of an inhabited home, floating home, or trailer coach where a gun is used; arson; attempted murder; kidnapping; continuous sexual abuse of a child; and carjacking (California Assembly, Analysis of SB 23X [August 26, 1994], http://www.leginfo.ca.gov [accessed July 30, 2009]).

7. CCPOA, "A Report Card for the Director—CYA Leader Fails Miserably," *Front Street* (June 2003), 6.

8. Legislative Analyst's Office, "Juvenile Crime, Initiative Statute" (n.d.), http://primary2000.sos.ca.gov/VoterGuide/Propositions/21analysis.htm (accessed July 30, 2009).

9. Jeff Thompson, "The Best Batch of Bills in 140 Years," *Peacekeeper* 12, no. 5 (December 1994), 28.

10. CCPOA, "The Magic 13," *Peacekeeper* 16, no. 2 (January/February 2000), 12.

11. "The Politics of Punishing: Building a State Governance Theory of American Imprisonment Variation," *Punishment & Society* 8, no. 1 (2006), 5–32.

12. Brian Janiskee and Ken Masugi, *Democracy in California: Politics and Government in the Golden State* (Lanham, MD: Rowan & Littlefield, 2008), 62–63.

13. Peter Schrag, *Paradise Lost: California's Experiment, America's Future* (Berkeley: University of California Press, 1998), 194.

14. California Secretary of State, *Ballot Initiative Summary* (Sacramento: California Secretary of State, 2003).

15. David Broder, *Democracy Derailed: Initiative Campaigns and the Power of Money* (New York: Harcourt Brace, 2000), 7.

16. Lord Windlesham, *Politics, Punishment, and Populism* (New York: Oxford University Press, 1998), 63.

17. Schrag, *Paradise Lost*, 213.

18. For statutory initiatives, sponsors must collect 5% of the votes that were cast in the most recent gubernatorial election. The percent of votes increases to 8% for

constitutional amendments. Sponsors must collect far more than the minimum number of signatures to account for inevitable duplicate and invalid signatures. Once an initiative becomes law, it is difficult for politicians and voters to alter it. A two-thirds vote of the legislature and the governor's signature are necessary to amend a constitutional amendment. The only way to amend a statutory initiative is by passing another voter-approved statute (California Secretary of State, *Ballot Initiative Summary*; Schrag, *Paradise Lost*, 193).

19. Schrag, *Paradise Lost*, 208.
20. Ibid., 192.
21. California Secretary of State, *Cal-Access*, http://cal-access.ss.ca.gov/ (accessed December 1, 2006).
22. Schrag, *Paradise Lost*, 269.
23. Barker. "The Politics of Punishing," 14.
24. Anthony Bottoms, "The Philosophy and Punishment and Sentencing," in C. Clarkson and R. Morgan (eds.), *The Politics of Sentencing Reform* (Oxford: Clarendon Press, 1995); John Pratt, *Penal Populism* (New York: Routledge, 2007).
25. Rosemary Gartner, Anthony Doob, and Franklin Zimring, "The Past as Prologue? Decarceration in California Then and Now," *Criminology and Public Policy* (forthcoming), 22.
26. Michael Tonry, "Rethinking Unthinkable Punishment Policies in America," *UCLA Law Review* 46, no. 4 (1999).
27. Franklin Zimring, Gordon Hawkins, and Sam Kamin, *Punishment and Democracy: Three Strikes and You're Out in California* (New York: Oxford University Press, 2001).
28. Ibid., chap. 2.
29. Joe Domanick, *Cruel Justice: Three Strikes and the Politics of Crime in America's Golden State* (Berkeley: University of California Press, 2004), 18.
30. Ibid., 41.
31. Zimring et al., *Punishment and Democracy*, 8.
32. Domanick, *Cruel Justice*, 87.
33. Ibid., 82.
34. Ibid., 104.
35. Ibid., 118.
36. Michael Vitiello, "Three Strikes and the *Romero* Case: The Supreme Court Restores Democracy," *Loyola of Los Angeles Law Review* 30 (1997), 1614.
37. Events such as the Klaas abduction and murder can serve as windows of opportunity, openings in which policymakers and cultural producers can harness public sentiment and shape policy outcomes. Michael Tonry says about the Klaas incident: "The death of Polly Klaas, and the reaction it provoked, could be seen as opening a window for more persuasive communication of moral views about deserved and severe punishments" (*Thinking About Crime: Sense and Sensibility in American Penal Culture* [New York: Oxford University Press, 2004], 94–95). The notion of a "window of opportunity" is similar to social movement scholars' concept of "political opportunity structures"—both ideas refer to social contexts that help collective actors achieve their aims. For an excellent, concise discussion of "political opportunity structures," see Doug McAdam, "Conceptual Origins, Current Problems, Future Directions," in Doug McAdam, John McCarthy, and Mayer Zald (eds.), *Comparative Perspectives on Social Movements: Political Opportunities, Mobilizing Structures, and Cultural Framings* (New York: Cambridge University Press, 1996), 23–40.

38. Ken Chavez, "Anti-Crime Measures Dominate Capitol: Fathers of Three Kidnap-Murder Victims Support Get-Tough Proposals," *Fresno Bee*, January 5, 1994, A1.
39. Sharon Hormell, "Debate Still Rages on '3 Strikes' Law," *Long Beach Press-Telegram*, October 4, 1994, D1.
40. Domanick, *Cruel Justice*, 130.
41. Don Novey, "A Wish for the New Year, *Peacekeeper* 11, no. 6 (November/December 1993), 7.
42. Katherine Beckett describes the Democrats' strategy to counter the Republican tactic of discrediting Democrats as "soft on crime" (and, therefore, soft on black and Hispanic "gang bangers" and "welfare mothers" in urban areas) (*Making Crime Pay: Law-and-Order in Contemporary American Politics* [New York: Oxford University Press, 1999]). Democrats—Bill Clinton in particular—tried to out-muscle Republicans on crime and punishment. Former California Governor Gray Davis fully embraced the "New Democrat" approach to crime and became more punitive than many of his law-and-order Republican colleagues. His stances on crime and punishment won him praise from the CCPOA and the union's crime victim allies.
43. Zimring et al., *Punishment and Democracy*, 6.
44. Domanick, *Cruel Justice*, 202.
45. California Secretary of State, *California Ballot Pamphlet: General Election, November 8, 1994* (Sacramento: California Secretary of State), 37. The proponents of Proposition 184 suggested in the ballot summary that crime victims' organizations sponsored the initiative. Mike Reynolds, one of the authors of the "Argument in Favor of Proposition" listed himself as "Board Member, Crime Victims United" (the CCPOA-sponsored organization led by Harriet Salarno). Jan Miller, chairperson of the Doris Tate Crime Victims Bureau (the other CCPOA-sponsored victims' group) coauthored the "Rebuttal to the Argument Against Proposition 184" (California Secretary of State, *Ballot Pamphlet*, 36–37).
46. Don Novey, "Support that Endures Long After the Victory Party," *Peacekeeper* 13, no.1 (January 1995), 7, emphasis in original.
47. CCPOA, "Public Safety: Government's First Responsibility," position paper (Sacramento: CCPOA, May 1995), 18.
48. Jeffrey D. Thompson, "Report of Lobbying Firm" (January 1, 1995–March 31, 1995); Jeffrey D. Thompson, "Report of Lobbying Firm" (January 1, 1996–March 31, 1996); Jeffrey D. Thompson, "Report of Lobbying Firm" (January 1, 1997–March 31, 1997); Jeffrey D. Thompson, "Report of Lobbying Firm" (July 1, 2000–September 9, 2000); Craig Brown, "Report of Lobbying Firm" (January 1, 2002–March 31, 2002); Crime Victims United of California, "Report of Lobbyist Employer" (January 2, 2002–March 31, 2002); Crime Victims United of California, "Report of Lobbyist Employer" (April 1, 2003–June 30, 2003); Paul Treat, "Report of Lobbying Firm" (April 1, 2003–June 30, 2003).
49. Domanick, *Cruel Justice*, 249.
50. Joe Domanick, "They Changed Their Minds on Three Strikes: Can They Change the Voters'?" *Los Angeles Times Magazine*, September 19, 2004, I10.
51. Ibid.
52. California Attorney General, *Proposition 66: Limitations on Three Strikes Law* (Sacramento: California Attorney General, 2004).
53. Interview, Nina Salarno-Ashford, March 24, 2004.
54. Californians United for Public Safety, "Opposition List" (October 27, 2004).
55. Field Notes, 16th Annual Victims' March on the Capitol, April 12, 2005.

56. California Secretary of State, *Cal-Access*, http://cal-access.ss.ca.gov/ (accessed December 7, 2006).

57. As of mid-October, three other organizations had made significant contributions to CUPS. The California Union of Security Employees (CAUSE) had contributed $10,000, the California District Attorneys Association had contributed $27,000, and the State Affiliated COPS PAC had contributed $25,000. The COPS PAC was an umbrella group of local and statewide law enforcement organizations. The CCPOA contributed $5,000 to the COPS PAC in 1993 (California Secretary of State, *Cal-Access*, http://cal-access.ss.ca.gov/ [accessed December 7, 2006]).

58. Californians United for Public Safety, "Felon a Day" (September 21, 2004).

59. Megan Garvey, "Big Money Pours in for 3-Strikes Ads," *Los Angeles Times*, October 28, 2004, B1.

60. Office for Victims of Crime, "2005 National Crime Victims' Rights Week Award Recipients," http://www.ovc.gov/cnvrw/2005/2005bios.htm (accessed March 15, 2006).

61. Nicholas had participated in the politics of incarceration before 2006. California Secretary of State documents show that in 1999–2000, the "Nicholas Family Trust," which lists Henry Nicholas as its principal contributor, spent $50,000 in support of Proposition 21, an initiative that made it possible to send certain juvenile offenders to state prison. Marcela Leech and CVUC strongly endorsed Proposition 21, which became law in 2000 (California Secretary of State, *Cal-Access*, http://cal-access.ss.ca.gov/ [accessed December 7, 2006]).

62. As discussed in chapter 2, the CCPOA funded commercials featuring Harriet Salarno of CVUC, which helped Pete Wilson win the governor's race in 1990.

63. Joe Mathews, "How Prospects for Prop. 66 Fell So Far, So Fast," *Los Angeles Times*, November 7, 2004, B1.

64. The California Union of Security Employees (CAUSE) added $50,000 to the $50,000 it had already spent against the measure. Assemblyman Todd Spitzer (one of the CCPOA's allies and a former law enforcement officer) contributed $50,000 through his PAC, "Friends of Todd Spitzer." The Republican Party contributed $251,750 to the anti-Proposition 66 efforts (California Secretary of State, *Cal-Access*, http://cal-access.ss.ca.gov/ [accessed December 7, 2006]).

65. CUPS paid McNally Temple Associates at least $1,282,492 for commercials and other expenses (e.g., bumper stickers and "fax bursts") (California Secretary of State, *Cal-Access*, http://cal-access.ss.ca.gov/ [accessed December 7, 2006]).

66. CUPS, "He Raped Me" (2004).

67. Leon Worden, "SCV Newsmaker of the Week: Edmund G. 'Jerry' Brown," (transcript of television interview, October 31, 2004), http://www.scvhistory.com/scvhistory/signal/newsmaker/sg103104c.htm (accessed June 2, 2006).

68. CCPOA, "The Enemies We Face" (n.d.). The "enemies" were state senator Richard Polanco, state senator John Vasconcellos, California Attorney General Bill Lockyer, "Inmate Rights Advocate" Cory Weinstein, Private Investigator Tom Quinn, and Oakland Mayor Jerry Brown. According to the CCPOA, these "enemies" "make the 'toughest beat' even tougher." The purpose of the brochure was to rally member support for the union's costly political program. The CCPOA routinely tries to rally members by depicting external threats to prison officers and the union.

69. David Garland explains that crime victims "serve as the personalized, real-life, 'it-could-be-you' metonym for the problem of personal security" ("The Culture of High Crime Societies," 351).

70. Tonry, *Thinking about Crime*, 91; Jonathan Simon, "Megan's Law: Crime and Democracy in Late Modern America," *Law and Social Inquiry* 25, no. 4 (2000), 1135.

71. Simon, "Megan's Law," 1138.

72. A spokesperson for the pro-Proposition 66 campaign commented, "The suddenness of it all was just stunning." He continued, "Everything changed in the last few days. They basically bought up every inch of unused air time that was available" (Joe Mathews, "How Prospects for Prop. 66 Fell So Far, So Fast," B1).

73. Keenan contributed at least $2,309,465 to the "Yes on 66" campaign. Soros, Sperling, and Lewis each contributed at least $500,000 to the campaign (California Secretary of State, *Cal-Access*, http://cal-access.ss.ca.gov/ [accessed August 4, 2009]).

74. California Secretary of State, *Cal-Access*, http://cal-access.ss.ca.gov/ (accessed December 7, 2006).

75. California Secretary of State, *Official Voter Information Guide* (Sacramento: Secretary of State, November 2, 2004), 46.

76. The arguments of the "Yes on 66" campaign about fairness seemed disingenuous considering that Proposition 66's main financial backer, Jerry Keenan, would have personally benefited from the initiative.

77. David Garland, *Punishment and Modern Society* (Chicago: University of Chicago Press, 1990), 264–265.

78. Arie Frieberg, "Affective versus Effective Justice: Instrumentalism and Emotionalism in Criminal Justice," *Punishment & Society* 3, no. 2 (2001), 269; Tom Tyler and Robert Boeckmann, "Three Strikes and You're Out, but Why? The Psychology of Public Support for Punishing Rule Breakers," *Law & Society Review* 31, no. 2 (1997), 255–256.

79. Field Notes, CVUC victims' dinner, April 11, 2005.

80. *Los Angeles Times* reporter Joe Matthews, who closely followed the Proposition 66 fight, makes a similar point: "The anti-66 campaign had been kept alive since the spring by the California District Attorneys Assn. and the state prison guards union, which hired the campaign's political consultants and paid for focus groups" ("How Prospects for Prop. 66 Fell So Far, So Fast," B1).

81. California Fair Political Practices Commission, "Big Money Talks" (Sacramento: Fair Political Practices Commission, March 2010), 42.

82. Legislative Analyst's Office, "Three Strikes: The Impact After More Than a Decade" (Sacramento: Legislative Analyst's Office, October 2005); Scott Ehlers, Vincent Shiraldi, and Jason Ziedenberg, *Still Striking Out: Ten Years of California's Three Strikes* (Washington, DC: Justice Policy Institute, July 1, 2004).

83. Erik Lotke, Jason Colburn, and Vincent Shiraldi, *3 Strikes & You're Out: An Examination of the Impact of Strikes Laws 10 Years After Their Enactment* (Washington, DC: Justice Policy Institute, September 1, 2004), 4–5.

84. California State Auditor, *California Department of Corrections and Rehabilitation*, Report 2009-107.2 (Sacramento: California State Auditor, May 2010).

85. Emily Bazelon, "Arguing Three Strikes," *New York Times Magazine*, May 17, 2010, MM40, http://www.nytimes.com/2010/05/23/magazine/23strikes-t.html (accessed May 24, 2010).

86. California State Auditor, *California Department of Corrections and Rehabilitation*, 23, 27.

87. Bazelon, "Arguing Three Strikes," MM40.

88. Zimring et al., *Punishment and Democracy*, 27.

89. In 1996 the California Supreme Court ruled in *People v. Superior Court (Romero)* that judges may "dismiss prior strikes in the furtherance of justice." The ruling reduced the effect that Three Strikes had on judges' discretion in sentencing repeat felons (Jennifer Edwards Walsh, *Three Strikes Laws* [Westport, CT: Greenwood, 2007], 63–64).

90. CCPOA, "Public Safety," 1.

91. "Three Strikes and You're Out" is a phrase used in baseball, America's "national pastime." The name suggests that Three Strikes is an "all-American" law that protects American citizens (and the mythical "American way of life") from "the criminal element"—understood as a foreign enemy. George Lakoff argues that Three Strikes exemplifies the principle of "moral strength"—the notion that "a show of strength is the best protection against evil"—which is a central element of contemporary conservative, "strict father" morality in the United States (*Moral Politics: How Liberals and Conservatives Think* [Chicago: University of Chicago Press, 1996], 200).

92. CCPOA, "Public Safety," 14, emphasis in original.

93. CCPOA, "Public Safety," 30.

94. Nina Salarno-Ashford, "Why We Should Have the Death Penalty," *Klaas Action Review: The Newsletter of the Marc Klaas Foundation for Children* 7, no. 2 (Summer 2001), 4.

95. CCPOA, "Public Safety," 27.

96. CCPOA, "Public Safety," 14.

97. Here I am drawing on the work of Joseph Gusfield, who insightfully wrote: "The fact of affirmation through acts of law and government expresses the public worth of one set of norms, of one sub-culture vis-à-vis those of others. It demonstrates which cultures have legitimacy and public domination, and which do not. Accordingly it enhances the social status of groups carrying the affirmed culture and degrades groups carrying that which is condemned as deviant" ("Moral Passage: The Symbolic Process in Public Designations of Deviance," *Social Problems* 15, no. 2 [Autumn 1967], 178).

CHAPTER 6

1. Charles Mahtesian, "The Uprising of the Prison Guards," *Governing Magazine* 9, no. 11 (August 1996), 38–41. For an analysis of the relationship between Thomas's scholarly and business endeavors, see Gilbert Geis, Alan Mobley, and David Shichor, "Private Prisons, Criminological Research, and Conflict of Interest: A Case Study," *Crime and Delinquency* 45, no. 3 (July 1999), 372–388.

2. CCPOA, *Public Safety: Government's First Responsibility*, policy paper (Sacramento: CCPOA, 2003), 35.

3. David Shichor, "The Corporate Context of Private Prisons," *Crime, Law, and Social Change* 20, no. 2 (1993), 124.

4. Christian Parenti, *Lockdown America: Police and Prisons in the Age of Crisis* (New York: Verso, 1999), 229.

5. Michael Jacobson, *Downsizing Prisons: How to Reduce Crime and End Mass Incarceration* (New York: New York University Press, 2005), 68.

6. The CDC was the state agency in charge of the prison system from the mid-1940s until 2005. As part of the reorganization of the state's penal bureaucracy in July 2005, the CDC was incorporated as part of the new superagency, the California Department of Corrections and Rehabilitation (CDCR). When discussing events that took place before 2005, I refer to the CDC. When discussing events after 2005, I refer to the CDCR.

7. Malcolm Feeley, "Entrepreneurs of Punishment: The Legacy of Privatization," *Punishment & Society* 4, no. 3 (2002), 324. Scholarship on the American "welfare state" shows that the private sector has been integrally involved in other major social service sectors, such as the delivery of health care (Jacob S. Hacker, *The Divided Welfare State: The Battle Over Public and Private Social Benefits in the United States* [New Haven, CT: Yale University Press, 2002]; Sheila B. Kamerman and Alfred J. Kahn (eds.), *Privatization and the Welfare State* [Princeton, NJ: Princeton University Press, 1989]).

8. Charles Thomas, "Correctional Privatization in America: An Assessment of Its Historical Origins, Present Status, and Future Prospects," in Alexander Tabarrok and Charles Logan (eds.), *Changing of the Guard: Private Prisons and the Control of Crime* (Oakland, CA: The Independent Institute, 2003), 57–124.

9. Loïc Wacquant, *Punishing the Poor: The Neoliberal Government of Social Insecurity* (Durham, NC: Duke University Press, 2009), 170. In 1996 CCA and Wackenhut controlled approximately 75% of the private prison market in the United States (CCA had 52% and Wackenhut had 25%) (Philip Mattera and Mafruza Khan, *Jail Breaks: Economic Subsidies Given to Private Prisons* [Washington, DC: Institute on Taxation and Economic Policy, 2001], 3).

10. William Sabol, Todd Minton, and Paige Harrison, *Prison and Jail Inmates at Mid-year 2006* (Washington, DC: Bureau of Justice Statistics, U.S. Department of Justice, June 2007), 4.

11. Wacquant, *Punishing the Poor*, 171.

12. Shelly Bookspan, *A Germ of Goodness: The California State Prison System, 1851–1944* (Lincoln: University of Nebraska Press, 1991).

13. Legislative Analyst's Office, "1996–97 Budget, Perspectives and Issues" (Sacramento: Legislative Analyst's Office, February 21, 1996); Legislative Analyst's Office, "Addressing the State's Long-Term Inmate Population Growth" (Sacramento: Legislative Analyst's Office, May 20, 1997).

14. Feeley, "Entrepreneurs of Punishment," 335.

15. The provision related to contracting out private services is in California Government Code section 19130. For detailed discussions of laws pertaining to California's civil service workers, see Donald Featherson, D. G. Thorton, and J. Greggory Correnti, "State and Local Privatization: An Evolving Process," *Public Contract Law Journal* 30, no. 4 (2001), 643–676.

16. Interview, Mark Nobili, August 15, 2005.

17. Eloise Rose, "CCPOA Opposes Private Prisons," *Peacekeeper* 6, no. 4 (April 1988), 2, 7.

18. Jeff Thompson, "Prisons for Profit," *Peacekeeper* 5, no. 2 (February 1987), 22.

19. Interview, Ryan Sherman, June 7, 2004.

20. Thompson, "Prisons for Profit," 22.

21. Rose, "CCPOA Opposes Private Prisons," 2.

22. Ibid., 7.

23. CCPOA leader Joe Baumann recalls that the union aborted the case because the union did not believe that the judge would agree that the CCFs produced "irreparable harm" to prison officers—the criterion needed to win the lawsuit. Interview, Joe Baumann, December 22, 2006.

24. *Sacramento Bee*, "Prisons-For-Profit Idea Gains Ground," June 7, 1987, A1.

25. California State Auditor, "Department of Corrections," Report #2005-1005 (Sacramento: Bureau of State Audits, September 2005), 7.

26. Legislative Analyst's Office, "Addressing the State's Long-Term Inmate Population Growth" (Sacramento: Legislative Analyst's Office, May 20, 1997).

27. California State Auditor, "Department of Corrections," 7–8.
28. Peter Schrag, *Paradise Lost: California's Experience, America's Future* (Berkeley: University of California Press, 1998).
29. *California Journal Weekly*, "Election 1994," November 14, 1994, http://web.lexis-nexis.com (accessed July 10, 2006).
30. Legislative Analyst's Office, *Accommodating the State's Prison Population Growth* (Sacramento: Legislative Analyst's Office, December 28, 1995).
31. Schrag, *Paradise Lost*, 95–96.
32. Cf., California Department of Finance, *A Performance Review, California Department of Corrections* (Sacramento: California Department of Finance, June 1996).
33. Interview, Bernie Orozco, June 5, 2004.
34. Ibid.
35. Thomas, "Correctional Privatization in America," 100.
36. Senate Subcommittee on Prison Construction and Operations, "The California Correctional Facilities Privatization Commission Act of 1996," committee analysis (April 9, 1996), http://www.leginfo.ca.gov/pub/95-96/bill/sen/sb_2151-2200/sb_2156_cfa_960408_151445_sen_comm.html (accessed April 19, 2006).
37. Marc Lifsher, "Private-Prison Advocates May Have to do Time Fighting Guards Union," *Orange County Register*, May 13, 1996, A1.
38. CCPOA, *Meeting the Challenge of Affordable Prisons* (Sacramento: CCPOA, n.d.).
39. Bill Lockyer, "California's Crisis in Corrections," memo (Sacramento: California Senate, December 4, 1995).
40. Interview, Ryan Sherman, June 11, 2004; interview, Bernie Orozco, April 2, 2007.
41. Marc Lifsher, "Lewis' bill to enable private-prison operations fails in Senate," *Orange County Register*, May 31, 1996, A24.
42. Interview, Richard Polanco, June 21, 2004; interview, Gwynnae Byrd, October 6, 2004.
43. In the beginning of 1998, Senator Polanco reintroduced the bill to create a Florida-style private prison commission in California. The legislation, SB 640, died in committee (i.e., it did not even get to the senate floor). This swift defeat led Polanco to conclude that large-scale prison privatization was not going to happen in California, at least not any time soon (interview, Richard Polanco, June 21, 2004; interview, Gwynnae Byrd, October 6, 2004).
44. Interview, Gwynnae Byrd, October 6, 2004.
45. Assembly Committee on Public Safety, "SB 818," committee analysis (Sacramento: California Assembly, July 9, 1997).
46. Interview, Richard Polanco, June 21, 2004.
47. Assembly Committee on Public Safety, "SB 818."
48. Ibid.
49. Ibid.
50. The Latino Caucus was quite powerful in the mid- to late 1990s, because legislators feared upsetting the growing Chicano/Latino electorate, energized by recent attacks by Governor Wilson who tried to use immigration as a wedge issue as he prepared to run for president of the United States.
51. Interview, Ryan Sherman, June 7, 2004. Philip Mattera and Mafruza Khan explain that between 1995 and 1998, the "private prison industry's reputation was . . . tarnished by a series of high-profile scandals about substandard conditions, poor management and brutality in facilities under its control" (*Jail Breaks*, 5). Mattera and Khan detail scandals that occurred in New Jersey (1995), Texas (1996 and 1997), and Ohio (1998).

52. Assembly Committee on Public Safety, "SB 818."
53. Jeff Thompson, "Attack of the Profit Giants!" *Peacekeeper* 18, no. 10 (November 1997), 17.
54. Interview, Richard Polanco, June 21, 2004; interview, Mark Nobili, August 15, 2005.
55. Interview, Richard Polanco, June 21, 2004; interview, Mark Nobili, August 15, 2005.
56. Robert Gunnison, "Privately Run Prison Planned for Mojave," *San Francisco Chronicle*, August 1, 1997, A22.
57. Jon Mathews, "Private Prison's Planned—State Unsure About Using It," *Sacramento Bee*, August 1, 1997, A4.
58. Gunnison, "Privately Run Prison Planned," A22.
59. Daniel Wood, "Private Prisons, Public Doubts," *Christian Science Monitor*, July 21, 1998, 1.
60. Gunnison, "Privately Run Prison Planned," A22.
61. CCA's stock dropped from $45 a share in 1997 to $.19 in 2000, and its long-term debt topped $1 billion in 1999 (Joseph T. Hallinan, "Federal Government Saves Private Prisons as State Convict Population Levels Off," *Wall Street Journal*, November 6, 2001, http://online.wsj.com/public/us [accessed June 10, 2006]).
62. Legislative Analyst's Office, "Analysis of the 2002–2003 Budget Bill—Judiciary and Criminal Justice Chapter" (Sacramento: Legislative Analyst's Office), D–32.
63. Interview, Richard Polanco, June 21, 2004; interview, Gwynnae Byrd, October 6, 2004; interview, Mark Nobili, August 15, 2005.
64. Interview, Mark Nobili, August 15, 2005.
65. I obtained the message from the CCPOA's 5150 hotline in January 2002 (emphasis added). I routinely checked the hotline and transcribed its messages while conducting fieldwork for this study.
66. Interview, Mark Nobili, August 15, 2005.
67. RF Communications, *Blood Money: The Killing of Two Award-Winning Programs* (Sacramento, 2002).
68. Kelly St. John, "Texas Prison Firm Broadcasts Argument for Keeping Facilities," *San Francisco Chronicle*, May 6, 2002, A8.
69. *San Francisco Chronicle*, "A Big Prison Paycheck," April 2, 2002, A16; *Los Angeles Times*, "Prison Guard Clout Endures," April 1, 2002, B10; *San Diego Union-Tribune*, "Big Pay-Back, Davis Makes Sop to Prison Guards' Union," March 19, 2002, B8.
70. It was common practice for lawmakers to rubber-stamp governors' labor pacts with state unions. In an attempt to end this custom, state senator Jackie Speier sponsored legislation in 2004 that mandated extensive analyses of and public hearings on the unions' contracts (Interview, Jackie Speier, May 5, 2006).
71. Interview, Gwynnae Byrd, October 6, 2004.
72. Senate Budget and Fiscal Review Committee (Budget Subcommittee No. 4), hearing (Sacramento: California Senate, May 17, 2002).
73. John Simerman and Sandy Kleffman, "Quid Pro Quo Issues Dog Davis' Campaign," *Contra Costa Times*, May 5, 2002, A1.
74. Arianna Huffington, "Governor Davis and the Failure of Power," *Salon.com* (January 27, 2001), http://archive.salon.com/politics/feature/2001/01/27/power/ (accessed March 20, 2007).
75. Interview, Mark Nobili, August 15, 2005.
76. Charles F. Bostwick, "Guards Union Targets Assemblyman," *Daily News of Los Angeles*, February 24, 2002, AV1; California Secretary of State, *Cal-Access*, http://cal-access.sos.ca.gov/ (accessed November 12, 2006).

77. Dan Morain, "Davis to Close State's Privately Run Prisons," *Los Angeles Times*, March 15, 2002, A1.
78. Gary Delsohn, "One of the Capitol's Savviest Players is Stepping Down," *Sacramento Bee*, July 27, 2002, A1.
79. Jenifer Warren, "When He Speaks, They Listen," *Los Angeles Times*, August 21, 2000, A1.
80. Interview, Mark Nobili, August 15, 2005.
81. Labor scholars Rick Fantasia and Kim Voss write in this regard, "Since 1947, twenty states, mostly in the South and West, have passed these 'right-to-work' laws that make unionism extremely difficult to maintain. The domestic equivalent of a 'banana republic,' the right-to-work states comprise a massive region of the country to which American corporations have long been able to move their operations in pursuit of an unregulated, unorganized, and, consequently, low-wage-paying business climate" (*Hard Work: Remaking the American Labor Movement* [Berkeley: University of California Press, 2004], 51).
82. Interview, Ryan Sherman, June 7, 2004.
83. Schwarzenegger's political action committees accepted, in 2003 and 2005, $68,000 from the Geo Group (previously Wackenhut), a leading private prison business (Andy Furillo, "Schwarzenegger Seeks $67 Million Boost for Private-Prison Operator," *Sacramento Bee*, March 9, 2008, A1.
84. Office of the Governor, "Prison Overcrowding State of Emergency Proclamation" (October 4, 2006).
85. Gail D. Ohanesian, *CCPOA v. Schwarzenegger*, ruling, Case No. 06CS01568 (February 20, 2007), 3.
86. Andy Furillo, "Crowded Prisons Get Reprieve," *Sacramento Bee*, June 5, 2008, A7.
87. Department of Corrections and Rehabilitation, Office of Public and Employee Communications, "Prison Reforms: Achieving Results" (Sacramento: CDCR, 2008), 2.
88. Office of the Governor, "Governor's Remarks: Schwarzenegger Calls Special Session to Address Prison Crowding, Recidivism" (June 26, 2006).
89. California Department of Corrections and Rehabilitation, "Governor Calls Special Session," press release (June 2006), http://www.cdcr.ca.gov/News/Reform_Archives/GovCallsSS.html (accessed August 10, 2009).

CHAPTER 7

1. John M. Wynne, Jr., *Prison Employee Unionism: The Impact on Correctional Administration and Programs* (Washington, DC: U.S. Department of Justice, January 1978), 3.
2. Wynne, *Prison Employee Unionism*, 62–63. See also James Jacobs, *Stateville: The Penitentiary in Mass Society* (Chicago: University of Chicago Press, 1977), chap. 7.
3. Wynne, *Prison Employee Unionism*, 3–4.
4. M. Robert Montilla, *Prison Employee Unionism: Management Guide for Correctional Administrators* (Washington, DC: U.S. Department of Justice, January 1978), 17.
5. Corrections Independent Review Panel, "Executive Summary," in *Reforming California's Youth and Adult Correctional System* (Sacramento: CIRP), http://cpr.ca.gov/Review_Panel/Executive_Summary.html (accessed November 8, 2007).

6. Joan Petersilia, *Understanding California Corrections* (Berkeley: California Policy Research Center, May 2006), 21.

7. Michael Rothfeld, "A Power Struggle Over Prisons," *Los Angeles Times*, September 25, 2007, A1.

8. Anonymous (Letter to the Editor), "Post-By-Seniority," *Peacekeeper* 3, no. 6 (June 1985), 8.

9. *Agreement Between State of California and California Correctional Peace Officers Association*, July 1, 1998 through June 30, 1999, at §12.07.

10. Managers may reassign officers as punishment for substandard annual performance reviews and conduct leading to adverse action, such as wrongful use of force. Officers only receive substandard reviews for consistent, documented behavior that occurred within the previous 12 months (reviews do not include behavior that occurred before the 12-month period). Managers may reassign officers for adverse action and substandard performance reviews in addition to the 10% that they may reassign for discretionary reasons (*Agreement Between State of California and California Correctional Peace Officers Association*, July 1, 2001 through July 2, 2006, at §9.01[B], §12.07[A]).

11. *Agreement Between State of California and California Correctional Peace Officers Association*, July 1, 1999 through July 2, 2001, at §12.07.

12. *Agreement Between State of California and California Correctional Peace Officers Association*, July 1, 2001 through July 2, 2006, at §12.07.

13. Petersilia, *Understanding California Corrections*, 25.

14. New York State Correctional Officers and Police Benevolent Association, *2003-2007 Security Services Unit Agreement*, at §24.3, http://www.goer.state.ny.us/CNA/current/nyscopbassu/index.html (accessed March 5, 2008).

15. "Warden Miller" is a pseudonym. The interviewee requested not to be identified in the book, citing fear of retaliation against relatives still working in the prison system. Interview, Warden Miller, July 6, 2004.

16. Petersilia, *Understanding California Corrections*, 26.

17. Senate Select Committee on Prison Management, *California State Prison, Corcoran: Department of Corrections' and the California Attorney General's Efforts to Investigate Incidents of Staff Brutality of Inmates*, vol. 4 (Sacramento: California Senate, August 3, 1998), 194.

18. Senate Select Committee on Government Oversight and Senate Select Committee on the California Correctional System, *Review of the State MOU Process and the Bargaining Unit 6 Contract* (Sacramento: California Senate, March 4, 2004), 164.

19. *Agreement Between State of California and California Correctional Peace Officers Association*, July 1, 2001 through July 2, 2006, at §9.09(D).

20. *Agreement Between State of California and California Correctional Peace Officers Association*, July 1, 2001 through July 2, 2006, at §9.09(A).

21. John Hagar, *Special Master's Final Report, RE Department of Corrections Post Powers Investigations and Employee Discipline*, no. C90-3094-TEH (U.S. District Court, Northern District of California, June 24, 2004), 104.

22. *Agreement Between State of California and California Correctional Peace Officers Association*, July 1, 2001 through July 2, 2006, at Side Letter #12–Regarding 9.09–CDC/CYA Personnel Investigations.

23. Hagar, *Special Master's Final Report*, 104.

24. Ibid., 115.

25. Ibid., 112, emphasis added.

26. CCPOA, "SB 1731—Oppose" (May 27, 2004), emphasis in original.

27. Interview, Chuck Alexander, August 11, 2006.
28. Senate Select Committee on Government Oversight and Senate Select Committee on the California Correctional System, *Review of the State MOU Process*, 170.
29. Ibid., 176.
30. Mark Arax, "Tales of Brutality Behind Bars," *Los Angeles Times*, August 21, 1996, A1. In the 1990s, California, Nevada, and Illinois were the only states that allowed firearms in cellblocks and exercise yards, and California was the only state that permitted officers to use lethal force to break up fistfights between prisoners. California State Prison, Corcoran, was the deadliest of the Golden State's deadly prisons. In October 1994 the *Orange County Register* reported, "California correctional officers with high-powered rifles and minimal training routinely shoot at inmates to break up fist-fights, a deadly practice that since 1989 has led to the killing of 27 convicts—more than three times as many as in all other U.S. prisons combined." In addition to killing 27 prisoners, officers had wounded by gunshot an additional 148 convicts (Kim Christensen and Marc Lifsher, "Prison Guards: Licensed to Kill?" *Orange County Register*, October 23, 1994, A1).
31. Arax, "Brutality Behind Bars," A1.
32. Mark Arax and Mark Gladstone, "State Thwarted Brutality Probe at Corcoran Prison, Investigators Say," *Los Angeles Times*, July 5, 1998, A1.
33. Mark Arax, "Ex-Guard Tells of Brutality, Code of Silence at Corcoran," *Los Angeles Times*, July 6, 1998, A1.
34. Arax and Gladstone, "State Thwarted Brutality Probe," A1.
35. Ibid.
36. Michael Lewis and Jerry Bier, "Guards' Union Restarts Ad Campaign; Advertising Unfolds Before Jury Selection for a Federal Trial of Correctional Officers," *Fresno Bee*, January 17, 2000, B1.
37. Mark Arax, "Stakes High as Prison Guards Go on Trial," *Los Angeles Time*, October 4, 1999, A3.
38. Kiley Russell, "8 Guards Cleared of Cruelty," *San Diego Union-Tribune*, June 10, 2000, A3.
39. Arax and Gladstone, "State Thwarted Brutality Probe," A24.
40. *Sacramento Bee*, "Corcoran's Taint Spreads: Investigators Say Governor's Office Aided Whitewash," July 12, 1998, F2.
41. Senate Select Committee on Prison Management, *California State Prison, Corcoran*, vol. 4, 196.
42. Mark Arax and Mark Gladstone, "Keeping Justice at Bay," *Los Angeles Times*, December 16, 1998, A1.
43. Mark Arax, "Union Crushed Bid to Let State Prosecute Guards," *Los Angeles Times*, July 19, 1999, A1.
44. Specifically, the state must negotiate changes with the union when the changes "would affect the working conditions of a significant number of employees in Unit 6," the "subject matter of the change is within the scope of representation pursuant to the Ralph C. Dills Act," and the CCPOA asks to negotiate with the state.
45. Daniel Weintraub, "Who Is In Control Inside Prisons? It's Negotiable," *Sacramento Bee*, April 19, 2007, B7.
46. Ibid.
47. Ibid.
48. Legislative Analyst's Office, *Correctional Officer Pay, Benefits, and Labor Relations* (Sacramento: Legislative Analyst's Office, February 7, 2008), 8.

49. Interview, Warden Miller, July 6, 2004. Neither the state nor the CCPOA maintains systemwide data on grievances filed at the institutional level. Therefore I was unable to evaluate the empirical basis of claims regarding the union's use of the grievance process at the local level.

50. I attempted to obtain data on binding arbitrations that would allow me to compare the CCPOA's use of the arbitration process with that of other state workers' unions, however, staff at the Department of Personnel Administration told me that the agency does not have that information accessible.

51. Nelson Lichtenstein, *State of the Union: A Century of American Labor* (Princeton, NJ: Princeton University Press, 2002), 62–63.

52. Earl Warren and Burdette J. Daniels, "California's New Penal and Correctional Law," *California Law Review* 32, no. 3, 229–241.

53. George Deukmejian, "It Is Time to Overhaul Corrections System," *Sacramento Bee*, September 19, 2004, E3.

54. Mark Martin, "Prison-Guard Union's Political Clout," *San Francisco Chronicle*, March 29, 2004, A1.

55. Pamela A. MacLean, "Strong Arm of the Law," *California Lawyer* 22, no. 11 (November 2002), 25–29.

56. Interview, Warden Miller, July 6, 2004.

57. Interview, Brian Parry, November 4, 2002.

58. Interview, Roderick Hickman, March 10, 2006.

59. Interview, Warden Miller, July 6, 2004.

60. Warden Miller referenced "Hawaii" because in 2002 the CCPOA hosted lawmakers in Maui for a legislative retreat. Among the attendees were three of the legislature's four leaders. The trip occurred right before lawmakers began negotiations over the state's then multibillion-dollar budget deficit (Kevin Yamamura, "Guards' Union Hosts Legislators in Hawaii," *Sacramento Bee*, December 5, 2002, A1).

61. Interview, Warden Miller, July 6, 2004 (emphasis added).

62. Jenifer Warren, "Guards Union is Giving Prisons Chief Hard Time," *Los Angeles Times*, November 15, 2004, A1.

63. Andy Furillo, "Slaying Ignites Prison Guards' Fury," *Sacramento Bee*, January 16, 2005, A3.

64. Ibid.

65. Rudy Bermúdez, press conference on murder of Manuel A. Gonzalez, February 10, 2005, http://www.ccpoa.tv/ (accessed November 10, 2006), transcribed by author.

66. David Goldstein, "Parole Agents Shuffle Sex Offenders—Statewide?" *CBS News*, February 10, 2006, http://cbs2.com (accessed January 2, 2007).

67. David Reyes, "No Molesters in Disney Area, Legislator Asks," *Los Angeles Times*, May 10, 2006, B1.

68. Interview, Roderick Hickman, March 10, 2006.

69. Ibid.

70. Laura Sullivan, "Folsom Embodies California's Prison Blues," National Public Radio, *All Things Considered*, August 13, 2009, http://www.npr.org (accessed August 13, 2009).

71. Ibid.

72. CCPOA, "Hold the Line," *Peacekeeper* 23, no. 1 (March 2006), 11.

73. Senate Select Committee on Government Oversight and the California Correctional System, "Reform of How Employee Investigations are Conducted at Youth and Adult Correctional Facilities" (Sacramento: California Senate, January 21, 2004), 7.

74. Political scientist Daniel Carpenter defines *administrative capacity* as "the collective talent of bureaucracies to perform with competence and without corruption and malfeasance" (*The Forging of Bureaucratic Autonomy: Reputations, Networks, and Policy Innovation in Executive Agencies, 1862–1928* [Princeton, NJ: Princeton University Press, 2001], 47).

75. Kietrich Rueschemeyer and Peter Evans, "The State and Economic Transformation: Toward an Analysis of the Conditions Underlying Effective Intervention" in Peter Evans, Dietrich Rueschemeyer, and Theda Skocpol (eds.), *Bringing the State Back In* (New York: Cambridge University Press, 1985), 52, emphasis in original.

76. Interview, Brian Parry, November 4, 2002.

77. Senate Select Committee on Prison Management, *California State Prison, Corcoran: Department of Corrections' and the California Attorney General's Efforts to Investigate Incidents of Staff Brutality of Inmates*, vol. 5 (Sacramento: California Senate, August 18, 1998), 30.

78. Rueschemeyer and Evans, "The State and Economic Transformation," 50.

79. Carpenter, *Forging of Bureaucratic Autonomy*, 28.

80. Corrections Independent Review Panel, *Reforming Corrections* (Sacramento: CIRP, June 2004), 1.

81. John Dilulio, *Governing Prisons* (New York: Free Press, 1987), 135.

82. Corrections Independent Review Panel, "Executive Summary," in *Reforming Corrections* (Sacramento: CIRP, June 2004). See also Youth and Adult Correctional Agency, *Strategic Plan* (Sacramento: YACA, January 2005), 15.

83. California State Auditor, *Bureau of State Audits, California Department of Corrections: Its Fiscal Practices and Internal Controls are Inadequate to Ensure Fiscal Responsibility* (Sacramento: California State Auditor, November 2001).

84. Corrections Independent Review Panel, "Executive Summary," emphasis added.

85. Legislative Analyst's Office, *Analysis of the 1997–98 Budget Bill, Judiciary and Criminal Justice Chapter* (Sacramento: Legislative Analyst's Office, February 18, 1997), D-18.

86. Carpenter, *Forging of Bureaucratic Autonomy*, 29.

87. California Department of Corrections and Rehabilitation, Division of Juvenile Justice, *Safety and Welfare Plan: Implementing Reform in California* (Sacramento: CDCR, March 31, 2006), 31.

88. *Findings of Fact and Conclusion of Law, RE Appointment of Receiver in Platt v. Schwarzenegger*, no. C01-1351-TEH (U.S. District Court, Northern District of California, October 3, 2005), 39.

89. For example, Little Hoover Commission, *Putting Violence Behind Bars: Redefining the Role of California's Prisons* (Sacramento: Little Hoover Commission, January 18, 1994).

90. California Bureau of State Audits, *California Department of Corrections and Rehabilitation: It Fails to Track and Use Data That Would Allow It to More Effectively Monitor and Manage Its Operations* (Sacramento: California Bureau of State Audits, September 2009).

91. Legislative Analyst's Office, "1997–1998 Analysis of the Governor's Budget" (Sacramento: Legislative Analyst's Office), D15–D16.

92. Cited in Hagar, *Special Master's Final Report*, 30.

93. Jerome Skolnick and James Fyfe, *Above the Law: Police and the Excessive Use of Force* (New York: Free Press, 1993), 117–118. In this quote, Skolnick and Fyfe describe the paramilitary organization of police departments. However, the authors note that prisons generally follow the same military model.

94. Interview, Warden Miller, July 6, 2004.

CHAPTER 8

1. Joe Mathews, "Prison Guards Union Shows Its Softer Side," *Los Angeles Times*, March 24, 2007, A1.
2. CCPOA, "From Sentencing to Incarceration to Release: A Blueprint for Reforming California's Prison System" (Sacramento: CCPOA, January 2007).
3. Ibid., 11.
4. Ibid., 12.
5. Little Hoover Commission, *Solving California's Corrections Crisis: Time is Running Out* (Sacramento: Little Hoover Commission, January 2007).
6. CCPOA, "From Sentencing to Incarceration," 13.
7. *The California Democratic Party 2007 State Convention*, San Diego, California, April 28, 2007, transcribed by author, emphasis added.
8. Eric Schlosser, "The Prison-Industrial Complex," *Atlantic Monthly* (December 1988), 51–77.
9. Sasha Abramsky, "Taming of the Screws," *Mother Jones* 33, no. 4 (July/August 2008), 54–55.
10. Ibid., emphasis added.
11. Mike Jimenez, "President's Message from Mike Jimenez" (Sacramento: CCPOA, June 30, 2008), http://www.ccpoa.org/news/?p=569 (accessed November 19, 2008).
12. Ibid.
13. Interview, Chuck Alexander and Mike Jimenez, August 11, 2006.
14. Ibid.
15. Jon Ortiz, "Read the Don Novey Emails to Mike Jimenez," *Sacramento Bee-The State Worker Blog*, December 19, 2010, http://www.sacbee.com/static/weblogs/the_state_worker/2009/12/read-the-don-novey-termination.html (accessed February 20, 2010).
16. Abramsky, "Taming of the Screws," 54-55.
17. Mathews, "Prison Guards Union."
18. Although the state has the right to implement a last, best, and final offer (LBFO) when it reaches an impasse with a bargaining unit (and the Public Employment Relations Board [PERB] verifies that the parties have reached that stage), *this was the first time that the state had imposed an LBFO on a state workers' union*. The move literally was unprecedented in California (*Sacramento Bee*, "State Moves Wisely with Guard Talks at Impasse," September 23, 2007, E6).
19. Hagar argued that Chief of Staff Kennedy held meetings with CCPOA President Mike Jimenez without notifying—much less including—Secretary Hickman (*Special Master's Draft Report, RE Status of State of California Corrective Action Plans for Administrative Investigations and Discipline; Recommendations*, No. C90-3094-TEH [U.S. District Court, Northern District of California, June 20, 2006], 27–30).
20. In a working paper, Kia Heise and I provide the results of a content analysis of these three newspapers' coverage of the CCPOA, which supports the claims I make in this section ("The Modern Octopus: Newspapers Take on the 'Powerful Prison Guards Union'," unpublished working paper).
21. *Sacramento Bee*, "Governor Panders on Prison Ideas," June 28, 2006, B6.
22. Legislative Analyst's Office, "Proposition 6" (Sacramento: Legislative Analyst's Office, July 17, 2008), http://www.lao.ca.gov/ballot/2008/6_11_2008.aspx (accessed September 24, 2009).
23. CCPOA, "5150 Hotline" (August 24, 2009), http://www.ccpoa.org/5150hotline_082409.shtml (accessed September 21, 2009).

24. Assembly Bill 14 X3 (Arambula) (Sacramento: California State Assembly, August 20, 2009), 219.
25. Ibid., 214.
26. Isabella Cota, "Parole for the sick to save the budget?" *KALW News* (on-line) (July 27, 2010), http://kalwnews.org/audio/2010/07/27/parole-sick-save-budget_493263.html (accessed August 1, 2010).
27. Rick Rogers, "Vietnam vet to head SD County vet court," *North County Times* (on-line) (September 10, 2010), http://www.nctimes.com/news/local/military/article_68cb0557-4ec9-5cc5-baf9-9709526b8ec3.html (accessed September 27, 2010).
28. California Department of Corrections and Rehabilitation, "CDCR Implements Public Safety Reforms to Parole Supervision, Expanded Incentive Credits for Inmates" (January 1, 2010), http://www.cdcr.ca.gov/News/2010_Press_Releases/Jan_21.html (accessed February 17, 2010).
29. Michael Jacobson, *Downsizing Prisons: How to Reduce Crime and End Mass Incarceration* (New York: New York University Press, 2005), 145–146.
30. Marisa Lagos, "Advocacy Group Sues Over Early-Release," *San Francisco Chronicle*, February 18, 2010, C2.
31. Saul Alinsky, *Rules for Radicals* (New York: Vintage, 1971), 50.
32. Ibid., 89.
33. The groups need not address an antagonist's positions on criminal punishment issues. Rather, they could focus on a target's key vulnerabilities—for example, a negative voting record on education or senior issues. The point, after all, is to provide consequences for supporting punitive segregation. The target would know the reason for the attack. More importantly, other politicians or state bureaucrats would know the reason too.
34. Jonathan Simon, *Governing Through Crime: How the War on Crime Transformed American Democracy and Created a Culture of Fear* (New York: Oxford University Press, 2007), chap. 3.
35. Franklin Zimring, *The Great American Crime Decline* (New York: Oxford University Press, 2007).
36. James Austin et al., *Unlocking America: Why and How to Reduce America's Prison Population* (Washington, DC: JFA Institute. 2007), 28.
37. The same questions should be asked of the rash of laws that blacklist and banish ex-sex offenders. As Loïc Wacquant demonstrates, in a thorough review of the literature on sex offender laws, these policies do not "work" in terms of decreasing sexual abuse. In fact, they appear to have the opposite effect in many cases (*Punishing the Poor* [Durham, NC: Duke University Press, 2009], chap. 7).
38. The terms "prisoner" and "convict" are sometimes used to suggest that the millions of imprisoned Americans share essential, negative characteristics. Therefore we allegedly *know* critical information about all prisoners (because convicted felons are all, at base, the same)—for example, they are dangerous, manipulative, immoral, and, for the most part, incapable of change. When used in these ways, the terms support punitive segregation. These terms need not be used to castigate imprisoned people. "Prisoner" can be employed as shorthand to designate a person that is behind bars and the term "convict" can be used to designate a legal status (one who is convicted). That is how I have used these terms in this book.
39. Wacquant, *Punishing the Poor*, 214.
40. Peter Sussman, "Media on Prisons: Censorship and Stereotypes" in Marc Mauer and Meda Chesney-Lind (eds.), *Invisible Punishment: The Collateral Consequences of Mass Imprisonment* (New York: New Press, 2002), 258–278.

41. Prison University Project, "Our Goals," http://www.prisonuniversityproject.org/
pages/about/about-us.html (accessed March 5, 2010); Prison Creative Arts Project, "About Our Organization," http://www.lsa.umich.edu/english/pcap/pages/
about_us.htm (accessed March 5, 2010).

42. Frank Provenzano, "U-M Site of Nation's Largest Prisoner Art Exhibit," *University
Record Online*, March 21, 2008, http://www.ur.umich.edu/0607/Mar19_07/12.
shtml (accessed June 3, 2010).

43. Studies show that the rehabilitative ideal still exists "on the ground"—that is,
penal staff such as prison managers and parole agents continue to believe in rehabilitation, even though limited resources, political pressure, and a strong emphasis on risk management make it extremely difficult to practice rehabilitation
behind the walls or on the streets (Candace Kruttschnitt and Rosemary Gartner,
Marking Time in the Golden State: Women's Imprisonment in California [New York:
Cambridge University Press, 2005]; Mona Lynch, "Rehabilitation as Rhetoric: The
Ideal of Reformation in Contemporary Discourse and Practice," *Punishment & Society* 2, no. 1 [2000], 40–65). As Mona Lynch argues, rehabilitation lives on primarily as rhetoric.

44. Michael Tonry, *Thinking About Crime: Sense and Sensibility in American Penal Culture* (New York: Oxford University Press, 2004), chap. 6.

45. Key indicators of this variation in punitiveness between California and Minnesota include imprisonment rates, propensity to send offenders to prison versus
other sanctions, length of prison sentences, policy differences (e.g., unlike California, Minnesota does not have the death penalty or a "three strikes" law), and
spending on corrections (Amy Lerman and Joshua Page, "Does the Front Line
Reflect the Party Line? An Embedded Work Role Perspective on Prison Officer
Attitudes," working paper).

METHODOLOGICAL APPENDIX

1. This study is not an example of "grounded theory." My theoretical proclivities
informed my observations, questions, and analyses. Drawing on my scholarly socialization, I immediately started to map out the structure and orientation of the
political and penal fields, to learn about the actions and dispositions of the agents
that operated in those social arenas, and to examine the relationship between the
structures and the agents. That is, the particular topic of this study—not my theoretical perspective—grew out of the exploratory research I conducted while volunteering in the senate. As describe in chapter 1, I use my case study to engage
and extend existing theories of labor, state, and punishment. In this vein, my
methodology resembles the "extended case method." For an explanation of the
extended case method, see Michael Burawoy et al., *Ethnography Unbound: Power
and Resistance in the Modern Metropolis* (Berkeley: University of California Press,
1991).

APPENDIX A

1. CCPOA, *Constitution, Bylaws, and Standard Operating Procedures* (2004), chap. 4.

SELECTED BIBLIOGRAPHY

Alinsky, Saul. *Rules for Radicals: A Pragmatic Primer for Realistic Radicals*. New York: Vintage Books, 1971.

Allen, Francis. *Decline of the Rehabilitative Ideal: Penal Policy and Social Purpose*. New Haven, CT: Yale University Press, 1981.

American Friends Service Committee. *Struggle for Justice: A Report on Crime and Punishment in America*. New York: Hill & Wang, 1971.

Anderson, Elijah. *Code of the Street: Decency, Violence, and the Moral Life of the Inner City*. New York: W. W. Norton, 1999.

Aronowitz, Stanley. *From the Ashes of Old: American Labor and America's Future*. New York: Basic Books, 1998.

Austin, James, Todd Clear, Troy Duster, David Greenberg, John Irwin, Candace McCoy, Alan Mobley, Barbara Owen, and Joshua Page. *Unlocking America: Why and How to Reduce America's Prison Population*. Washington, DC: JFA Institute. 2007.

Barker, Vanessa. "The Politics of Punishing: Building a State Governance Theory of American Imprisonment Variation." *Punishment & Society* 8, no. 1 (2006), 5–32.

———. *The Politics of Imprisonment: How the Democratic Process Shapes the Way America Punishes Offenders*. New York: Oxford University Press, 2009.

Baumgartner, Frank R., and Beth L. Leech. *Basic Interests: The Importance of Groups in Politics and in Political Sciences*. Princeton, NJ: Princeton University Press, 1998.

Beckett, Katherine. *Making Crime Pay: Law and Order in Contemporary Politics*. New York: Oxford University Press, 1997.

Beckett, Katherine, and Theodore Sasson. *The Politics of Injustice: Crime and Punishment in America*. Thousand Oaks, CA: Pine Forge Press, 2000.

Best, Joel. "Victimization and the Victim Industry." *Society* 34, no. 4 (1997), 9–17.

Bookspan, Shelly. *A Germ of Goodness: The California State Prison System, 1851–1944*. Lincoln: University of Nebraska Press, 1991.

Bottoms, Anthony. "The Philosophy of Punishment and Sentencing." In *The Politics of Sentencing Reform*, edited by Chris Clarkson and Rod Morgan, pp. 17–49. Oxford: Clarendon Press, 1995.

Bourdieu, Pierre. *Language and Symbolic Power*. Cambridge, MA: Harvard University Press, 1999.

———. *Pascalian Meditations*. Palo Alto, CA: Stanford University Press, 1997.

———. *Practical Reason*. Palo Alto, CA: Stanford University Press, 1998.

———. *Sociology in Question*. New York: Sage, 1995.

Bourdieu, Pierre, and Loïc Wacquant. *An Invitation to Reflexive Sociology*. Chicago: University of Chicago Press, 1992.

Braman, Donald. *Doing Time on the Outside: Incarceration and Family Life in Urban America*. Ann Arbor: University of Michigan Press, 2007.

Broder, David. *Democracy Derailed: Initiative Campaigns and the Power of Money*. New York: Harcourt, 2000.

Bunker, Edward. *Education of a Felon*. New York: St. Martin's Press, 2000.

Burawoy, Michael, Alice Burton, Ann Arnett Ferguson, Kathryn J. Fox, Joshua Gamson, Nadine Gartrell, Leslie Hunt, Charles Kurzman, Leslie Salzinger, Josepha Schiffman, and Shiori Ui. *Ethnography Unbound: Power and Resistance in the Modern Metropolis*. Berkeley: University of California Press, 1991.

Burton-Rose, Daniel, ed. *The Celling of America: An Inside Look at the U.S. Prison Industry*. Monroe, ME: Common Courage Press, 1998.

Cain, Bruce, and Thad Kousser. *Adapting to Term Limits: Recent Experiences and New Directions*. San Francisco: Public Policy Institute of California, 2004.

Campbell, Michael. "Agents of Change: Law Enforcement, Prisons, and Politics in Texas and California." PhD dissertation, University of California, Irvine, 2009.

Carpenter, Daniel. *The Forging of Bureaucratic Autonomy: Reputations, Networks, and Policy Innovation in Executive Agencies, 1862–1928*. Princeton, NJ: Princeton University Press, 2001.

Chàvez, Lydia. *The Color Bind: California's Battle to End Affirmative Action*. Berkeley: University of California Press, 1998.

Chiricos, Ted, Kathy Padgett, and Marc Gertz. "Fear, TV News, and the Reality of Crime." *Criminology* 38, no. 3 (2000), 755–785.

Clemmer, Donald. *The Prison Community*. New York: Rinehart, 1958.

Cullen, Francis, and Karen Gilbert. *Reaffirming Rehabilitation*. Cincinnati, OH: Anderson Publishing, 1982.

Cummins, Eric. *The Rise and Fall of California's Radical Prison Movement*. Palo Alto, CA: Stanford University Press, 1994.

Davidson, Theodore. *Chicano Prisoners: The Key to San Quentin*. New York: Holt, Rinehart, and Winston, 1974.

DeLord, Ronald G. *Police Association Power, Politics and Confrontation: A Guide for the Successful Police Labor Leader*. Springfield, IL: Charles C. Thomas, 1997.

Dilulio, John. *Governing Prisons*. New York: Free Press, 1987.

Domanick, Joe. *Cruel Justice: Three Strikes and the Politics of Crime in America's Golden State*. Berkeley: University of California Press, 2004.

Durkheim, Emile. *The Division of Labor in Society*. New York: Free Press, 1984.

———. *The Elementary Forms of Religious Life*. New York: Free Press, 1995.

———. *Rules of the Sociological Method*. New York: Free Press, 1982.

Elias, Robert. *The Politics of Victimization: Victims, Victimology, and Human Rights*. New York: Oxford University Press, 1986.

———. *Victims Still: The Political Manipulation of Crime Victims*. Newbury Park, CA: Sage, 1993.

Eschholz, Sarah, Ted Chiricos, and Marc Gertz. "Television and Fear of Crime: Program Types, Audience Traits, and the Mediating Effect of Perceived Neighborhood Racial Composition." *Social Problems* 50, no. 3 (December 2003), 395–415.

Fantasia, Rick, and Kim Voss. *Hard Work: Remaking the American Labor Movement*. Berkeley: University of California Press, 2004.

Faherty, Sara. *Victims and Victims' Rights*. Philadelphia: Chelsea House, 1999.

Featherson, Donald, D. G. Thorton, and J. Greggory Correnti. "State and Local Privatization: An Evolving Process." *Public Contract Law Journal* 30, no. 4 (2001), 643–676.

Feeley, Malcolm. "Entrepreneurs of Punishment: The Legacy of Privatization." *Punishment & Society* 4, no. 3 (2002), 321–344.

Feeley, Malcolm, and Edward Rubin. *Judicial Policy Making and the Modern State*. New York: Cambridge University Press, 1998.

Feeley, Malcolm, and Jonathan Simon. "The New Penology: Notes on the Emerging Strategy of Corrections and Its Implications." *Criminology* 30, no. 4 (1992), 449–474.

Freiberg, Arie. "Affective versus Effective Justice: Instrumentalism and Emotionalism in Criminal Justice." *Punishment & Society* 3, no. 2 (2001), 265–278.

Frost, Natasha. "The Mismeasure of Punishment: Alternative Measures of Punitiveness and Their (Substantial) Consequences." *Punishment & Society* 10, no. 3 (2008), 277–300.

Garland, David. *The Culture of Control: Crime and Social Order in Contemporary Society*. Chicago: University of Chicago Press, 2001.

———. "The Culture of High Crime Societies: Some Preconditions of Recent 'Law and Order' Policies." *British Journal of Criminology* 40 (2000), 347–375.

———. *Punishment and Modern Society*. Chicago: University of Chicago Press, 1990.

Gartner, Rosemary, Anthony Doob, and Franklin Zimring. "The Past as Prologue? Decarceration in California Then and Now." *Criminology and Public Policy* (forthcoming).

Geis, Gilbert, Alan Mobley, and David Shichor. "Private Prisons, Criminological Research, and Conflict of Interest: A Case Study." *Crime and Delinquency* 45, no. 3 (July 1999), 372–388.

Gilmore, Ruth Wilson. *Golden Gulag: Prison, Surplus, Crisis, and Opposition in Globalizing California*. Berkeley: University of California Press, 2007.

Glassner, Barry. *The Culture of Fear: Why Americans Are Afraid of the Wrong Things*. New York: Basic Books, 1999.

Goffman, Erving. *Asylums*. New York: Anchor Books, 1961.

Gottschalk, Marie. *The Prison and the Gallows: The Politics of Mass Incarceration in America*. New York: Cambridge University Press, 2006.

Gusfield, Joseph. "Moral Passage: The Symbolic Process in Public Designations of Deviance." *Social Problems* 15, no. 2 (Autumn 1967), 175–188.

Hacker, Jacob S. *The Divided Welfare State: The Battle Over Public and Private Social Benefits in the United States*. New Haven, CT: Yale University Press, 2002.

Haley, Alex, and Malcolm X. *The Autobiography of Malcolm X*. New York: Ballantine Books, 1973.

Haney, Craig. "Mental Health Issues in Long-Term Solitary and 'Supermax' Confinement." *Crime and Delinquency* 49, no. 1 (2003), 124–156.

Irwin, John. *Lifers: Seeking Redemption in Prison*. New York: Routledge, 2009.

———. *Prisons in Turmoil*. Boston: Little, Brown and Company, 1980.

———. *The Warehouse Prison: Disposal of the New Dangerous Class*. Los Angeles: Roxbury Publishing, 2005.

Jacobs, David, and Ronald Helms. "Collective Outbursts, Politics, and Punitive Resources: Toward a Political Sociology of Spending on Social Control." *Social Forces* 77, no. 4 (1999), 1497–1523.

Jacobs, James. *New Perspectives on Prisons and Imprisonment*. New York: Cornell University Press, 1983.

———. *Stateville: The Penitentiary in Mass Society*. Chicago: University of Chicago Press, 1977.

Jacobson, Michael. *Downsizing Prisons: How to Reduce Crime and End Mass Incarceration*. New York: New York University Press, 2006.

Janiskee, Brian, and Ken Masugi. *Democracy in California: Politics and Government in the Golden State*. Lanham, MD: Rowman & Littlefield, 2008.

Johnson, Ray (with Mona McCormick). *Too Dangerous to be At Large*. New York: New York Times Book Co., 1975.

Johnston, Paul. *Success While Others Fail: Social Movement Unionism and the Public Workplace*. Ithaca, NY: ILR, 1994.

Kamerman, Sheila B., and Alfred J. Kahn, eds. *Privatization and the Welfare State*. Princeton, NJ: Princeton University Press, 1989.

Kruttschnitt, Candace, and Rosemary Gartner. *Marking Time in the Golden State: Women's Imprisonment in California*. New York: Cambridge University Press, 2005.

Lakoff, George. *Moral Politics: How Liberals and Conservatives Think*. Chicago: University of Chicago Press, 1996.

Lamont, Michèle, and Virág Molnár. "The Study of Boundaries in the Social Sciences." *Annual Review of Sociology* 28 (2002), 167–195.

Leon, Chrysanthi S. "Compulsion and Control: Sex Crime and Criminal Justice Policy in California, 1930–2007." PhD dissertation, University of California, Berkeley, 2004.

Lichtenstein, Nelson. *State of the Union: A Century of American Labor*. Princeton, NJ: Princeton University Press, 2002.

Lopez, Steven. *Reorganizing the Rust Belt*. Berkeley: University of California Press, 2004.

Lynch, Mona. "Rehabilitation as Rhetoric: The Ideal of Reformation in Contemporary Discourse and Practice." *Punishment & Society* 2, no. 1 (2000), 40–65.

———. *Sunbelt Justice: Arizona and the Transformation of American Punishment*. Palo Alto, CA: Stanford University Press, 2010.

MacKinnon, Catherine. *Sexual Harassment of Working Women: A Case of Sex Discrimination*. New Haven, CT: Yale University Press, 1979.

Martin, Isaac. *The Permanent Tax Revolt: How the Property Tax Transformed American Politics*. Palo Alto, CA: Stanford University Press, 2008.

Martin, Susan, and Nancy Jurik. *Doing Justice, Doing Gender*. Thousand Oaks, CA: Sage, 1996.

McAdam, Doug, John McCarthy, and Mayer Zald, eds. *Comparative Perspectives on Social Movements: Political Opportunities, Mobilizing Structures, and Cultural Framings*. New York: Cambridge University Press, 1996.

McCarty, Heather Jane. "From Con-Boss to Gang Lord: The Transformation of Social Relations in California Prisons, 1943–1983." PhD dissertation, University of California, Berkeley, 2004.

McCoy, Candace. *Politics and Plea Bargaining: Victims' Rights in California*. Philadelphia: University of Pennsylvania Press, 1993.

McGee, Richard. *Prisons and Politics*. Lexington, MA: Lexington Books, 1981.

Melossi, Dario. "Gazette of Morality and Social Whip: Punishment, Hegemony, and the Case of the USA, 1972–1992." *Social & Legal Studies* 2 (1993), 259–279.

Miller, Lisa. *The Perils of Federalism*. New York: Oxford University Press, 2008.

Mitford, Jessica. *Kind and Unusual Punishment*. New York: Vintage Books, 1974.

Montilla, Robert. *Prison Employee Unionism: Management Guide for Correctional Administrators*. Washington, DC: U.S. Department of Justice, 1978.

Morris, Norval. *The Future of Imprisonment*. Chicago, IL: University of Chicago Press, 1974.

Owen, Barbara. *The Reproduction of Social Control: A Study of Prison Workers at San Quentin*. New York: Praeger, 1988.

Page, Joshua. "Eliminating the Enemy: The Import of Denying Higher Education to Prisoners in Clinton's America." *Punishment and Society* 6, no. 4 (2004), 357–378.

———. "Manufacturing Affinity: The Fortification and Expression of Ties between Prison Officers and Crime Victims." *Journal of Contemporary Ethnography* 37, no. 6 (2008), 745–777.

Parenti, Christian. *Lockdown America: Police and Prisons in the Age of Crisis*. New York: Verso, 1999.

Perkinson, Robert. *Texas Tough: The Rise of America's Prison Empire*. New York: Metropolitan Books, 2010.

Petersilia, Joan. "Crime and Punishment in California: Full Cells, Empty Pockets, and Questionable Benefits." In *Urban America: Policy Choices for Los Angeles and the Nation*, edited by James Steinberg, David Lyon, and Mary Vaiana, pp. 157–205. Santa Monica, CA: Rand, 1992.

———. *Understanding California Corrections*. Berkeley: California Policy Research Center, 2006.

———. *When Prisoners Come Home: Parole and Prisoner Reentry*. New York: Oxford University Press, 2003.

Pew Center on the States. *One in 100: Behind Bars in America 2008*. Washington, DC: Pew Center on the States, 2008.

Pratt, John. *Penal Populism*. New York: Routledge, 2007.

Reynolds, Mike, Bill Jones, and Dan Evans. *Three Strikes and You're Out: A Promise to Kimber*. Fresno, CA: Quill Driver Books, 1996.

Rhodes, Lorna. *Total Confinement: Madness and Reason in the Maximum Security Prison*. Berkeley: University of California Press, 2004.

Robertson, James E. "Houses of the Dead: Warehouse Prisons, Paradigm Change, and the Supreme Court." *Houston Law Review* 34 (1997), 1003–1063.

Rothman, David. *Conscience and Convenience*. New York: Aldine de Gruyter, 2002.

Rueschemeyer, Kietrich, and Peter Evans. "The State and Economic Transformation: Toward an Analysis of the Conditions Underlying Effective Intervention." In *Bringing the State Back In*, edited by Peter Evans, Dietrich Rueschemeyer, and Theda Skocpol, pp. 44–77. New York: Cambridge University Press, 1985.

Savelsberg, Joachim. "Knowledge, Domination, and Criminal Punishment." *American Journal of Sociology* 99, no. 4 (1994), 911–943.

Schrag, Peter. *California: America's High-Stakes Experiment*. Berkeley: University of California Press, 2006.

———. *Paradise Lost: California's Experience: America's Future*. Berkeley: University of California Press, 1999.

Shapiro, Bruce. "Victims & Vengeance: Why the Victims' Rights Amendment is a Bad Idea." *The Nation* 264 (February 10, 1997), 11–19.

Shichor, David. "The Corporate Context of Private Prisons." *Crime, Law, and Social Change* 20, no. 2 (1993), 113–138.

Schoenfeld, Heather. "The Politics of Prison Growth: From Chain Gangs to Work Release Centers and Supermax Prisons, Florida, 1955–2000." PhD dissertation, Northwestern University, 2009.

Simon, Jonathan. *Governing Through Crime: How the War on Crime Transformed American Democracy and Created a Culture of Fear*. New York: Oxford University Press, 2007.

———. "Megan's Law: Crime and Democracy in Late Modern America." *Law & Social Inquiry* 25, no. 4 (2000), 1111–1150.

———. *Poor Discipline: Parole and the Social Control of the Underclass, 1890–1990*. Chicago: University of Chicago Press, 1993.

Skolnick, Jerome, and James Fyfe. *Above the Law: Police and the Excessive Use of Force*. New York: Free Press, 1993.

Sussman, Peter. "Media on Prisons: Censorship and Stereotypes." In *Invisible Punishment: The Collateral Consequences of Mass Imprisonment*, edited by Marc Mauer and Meda Chesney-Lind, pp. 258–278. New York: New Press, 2002.

Sutton, John. "Imprisonment and Social Classification in Five Common-Law Democracies, 1955–1985." *American Journal of Sociology* 106, no. 2 (2000), 350–386.

Sykes, Gresham. *The Society of Captives: A Study of a Maximum Security Prison*. Princeton, NJ: Princeton University Press, 1971.

Thomas, Charles. "Correctional Privatization in America: An Assessment of Its Historical Origins, Present Status, and Future Prospects." In *Changing of the Guard: Private Prisons and the Control of Crime*, edited by Alexander Tabarrok and Charles Logan, pp. 57–124. Oakland: Independent Institute, 2003.

Tonry, Michael. *Malign Neglect: Race, Crime, and Punishment in America*. New York: Oxford University Press, 1996.

———. "Rethinking Unthinkable Punishment Policies in America." *UCLA Law Review* 46, no. 4 (1999), 1751–1791.

———. *Thinking About Crime: Sense and Sensibility in American Penal Culture*. New York: Oxford University Press, 2004.

Tyler, Tom, and Robert Boeckmann. "Three Strikes and You're Out, but Why? The Psychology of Public Support for Punishing Rule Breakers." *Law & Society Review* 31, no. 2 (1997), 255–256.

Vitiello, Michael. "Three Strikes and the *Romero* Case: The Supreme Court Restores Democracy," *Loyola of Los Angeles Law Review* 30 (1997), 1601-1666.

Wacquant, Loïc. "Deadly Symbiosis: When Ghetto and Prison Meet and Merge." *Punishment & Society* 3, no. 1 (2001), 95–133.

———, ed. *Pierre Bourdieu and Democratic Politics*. Cambridge, UK: Polity Press, 2005.

———. *Punishing the Poor: The Neoliberal Government of Social Insecurity*. Durham, NC: Duke University Press, 2009.

Walsh, Jennifer. *Three Strikes Laws*. Santa Barbara, CA: Greenwood, 2007.

Warren, Earl, and Burdette J. Daniels. "California's New Penal and Correctional Law." *California Law Review* 32, no. 3 (1944), 229–241.

Weitzer, Ronald, and Charis Kubrin. "Breaking News: How Local TV News and Real-World Conditions Affect Fear of Crime." *Justice Quarterly* 21, no. 3 (2004), 497–520.

Western, Bruce. *Punishment and Inequality in America*. New York: Russell Sage Foundation, 2006.

Whitman, James Q. *Harsh Justice: Criminal Punishment and the Widening Divide Between America and Europe*. New York: Oxford University Press, 2003.

Wicker, Tom. *A Time to Die: The Attica Prison Revolt*. Lincoln: University of Nebraska Press, 1994.

Windlesham, Lord. *Politics, Punishment, and Populism*. New York: Oxford University Press, 1998.

Wright, Erik Olin. *The Politics of Punishment*. New York: Harper & Row, 1973.

Wynne, John M., Jr. *Prison Employee Unionism: The Impact on Correctional Administration and Programs*. Washington, DC: U.S. Department of Justice, 1978.

Young, Jock. *The Exclusive Society: Social Exclusion, Crime and Difference in Late Modernity*. New York: Sage, 1999.

Zimring, Franklin. *The Great American Crime Decline*. New York: Oxford University Press, 2007.

———. "The New Politics of Criminal Justice: Of 'Three Strikes,' Truth-in-Sentencing, and Megan's Laws." Perspectives on Crime and Justice: 1999–2000 Lecture Series 4. Washington, DC: National Institute of Justice, March 2001.

Zimring, Franklin, and Gordon Hawkins. *The Scale of Imprisonment*. Chicago: University of Chicago Press, 1991.

———. *Prison Population and Criminal Justice Policy in California*. Berkeley, CA: Institute of Governmental Studies, 1992.

Zimring, Franklin, Gordon Hawkins, and Sam Kamin. *Punishment and Democracy: Three Strikes and You're Out in California*. New York: Oxford University Press, 2001.

INDEX

activists at Folsom Prison, 161
class-action suit against CDC, 33–34
death penalty, 27
formation, 15, 30
independent association, 37
Novey as president, 40–41
organizational chart, 42*f*
"pizza and beer" outfit, 15–16
Prisoners' Union, 27–29
prison officers and, 20
radicalization of, 25–29
safety measures, 26–27
transformation to CCPOA, 13, 161
California Correctional Peace Officers
    Association (CCPOA)
5150 hotline, 152, 260*n*65
abstention on sentencing policies,
    112–13
*Behind the Wall: The Toughest Beat in
    California* video, 69, 81–82
bond with CVUC, 91–92
California Correctional Officers
    Association (CCOA) becoming,
    13, 161
candidate endorsements, 63–64
candidates for elections, 245*n*85
committees, 227–28
contributions to legislative leaders,
    62t, 243*n*44, 245*n*82
Corcoran prison scandals, 167–71,
    184–85
creation, 43
development of CVUC and CVB, 87
diversity, 49–50
economic resources, 44–45
formation of CUPS, 124
grievance and arbitration, 190–91
gubernatorial ties, 58–62
*Hard Time: A Walk on the Toughest
    Beat in California* video, 70–72
independent investment strategy,
    Wilson, 60–61
influence on prison operations,
    191–93, 216–17
journalistic and activist writings,
    232*n*18
juvenile incarceration bills, 113–14
lawsuit against state, 141–42
legislative ties, 62–63
magazine *Peacekeeper*, 72–75

Magic 13 questions for endorsement,
    55–56, 115, 121–22, 157
media campaign and Wilson, 59–60,
    244–45*n*66
membership, 48, 49f, 242*n*20
nonpartisanship, 54–55
partnership with crime victims'
    advocates, 84–91
political action committees (PACs),
    229
politically realistic unionism, 44
political realism, 50–54
prison privatization, 138–39, 156–59
public ceremony, 91–99
*Public Safety: Government's First
    Responsibility*, 70
public service announcements
    (PSAs), 75
public vs. private incarceration, 5–6
punishing enemies, 64–68
punitive segregation, 111–12
relationship with penal field, 12,
    13–14
research, 221–25
rewarding friends, 54–64
Section 27.01, 171–72
sentencing commission, 203–5
specter of the, 44, 64–68, 138, 149,
    156, 158, 167, 170, 177, 192, 217,
    225, 246*n*99
tough on crime, 112–15
unionization results, 76–80
warden confirmations, 175–79
California Crime Victims for
    Alternatives to the Death Penalty,
    100, 109
California Democratic Party, 54–55,
    243*n*42
California Department of Corrections
    (CDC)
administrators, 161
basic academy for, 74
class-action suit against, 33–34
community correctional facilities
    (CCFs), 140–43
creation, 17
director McGee, 17, 236*n*13
directors, 188*f*
"get tough on crime" theme, 46–47
medical system, 189

California Department of Corrections
(CDC) (*continued*)
negotiations with Prisoners' Union,
28–29
organizational dysfunction, 186–87
parole reform, 105
"prison guard" to "correctional
officer," 18–19
prison privatization, 138–39
reorganization, 257n6
violence control program, 222
California Department of Corrections
and Rehabilitation (CDCR), 161,
213, 257n6
California District Attorneys
Association, 127, 255n57
California Highway Patrol officers, 29,
77, 163
California Medical Association, 57
California Police Chiefs Association,
129
California Public Employee Relations
Board (PERB), 30, 42
"California Recovery Team,"
Schwarzenegger, 127
California Rehabilitation Center, 90
California Republican Party, 54–55, 61
California State Auditor, 189
California State Employees Association
(CSEA)
bosses, 36–37
Folsom activists, 36
campaign to represent prison officers,
30
plights of prison officers, 36–37
union, 54, 59
California Statewide Law Enforcement
Association (CSLEA), 80
Californias United for Public Safety,
Independent Expenditure
Committee (CUPS-IEC), 124, 125
California Supreme Court
Dills Act, 30
People v. Superior Court, 257n89
California Teachers Association, 54, 59,
60, 108, 155, 243n42
California Union of Security Employees
(CAUSE), 255n57, 255n64
Californians United for Public Safety
(CUPS), 52, 126

California Youth Authority (CYA), 16,
54
basic academy for, 74
juveniles to adult prison, 114
victims' advocates, 100
Camacho, Moe, 27
Campbell, Tom, parole model, 106
career criminals, term, 212
Carpenter, Daniel, 187–89, 265n74
CCPOA. *See* California Correctional
Peace Officers Association
(CCPOA)
Center for Juvenile and Criminal
Justice, 246n90
Change to Win coalition, 8
Chapman, Jane, women officers,
239n80
Chicano Correctional Workers Associa-
tion, 49
child safety, "Thumbs Up!," 75
Christmas, William, 23
Citizens Against Homicide, 93, 125
Citizens for Law-and-Order, 93, 99,
106
Citizens for Prison and Parole Reform,
25
civil rights movement, prisoners, 21
Civil Service Act, 141
Clauder, Sam, Proposition 66, 123
Clinton, William J., 117, 120,
254n42
Clutchette, John, Soledad incident, 22
code of silence, 165–66, 179, 199
"code of the street," 9
collateral consequence,
hyperimprisonment, 216
Commission on Judicial Performance,
Salarno, 100
commitment offense and sentencing,
prisoners, 70
community correctional facility (CCF)
California Department of Corrections
(CDC), 140–43
Governor Davis, 151–55
Hidden Valley Ranch, 140
zeroing out, 150–56
compensation, California prison
officers, 76, 247n126, 247n127
competition, prison agencies, 190–91
"con bosses," 236n9

last, best, and final offer (LBFO), 199, 266n18
late modernity, punitive turn and, 233–34n35
Latino Caucus, 259n50
"law and order"
  conservative politicians, 9
  penal field transformation, 215–16
  punitive segregation, 239n62
  victims of crime, 212
Law-and-Order Campaign Committee, foundation, 28
Law Enforcement Assistance Administration, 83
law enforcement associations, 10
lawsuit
  CCPOA against state, 141–42
  Plata v. Davis, 189
  Valdivia settlement, 104t, 105
Leach, Marcella
  Justice for Homicide Victims, 125, 126
  "No on 66" campaign, 132
  Proposition 21, 255n61
  Propositions 6 and 9, 203
leadership
  prison system, 187–89
  Youth and Adult Correctional Agency (YACA), 183, 186
Legislative Analyst's Office (LAO), 190
legislative ties, CCPOA, 62–63
Leonard, Bill, union politics, 64–65
Lewis, Peter, Proposition 66, 130
Lichtenstein, Nelson, 240n92
Little Hoover Commission, parole reform, 103–4, 242n17, 251n54
lobbying. *See* California Correctional Peace Officers Association (CCPOA)
  Crime Victims United of California (CVUC), 86–87
  Doris Tate Crime Victims Bureau, 103, 121
  federal government and, 243n39
Lockyer, Bill
  investigating prison employees, 170–71
  Nina Salarno-Ashford, 100
  prison overcrowding and SB 2156, 145

Los Angeles Police Protective League, 80
Los Angeles Times
  CCPOA leak, 66
  CCPOA's softer side, 194–95
  criticism of CCPOA, 200
  death of bill SB 451, 170–71
  editorials on California prisons, 6
  Hickman, 179
  Jimenez's sons, 199
  jury bias and union, 169
  Novey interview, 67–68
  prison officers and Native Americans, 52–53
  private prisons, 154
  Schwarzenegger administration's strategy, 100
"Lost Child," public service announcement, 75
Louisiana, prison reforms, 7
Lungren, Dan, CCPOA, 61

Macarro, Mark, Pechanga tribe, 53
McClain, James, court and hostage taking, 22–23
McCoy, Candace, 45
McGee, Richard
  California Department of Corrections (CDC), 3, 17, 236n13
  "correctional officer," 246n109
  rehabilitation components, 17–18, 19, 20
Machiavelli, Nicolló, 51, 52
McHugh, Gavin, 54, 90
McHugh, Shari, 54, 90
McNally Temple Associates, 90, 127, 255n65
Magee, Ruchell, McClain court proceeding, 22–23
Magic 13, endorsement decisions, 55–56, 115, 121–22, 157
Malcolm X, 237n27
management
  "entire agreement" provision, 171–72
  grievance and arbitration process, 173f
  Peace Officer Bill of Rights (POBR), 165
  personnel investigations, 164–67, 171–75
  post-and-bid system, 162–64

California Correctional Officers
Association (CCOA), 38–39, 40–41
campaign against Proposition 66,
132
CCPOA, 61, 63, 78, 194–95, 197
CCPOA and CVUC, 91
CCPOA fires, 198
challenging management rights, 161
crime victim rights, 80, 84–87, 99,
108
emails to Jimenez, *Sacramento Bee*,
198
influence outside California, 79
Michael Salarno, 89–90
MILE PAC, 49
parole model, 108
personnel investigations, 164
photograph, 67*f*
political consultant for CCPOA, 198
political consultant for CSLEA, 80
political consultant for LAPPL, 80
prison violence, 81
Myers, CCA, 150
punitive segregation, 111, 208
resigns as CCPOA president, 197
Salarno's first meeting with, 85–86,
88–89
specter of the CCPOA, 67–68
Three Strikes campaign, 119–20
unions and politics, 50–52, 58–59,
66–68
Nuestra Familia, prison gang, 238*n*41

Office for Victims of Crime, Reagan
administration, 83
Office of Inspector General, 182–83,
189, 190
Oklahoma, private prisons, 159
Omnibus Crime Bill (1994), President
Clinton, 117
"one-for-one" doctrine, Jackson's, 22,
24
orientation, penal field, 11–12
Orozco, Bernie, prison privatization
bill, 144
overcrowding
California's prison dilemma, 142–43
Schwarzenegger and state of emergency, 158–59
Owen, Barbara, sexual harassment, 32

Pacheco, Nick, 66
Pacheco, Rod, SB 818, 148–49
paramilitary organization, police,
265*n*93
paramilitary organization, prison, 160,
192
Parenti, Christian, 138
Parents of Murdered Children, 83, 93,
125
Parents of Murdered Victims, 93
parole boards, Prison Reorganization
Act, 20
parole policy, 236–37*n*16
parole reform
chronology of, in California, 104*t*
crime victims' organizations, 105
Little Hoover Commission, 103–4,
242*n*17, 251*n*54
"New Parole Model," 105–6, 251*n*58
Schwarzenegger, 104–5, 107–8, 131
Valdivia settlement, 104t, 105
Parry, Brian, 177–78, 184
path, 228
Paulson, David, anti-Proposition 66,
127–28
"pay-to-play" politics
editorials on CCPOA, 200
Gray Davis, 154–55
Peace, Steve, community correctional
facilities, 154
Peacekeeper
CCPOA magazine, 72–75
cover of, 73*f*
crime victims and victim advocates,
88
job assignments, 162
research, 224
Thompson, 64
Three Strikes campaign, 120
truth-in-sentencing bill, 113
victims of violent crime, 88
victory for CCPOA and allies, 98
Peace Officer Bill of Rights (POBR), 165
Pechanga tribe, 53
Pelican Bay State Prison, 165–66, 170
penal bureaucracy
administrative capacity, 183
Office of Inspector General, 182–83
organizational structure, 185–87
purposes and goals, 183–85

penal bureaucracy (*continied*)
　reorganization, 190
　resources, 185–87
penal field
　actors, 207–11, 217
　approaching punishment, 216–19
　Bourdieu, 10, 235*n*42
　challengers in, 209*t*
　composition, 207–11
　culture, 211–16
　definition, 10
　description, 10–11
　orientation, 11–12
　relationship with CCPOA, 12, 13–14
　sporting field analogy, 235*n*43
　transformation, 215–16
People v. Superior Court, California
　　Supreme Court, 257*n*89
personnel, group therapy, 237*n*19,
　237*n*23
personnel investigations
　Corcoran prison, 167–71
　grievance and arbitration, 190–91
　prison management, 164–67,
　　171–75
Petersilia, Joan
　California prison population, 70
　parole expert, 20
　post-and-bid rules, 164
　prison management, 161
　prison officers' pay, 76, 77
　punitive segregation, 46
Plata v. Davis, medical lawsuit, 189
players, term, 235*n*45
Polanco, Richard
　CCPOA, 66, 103
　community correctional facilities
　　(CCFs), 151, 154–55
　prison privatization, 145–49,
　　259*n*43
　SB 818, 147–49
policymaking, interest groups and
　criminal justice, 10–13
political action committees (PACs),
　CCPOA, 52, 57–58, 87, 108
political districts, California, 243–
　44*n*52
politically realistic unionism, 44, 241*n*2
political opportunity structure, 241*n*1
political production, means of, 208

political realism, California
　　Correctional Peace Officers Associ-
　　ation (CCPOA), 50–54
politicization, penal policy, 7
politics
　California Correctional Peace Officers
　　Association (CCPOA), 5, 44, 50–54,
　　229
　prison privatization, 143–49
population
　California adult prison (1965–2008),
　　48*f*
　California prisons, 4
　drawing down prison, 206–7
post-and-bid system, prison officers,
　162–64, 199
power
　Alinsky, 208
　confrontation, 210–11
power by proxy, 13, 82
Presley, Bob, inmate rights, 98
prison agencies, unequal competition,
　190–91
Prison Committee, 143–44, 221–23
Prison Creative Arts Project (PCAP),
　213–15
prisoners
　commitment offense, 70
　media ban, 213
　opposition to rehabilitation, 20
　promoting expression of, 213–15
　speaking out, 213–15
　term, 267*n*38
prisoners' rights
　Black Muslims, 21
　Convict Bill of Rights, 24, 98–99
　Prisoners' Rights Union, 114
Prisoners' Union, 23, 27–29
prison gangs, Black Guerilla Family
　(BGF), 24, 238*n*41
prison guards, reclassification to
　"correctional officers," 18–19
prison-industrial complex (PIC), term,
　196
"prison intelligentsia," Irwin, 237*n*27
prison officers
　affirmative action, 35
　conflicting aims, 184
　disparaging highway patrol, 39–40
　labor union, 5

cabinet position for crime victim
advocate, 100
"California Recovery Team," 127
CCPOA's contract, 174
criticism of CCPOA, 200–201
Fisher to parole board, 99–100
Hickman's resignation, 182
"last, best, and final" offer (LBFO),
199, 266n18
parole reform, 104–5, 107–8, 131
prison overcrowding, 158–59
prison population proposals, 206–7
private prison contributions, 261n83
Proposition 66, 126, 128
punishment focus shift, 93
selection, 179
sentencing commission, 204
state of emergency, 158–59
Three Strikes, 122
Valdivia lawsuit, 104–5
warden confirmations, 178
Scribner, A. K., Duel Vocational
Institute, 37–38
Section 9.09, contract provision, 165,
166
selective retaliatory violence, Jackson,
22
Senate Committee on Public Safety,
Boatwright, 143–44
Senate Rules Committee, confirmation,
175–76
seniority systems, affirmative action,
240n92
sentencing commission, CCPOA
opposing, 203–5
sex offenders, 267n37
housing issue, 181
one strike for violent, 113
sexual harassment
female officers, 240nl.84
Folsom, 32
sexual predators, term, 212
Shapiro, Robert, vengeance-rights
lobby, 84
Sherman, Ryan
CCPOA lobbyist, 68, 90, 103
warden appointments, 176
Shichor, David, prison privatization,
137–38
Shur, Dan, Lungren's campaign, 61

Side Letter 12, contract provision,
165–67, 168
Simon, Jonathan
crime victims, 84, 251n68
parole policy, 236–37n16
predator and prey, terms, 129
war on crime, 109
"social facts," definition, 246n99
Soledad Brother, Jackson, 22
Soledad Incident, white officer murder,
22–23
Soros, George, Proposition 66, 130
Speier, Jackie
Novey, 68
politics and union, 51, 65, 260n70
prison officer union, 6
Sperling, John, Proposition 66, 130
Speth, Percy, CCPOA, 90
Spitzer, Todd, 94, 255n64
State Department of Industrial
Relations, San Quentin, 25
State Employees International Union
(SEIU), 158
State Employer–Employee Relations
Act, (Dills Act), 30
State Personnel Board, 190
Steinberg, Darrell, CCPOA, 78
Stender, Fay, prison movement
attorney, 22
Stevens-Roby, Dorothy, affirmative
action, 34
Stockton Record, voice of victims, 101
Strickland, Donald, Kings County,
169–70
Struggle for Justice, American Friends
Service Committee, 29
Supreme Court, Black Muslims, 21

Tate, Doris, 99, 109–10. *See also* Doris
Tate Crime Victims Bureau
tax revolt, Proposition 13, 116
Teamsters
CCOA campaign against, 43
The Granite writers, 37
Hoffa, 67
Teddy Bear Project, Crime Victims
United, 248n19
Tennessee, private prisons, 143, 157,
159
term limits, Proposition 140, 53

CPSIA information can be obtained
at www.ICGtesting.com
Printed in the USA
BVOW00s0035040117

472514BV00003B/99/P